The Colour of God

The Colour of God

Ayesha Siddiqua Chaudhry

ONEWORLD

A Oneworld Book

First published by Oneworld Publications in 2021

Copyright © Ayesha S. Chaudhry 2021

The moral right of Ayesha S. Chaudhry to be identified as the
Author of this work has been asserted by her in accordance
with the Copyright, Designs, and Patents Act 1988

ISBN 978-1-78607-925-1 (hardback)
ISBN 978-0-86154-085-3 (export paperback)
eISBN 978-1-78607-976-3

Typeset by Hewer Text UK Ltd, Edinburgh
Printed and bound in Great Britain by Clays Ltd, Elcograf S.p.A.

Oneworld Publications
10 Bloomsbury Street
London WC1B 3SR
England

Stay up to date with the latest books,
special offers, and exclusive content from
Oneworld with our newsletter

Sign up on our website
oneworld-publications.com

For

Light dancing on titlywings.
My Medina.
Chiryasong of my dil.

صبغة الله ومن أحسن من الله صبغة ۝

The colour of God. And what is better than the colour of God?

—The Qur'an

Contents

What is your name, li'l munna?

My name is Sibghatullah.

What does your name mean?

The colour of God.

And what is the colour of God?

Ummm . . . green, I think . . . or maybe light brown.

PART I

Anguish

It is not my place to tell his story. Only my own. And my story is formed by him. So, should I start with the day he was born, on a cold, wintry December night, snowflakes drifting lazily in the yellow glow of street lamps? Or with the day he died, on a warm, rainy summer night in June, four and a half years later?

There's no right place to begin, so let's start with his death. His death made me go back and rethink everything. Made me see that the most fundamental facts of life are unstable, shaky. Like time. Time does not just march forward. Sometimes it skips ahead, rushing through long stretches of life, and other times it resists forward motion, moving unbearably slowly, dragging itself out, refusing to move along. Like a puppy resisting the leash, digging his feet into the pavement, preferring to rip his pads than give in to the demands of his walker. And sometimes it loops right back, keeping you stuck in a nightmare from which you cannot wake. Like water endlessly circling the drain, never emptying out. His death floods my mind, it seeps into every corner of my brain, it drenches every memory.

It's June 28, 2005 and I am twenty-four years old. I have been married for about six months. I fought tooth and nail, prayed my heart out to marry this boy, not yet a man. He is two months younger than me. His parents opposed our marriage. They didn't come to the wedding, even though he got on his knees and begged them.

If you marry her, you're not welcome back here, they said, and then followed through.

My family was full of trepidation about our wedding, about my marrying a person whose parents disowned him. They wondered aloud if I could trust him. *Does he know what he's doing? Will he change his mind tomorrow?*

Yes, he does and *No, he won't*, I told them, with more confidence than I felt.

We got married in Las Vegas, though that's less scandalous than it sounds. My sister was living there at the time and offered to host the wedding. My parents, my siblings with their growing families and a few friends gathered, taking up too little space in a vast green prayer hall at a mosque just off the Strip. The day was December 18, 2004, Sibghatullah's fourth birthday. Whose bright idea was it for us to get married on his birthday? One of us must have thought up this plan but all of us thrilled at the harmony and beauty of it. Love upon love. Baraka multiplied. His mother, my older sister, single-handedly organised the wedding – made the arrangements at the mosque, booked the reception at a restaurant, made the salon appointments, waxed my legs, arms and face the night before, hosted my entire family of six siblings, spouses, children and parents in her two-bedroom apartment.

Sibghatullah had been involved in all the planning. He had opinions about the hairstyle his mother chose for me, the cake she picked out, the clothes I would wear. He thought that the wedding was his, that he was the one marrying me, and was scandalised to learn that his Ayesha Khala wasn't coming to marry him at all, but some random guy named Rumee. He expressed his disappointment by icing him out. He never really warmed up to Rumee. I'm sure he would have eventually. But there wasn't enough time.

Back to that June evening. I've been married for six months and ten days now and I don't know what I'm doing. I do not understand marriage. I've never been in a romantic relationship before. Neither has Rumee. It took us three weeks to figure out how to have sex. If sex is instinctual, our instincts were buried so deep we didn't know where to look. Rumee's friend advised him, *Just get in there and explode.*

Well, it took a while for him to *get in there*. For weeks, as we tried to figure out what comes naturally to animals, Rumee would ask, *Am I in?* And I'd say, . . . *I think so?*

When he was finally in, we both knew. He didn't ask and I didn't respond with a question. It felt good.

Rumee's parents were not speaking to him. Some of my family members were not speaking to each other. There were several fights before and after the wedding. Sometimes, families use reunions to air their grievances. Some of the fights were over money, as though money could heal years of trauma. When the visit was over, my father departed in a huff, without saying goodbye or hugging Sibghatullah. Even at his young age, he noticed and was hurt.

Why is Nana angry? he asked.

This haughty and momentary lapse on my father's part will haunt us for the rest of our days. Some of our mistakes are carried by those we love.

Six months after the wedding, my older sister is in transit, moving from Las Vegas to a small town in New England. I have just moved myself from New York to Rumee's apartment in Baltimore so that we can play house, but I'm not expecting the relationship to work out. He's working at some nine-to-five job instead of finishing his PhD. I'm at home, all day, preparing for my comprehensive exams. I'm doing a PhD in Islamic Studies at New York University, and on that campus and in that city I had a social network. I have no friends here. There is nowhere to walk. I am eating too much ice-cream.

On June 28th, Rumee convinces me to work out with him at the gym in our apartment complex. I reluctantly agree after much whining about how much I hate sweating. To my twenty-four-year-old mind, sweating is gross and sweating in hijab is more gross. I find fitness clothes obscene, at odds with my notions of modesty. I wear too many clothes when I work out; long yoga pants for jogging, the bottom half of the legs flared so they don't excessively hug my curves. On top I wear a long-sleeved shirt, but this is too revealing and the shape of my butt shows through the yoga pants. To fix both these problems, I wear an extra-large men's cotton T-shirt over my outfit. This hides all my curves, my butt, waist and bust. Now for the head. I tie a small, non-slip cotton kerchief on my head. This will ensure that the hijab I wrap over the kerchief doesn't move from physical exertion. I look in the mirror. *Do I look modest enough?* Rumee thinks so. My mother's voice in my head disagrees. I ignore her and head to the gym.

I climb the elliptical machine and, momentarily, I feel much, much better – the endorphin release eases my gnawing anxiety and distracts me from the judgemental voices in my head. As we are about to head back to the apartment, it starts pouring rain. Hard, East Coast summer rain. Warm and strong. We look at each other and realise there is no way around it, we are going to get drenched. At first, we run with our shoulders hunched, as if to shield us, but pretty soon our apprehension melts into childish glee as we run through the heavy downpour, bodies open, laughing, our clothes wet and heavy, our shoes squelching.

We get home, buzzing with energy as we shower and change into dry, comfortable clothes. I make myself a hot chocolate. Rumee sits to write something at the desk in the den. I curl up on the floor behind him, my legs folded under me as I lean forward to read another book for my exams. I remember the book, *Qur'an, Liberation and Pluralism* by Farid Esack.

At around 10:30P.M. my phone rings. It is a flip phone, my first cell. There is a red light on top that flashes when it rings. I pick up and hear a sound that is impossible to describe but that imprints itself forever in my brain. It is a wail, or a lament, the sound of an animal wounded deeply and irreparably.

Hello? Who is this? I ask tentatively. I look at the number; I don't recognise it. The phone disconnects.

I call the number back and a man answers. He says he is with my older sister. I know immediately that he is a stranger because he mispronounces her name. He gives her the phone. She is wailing, screaming, hysterical.

No, no, no! He's gone! He's gone! Sibghatullah is gone! I want him back, I want my baby back!

What do you mean he's gone? Who took him? Of course you can have him back! I assure her as I frantically try to figure out what is going on.

She hangs up and I feel a wild panic rise within me.

What is going on? I ask Rumee. Who took Sibghatullah? Why did they take him? Was he kidnapped? Was it the government? No thought is outlandish in light of the most outlandish thought of all – that Sibghatullah could be gone. Gone where?

The phone rings again. This call is from Canada, my parents' house. My younger sister is on the phone.

Are you sitting down? she asks.

Sure, why? What's going on? I got a really strange call from –

Sibghatullah was feeling sick, she took him to the hospital. He just died.

She just says it. Quietly. Firmly. Clearly.

What? No. That can't be true! Are you sure? What do you mean, he's dead?

I hang up the phone. I cannot repeat the words. Emotions overtake me. I cannot process them, I have no tools to manage them. My body tries to dispel the feelings. First, I vomit. Then I hit my head against the wall. As a child, I once saw my mother do this when she was upset. I bang my head against the wall, pull my hair and finally understand the sound I heard in that first phone call. It is the sound of a mother having just – moments ago – lost her child.

It is the sound of anguish.

PART II

Assimilation

The story of covering my hair, my face, my entire body, including my hands, is rooted in my mother's story. And her story of covering is wrapped up in her relationship with immigration and assimilation. Like the other girls in her hometown in Pakistan, my mother started covering her hair when she was a young child. But for the first few years after immigrating, she and my dad tried to assimilate into a white Canada. My father immigrated in the sixties with a twelfth-grade education and a diploma in metallurgy. He worked in construction as a welder and pipe fitter. He 'brought' – his words, not mine – my mother to Toronto after marrying her. She was eighteen years old and bewildered by everything she saw. In the winter she was stunned by the extreme cold; in the summer she was horrified at the white bodies lounging in the sun around the swimming pool located in the centre of the apartment complex where she lived. She would peer down from her tiny apartment, dazed and disgusted by the lack of shame. She hated her tiny apartment, she always said it made her feel like an animal in a cage. She missed the courtyards and fresh air of Pakistan. She was terrified of escalators. I inherited that fear from her. To this day, my heart quickens a bit just before stepping on.

But still, under my father's influence, she tried to assimilate. They both did. Pictures of my parents from the seventies capture the people they were trying to be. My father is sometimes clean-shaven, and other times sports a fashionable trim beard. He looks a bit dodgy in his three-piece, checkered, mustard suits, and handsome in his flared pants and Ray Ban sunglasses. He poses in front of his Mustang, sometimes leaning against it, other times standing behind its open front door. My mother smiles uncertainly in bell-bottoms and a vest, with a kerchief on her head, pushing a stroller in High Park.

These pictures show two young South Asians desperately trying to fit in, to be accepted, to be white. But they were not white, they were brown. And 1970s white Canada did not let them forget it. 'Paki' is the only slur they shared with us. Even now, when they say it, I get a sense of how much it hurt them. How it took the wind out of their sails. How it made them want to give up and go back home. And they did both of those things – gave up and tried to go back home.

Many immigrants talk about the 'Dream of Return'. *One day, I'll go home. I'll make enough money to go back, back to a country I belong in, to a place that feels like home.* But the cruel fact of immigration is that once you leave, you never really have a home. You and the place you leave behind transform, ceaselessly, infinitely, so that when – if – you encounter each other again, you are unrecognisable to one another. When you visit the neighbourhood you grew up in, you wonder, *Is this the street our house was on? Or was it the next street over? Are we even in the right area?* Your relatives and friends marvel, *Is that really you? My god, I didn't recognise you!* But still, the Dream of Return remains strong; it is a dream that those immigrants cling to most desperately who do not find home in the places to which they immigrate, where they become citizens, where they pay taxes, where they have their children, where they lose their children.

I'm talking about immigration out of necessity, out of desperation. A better word for this might be 'exile', except it's not that you've been banished from your country of origin, but rather that the sorry state of the nation you're born into and your own socio-economic class leave you no choice but to try your luck elsewhere if you dare hope for a better future.

Whatever the geopolitics of the region, or the forces of the global capitalist system that led you to find yourself in this position, it does not really matter to you. All that matters is that you would rather stay home, but you know there is no hope for you there. If you want a better future, you must leave. And you must go to a wealthier nation, a nation that is privileged by the global structures of inequality. You leave because you understand the bleak future that lies ahead. And if you're really lucky, maybe you'll amass enough wealth to return home and help your parents and siblings and extended family. They'll need it, because if they stay put – as most of them will – their future will turn out even bleaker than you could have ever imagined. Poverty will destroy your family, it will ravage the bodies of your loved ones, they will fight over scraps, they will die young from preventable diseases, without access to the basic medical attention that might have saved them.

It is these immigrants that hold tight to the Dream of Return. This immigration is not the immigration of the wealthy elite of this world. It is not the immigration of those who hop nations and continents in pursuit of adventure, hobbies, an escape from boredom. Those people never actually immigrate, though in conversation they might stop and ponder with unnecessary profundity, *I guess I'm an immigrant, too!* These people don't really think of themselves as immigrants at all; they're expats. People who always belong somewhere – somewhere else – and always have the luxury to head home, their real home, anytime they so desire.

But immigrants of my parents' ilk cannot do this, they cannot just head home. They must accumulate wealth so that they can survive when they get back to a home they no longer recognise. For such immigrants, the Dream of Return remains just that, a dream that motivates them those first years and then slowly wanes and dies as they age. The Dream of Return dies for most immigrants well before they are buried in the foreign land that will become the closest thing to home that they will ever know.

My parents did not take their rejection well. They resented and bristled at the racism they experienced, at the regular insults and demands to 'go home'. So, after about a decade of trying the assimilation route, they decided to go back to Pakistan. On this front – going home – they failed, though they tried four times – no small feat with six children. Each time, they sold everything, said goodbye to their friends and adios to Canada, and relocated to Pakistan *for real this time*. Each time, their businesses flopped, they were cheated out of their money, or some such thing, and they came back to Canada to try again.

There was no possibility in their minds of remaining forever in Canada and making it their home. Under a steady barrage of racism and xenophobia, my parents gave up on trying to assimilate into Canadian society. *Fine, if you won't have us, we don't want to belong to you anyways.* Classic bitter grapes strategy. I know it is supposed to be 'sour grapes', not 'bitter grapes', but when you are born and raised in Canada speaking Urdu as your first language, you're going to mess up metaphors. And when you do, you come to expect the superior looks and condescending corrections, even when they don't make sense. I mean, 'bitter grapes' makes more sense than 'sour grapes'. Concord grapes are sour and they taste awesome. Bitter grapes makes more sense. Think about it.

Anyways, the year I was born, my mother started wearing a hijab. She retired her pants, and sewed herself some shalwar kameez. My father grew out his beard like the

Prophet's, at least one fist-length long. And they both brought their children along for the ride on this anti-assimilationist train. Surely they thought they were protecting us, saving us from the rejection that had scarred them so deeply. If we never wanted to belong in the first place, we wouldn't care when people mocked us, treated us with contempt, were unfriendly to us. My parents pulled my older brother and sister out of choir, chess club, track and all other extra-curricular activities. They got rid of the TV, stopped listening to music and quit reading anything that could be a purveyor of 'Western' culture. Instead, they focused their energies on studying Islam, learning to recite the Qur'an properly, listening to Islamic lectures from Urdu-speaking preachers on audio cassettes. If all they were going to be was 'Paki', they might as well be proper Pakis, learn their culture and their religion. Be the people they were going to get shit for being.

The way my mother tells the story, she gave up on assimilating and put on a hijab to symbolise her rejection of Canadian society and her decision to choose 'Islam' over 'Western' culture. I find this choice fascinating. In response to being rejected for being 'Paki', my mother decided to dress in an identifiably 'Muslim' way. Her response to racial discrimination was to hyper-emphasise her religious identity. She couldn't quite stop being 'Paki' but she could change the direction of the discrimination, shift it from being racial to religious. This gave her a sense of control over her persecution; she'd rather be hated, mocked, derided, cussed at for something she was choosing to wear, rather than something she could not change about herself.

The irony is that the style of hijab my mother chose to adopt was itself Western – influenced by her time in Canada, and her interaction with Canadian Muslims of different ethnicities, races and cultures. Her hijab was a square cloth, folded into a triangle and pinned at the chin. This hijab was not like the chadors and dupattas she grew up wearing in Pakistan.

Here's a brief catalogue of ways that women cover in Pakistan:

Chadors are rectangular, opaque, soft pieces of fabric that are draped over a woman's head. There are no pins or strings or ties on this fabric. The chador conceals fluidly, so you can use it to cover more or less of yourself, depending on the situation. Chadors come in various sizes. If you're out and about, you'd wear a large chador that might envelop your entire body, head to toe. If you're cooking at home while company is over, you might wear a smaller chador. Since chadors aren't pinned or tied, they don't stay put. They slip. You have to devote a good deal of energy and attention to keeping them on.

A dupatta is a gauzier version of a chador. It is also rectangular, on the smaller side, but it is light and airy. Though many women wear a dupatta at home and a chador outside, more 'modern' women will wear a dupatta outside rather than a chador. Dupattas can be fashionable. They often come with matching outfits.

A burqa, also relevant to this story, is the most conservative of coverings – it is specifically designed for outdoor wear, where your hands might be otherwise occupied and you cannot afford to use them to hold a chador in place or adjust it when it slips from its place. A burqa consists of a long, loose-fitted flowing gown and a headpiece that is tied at your chin or the back of the neck, with a face veil, a niqab, that is usually clicked into place with a tich button. Burqas are generally black, a sensible colour when you think of how often you'd have to wash a lighter-coloured burqa after walking through dusty streets. And if you don't have a washing machine, as is the case with the majority of Pakistanis, then a lighter-coloured burqa is a real hassle. A burqa makes it easier to carry groceries, herd children and be otherwise engaged in public activity. But it is also more concealing, so there isn't any chance of it slipping accidentally, and maybe revealing some hair or your face to someone you might be flirting with. A chador may require more consistent attention, making it cumbersome to be in public efficiently, but it has more fluid-ity; it can be less revealing should you so desire.

My mother had worn all three types of covering in Pakistan – a dupatta, a chador and a burqa. And in those early years when she was trying to assimilate in Canada, she felt deep shame at removing all her coverings. She felt naked, 'nangi'. She said she felt so much shame, she would rather the earth itself open and swallow her whole than be seen nangi by her father. And that's the thing, the key to understanding this story: she wasn't ashamed before God so much as she was ashamed before her dad. It's almost like they were merged for her, her father a human stand-in for God, God personified.

My mother describes her father, my grandfather, as a fiercely pious man. His name was Asad-ur-Rehman, 'Lion of the Merciful', Mercy being one of the names of God. Asad-ur-Rehman, the Lion of the Merciful, was known for living up to his name. Legend had it that his piety was so fierce that women who didn't normally cover themselves would at least wear a dupatta when passing through his street, out of respect for Asad-ur-Rehman's convictions. And his conviction was that women ought to be modest and express their modesty by concealing themselves. In these stories, my mother always mentions two airline hostesses who would only wear their dupattas when passing by my grandfather's street. In these stories, the street became his too. She was really proud of this, that her father commanded such respect and influence, that women were afraid to pass through his street without covering themselves. I was proud of him too when I heard these stories as a child. I was proud of my maternal lineage, proud to be the granddaughter of such a fiercely pious man.

Funny thing about stories you learn as a child: they seem so self-evident, so true, so natural. Like the sky being blue or the grass being green. Why would you doubt these facts? Why would adults say anything misleading, why would they not know something? Then you grow up and realise that adulthood is a myth. We are children in ageing bodies, stumbling through life, pretending to know more than we do, acting like we have more control than we have.

It wasn't until I recounted this story about my grand-father to my partner that I realised – both from his widening eyes and from hearing the words coming out of my mouth – that, in this story, my grandfather comes across as a patri-archal, misogynistic tyrant. There had to be a reason why women covered themselves temporarily to pass by his house. He might have harassed them or shamed them. I shudder to think what he did or said that made all the women in the neighbourhood extra careful when walking down his street.

But in my mother's narrative, her father is the good guy. The guy whose piety is so great that women covered out of respect for him. Respect rather than fear. And she was terribly disappointed in herself for not covering in Canada. And when she thought about her father seeing her in her state of 'nakedness', which is what she called it even though she was completely covered except for her head and hands, she wished that the earth would swallow her rather than she see the disappointment on his face.

All this is the backstory for what follows. And the story is this: at some point, during that early assimilationist phase, while they were still trying to be 'Canadian', my parents went back to Pakistan for a visit. They had two kids at the time, my older siblings, five and three years old. My mother was around twenty-four. I wasn't born yet. She was excited about going to Pakistan, but also nervous. Although she wasn't covering in Canada, she packed a burqa in her suitcase. She figured she would take it out when they got to the airport in Lahore, and then wear it before the hours-long journey over potholed roads to her hometown, Gujranwala. Her parents were still alive and she was going to be staying with them. Her older brother would be there to pick her up from the airport.

My parents arrived in Pakistan having survived an over eighteen-hour flight from Toronto to Lahore, with a layover in Europe. The children were exhausted, hungry, crying and too hot in the summer heat. My mother was sleep deprived. The flight was delayed coming in, so her brother had been waiting for several hours already. Now, when my mother started going through her luggage to find her burqa, her brother, himself tired and hungry, dissuaded her. *What's the big deal?* he asked. *We're just going to get in the car and drive home. No one will see you.* He was anxious to hit the road and get home. Everyone was expecting them.

And just like that, my mother was dissuaded.

In her telling, she blames this on the crying children, her own fatigue, her brother's counsel, but I wonder if a part of her wanted to share this new Canadian version of herself with her family. Maybe a tiny part of her wanted her parents and siblings to meet and love this new person she was becoming. After all, she'd spent several years abroad, change was inevitable, and sometimes enviable. In Urdu, they use the word 'bahir' for 'abroad'. Literally, 'bahir' means 'outside', so that Pakistan is 'inside' and the rest of the world is 'outside'. It is a commonplace way to think of the private and the public, with the nation itself as the private sphere and world as the public sphere. Like domestic and foreign. The term 'bahir' can be used variously to convey a mixture of pride, contempt and envy. It can signify your connection to the outside world, perhaps a possibility for escape, perhaps a certain cosmopolitan sophistication, or it can be used as a put-down to describe visiting relatives who might be putting on airs.

At any rate, my mother did not put on her burqa. She did not cover her head to go home. Unlike the neighbour-hood women and the air hostesses, who covered their heads to pass by her father's house, my mother arrived at his house, after years away, head uncovered. Maybe she was unconsciously trying to push boundaries, to see if she was loved unconditionally. Perhaps it was an assertion of inde-pendence. *I don't live by your rules anymore.*

Whatever the (sub)conscious impulse for this decision, my mother managed to create the very scene she had dreaded for years. The scene where her father catches her, head uncovered, in public. The man who makes random women cover their hair just to pass by 'his' street encounters his very own daughter uncovered, nangi. Except, instead of this happening in Canada, which was impossible since my grandfather had no intention of ever visiting, my mother staged this scene in Pakistan, at my grandfather's very own house, on his very own street.

My parents arrived at my grandparents' house in Gujranwala. The car pulled into the narrow brick lane, stopping in the gully in front of my grandparents' home. The brick lane is slightly rounded, the middle higher than the sides, so water rolls off when it rains. Cars are always on a slant in the lane, motorcycles lean one way or the other, but horse carriages do just fine with their big wooden wheels on either side, taking up the whole lane. On either side of the lane is a small channel, with greenish-black water running through. Outdoor plumbing. This used to be the nice part of town, the one with plumbing and a sewer system from colonial times. It was called 'Civil Line'. My grandparents' house sits on the corner of two lanes, a typical house for the area. The first thing you encounter is its high stone walls. And the door, a large wooden door, with metal bolts. The walls and door yell *Private!*, and you never actually know what you'll find if you're allowed through, beyond the outer walls.

My parents came inside quickly and started to settle into the room that they would share with their children for the next few months. My grandfather was home when they arrived. He was expecting them. He saw my mother. He didn't say anything about the situation with the nakedness. Not yet, anyways. They exchanged pleasantries. It was already evening. They had dinner with the extended family, my mom's brothers and sisters, and their families. She is one of thirteen siblings. There were a lot of people, a lot of children, there was a lot of commotion. Then everyone started retiring for the night, either to their rooms or to their homes nearby. As things got quieter, my mother became more and more anxious. She knew her father wasn't going to let this go. He was going to, at the very least, say something. She wished she could just say something herself and get the anticipation over with, but she was too frightened, she didn't have the courage.

Finally, she retired to her room. The lights started to turn off. My mother's room had a window that opened on to the courtyard of this large house. Courtyards make cloistered spaces more friendly for women. They can enjoy the outdoors, the winter sun, the monsoon rains, without leaving the house. In the courtyard tonight, my mother watched her father pace back and forth, smoking cigarettes. She heard his slow, measured footsteps, watched the red burning tobacco, as he paced steadily, deliberately, from one end of the courtyard to the other and back.

She knew he was going to say something to her. What would he say? She hoped he wouldn't be cruel and humiliate her in front of her husband and children. She didn't want him to do her 'bay-izzati'. 'Izzat' means 'honour' or 'dignity'. When someone does your bay-izzati, they rob you of your honour, your dignity. What if he yelled and screamed and kicked them out of his house? She made calculations in her mind: where would she go? One of her sisters' places? Their husbands might not be inclined to host a family of four to whom they had no patrilineal obligation. One of her brothers' places? Most were too poor to host them.

She followed the red embers of the cigarette as it moved back and forth across the courtyard, my grandfather's face obscured in the dark. Finally, he walked toward her room, opened the door and walked in. My mother was ready for him, sitting on the chaar-pai.

If you're wondering where my dad is in this story, you raise a good point. In telling this story, my mother barely mentions him. Is he sitting with her, anxiously wondering what will happen next? After all, his fate is tied to hers. If her father throws them out, he will have to fend for the family. The tension between my mother and her own father is so intense in this moment that it erases everyone else. Her husband and children are no longer. All that remains is the bond between father and daughter. Will it survive this moment?

And the fact that my grandfather can just walk into their room – a grown, married couple with children, after bedtime – is an expression of power and entitlement. This is, after all, his house. He may go where he pleases. He's not worried about etiquette. My parents are guests in his house, they are at his mercy. He can let them stay or throw them out. He can tell them what to do, what to wear. His opinion matters. His feelings matter.

My mother is half relieved and half terrified that the moment she has been dreading is finally here. My grandfather sits across from my mother, avoids eye contact, looks away from her, looks at the floor. He speaks quietly.

Did I see correctly that you arrived at my house with your head naked?

Yes, she whispers.

He nods his head thoughtfully, slowly.

I wondered if I'd seen correctly, if perhaps my eyes were lying to me. She is silent. He continues.

I thought it can't be, that my own Baby would come to my home with a nanga head.

That is actually my mother's nickname. Not Urdu for 'baby', but the English word itself. Colonialism made English the official language of Pakistan, alongside Urdu.

Not when the neighbourhood women wouldn't dare walk by my house with naked heads. Baby wouldn't come to my house with a naked head.

I'm sorry, Abba-ji. I didn't mean to disrespect you. I wanted to unpack the burqa at the airport but Bhai said not to worry about it.

She blamed her brother. In doing so she admits that she doesn't wear a burqa in Canada, and was planning to take it out at the airport. Her father doesn't seem to care. He's fixated on her not wearing it around him, not wearing it when she comes to *his* house, *his* street. This is about him. His reputation.

Your brother is a son of a bitch. You shouldn't have listened to him. Do you cover for him or for Allah?

Even though he says she should cover for God, he means himself. And it is from him that she asks forgiveness.

I'm sorry, Abba-ji. I made a mistake, please forgive me.

He does forgive her, but not without shaming her. He speaks the words she has expected to hear for years, the words she believes she deserves to hear, the words she's dreaded since the day she stopped covering her hair. The words she did not want to hear so badly, she wished the ground would swallow her up instead. But also the words she gave her father the chance to utter, by somehow not covering her head when she came to visit, becoming – as we sometimes do – the architect of her own nightmare.

He said, *The neighbourhood that would rather cover its women than have them pass by the house of Asad-ur-Rehman with naked heads, today that neighbourhood saw my own daughter disembark from a car and enter the threshold of my house with her head naked. You have made a mockery of me. Today, you made me hang my head in shame. I will not be able to raise it again.*

Then he left and never brought up the conversation again.

And my mother saw him for only a few more years, with her head always covered. By the time he died, she was burqa-clad in Canada.

It would be easy to say that this encounter between daughter and father, between my mother and my grandfather, is the reason my mother eventually donned a burqa in Canada. But the truth is far more complicated than that. Remember, my grandfather was only upset that my mother came to his threshold, his house, his neighborhood, without her burqa. He didn't care what she wore in Canada.

The story between my mother and her father, that's a script we're familiar with, we've heard this story before. Muslim patriarchy suffocating Muslim women. But this story is bigger than that. The reason, in the end, that my mother decided to wear a burqa in Canada was not because of Muslim patriarchy, but because of racism, because of a decade spent trying to assimilate but failing – and it felt like failure – to be accepted as Canadian.

When my mother donned a burqa in Canada, years after this incident with her father, it was as a shield from racism. It was racism that would eventually make fundamentalist Islam appealing to her. Wearing a niqab did not increase the persecution and discrimination my mother faced. But now, instead of the insults, the cruel words and harsh looks hurting her feelings – *Why do you hate me because of my colour?* – my mother could believe that her persecution was a measure of her sincerity, her worthiness. Enduring religious persecution is noble, honourable, principled, meritorious; it is heroic. To be persecuted for your beliefs and to remain steadfast in the face of persecution, that is the stuff of legend.

And this is how it came to be that I was born into a house filled with the religious zeal of new converts, and why I began wearing a hijab when I was young. So young as to not remember when I started. Raised in the cradle of a religious identity fashioned as a shield, a protection from racism.

Second Generation

I started wearing hijab before consciousness, before I have any memory of putting it on. It is as if I emerged into being with my head already covered. I only know how I came to wear hijab from stories my mother tells. She tells me that I started wearing it when I was five years old. She's really proud of this. She says she didn't force me to wear it; on the contrary, I had insisted. I was a strong-willed child. I didn't like 'no' as an answer. I still don't. Does anyone?

My mother herself started wearing hijab the year I was born. By the time I started kindergarten, I asked if I could wear hijab too. My mother tried to dissuade me.

You're too young. When you're older you can wear it for sure.

But I want to wear it now!

You're too young, what will people say? They'll think I'm forcing you!

She tells me that I started stealing her hijabs, wearing them to school and then coming home, dragging them behind me, all muddy and dirty. Her hijabs were too big for my tiny body. After enough ruined hijabs, she relented and sewed me some my size; square fabric, which you folded into a triangle and then pinned at your chin, but really your throat, with a safety pin. At that age, I doubt my mother pinned the hijab at my throat. She probably just tied it under my chin, like a kerchief that elderly Eastern European women wear on their heads sometimes. I would graduate to the safety pin.

My earliest memory of wearing hijab is having forgotten to wear it. I was attending the Islamic School in Toronto. There were Muslims from all over the world at this school. The Sudanese principal had a thin, white metal rod, four feet long, that he carried around the school with him. He would use it to discipline misbehaving children, sometimes with a sharp, stinging strike to their hands. He believed in public punishment so that the other children would know what to expect if they misbehaved. I saw him hit a young boy once. The child shrieked, his face crumpling with pain and shame, reddening, his eyes squinting as he hopped frantically from one foot to the other. I feel I was hit by this rod too. I have a vivid memory of how it felt on my hand. I say 'feel' because I'm not sure if I've conjured up this experience with my elaborate childhood imagination. Maybe I was hit and I blocked out the details. Or maybe I spent so much time and emotional energy terrified, imagining how it would feel to be hit by the rod, that I imagined that it happened. Either way, we were all terrified of the principal's rod. Terror is only effective when it takes hold of our imagination.

But the principal was also very nice to me. One evening after a fundraising event, when people milled about after dinner in a sparse and cavernous community hall, with walls painted white, the floor a beige linoleum and lights fluorescent and bright, I remember he played with me, lifting me off the floor and twirling me around. I loved the attention. He asked my parents if he could adopt me for a few years. He promised to teach me flawless Arabic.

Your daughter is special, he told them. *She could be a great scholar.*

There were Canadians from all over the world at the Islamic School: South Asians from India and Pakistan; Arabs from Saudi, Syria and Egypt; converts, European and Japanese. Everyone came with their own cultural background, their own vision of a pristine Islam. All these visions jostled with one another to create a mosaic, an Islamic mosaic, at this school.

But my parents didn't think Islam should be a mosaic. They didn't like the way Islam was being practised there – it was too diluted, too weak, too Western. There was too much mixing between the genders. Why did this school have co-ed classes? Did they care nothing for Islam? Qur'an memorisation, or lack thereof, was a particular sore point for my parents. I'd learned to recite the Qur'an very early, and had read it in its entirety by the time I was five years old. The Qur'an is divided into siparas, thirty sections of roughly equal length. I had memorised the last sipara in its entirety by the time I was seven, and my parents expected me to keep pace with memorisation at the Islamic School. But my peers were still only just learning to recite the Qur'an, and they were way behind me on the memorisation. And to make matters worse, the Islamic School was an hour-long bus ride away, and the long commute meant less time to keep up with my memorisation when I got home. So what was the point of sending me to Islamic school if I wasn't learning anything Islamic, not even the Qur'an?

I wonder if my parents also pulled me out of the Islamic School because they couldn't afford to pay the fees. How were they going to send all six children there? Whatever the reason, by third grade, I was back in public school.

But while in Islamic school, one winter morning, in between grabbing my lunch, pulling on my jacket, leg warmers, gloves and hat, I forgot to also wear my hijab. I didn't realise this until I was on my way to school. As I warmed up on the bus, I went to remove my hat and discovered, with horror and shame, that I'd forgotten to wear my hijab! The realisation knocked the breath out of me. I froze. My ears started ringing. I quickly replaced the hat on my head, looked around guiltily to make sure no one had seen my hair and tried to disappear into the bus seat. At school I whispered what had happened to my teacher, Sister Nobuko.

Something really bad has happened. I trembled, *I forgot my hijab.*

To my surprise, she was nonchalant. *Oh, well, you don't have to wear it today.*

What? Had she lost her mind? I was a Muslim girl, I had to wear hijab. You couldn't just not wear it. I felt naked without my hijab. Like I'd forgotten to wear pants and everyone was just rolling with it. *Oh well, that happens sometimes. Spend the day without pants and tomorrow you can remember to wear them.* What the fuck?

Sister Nobuko saw that I was going to have trouble participating in class, because I stood frozen in place, looking at the floor in shame. She took an exasperated sigh and said, *Well, we can grab one from the bin of extra hijabs we keep for prayer time. Would you like one of those?*

I gratefully accepted this offer, taking the hijab from her hands with a mixture of urgency and relief. I don't know the last time that hijab had been washed. The smell of many heads mingled in the scent of the hijab to create a pungent, spicy perfume. I didn't care. I'd rather wear a dodgy-smelling hijab than walk shamelessly with my head uncovered all day. As relief washed over me, energy returned to my body. I stood taller, uncrumpling myself. Once again, I felt comfortable at school; I was chatty and enthusiastic. I added my own scent of oiled, thick Pakistani hair to that hijab.

Once I started public school, hijab moved from being a personal expression of my religious conviction to a central part of my identity. At the Islamic School, no one was hung up on my hijab, but in public school, it became the first and sometimes the only thing people saw of me. It's like they had this reductive, simplistic idea of the hijab and Muslims, and they just projected that on to me. They couldn't even see me. They didn't see my adorable face, or my oversized eye glasses. (I always wanted the biggest glasses – they made me feel like an adult, and this was the eighties.) They didn't notice my outgoing, chatty, even spunky personality. Instead, they noticed and commented on my hijab. Even though I didn't spend every waking moment thinking about it – it was just something I wore, and like all regularly worn things I forgot I was wearing it – no one else could get over it.

Why are you wearing that? they'd ask.

Where are you from?

Is that from your religion?

What would happen if I saw your hair?

Do you wear it when you sleep?

Do you wear that in the shower?

Aren't you too hot?

Who made you wear it? Your parents? Like their parents didn't make them wear the clothes they were wearing.

The questions were ceaseless and incessant. Sometimes they were asked out of curiosity, other times pity, moral judgement, suspicion. The questions always betrayed the privilege of the questioner. To feel that you have the right to walk up to a stranger and ask them why they are wearing what they are wearing, this comfort lies with those who do not have to ask themselves the same questions. Always, the questions made me feel like an outsider, like I didn't belong, demanded that I explain myself, justify my very existence.

Canada is a cultural mosaic, we were taught in our curriculum. *As a country of immigrants, we value everyone's cultural and religious contributions. You don't have to leave your culture and religion behind to belong here; we accept all of you. Your cultural and religious characteristics are small, colourful tiles; each one adds to the beauty of the larger mosaic that is Canada.*

But some cultures and religions belonged more than others. Some clothes were more 'Canadian' than others. The hijab hadn't, and still hasn't, made it into the cultural mosaic.

I became good at answering the questions, they were so frequent, so predictable, so . . . boring. Like everyone was working with the same script, asking the same questions over and over and over again. I was so much more than my hijab. I had ideas about things. But most people couldn't get past the fabric on my head to hear me. Not my classmates, not my teachers, not strangers in the supermarket. I'd answer patiently, calmly, mindlessly. Other times, my answers were testy, frustrated, annoyed.

I wear this because of my religion. I am a Muslim.

Nothing would happen if you saw my hair.

No, I don't wear it to sleep.

No, I don't wear it in the shower. How would that even work?!

No, I'm not too hot. And it's hotter in Hell.

I'm from here! I was born in Canada.

And then, in my head, *This is what a Canadian looks like, motherfuckers.*

I felt so defiant and self-righteous saying this, even just in my head. I relished sullying what was clearly pure and pristine in their minds, by turning the pollution into the thing itself. This was not the first time my body was cast as a pollutant, tainting, spoiling what is pure. In some, but not all, Islamic legal texts, women's bodies are seen as polluting to communal rituals and sacred spaces; and here was my body cast as a pollutant again, but this time defiling the idea of a Canadian. The people who saw me as an outsider had an idea of what a 'Canadian' looked like, they saw themselves reflected in this idea, this idea was precious to them. I did not fit in their vision, in their self-image; my existence corrupted their vision. But what if I were the vision itself? What if I could ruin how they looked at themselves? Ruin their self-image.

What I did not understand then is that my desire to be 'Canadian', to be accepted as such, was shaped by fear. In claiming the identity of a 'Canadian', I was holding on to the very thing that was being used to reject me. I was looking for stability in the thing that was creating precariousness for me to begin with – citizenship. But what does it mean, really, to 'look' Canadian, to 'be' Canadian? What does it mean for me to claim this identity as a South Asian woman, a progeny of a double diaspora, displaced by colonialism and into a settler colonial state?

Any joy I might squeeze from this petty rejoinder was short-lived. For to say the sentence itself, to claim 'Canadianness' at all, is to already be ensnared by the logic of the state.

The state artificially creates the conditions of its own citizenship, in which some are embraced while others are rejected. It draws a line around itself, telling all outside the line that it owes them nothing, and demands that all inside the line become subjects of the state, whether they like it or not. It represents itself as the solution to the very problems it creates.

In claiming citizenship, I was begging to inherit the sins of the state. The genocides, the war crimes, the selling of arms to dictators, the structural racism, the institutionalised patriarchy. Blind patriotism demands a great deal of forgetting and selective remembering. It requires a whitewashing of history, so we can feel virtuous as we kill and oppress and dispossess in the name of the nation. We forget, no, we erase the sins so we can celebrate ourselves simply, which requires us to first craft simplistic stories about ourselves. If erasing our sins means erasing entire peoples and histories, including our own, so be it. We demand this forgetting, this erasure, as the cost of 'good citizenship', and we are angry, frustrated, annoyed when people refuse to participate in the erasure, when they insist on reminding us of our sins, when they insist on remembering.

By its very existence, the Canadian state displaces and alienates those who are indigenous to the land it lays claim over; it demands they justify their right to continue existing on land they are already living on, and defend that right to foreign, unwelcome colonisers. In other words, the state creates a hell from which citizenship to this same state becomes the only respite, maybe the only reprieve. What I'm saying is, by making citizenship a form of belonging, the state turns itself into a refuge from itself. And this is how God describes Herself in the Qur'an:

لا ملجأ من الله إلا إليه

There is no refuge from God except in God.

When the state turns itself into a refuge from itself, the state turns itself into a god. Worshipping a god that is not God is a sin called 'shirk'. Shirk is the only unforgivable sin in Islam.

Theft

When I was little, say maybe four or five years old, I joined my mother on a visit to her friend's house. We didn't grow up wealthy. My mother managed our home, produced and raised six children. She did this mostly alone, because my father worked long hours and was often at work when we were awake. When I was young, we lived in rental apartments, and whenever we had to move and my parents had to find a new apartment to rent, they would leave us with friends. They would hide the fact that they had so many children. They would hope that the landlord would not ask them how many children they had, so that they wouldn't have to lie. But they lied when necessary. Most landlords would balk at the idea of three, four, five, and eventually six children living in a small space. It was difficult to explain to them that we weren't spoiled and undisciplined, like gora children. We were South Asian and Muslim, and unable to afford living in large houses; we weren't going to be allowed to misbehave, run wild and destroy our chances of living somewhere.

At the time of this visit, when I accompanied my mother to her friend's house, we were living in a small apartment in Toronto, four children in a two-bedroom apartment. We didn't have a lot of furniture. We had a couch for entertaining, a kitchen table and chairs, but we didn't have beds. My parents thought wall-to-wall carpeting was amazing. Who needed beds? Just throw down a sheet and pillow and you're set! Plus, beds were expensive and took up a lot of space. What was the point? My father worked as a pipe fitter and a welder. He sent extra money back home to Pakistan to support extended family on both sides, and Islamic causes. We were fortunate to have so much.

But when we visited other people, I saw how little we had. Other people had fancy bedroom furniture, dressers, side tables, elegant beds. Some girls had princess beds with a canopy! Oh, how I envied these children. They had TVs, they could watch movies. My mother's friend even had a cabinet full of only decorative stuff! She had little crystal figurines in it, like a bird or a bear, and I watched the light create dazzling colours as it filtered through the crystal. I could see purples and pinks and greens. I became mesmerised and obsessed with one figurine of a bird, its wings just spread for flight. It was so elegant, so beautiful, so bewitching. I touched it; it was stunning. I couldn't part with it. Before we left this aunty's house, I pocketed it. She had other beautiful things. She wouldn't miss it. And I *needed* to have it. So, I stole it. Except, I was too young to understand the concept of theft.

But the adults understood. Her friend called our home later that night and told my mother that the figurine was missing. My mother assured her that she would deal with it. And she did. By teaching me about stealing, which is taking something that belongs to someone else without their consent. Apparently, it didn't matter how much you liked it or needed it.

When my parents consulted with one another and considered how they would teach me about stealing, the conversation portion of the lesson wasn't immediately followed by a lesson on forgiveness, where I return the figurine to its owner, apologise and am forgiven. That *did* happen. Eventually. But first, there was a theatrical detour.

In Islam, my parents taught me, *if you steal, your hand gets chopped off.*

And since I had stolen, I deserved to have my hand chopped off. My father was to do the deed.

And this is how it came to pass that I remember crouching behind the couch we used for entertaining, squeezed between the wall and the back of the couch, terrified, looking up, as I see my father peering down at me, brandishing an axe. Or at least that is what I've believed my entire life, until recently, when recounting this story to a group of friends, they convinced me that it was, more likely, a hatchet. Obviously, I didn't know the difference. I was crying, and at some point my mother pulled me out, hugged and consoled me, assured me that though I'd narrowly escaped punishment this time, there were no guarantees next time. Better not steal again.

I think my parents were proud of themselves for doing such a great job teaching me a valuable lesson. It wouldn't do to have their children stealing. This was serious. You couldn't fuck with the law. They were uncertain of how they'd help me if I got in trouble with the law, if I got in the habit of stealing. Better nip this in the bud.

In his book *Between the World and Me*, Ta-Nehisi Coates talks about how his parents beat him out of fear for what might happen to him in the streets, at the hands of white authorities. The beating was meant to be a kind of protection, a kind of love. It seems they believed that the violence they employed to educate Coates would serve him well, especially if it saved him from violence beyond the house. As long as they were doing the hitting, they were in control of it. They loved him. So they wouldn't hurt him irrevocably. He wouldn't die at their hands. In this way, violence becomes a teaching, a kindness, a mercy even.

My mother always says, محبت کی مار مکھن سے بھی نرم ہے

A beating from love – a 'love-beating', perhaps – is softer than butter.

Maybe Coates's parents figured that there was some algorithm that determined the amount of violence in the world, like we were all owed a portion of it, and if they administered it themselves, they could control it, be measured and merciful with their son's quota. Because they couldn't trust the authorities, the state, to be measured or merciful. The state and its apparatus are monstrous, murderous, careless, merciless with bodies of colour, especially with

black bodies. Or maybe they thought a certain level of
violence was necessary to keep him in line, so that he might
never encounter the authorities. Which feeds the myth that
the 'authorities' are only ever involved when we step out of
line. Or maybe . . . or maybe . . . or maybe . . .

This is what the state does to the populations it margin-
alises – it dominates us with such ferocity, the mere threat of
its violence is so terrifying, it fools us into imagining that our
controlled violence against our own, against ourselves, will
spare us greater, more fearsome violence. And so, the state
comes to appear benevolent in the face of our own monstros-
ities. And we hurt the ones we love, in the name of love. And
protection. Through violence.

I have only two memories of my grandfather, both from
family trips to Pakistan. In one, he's in a bed in one of the
rooms in my mamoo's portion of the house. The room is
painted a light shade of green. It is a house that my grandfather claimed after Partition. He fled to Pakistan from
India with his family, leaving behind farmlands, cattle and a
haveli, a compound of houses – immovable wealth.
Apparently, the way it worked during Partition was that if
you survived the massacres in your home town, escaped the
knives of your neighbours, jewellers, butchers and school
teachers, once-friends now turned enemies based on lines
drawn by white men over lunches in posh rooms; if you

survived the violence along the way, on the roads and train stations, stations turned – for a little while – into battlefields and slaughterhouses, running red with rivers of blood; if you finally made it to the place where you were supposed to be, which wasn't your home because that had been left behind, but the place where it had been decided by the people who would never be called thieves that you'd have to start your life over, then what you would do is find an empty house, another displaced family's home, and move into it and claim it as your own. Finders keepers following partition, displacement and massacre.

The house my grandparents settled into is a large home that used to belong to a Punjabi Hindu or Sikh family; we know this because it was abandoned. My grandfather claimed it. Growing up, I heard this was a wealthy family's house, evidenced by the fact that they left behind an entire trunk full of chocolates. Now the house is partitioned in two as my grandfather lies weak, ill and dying, surrounded by his children and grandchildren in a room in a part of the house that two of his seven sons live in. The other half is occupied by another son. The sons split the house in two, and the partition was not amicable. The brothers fought over portions of the house, each feeling cheated out of his fair share. And the three who claimed the house, two in one section and one in the other, screwed their remaining siblings – including my mother – out of their rightful claim over a house the family barely had a claim over to begin with.

I'm not sure how old I am in this scene, maybe I'm five. The white-bearded, light-skinned, frail man on the bed, my grandfather, is dying. Some people are weeping, speaking in hushed tones. There is a sense of great importance in the room; something is about to happen. I'm not there when it does. I am told that just before he died, he smelled blossoms, asking, *Where are all these flowers coming from?* There were no flowers in the room. This is a good sign. The smell of flowers means he is headed to Jannah, the Garden, Paradise, encountering its smell before its sight. He smelled Heaven while still alive, in the liminal space between life and death, when he could still communicate, when he could still tell us, *There are flowers in Paradise! I smell them!*

The next time I see him, he is dead. His washed body lying on a chaar-pai. There is a huge slab of ice the size of a coffin underneath the chaar-pai, cooling the body from below so it doesn't rot. The body, the chaar-pai, the coffin-sized block of ice are all in the courtyard of the house. I think it is summer, and early evening, so likely about 7:00P.M. Some of the adults are wailing. My mother's sister brings me close to the body.

Go ahead, look at him. He's your nana.

Your grandfather. Your mother's father. The words for maternal and paternal grandfather are different in Urdu, 'nana' and 'dada', respectively. The difference between these grandfathers is significant. You have different claims over each. They have different kinds of power over you.

Go ahead, look at him. He's your nana.

Even now, as I remember or manufacture this scene, I am aware that she means to convey something important to me, but I don't get it. Not then, not now. What is she trying to tell me? Maybe she wants me to know where I'm from, my maternal lineage. Maybe she's just overcome with grief and this encounter has nothing to do with me. That's more likely; this is about her. But I don't know that when I'm five. And more than thirty years later, I remember that exchange, but I doubt she has any recollection of it.

I go into a dark back room off the courtyard, crossing into another section of the house, and hang out with my cousins, who are also children. We discuss, try to process what has just happened, and how we should behave.

Our grandfather just died, says one cousin.

We should be sad, says another.

Let's cry, suggests a third.

Good idea, we agree.

So we try to make ourselves cry, mimicking the adults, forcing feelings of sadness I don't actually feel. After all, I never had a relationship with this man who has just died, this man named Asad-ur-Rehman. Beautiful name when you think about it. Not the 'Lion of God', but the 'Lion of the Merciful'. A name that holds opposites, that imagines fierceness and mercy together, at once.

As I think back on this strange memory of being in a dark room that feels like a cave, the walls made of stone and brick, moisture seeping through them so the room feels damp, pretending to be sad, fake crying at the death of a

grandfather I never knew, I wonder, is this the first memory
I have of feeling like a fraud? I wonder too, can grief be
stolen? What I'm really asking is, can grief be owned?

There is a contested story about the British East India
Company involving the thumbs of Bengali weavers.
According to oral accounts, the thumbs of Bengali weavers
were cut off by the British to prevent them from competing
with the East India Company in the textile trade. But a written account, by a colonialist himself, states that the East
India Company's labour practices were so horrific that
Bengali weavers cut off their own thumbs rather than allow
their labour to be stolen by the British. Where does the truth
of the missing thumbs lie, in the oral history of Indigenous
peoples or the written history of colonisers? Memories, too,
it turns out, can be stolen.

In the episode with the hatchet, I was never physically hurt.
The mere threat of violence was enough to put the fear of
God in me. The fear of God can be more merciful than the
fear of the state. God can be shaped and reshaped by us, but
we are helpless before the state.

And it worked. I learned the lesson I was supposed to.
That people and things can be owned. That some people

own more things than others. That ownership is virtuous and, even more, it is a protected right. Taking something that someone else claims ownership over is called 'theft'. It does not matter how little you have, or how much they have, or how they came by what they have, taking it is a crime and a sin. The crime is both moral and legal. Laws – religious and secular – punish the thief. The punishment is often physical, whether it involves cutting off a hand, or confining you to a cage, stealing years from your life.

I learned this lesson living on stolen land, land stolen by Europeans from the Indigenous peoples whom they mistook as 'Indians' and then called 'Indians' anyways. Stealing their identities, their names, their land, their kin, their children, their language. Teaching us that what is not owned can still be stolen.

So the lesson I learned was this: the powerless have only a merciful God to rely upon, whereas the powerful can rely on the mercy of the state.

Unexpected Visitors

Whenever I hear about incredible, selfless people who devote their lives to the service of others, who sacrifice their own needs so they may help others in need, I wonder about the ways they fail their own families to be these people. It's not that I don't admire them, that I'm not impressed by their sacrifices. It's just that I know that the 'self' in 'self-sacrifice' more often than not includes the sacrifice of other 'selves', the selves in one's family, those known as 'loved ones'. These people – one's own partners, children, siblings, parents – don't count in the category of 'others', the 'others' whom one helps. So, when I hear about Mother Teresa, I wonder about her family. What did they think of her? What did she do for them? What did they give up? Same thing with Martin Luther King, Jr., Gandhi, even Jesus.

Here, I'm reminded of that passage from the New Testament, where Jesus is with the believers, preaching to the crowds. He's having a moment with his congregants, and suddenly, this moment is interrupted by an announcement.

Your mother and brothers are standing outside, wanting to speak with you.

How long have they been there, waiting outside, waiting to be let in, to see Jesus, to speak to him, waiting for his permission? Why are they even waiting outside? Why haven't they just come in expecting to be welcomed? Are they being kept outside by a guard, or some equivalent of a bouncer?

I expect Jesus to jump up and run outside, to greet his family, to apologise for their wait, to say, *Yes, yes, of course, let them in!*

But he doesn't do that. Instead, he responds in a way that strikes me as rude, insulting even. Instead of responding with a gesture of welcome and respect, he rejects his family's claim over him while paradoxically expanding the notion of kinship itself.

Who is my mother, and who are my brothers? he asks.

His question is a spurning, a turning away. His question makes a stranger of his mother, the woman who carried him in her womb for nine months, who nourished him from her body, providing him nutrients by draining them from her own bones, then suckled him, cared for him, bore ostracism because of him. How can she make a claim over him if he doesn't even recognise their relationship?

Then Jesus points to those around him, to the disciples, to the crowds, people whom he has known for years, and people whom he met only months ago, weeks and days ago, maybe even moments ago. There are people in the crowds whom Jesus has never met before, he does not even know their names. Yet he says, *Here are my mother and my brothers. For whoever does the will of my Father in Heaven is my brother and sister and mother.*

I found myself studying this text with some Christian theologians at Cambridge University, and they insisted that this passage was about the radical inclusion of Christianity. That in this sentence, Jesus' family, his mothers and his brothers and his sisters, are multiplied manifold. His sense of obligation to family is expanded to include strangers. *How benevolent!* they said, wanting me to see the generosity, the magnanimity of Christ.

But I found myself standing outside with Jesus' mother and his brothers. What did his words mean to them? How did they receive them? How much pain did it cause them? Are they let in, or are they turned away after this little lesson about how unspecial they are and how special everyone else is? And how special is family if it can be undone so easily, so lightly? Would you want to be the mother or brother of a man who so easily disowns his own?

My Christian theologian friends had a point: it is great to have an expansive notion of kinship. But they could not see, or would not see, that in this case, expansion is achieved through exclusion, by making expendable Jesus' mother and brothers. Sure, in saying, *Here are my mother and my brothers,* Jesus' mother and brothers are indeed multiplied manifold. But this sentence comes in response to a question posed by Jesus, *Who is my mother, and who are my brothers?* And this question is a misrecognition; it excludes his sense of obligation to his blood kin in service of the kinship of faith that he is trying to create.

Each person only has a limited amount of energy. When we spend our time and energy on some, we neglect others. It's always a trade-off. Self-sacrifice for others comes at the

expense of family. They are a part of the self that is perhaps
too easily sacrificed.

In my family, we did not celebrate birthdays. When you
grow up in a religiously zealous household, religious reasoning is used to explain, justify, a lot of things. Many of these
things may not be about religion at the start. It may be that
your family does something because of pragmatic financial
reasons, but then, once it has been explained and justified
using religious reasoning, it becomes infused with virtue and
piety, taking on a life of its own.

I don't know exactly why my parents decided not to
celebrate birthdays. There could be many reasons. For one
thing, it is not a very South Asian thing to do. I mean, South
Asians do celebrate birthdays now, but that is more a function of globalisation than of South Asian culture. South
Asian Muslims have a long tradition of celebrating the
birthdays (and death days) of important people, like the
Prophet Muhammad, but not necessarily the birthdays of
family members. Also, in a continent where birthdays
weren't even recorded until recently, birthday celebrations
don't make a lot of sense. And this isn't in the ancient past
either. We don't know what day, month or even year my
father was born – he believes he was born in 1942 or 1944.
When my father was applying for a Canadian visa, he just
made up his birth date, picking the first day of a month. His

first daughter and second child would later be born on that very same day. Now they share a birthday, but his is made up.

It's always interesting to me when my white friends talk about their genealogies, how they can trace their family tree back several generations to so-and-so, how they have written records of their ancestors. I can't do that, because I don't have written records dating back even two generations. This is the result of being born to a people whose culture isn't obsessed with writing and bureaucracy. That is the easy and bullshit and racist way to explain it. But really, it is the result of belonging to a people ravaged by colonialism, by a colonialism where white people kept a record of themselves in India, but didn't think to record details – and outright destroyed records – of a people they considered on a par with dogs. British colonialism in South Asia is a story soaked in barbarity and inhumanity dressed up as civilisation. Formal British colonialism ended with genocide, resulting in the mass migration and displacement, forced expulsion, of my parents' generation. Millions of people were displaced, forcibly moved between India and Pakistan. That this genocidally motivated expulsion is called 'migration' in popular historical narratives demonstrates how violence is sanitised and experiences of entire peoples erased to keep the powerful from taking responsibility for their crimes.

When running from their homes, as news arrived of violence close at hand, because they belonged to the wrong religion and lived in the wrong place, my grandparents couldn't be burdened with tomes of paper when they needed to be light and quick. They could only take with them what they could literally carry. Maybe they thought they would return home later and collect their belongings, their lives, left behind at a moment's notice. But it turned out they were lucky just to have survived. They would never see home again. For the rest of their lives, they'd carry instead the loss of home, the loss of a sense of belonging, dreams of the past, a place where they were born, had lived for generations, a home abandoned to memory. And their records, hastily left behind, were likely destroyed by the families that replaced them in their homes, who put down roots for a new future, a new start, a new story of a different family.

Birthdays are also very expensive, what with all the presents and cakes. If you have six children, the dollars add up. And if you want to throw a party, then you have to go to other children's birthday parties too. Suddenly, you're buying presents for dozens of children every year. So it makes sense that my immigrant parents, who lived with six children on a single blue-collar income, might have decided not to celebrate birthdays due to financial constraints. But that's embarrassing. It's hard to tell your kids you can't afford to celebrate their birthdays in a culture where birthday celebrations are normal. And how do you explain to them that they are also not allowed to celebrate their friends' birthdays, that they must decline invitations to their birthday parties, that you can't buy them presents?

What if there was a way to feel good, righteous, about not celebrating birthdays? Ah, but there is: religion! Instead of telling us that celebrating birthdays was really expensive and that they couldn't afford the ritual, or that celebrating birthdays was a culturally strange ritual for them, this is what my parents, god bless them, said to us:

We don't celebrate birthdays because we are Muslim and Muslims don't celebrate birthdays. What is there to celebrate anyways? You're a year closer to death and what do you have to show for it? Muhammad bin Qasim conquered India at the age of eighteen, what have you done?

When I was young, I bought into this. Why *did* people celebrate birthdays? What was the point? We *were* a year closer to death every year. As morbid as that thought was, it was true. And, truth be told, I was insecure about Muhammad bin Qasim. How did he conquer India when he was so young? Why was I so unaccomplished compared to him? My concerns seemed petty compared to his. I worried about exams and papers, while he brought glory to Islam and Muslims. Why couldn't I be more like him?

Only later would I understand the importance of perspective in experiencing the grandness of life. As in the case of the half-filled glass, where you can focus on it being half empty or half full, birthdays could be an opportunity to reflect – with gratitude – on the days enjoyed on Earth, or a moment to consider – with sorrow and regret – the loss of yet another year in the ceaseless passage of time. And it would be a while still before I learned about privilege, how Muhammad bin Qasim was a privileged male, son of a governor, and that he probably had little to do with earning the credentials to lead an army to conquer any place. Likely, his bloodline, birth order and genitals determined this role for him. And that the conquest of India, as with any conquest ever, was a nasty event, involving the death and displacement of countless and forever unremembered and unrecorded people.

Growing up, our house was always filled with people. Not just our ever-expanding family of six children, then their spouses, then their children, but also people unrelated to us, strangers. My parents' commitment to anti-assimilation meant that they tried to keep us at home as much as possible. If we were away from home, they could not watch and control us. Who knows, we might watch TV if we visited a friend in their home, cavort with the opposite sex if the homes weren't gender segregated, which they never were. Who knows what shenanigans we might get up to; we might go to the mall, go outside, unsupervised. So, as a rule, we weren't allowed to visit friends' homes or play with them outside. They had to come over to our TV-less, music-less, novel-less, mostly toy-less home if they wanted to hang out. But since there was little to do at our place, you can imagine that our house wasn't a prime destination. Still, if we were working on a project, friends might come over. Or they might stop by to just hang out and talk.

Mostly, the visitors were my parents' friends and their kids. But my parents also welcomed strangers who were going through a transition period and needed a place to live for a few weeks or months as they immigrated to Canada, or a husband who went to work in the United States and his pregnant wife waited for her visa to arrive, or families that wanted to spend a weekend away from their own home, or families who had moved away but were in town visiting friends, people connected to my parents through friends, or friends of friends. Sometimes the visitors arranged their visit beforehand, they showed up according to plan on a certain date and time; other times they dropped by unannounced and unexpected.

My mother loved unannounced and unexpected visitors. For her, these people recreated the feeling of growing up in post-Partition Pakistan, when people didn't call ahead before stopping by for a visit. Not everyone had phones back then, so there might have been a technological barrier for calling ahead. But even after phones became accessible and widely available, people persisted in unannounced visits. In the cloistered lives of women in my mother's family, who needed a legitimate excuse and permission to leave the house, these kinds of visitors were delightful. I suppose that as a homemaker with six children, the primary place my mother socialised was in private spaces – her own home and her friends' homes and, of course, the masjid. The fact that the masjid was a place for my mother to socialise was a unique feature of her life in Canada, since most masjids in Pakistan architecturally exclude women.

Having a friend drop by unexpectedly was akin to running into someone on the sidewalk or subway and having a pleasant conversation. It broke the monotony of the day. It added a new challenge. And somehow, my mother managed to find a whole group of people in Canada who were also nostalgic for the freedom to drop by unannounced, unexpected. This community relished the comfort and freedom of just showing up to someone's house and expecting to be hosted graciously. The unwitting hosts don't complain; on the contrary, they're thrilled to see you, they see it as a compliment and an honour, a sign of familiarity and kinship in this foreign land whose formality turns family into strangers. They consider it a blessing that you would show up because you felt like it, just because, without needing to ask permission. They looked down their noses at people who acted like goras, making appointments to see each other, like they were visiting a doctor rather than a friend. They saw it as putting on airs.

Generosity and graciousness were important qualities of hosting. You offered your guest not just what you had, but the best of what you had to offer. They'd come to your door, at your mercy, you had to treat them well. This is where things got tricky. What if the best of what you had to offer wasn't technically yours? What if it belonged to someone else in your house, like to your child – could you take it without asking and give it away to someone else? Was that an act of generosity or theft?

It was this conundrum precisely that we confronted on my twenty-third birthday. By this time, we – my siblings and I – had cautiously started celebrating birthdays, in a really low-key way, not with presents and parties but by making gestures of appreciation for the person whose birthday it was. This was tenuous and unstable ground; we walked cautiously around the birthday celebrations, on our best behaviour to ensure that birthday privileges wouldn't be revoked. Sometimes, we celebrated a birthday secretly. On one of her birthdays, my brother snuck my sister out to the Hershey Centre to watch ice-skating. Her eyes still light up when she talks about it all these years later.

My twenty-third birthday was the last birthday I would celebrate while still living at home. I'd been accepted to New York University for doctoral studies and was, against my parents' wishes, moving out that fall. My youngest sister was fourteen at the time, and wanted to celebrate. She loved baking cakes and knew of my obsession with cheesecakes, so she baked me one for my birthday. She put a lot of time and energy into the enterprise. She searched and found a recipe – this was the era before Google – asked my dad to buy her the necessary ingredients and baked a cake. She decorated it with red icing, writing 'Happy Birthday Ayesha' on top. Then she covered it delicately with plastic wrap and announced that she was putting it in the fridge to eat after dinner. We were excited, a reward for the end of the day. I was moved by the gesture, touched by this act of kindness and love, which made me feel special. Feeling special feels really good.

It was a beautiful spring day. I love having my birthday in April. It is such a transitional time of year on the East Coast. The ground is beginning to thaw, there are tiny buds on trees, some flowers are already blooming, the smell in the air is of resurrection. We prayed Asr as a family – it's the prayer offered in the afternoon, when a shadow is twice the length of the body. The fact that the sun and shadows play such a crucial role in determining prayer times reminds us that Islam originated in the desert, where you're guaranteed to see your shadow. This is not an East Coast religion, where heavy, low clouds dominate the skies, blotting out the sun for weeks on end.

Just as we finished Asr, the doorbell rang. Visitors. A mother and her two young children, a one-year-old and a four-year-old. This woman was a student of my mother's, she was a recent immigrant from Pakistan. She attended my mother's Sunday morning class, where a group of South Asian women studied the Qur'an, memorising the meaning of each Arabic word in Urdu. The Qur'an, in this class, was like a giant vocabulary list, so that if students learned the Urdu translation of every single Arabic word, then they would be able to understand the Qur'an when they heard it recited. This technique of Arabic language instruction is called 'Tarjuma Qur'an' (Qur'an in translation), and I learned the Qur'an like this from my mother. My mother also offered commentary on each verse under study, based on her own readings, experiences and opinions. Sometimes she'd say, *Mawlana Maududi says this verse means x, but I think he wasn't seeing the full picture . . .*

So, anyways, this young mother came to our house after Asr prayers because she was missing her own mother and wanted to get out of the house. My mother welcomed her warmly and quickly started to boil water and milk – separately – for chai, relishing the pressure of providing hospitality for a guest with what was at hand. We told our mother we were heading upstairs while she socialised with this unexpected guest, but please, could she get rid of her before dinner? We wanted it to be a family dinner. We had to ask, because it was likely that she would invite the woman to stay for as long as she wanted. My mother glowered at us, angry at our lack of generosity and graciousness.

We went upstairs and hung out until we heard the guests leave. Thankfully, she hadn't stayed for dinner, though I am certain my mother invited her to join us, likely more than once. As we began prepping for dinner, my sister went to pull the cake out of the fridge. She wanted it to sit out for a bit so she could serve it at room temperature.

She shrieked, *What happened to my cake, Mommy?!*

My mother was nonchalant. *What? Oh, I gave a piece to the kid. He wanted some.*

My sister was beside herself. She was crying, upset that her hard work had been ruined. She'd had a vision of how this evening would go, how she'd feel when she served the cake. And now, instead of looking like it had been baked for me for my birthday, it looked like some leftover cake that had already been picked through. And all this because some random person decided to show up to our house, unannounced, and my mother offered her the best of what she had, even though the best of what she had wasn't really hers to offer.

You didn't have to give him the cake! my sister cried. *You could have given him anything else. He didn't even know about the cake! It was a birthday cake!*

My mother yelled back, the mood in the house turning angry and sour. Storm clouds gathered in her face. *Who cares about birthday cakes? So what if there is a piece missing from it? Why are you so stingy? I didn't raise you to be this way!*

It can't have a piece missing from it because it is a birthday cake! You ruined my cake!

Why can't it have a piece missing? Who came up with that rule? This is why we don't celebrate birthdays, we're not goras! What's there to celebrate anyways? You're a year closer to death. You should be crying rather than celebrating. What have you to show for all your years?!

I sat at the kitchen table, hot tears rolling down my face as I looked at the cheesecake in its rectangular Pyrex dish, a corner piece missing.

This is how I'll always remember my twenty-third birthday, I thought melodramatically. *Why can't anything be easy? Why does everything have be a big deal? Why can't we just celebrate a fucking birthday without drama?!*

We had a sober dinner and ate the cake quietly. Later, we laughed about the incident, but not without pain. Before long, our entire family would celebrate Sibghatullah's fourth birthday in Las Vegas. We celebrated the night before, because for some reason I was getting married on his birthday. There were party hats for the four kids running around, there was delicious food and my sister's two-bedroom apartment felt full to the brim with fifteen people talking, laughing and eating. Rumee and I bought Sibghatullah a small boom box as a present, and Rumee showed him how he could carry it on his right shoulder and walk around with it, looking cool. Sibghatullah was shy, smiling sweetly as he tried to carry the boom box on his shoulder, which looked enormous on his tiny frame. His attempt to imitate Rumee made us all laugh.

Six months later, death would visit our family. Unexpected and unannounced. And we'd stop saying that birthdays meant you were a year closer to death.

I am standing in a room in Credit Valley Hospital. It is late afternoon, the light is turning from blinding brightness to a soft gold. It is filtering through the blinds on to the floor, hitting the hospital furniture – the plastic chairs, the bed covered with thin cotton sheets, the machines and their wires and tubes. There are several older women in the room, some wearing shalwar kameez and chadors, some with burqas. They are crying softly, burying their faces into their chadors and hijabs. A young woman sits on the hospital bed holding a tiny baby. I can't see his face, but I can hear him. There is a sound coming from him that fills the room. It is the sound of laboured breathing. It is the sound of breath being painfully forced out of a tiny body. The sound is so strange, it is barely recognisable as human. I've never heard anything like it and I don't hear it again until decades later, while on a fellowship at Radcliffe. A friend, who is a composer, shares music she's written for a hundred-year-old broken accordion she named Annette. Hearing Annette, I recognise the sound. I have a place for this sound in my head. It is the sound of a child laboriously breathing through failing lungs. It is the sound of a child dying, trying to catch one more breath before he will not breathe again. Others in the room do not hear Annette this way. How could they? They weren't there, in that hospital room with me.

Why am I in this room? I've been brought here by my mother to console the grieving family, to lend another body to carry the grief that is hovering, both already here and about to descend upon this family, to help out in any way that I can. But I'm not needed here. I stand silently and helplessly in the corner. I watch the women look at my mother with trusting eyes. They are grateful she is here. She takes her place next to the young woman holding her dying child. She strokes her arm, recites from the Qur'an, whispers reassuring words to her. Words about the afterlife, words about patience, and fortitude, and faith. The women lean in, they listen, intent, hungry. My mother recites prayers, she offers them vessels to carry their grief, she gives them words that catch and hold their pain in different shapes and sizes and colours.

Hours pass like this. The slow, laborious breath getting slower. Eventually it will stop. It is so clear. So inevitable.

It is only a matter of time. A few hours later, I go home. I get a ride from an aunty, one of my mother's friends. My mother stays. She belongs there, in that room. This is her place. She is needed here. She is providing real comfort and solace.

We have dinner without her at home, pray Isha and go to sleep. She stays there, at the hospital, with the mother and child till 1:00A.M., till after the baby passes, till the body is collected and stored in a refrigerator. Later, the baby's body will be bathed – my mother will do that with some of the other women – and then the men will bury him. When I leave, my mother stays.

She is with her family.

She loves them. She is loved by them. I know that when she passes, there will be others to help me carry my grief. And I will be grateful for her service.

Early Talker

I have always been a talker and I have always gotten in trouble for it. My talking caused me a great deal of anxiety growing up. I'd talk so much that, inevitably, I was bound to say the wrong thing, divulge private information, betray a confidence, say something offensive. Then I'd get in trouble. And yet, try as I might to shut up, I could not. The words just poured out of my mouth in a stream, flowing ceaselessly, spilling everywhere, surrounding me in a pool that threatened to drown.

My family's primary form of entertainment – because we didn't watch TV, play sports, read novels – was socialising. We'd get dressed up to go to one of my parents' friends' homes and we'd spend several hours there, in small apartments in musty buildings perfumed with the fragrance of cumin, sitting on floral-patterned couches, the men smoking and talking politics, raising their voices sometimes in passionate disagreement that sounded like anger to us – that probably was anger, too – the women cooking, serving food (which the men took first), then cleaning the piles of dirty dishes while making chai and serving dessert. These apartments had concrete balconies, and the kids would hang out there, or in one of the kids' bedrooms. If the friends had houses, the men would usually be upstairs, the women and babies on the main floor and the children running around in an unfurnished basement. The complete segregation of men to the top floor made it easier for the women to prepare the food and clean up without worrying about modesty, without worrying about their dupattas slipping off, exposing their heads, or necks, or the shapes of their breasts to the eyes of men.

My problem was that I liked talking more than playing with the kids. I found the kids boring. They would play video games, or with dolls, and that was fine for a bit. But I didn't really get it. My parents weren't into toys. Another fact of economic constraint dressed up as virtue, I suppose. Dolls seemed theologically problematic to them; they were a kind of graven image, as were all images of humans and animals. For a few years, they even refused to take photos. If photos, like statues and drawings of people, encroached upon God's creative skills – only *He* could create humans, we weren't supposed to compete – then dolls posed a pretty serious problem. So, instead of staying in my niche social group at these parties, I'd run to the adults, men and women, and charm them with stories, try to impress them with my Qur'an recitation skills. And sometimes, I'd share information my parents would have preferred to keep private.

You talk too much was a common criticism I got. Sometimes my parents would try to use their words lovingly, patiently, to help me understand that I shouldn't talk so much. They'd warn me before the party, *Now, remember Ayesha, don't talk too much!* Other times, they'd yell at me afterwards. Sometimes, they tried hitting. I think we call that 'spanking'. That's a word invented to make parents feel better about hitting their children. It's funny, the words we conjure up to make violence sound like something else, like virtue, or kindness, or something good.

It was all futile because, even though I desperately wanted to, I could not stop talking. I'd know I was talking too much even as I was doing it. And then I'd get stressed out and talk more. And as we prepared to leave, when everyone was in the foyer, surrounded by a sea of shoes, everybody wiggling their feet into their own pair, bending down, tying laces and clasps, the hosts standing around, hovering, all of us saying our goodbyes, I'd seize the opportunity to secure a verbal agreement from my parents in front of everyone that I hadn't spoken too much and that, at any rate, there wouldn't be any punishment.

I didn't talk too much, did I? I'd ask anxiously and loudly, *I'm not going to get into trouble, right?*

I believed that if I got my parents to agree in front of other adult witnesses, then I'd be spared. My parents laughed uneasily at the questions, half amused, half embarrassed. Later, they made it clear: asking those questions *was* talking too much.

My parents weren't the only ones who thought I talked too much. Others did too. And, as it turns out, they felt comfortable policing my behaviour. In every patriarchal society

– so, in most societies – there is an ideal form of femininity and masculinity, mythical standards that everyone is held to. You'd better belong to one of two genders, male or female. And then you have to act your part. If you don't, people try to set you straight – your peers, your family, perfect strangers. People freak the fuck out when you don't act 'appropriately'. They have fancy words to describe the behaviour of people who don't conform – *uncouth, uncivil, disruptive, dangerous, emotional, uncivilised, irrational, inappropriate, wayward, nashiza, bay haya, undisciplined.*

One of the assignments I offer my students is to invite them to pay attention to the ways they perform their gender in their everyday lives, and once they can see their performance, we wonder what would happen if they 'break' one of these performances. They can break their performance in ways big or small; the point is to observe the interplay between their own performance of gender and the social policing of their behaviour. The exercise, which I did not come up with, is meant to draw attention to how much we police our own behaviour in order to avoid having our behaviour policed by others. My students return to class stunned. Female students are told by their mothers to *sit like a lady* when they place their elbows on the table, or they are asked by their brothers, *Why are you sitting like a dude?* when they sit comfortably on the couch, legs spread apart, arms draped over the back of the seat. Male students are told by four-year-old children, *But you're not a girl,* when they offer to paint nails with them.

In my case, it was an amalgamation of 'Canadian', 'Pakistani' and 'conservative Muslim' values, a particular layered manifestation of overlapping patriarchies, that saw my speaking too much as a problem. One friend of my mother's, Zahida, another Pakistani immigrant who lived in the same building as ours, a building dubbed 'Paki Palace', had a big problem with my chatter. She found it irritating and unbecoming. She hated that I monopolised the conversation when she visited my mother. It bothered her that when she visited, tiny little me would instruct my mother to go ahead and prepare chai for the guest while I entertained her with my Qur'an recitation.

A brief interlude on Qur'an recitation here: essentially, this was me serenading my guests in the only way I knew how. By the time I was born, my parents were following a puritanical version of Islam. They were anti-music as part of their anti-assimilation project. Music was the devil's gateway, his entry point. It made you want to move your body, it made you forgetful of God. It's easy for dancing, which is pleasuring in your body, to slip into sexual pleasure. According to the puritans, there is a straight line from music to sex. Muslims aren't the only ones with this precious insight into the evils of music. And, of course, most Muslims have no problem with music, but I didn't know that. As far as I was concerned, music and Islam were mutually exclusive. So, I grew up with the Qur'an as my music. To this day, I relate to it like that. Whenever I listen to it, which is

more and more often as I get older, I am nostalgic and I
recite along with gusto and passion and wistful sadness.

At any rate, when Zahida visited, she didn't see me as a
child starving for attention, a child with two older siblings
and a brother just one and a half years younger than her, a
child who at a tender age had to make emotional, physical
and psychological room for another, more fragile sibling,
after already being the third child herself. No, she saw a
spoiled brat whose parents were not disciplining her
enough. She saw a child that needed to be 'straightened',
'fixed', for her own good. After all, what an undesirable,
ugly quality for a girl to have, the quality of talking too
much, of not knowing when to shut the fuck up. So, she
decided to take matters into her own hands. If my mother
wasn't going to set me straight, Zahida would take on this
task for her.

The first step in teaching me a lesson was to find a way
for us to be alone, without my mother around. This was
going to be difficult. As a rule, my mother was extremely
suspicious of other adults around her children. However
she came to be this way, she never says. But she did teach us
to never trust people. We, her children, absorbed this lesson
in our bones. But Zahida nevertheless tried to convince my
mother to let me visit her alone; she persisted through all
the refusals, pretended to adore me, said that she wanted to

spend quality time with me, until, finally, she prevailed. She played the infertility and lonely immigrant cards.

My husband and I are trying to have children, but it's not working. I'm so sad and lonely in this country, please let Ayesha come and spend an afternoon with me, it'll cheer me up.

Cheer me up – دل خوش ہو جائے گا The Urdu expression for this translates literally to *my heart will become happy*.

Won't you please let her come? She'll have so much fun. I'd love to hear her chatter all afternoon.

My mother finally relented. The afternoon I was to go over to Zahida's house, my mother prepped me. I was show-ered, doused with what turns out to be cancer-causing baby powder, dolled up in a dress. My mother psyched me up for the trip.

You'll have fun at Zahida Aunty's house. She loves kids. You're lucky you get to go over there. Don't worry, I'll be right here and I'll come get you in a few hours. Remember, though, behave like a good girl while you're there. Don't talk too much!

Zahida took me up to her apartment and told me that I had a problem.

You talk too much, she said, *and now you're going to learn a lesson.* She took me to her bedroom closet, where there was a stuffed lobster hanging on a plaque. Her husband had bought it for her when he was on some trip, and she hated it. It creeped her out, so she'd hung it in their closet for some reason.

Now, she took me to the closet, pointed at the lobster and said that it was a monster that would eat me because I talked too much. Then she pushed my struggling body into the closet and locked me in. I was alone in there, in the pitch dark, with an image of the fucking lobster seared in my brain, screaming and crying until I could no longer breathe. The panic filled my chest and my brain, it clouded my vision, so the room became darker still. I kicked and pushed against the door to no end. I don't know how long I was in there. It doesn't really matter, does it? Because children cannot tell time – an hour and a day can feel the same. It felt like eternity. And I wonder now, if I might have passed out from the sheer panic, because I don't remember being freed from the closet. There is no record in my mind of the door opening, light flooding in, of her pulling me out.

I just remember my throat being sore, my voice so hoarse I couldn't speak. She gave me ice-cream and told me I'd better not tell anyone what had happened. If I did, the monster in the closet would know and it would come eat me. I believed her; of course I did. I remember eating that ice-cream. Taking pleasure in its sweetness. It was quiet in my head. I had nothing to say. I walked around her living room, eating that ice-cream, not at all hating or angry or afraid of the woman who had essentially kidnapped and tortured me.

At some point my mother called to check in and asked to speak with me. She says that the minute she heard my voice, she knew that something was wrong. She insisted on coming and getting me right way. When she picked me up, I was subdued, quiet. I wasn't talking. This wasn't like me.

Did you have a good time? she asked. I nodded, yes.

She narrowed her eyes at Zahida. *Did something happen? Is everything alright? Why is she so quiet?*

She's fine, we had a great time. She must be tired.

My mother took me home. I was quiet all evening. I fell asleep and woke up screaming, hysterical, burning up with a fever.

It's going to eat me, it's going to eat me!! I yelled.

What's going to eat you? my parents asked, bewildered. I kept pointing to something in the distance. My parents finally called Zahida in the middle of the night, waking her and her husband.

What did you do to our daughter? She's feverish and saying she's afraid something is going to eat her and she won't tell us what.

Well . . . and she confessed. My parents were furious. They told her to never come around again. They shamed her – rightfully – for traumatising their daughter. They assured me that the stuffed lobster was not a monster and that it could not eat me.

For years after, I recoiled at the sight of lobsters. And my body reacts terribly to strong emotions, often passing out almost before I can register them.

A few years ago, Zahida called my mother. She was visiting Canada from the Emirates, where she had relocated. She has grown daughters now. My mother was polite but firm

– she wasn't interested in making time to see her. There are some things you don't come back from, I guess.

Recently, after I fainted at a reception held by the Dean of the Radcliffe Institute for Advanced Study, my mother wondered out loud if what Zahida did still had a lingering effect on how I handled my emotions. She worries and feels guilty, I suppose, for not protecting me from her psycho neighbour friend. It's not her fault. Though she, too, would have preferred it if I didn't talk so much.

But after all that, after all the scolding, the shaming, the hitting, the traumatising; none of it worked.

I still talk a lot, too much according to some. Just this week, I was in a conversation with Rumee and a senior colleague, a white man, a scholar of Jewish studies. We were discussing the ways in which speech is regulated in formal settings to reduce the free exchange of ideas, and he asked Rumee, *Wouldn't it be great for your relationship if her speech was regulated?* And then he laughed hysterically, as if he'd said something witty.

What's the joke? I wanted to ask.

But I didn't. I stayed quiet.

When I was writing my first book, I spent years reading texts by medieval Muslim male scholars, the respected luminaries of my religious tradition, justifying the right of husbands to hit their wives. Their words cast shadows across my heart.

These luminaries found women threatening. They wanted to snuff out our light, straighten us. They said husbands could hit their wives in order to set them straight, to discipline them. They could hit their wives for 'disobedience'. They could hit them for their 'nushuz', for their 'audacity' and, you guessed it, they could hit them for their 'sharp tongues'.

But they also conceded that husbands would never fully straighten their wives. *Eve was created from the rib of Adam*, these Muslim men said, relying on the Judeo-Christian creation story and ignoring the more egalitarian Islamic one. *And so they are crooked*, they said, *like a rib. Don't try to straighten them too much, lest you break them.*

But try anyway, they said.

I wish I could end by saying that I'm done feeling guilty about talking too much. That, *Damn it, I talk too much and the world is better off for it!* That I celebrate this part of myself, that I thrill in the exhilaration of breaking the moulds of ideal femininities. But the fact of the matter is that traumatic experiences of community policing do real damage. They rob a part of you. They break something inside of you, so that, even after years of therapy and trying to glue those parts back together again, like Humpty Dumpty, it doesn't quite work. The cracks and fractures remain, weak points in your psyche, always susceptible to manipulation, to breaking again.

I'm smarter about talking now. But I often worry about talking too much. A part of me still believes I talk too much. In social settings, I regularly check in with myself to see if I've talked too much, pausing to self-examine. And I watch the men and white people do most of the talking. When I speak – especially if I express an opinion – they look at me, suddenly aware of my presence, like they are seeing me for the first time; they might smile or purse their lips as they say, *You are just too much!* Which, of course, is another way of saying, not enough.

Education

The year I was born, my family joined a cult. And this cult's ideology formed the curriculum of my childhood. The cult's ideology aimed for a political order in which God, not humans, had sovereignty. This utopia was called a 'khilafa', and it was meant be ruled by a man called the 'khalifa'. The cult's ultimate goal was to establish shari'a as a global law, to be followed by everyone on Earth. This dream of the future was fuelled by a dream of the past: before colonialism, dreamed the cult leader, Muslims had been God's vicegerents on Earth. This was the original purpose of human creation; Adam was God's first vicegerent on Earth, and we were meant to continue his legacy through the establishment of the khilafa. But Adam, the original khalifa, never headed up a political organisation or a country, so the idea of the khalifa was only loosely styled on him. The cult viewed khilafa as a promise for justice; in the khilafa, God's law would reign supreme, and since God was just, His law was the only just law.

This might sound scary to some, what with Islamophobia and its concerns about 'creeping shari'a'. But don't worry, the cult's ideology was not inherently violent. In fact, the cult believed in 'neither the ballot nor the bullet' as the ideal course for political action. They wanted a non-violent revolution of the mind that would lead to a political revolution.

You might be wondering too about the use of the word 'vicegerent'. The cult leader insisted on the word 'vicegerent' because his vision of an Islamic state, of the khilafa, was formed in the wake of colonialism. The Queen of England always had someone to represent her and her interests in India, and this person was known as her vicegerent. So, the cult leader, living in India and then later Pakistan, imagined an Islamic State that mimicked the British Empire. He maintained the dream of an empire that dominated the globe, on which the sun never set; he wanted to keep the structures of the British Empire in place, but replace all the key players with Muslims. Muslim supremacy replacing white supremacy. In the khilafa, God took the place of the Queen and the cult leader claimed the role of the khalifa, God's vicegerent, for himself. The cult's 'Islamic' theology was very much forged in the fires of British colonialism. Among the crimes of colonialism is that it stole our imaginations, so that even our imagination of ourselves, even our resistance is fashioned in its image.

The cult was post-colonial, nationalist and Pakistani, adhering to and propagating a puritanical version of Islam. It was a fundamentalist organisation. The cult leader used that word.

We are fundamentalists and proud of it, he said. *We aim to return to the fundamentals of Islam.*

He dreamed, out loud, of a pure, clean, simple Islam. An Islam before modernity, before colonialism, before the confusions of the medieval period, the irregularities of empire and cosmopolitan urban centres, an Islam as pure as its birth, in the desert, to a prophet with a small community. A free and liberating Islam. An Islam as desert spring – clear, cool, refreshing, nourishing.

To join this cult, my parents took a bay'a, an oath of allegiance, to *listen and obey* the cult leader in all matters and to tithe their wealth to him. My dad put his hand in the cult leader's hand, like the men of Medina had put their hands in the Prophet's. They made a promise solidified by physical contact. My mother couldn't put her hand in his, though; cross-gender touching could be nothing but sexual. So, for the women, the cult leader again imitated – poorly – the Prophet. In Medina, Muhammad held a rope to connect himself to the women, playing on the rich imagery of the Qur'an:

وأعتصموا بحبل الله جميعا

Hold fast to the rope of God, all together.

The cult leader couldn't find himself a rope, which was surely more readily available than in the Prophet's time, so instead, he held on to a twisted bed sheet simulating a rope. The bed sheet imitated a rope, and the cult leader imitated the Prophet. He held one end of the sheet as the women held the other. Not touching each other physically, but touching metaphorically, through a sheet impersonating a rope, connected to a man impersonating a prophet. The words they uttered, in a call and repeat fashion, were taken from the Qur'an, the very words the women in Muhammad's own community uttered when they gave the Prophet their allegiance. The words the men said for their oath aren't recorded in the Qur'an, but the women's words are:

> *O Prophet, when the believing women come to you pledging that they will not associate anyone with Allah, and will not steal, and will not engage in illicit sex, and will not kill their children, and will not bring slander concocted between their hands and their feet, and will not disobey you in what is good, accept their pledge and ask forgiveness for them from Allah. Indeed, Allah is Forgiving and Merciful.*

And so, in the living room of an apartment in Toronto, South Asian men and women play-acted, repeating the words and the roles of the Prophet and his early community, a prophet whose religion would grow wildly, flourishing for almost 1,500 years now, becoming one of the world's largest religions. Now, some adherents of this religion, a few of over a billion, sat on the floor, trying to recreate the feelings of that first community. They felt echoes of the persecution of that community, and they shared the urgent, feverish dream that their future could be changed by a new belief. If these women sitting on the floor, draped in chadors and hunched over in humbled and submissive postures, gripping the twisted sheet and repeating the words of the Oath of Allegiance, were like the Arabian women who took the Oath of Allegiance recorded in the Qur'an over 1,400 years ago, then maybe the heavyset man who sat on a chair, tall, looking down at the women, and uttering the words they were to repeat, maybe he was like the Prophet. Not *the* Prophet, of course, but surely he fancied himself, at least, *a* prophet.

Uff. I'm struggling to tell this story of my family and the cult. I need to tell it because it is part of my story, it explains so much of who I am, but I resent telling this story because it is too perfect. It gets too much attention. It is titillating and exciting. Some of my white friends love this story. I've been asked to tell it at dinner parties, and I've used it to sing for my supper, offered it as a course to be consumed. But over the years, I find myself telling the story less and less. Even though this story forms me to my core, I hate that it also fulfils stereotypes of Muslims in our particular political moment. And though this experience is an essential part of my personal story, it is marginal, exceptional among Muslims. It doesn't represent mainstream Islam or Muslims. Cults, by definition, are not mainstream. But in other ways, this is a universal story, a story about belonging and alienation, about finding community and meaning in the construction of a life.

This story gives me strength, but it is also a source of weakness. It gives me credibility, but it also gets me the sort of attention I'd rather not attract. The attention of racist people who do not think of themselves as racist at all, and think of me as too courageous, too brave, for becoming the person I have become. I'm not looking for admiration, I do not care for this kind of attention. I ask you, dear reader, to please avoid simplistic, exotic, dehumanised conclusions from this story. Try to find yourself in it. Look harder. You are here.

Okay, back to the story. After a decade of trying to assimilate into Canada, the year I was born, my parents finally gave up. They traded in their racial identifiers for religious ones. It's not that they gave up on being brown – how could they? – but they gave white Canada something else to identify them with. Rather than just being 'Pakis', they became 'Muslims'. Now, when people saw them, they'd notice their attire – strange, foreign, Muslim. My dad's long beard and my mother's hijab.

This was a power move. They inverted the assimilation game and, in doing so, they tried to invert the hierarchy, so that instead of being underneath, looking up at the racists who rejected them, they were above, peering down at Canadians who lived their lives without the truth and enlightenment of Islam. Every time racist white people hurled insults at them, technically, my parents had something to feel good about. They were facing hatred because of something they were choosing to do. And it was worth something, this religious persecution – it accrued them religious merit points. Every racist, hateful, bigoted encounter deposited piety points to their religious bank accounts. And Muslims who successfully assimilated into white Canadian culture became failures; they were weak, lost people who had too readily given up the sacred and precious treasure of Islam in the pursuit of false idols.

But the irony is that the religious identity my parents fashioned in resistance to racism was formed by that racism. It was a new religious identity, an identity encountered, learned and embraced in Canada; not one they had been raised with in Pakistan. In their attempt to outmanoeuvre white supremacy, they submitted to it, moulded themselves to it, created an entirely new identity for it. They became, in some ways, the very caricatures of 'Muslim' conjured up by white people – in their literature, their movies, their popular imagination.

My parents' decision to change their strategy from assimilation to anti-assimilation can be traced back to a particular moment, to a Jumu'a prayer at the Jami' Mosque in downtown Toronto. My father wasn't a very religious man. He did not pray five times a day. But somehow, one Friday afternoon, he found himself at the masjid for Jumu'a. The man delivering the khutba that day happened to be a Pakistani medical doctor turned religious scholar. He had no formal degrees in Islamic Studies. It turns out there are a good number of medical doctors who fancy themselves religious authorities. I guess they figure, *I'm smart, my perspective is probably better than that of the average person.* And they're used to playing God in their profession, used to receiving the supplication and gratitude of their patients and their families. But they should know better – just like having a body doesn't make you a medical expert, being religious doesn't make you a scholar of theology.

On the Friday my father decided to go to Jumu'a, the man delivering the khutba was just such a medical expert. He was a doctor by the name of Israr Ahmed and he believed that his perspective and experience made him a religious authority, worthy of reverence and obedience. Before the creation of Pakistan, Israr Ahmed had been a member of a fundamentalist political party in India with the highly uncreative name Jamaat-e-Islami (The Islamic Group). Soon after 1947, Jamaat-e-Islami's leader, Maulana Maududi, made a controversial decision to run his party in the upcoming Pakistani elections. Israr Ahmed viewed Maududi's decision to participate in the electoral process as a betrayal. If the end goal was khilafa, with the intention of returning sovereignty to God, then participating in a democratic political process that ceded sovereignty to human beings betrayed the cause. Instead, he argued, a khilafa must be run by a khalifa, someone chosen not by a vote, but by the strength of his religious convictions. After all, the khalifa was supposed to represent God, not the people. According to him, voting for the khalifa, making him accountable to people's whims, made a mockery of the whole system.

Branding Maududi a moderate sell-out, Israr Ahmed created his own political religious group. Carrying on the unimaginative tradition of fundamentalism everywhere, he named this new group Tanzeem-e-Islami (The Islamic Organisation). Tanzeem, he said, would never sell out its core message that sovereignty belongs only to God. They would work tirelessly to bring about a revolution that would establish a khilafa that would truly represent God on Earth. And as the leader and mastermind of the movement that would establish this khilafa, it stood to reason that Israr Ahmed himself would be the ideal khalifa.

Israr Ahmed's message caught on among enough people that he started forming local chapters of his Tanzeem in various cities, first in Pakistan, and then increasingly abroad. Some chapters had five or six members, whereas others had hundreds. In 1979, he was visiting some of his acolytes in the Toronto chapter, and happened to be delivering the khutba the day my dad decided, on a whim, to show up to a masjid in downtown Toronto for Jumu'a. A masjid that had itself converted, not long before, from a church to a mosque.

Israr Ahmed was a fiery, charismatic preacher. He was a rotund man, and he stuck his tummy out when he stood, arching his back like he was pregnant. He had a deep baritone voice, almond-shaped eyes and dark brown skin. He sported a beard that was beginning to whiten and a Qaid-e-Azam hat, which is sort of like the cap naval officers wear but made of lambswool. Israr Ahmed preached a version of Islam that was anti-colonial, Pakistani nationalist and Salafi. He saw a return to the fundamentals of Islam as the solution to all problems – not just the problems of Muslim communities, but of all humanity. A simple, clear, universal solution to all problems, past and future. And Muslims, especially Pakistanis, had a special role to play in this solution. According to Israr Ahmed, God created Pakistan as a homeland for Muslims, and its destiny was to be the seat of the khilafa that would bring peace and justice to the world. But for that dream to be realised, we first needed to stop being ashamed of our Islam and of being Pakistani.

Don't dilute and change your ways, be strong, be proud of yourselves, he told the congregants. *Why would you try to be like white people and Christians and secularists? You're not lost, they are! You shouldn't be following them, they should be following you!*

My father connected deeply with this message. This was the belonging he'd been searching for the whole time, except that he'd had it upside down. Instead of trying to assimilate, he should have been trying to resist assimilation. He was special. He was important. He had a crucial, even historic role to play. He was Muslim. He was Pakistani. He had the cure for what ailed humanity right at his fingertips. He could become a leader, the one who got respect, the one whom others followed. Israr Ahmed would show him the way. But first he'd need to join his Tanzeem, take an oath of allegiance, promise to *listen and obey*, tithe his wealth and join a local chapter, called an 'usra', which means 'family'.

My father is an easily excitable man. It's one of the things that makes him both lovable and exasperating. When he felt his heart soar at the message of Israr Ahmed, like a helium balloon floating into the sky, he didn't stay on the ground, looking up, watching it float away. Nope. He jumped up and caught the string and floated with it, into the unknown, wherever it might take him. After the khutba, a group of men spontaneously pledged their allegiance to Dr Israr Ahmed. My father was one of them.

That evening, he hurried home to tell my mother about Israr Ahmed, and Tanzeem-e-Islami, his new family, and our new life path.

My mother was always the more religious of my parents. She'd been pulled out of eighth grade to become a full-time caregiver for her maternal grandfather. He was blind and needed full-time care. At first, my khala, my mother's sister, cared for him. But then she got married off and it was decided that my mother would be his caregiver. It goes without saying that this decision was made for her, she was not consulted. She didn't want to be pulled out of school. She loved school. Her father made the decision. She says that when she heard the news, she cried for days. He waited her out. Eventually, she ran out of tears and realised that her resistance was futile. Her father's mind was made up and there was no way around it. She eventually got over her grief and went upstairs to her grandfather's room, ready to care for him. He apologised to her, said he knew she was sad and that he'd rather that she not have to sacrifice her education for him.

But she did. And he let her.

Patriarchy is cruel to women in such complex ways. In a patriarchal culture, women's education is of little value. If you're just going to be married off to produce children, then education is a luxury that can easily turn into a burden. Education requires investment of the family's resources – money, time, labour – for little return. Girls' time can be better spent learning practical skills. Instead of sitting in a classroom and poring over homework, they could be learning to cook and mend clothes. The monetary investment in school fees and uniforms, notebooks, pens, etc., have little value if you aren't expected to enter the workforce and provide for the family. So you can see how this trade-off between education and free labour made for an easy choice for my grandfather. I doubt he agonised over his decision.

But the only reason he was faced with this choice to begin with was because of a failure of patriarchy. You see, my mother's blind maternal grandfather, my great-grandfather, was the responsibility of his son, not his daughter. And my great-grandfather had a son who was a wealthy businessman who had the means to care for him, and in fact offered to do so. But this son wanted to hire help to provide that care, and my great-grandfather found this insulting. He was disappointed and ashamed that his very own son, whom he had *raised with his own hands*, with an over-abundance of love and care, would abandon him in his old age to the care of hired help. He wanted not only to live in his son's house, but to be looked after by his son – which really meant, cared for by his son's wife and daughters.

This is a theme that finds itself in the nursing-home debate currently raging in South Asian immigrant communities. The expectation is that in old age, people receive fundamentally different care from their relatives than they do from strangers. Strangers, also known as 'professionals', don't love the people they are caring for, they are not indebted to them, they cannot be readily manipulated by guilt and shame. Of course, this is not a self-evident truth – that you receive better care from loved ones than from paid professionals. And elder abuse by family members and professionals alike is a real phenomenon. But the conceit that family takes better care of you is strong, rooted in a mythical conception of the 'family' as a womb-like place, a simple place of symbiotic love and respect. Where parents are gods who only want what is best for their children, who sacrifice everything for them, and who are then rewarded, in the end, with obedient children whose happiness springs from caring for and serving their parents. To hire help, or to – god forbid – put one's parents in a nursing home, ruptures the myth of the family and is thus a vile, unforgivable sin. Human weaknesses, and desires, and constraints, and failings, and limitations have no place in the myth of the family.

It was this myth laid bare, exposed as false, that was at play in the conflict between my blind great-grandfather and his son, that landed my great-grandfather at his daughter Rehmat's doorstep. He arrived in the afternoon, unguided, by himself, vulnerable and alone, dignity in hand, at the mercy of his daughter's fiery-tempered husband, Asad-ur-Rehman.

Only Rehmat was home when he arrived. He said: رحمت کمرہ چاہیے، کمرہ دے سکتی ہو؟ *Rehmat, I need a room, can you spare a room?*

Rehmat said, کمرہ ہے، لیکن پوچھنا پڑے گا *There is a room, but I'll have to ask first.*

Disappointed by her answer, my great-grandfather headed out, but as he was leaving, he ran into Asad-ur-Rehman, who was just returning home. Asad-ur-Rehman took his father-in-law's hand and asked, *What's going on? Have you had chai?*

No. I came to ask Rehmat for something.

Well, come back in, have some chai!

Over chai, Asad-ur-Rehman asked, *So, what did you come to ask for?*

I came to ask for a room.

What did she say?

She said she had to ask you first.

My grandfather took his father-in-law's hand a second time that afternoon and walked him around the house, telling him the measurements of each room, the number of windows, telling him, *Any room you want in this house is yours.*

Asad-ur-Rehman was annoyed with his wife, that she hadn't just said *yes* to her father, that she didn't know that her husband was the kind of magnanimous and generous man who would of course accommodate his father-in-law's request.

But she didn't know. So she had to ask.

In addition to a room, Asad-ur-Rehman also offered up his daughter, my khala, to be his father-in-law's primary caregiver. After a few years, my khala was arranged to be married. As she sat in the courtyard, on a takht-posh, at her rukhsati – which is a sort of 'send-off', where the girl leaves her family to now live with her husband and his family – Asad-ur-Rehman found himself overcome with emotions, and his eyes welled up. As he wiped away his tears, he noticed his blind father-in-law crying too. He was confused. *I'm crying because my daughter is leaving,* تسی کیوں رورے ہو؟ *Why are you crying?*

His father-in-law replied, آج میں محتاج ہو گیا *Today I've become dependent, a burden*, because his primary caregiver was leaving the house, being married off.

Without any hesitation, Asad-ur-Rehman offered up his youngest daughter, my mother.

You're not muhtaj, میرے پاس ایک اور بیٹی ہے *I have one more daughter.*

And so, in another act of dramatic generosity, Asad-ur-Rehman screwed my mother out of an education. Even though her grandfather would apologise to her for this unfortunate situation, he effectively made it happen by refusing the care of hired help, by demanding that his full-time caregiver share his blood. A family member had to be sacrificed for his demands.

In some ways, my mother made peace with this traumatic event. She certainly forgave both her father and her grandfather. Indeed, she speaks highly of them, reverentially, even. It meant a lot to her that her father cried when, some years later, he stumbled upon her notebooks and saw her fine penmanship. He said he wished he hadn't pulled her out of school.

And my mother loved those few years with her grandfather. He was a highly organised and well-disciplined man. In her memories, he lived his days in a regimented fashion, was strict about his diet, ate only a small amount at fixed times. If a meal was late, he'd skip it. This behaviour could be seen as childish and vengeful, but she saw it as noble. Since he was blind, he loved being read to, to pass the time. So my mother read to him from weekly magazines, some of which were put out by Jamaat-e-Islami. These magazines were full of the teachings of political Islam, especially those of the founder of Jamaat-e-Islami, Maulana Maududi. The teachings in these magazines formed the foundation of my mother's knowledge about Islam. They taught her how a Muslim should behave and this understanding was deeply gendered, with Muslim women playing supporting roles for their husbands, and fathers, and brothers, and sons. Later, she would struggle with these values as an immigrant trying to assimilate into Canada. And when she finally decided to ditch the assimilation project, these values gave her a soft place to land. Tanzeem offered her a sense of purpose and control, a sense of belonging to something greater than family, a chance to be part of a movement, to become an actor in history, a way to move beyond her domestic role of caregiver.

Despite the warm memories of caring for her grandfather, my mother lamented being pulled out of school for
the rest of her life. She tried going back when her first two
children started school themselves. I think she imagined a
different future for herself, apart from the roles of mother
and wife. She enrolled at a local high school, but the
language barrier was difficult to overcome. She struggled to
fulfil her duties as a mother and wife alongside school. And
my dad's brother and a friend, who were living with them at
the time, whom my parents had sponsored from Pakistan,
who were sharing my parents' tiny apartment and eating
their food, mocked her when she'd come home from school.
Rather than helping out, they derided her dreams. Who did
she think she was, that she'd get a chance to go to school
again, get an education? Did she think she could get a job?
It all proved too much.

A few years ago, I enrolled her in adult education English
classes. I took her to her first class. She was scared, but she is
brave. She stuck with the classes for four years, waddling to
school with her bad knees, wearing a jilbab and hijab. She
finished grade twelve English. But she didn't take the extra
few classes necessary to get a high school diploma. She was
overwhelmed with fear at having to take a mathematics course;
math scared her. It's not the numbers and the equations that
scared her so much as the very real possibility that she might
not be good at it, or, even worse, work hard at it and still fail.
She doesn't want to fail or to be at the start of things. I get it.
It's exhausting when so many of life's basic experiences are

new and unfamiliar. Easier and safer to stick to what you know and come to terms with how life turned out.

Still, she did well for herself. She put six children through university. She became a religious scholar in her own right. She taught herself Qur'anic exegesis, reading Qur'an commentaries in Urdu, in her basement study, poring over books, transcribing audio lectures verbatim. She's taught Qur'an classes in that basement for several decades, and continues to do so today. She taught generations of children to recite the Qur'an. She's educated dozens of women in her Sunday classes, where they study Qur'an translation and interpretation. And she has lectured on the Qur'an to all-female audiences on the first Saturday of every month for three decades now.

When people ask me how I came to be a professor in Islamic Studies, the answer is obvious. I'm just trying to be like my mother.

I don't know much about my father's past. He was born in India, we don't know what year exactly. He was named after an older brother he never met. His older brother was around eighteen years old and bathing in a talaab (reservoir) on farmlands nearby when he drowned. People said that Hindu and Sikh boys held him under water until he died. My father was his namesake and his stories swirled around my father's childhood.

When he was around five years old, my father's family fled to Pakistan. His father, my paternal grandfather, heard about the coming inter-religious and ethnic violence that accompanied Partition, where mobs burned villages, killed everyone in their path, where butchers and neighbours and friends and teachers slaughtered long-held, respected clients, and neighbours and friends and students. My grandfather started slowly selling his precious household items in preparation for the moment they'd have to flee. When word came that the mobs were close, a group of families fled together, staying in refugee camps along the way, until the violence approached again, and then they hopped trains until, finally, they disembarked together, in a city in Pakistan called Toba Tek Singh. My father went to school until twelfth grade, and then he got a diploma in metallurgical arts. His art: welding.

My father had no dreams of coming to Canada, but found himself filling out an application for a visa when visiting the Canadian embassy with a friend who wanted to move there. *Why not submit an application, too?* his friend asked. So he applied. His friend didn't get a visa, but my father did – Canada needed welders.

When my father went in for the interview, the officer asked him, *Where do you want to go in Canada?*

My father replied with a question, *Where are the jobs?*

Toronto.

I'll go there, then.

So he moved to Toronto. He went back to Pakistan to get married and returned with my mother. He had his children in Toronto. He met Israr Ahmed in Toronto. He found meaning for his life in Toronto. Tanzeem gave my father a purpose, a sense of belonging to something bigger than himself. It made him less lonely. Each local chapter was called an 'usra', a 'family', and the members did what they could to make it feel that way. In diaspora, Tanzeem was a lifeline.

My father spent most of his life at his job, working long, hard hours, toiling with his body, negotiating social terrain from a low rung on the social hierarchy. He spent his free time making copies of Israr Ahmed's audio tapes, selling or distributing them for free to friends and others at various mosques. Israr Ahmed's message was for Muslims, it was meant to convert Muslims first and foremost. My father bought boxes of TDK cassette tapes, each wrapped in shiny black and red packaging. He gingerly opened the covers, he pulled at the little tab that makes for easy removal, he carefully labelled and recorded the tapes. At first, he recorded the cassettes one by one on a tape recorder, but then he bought an expensive and fancy machine that made three copies of each cassette at once, and in a matter of minutes. He spent hours making those tapes. Sometimes we would join him, a family production. Then, at Eid prayers, or Jumu'a, or at Muslim bazaars, we'd distribute them, trying to convince other, weaker, lost, failing Muslims to join us, to join our Tanzeem. Most of them weren't into it, but once in a while we got some new members. It felt like sweet victory. Immediately, we'd treat them like family, because they were in our usra now. Our family. We didn't need to build trust, take time to learn about each other first, because we were already family, we were committed to the same cause. Khilafa. God's sovereignty. Justice on Earth. We had taken an oath on the same man's hand. We would visit each other's houses. My mother would lecture the women, and my father would play Israr Ahmed's cassettes for the men. The women would listen to my mother's lectures, sometimes willingly, other times resentfully, and the men would sit around silently listening to the tapes. Inevitably, there would be fallings out, betrayals, raised voices, hurt feelings.

In time, like Hajra so many centuries ago, we learned that our shared values, expressed in the ritual of communal oath-taking, were not enough to make a family. An oath taken on the hand of the same man does not always prove lasting. Imagined values cannot do the work that blood fails to do. In the end, we would learn, family is elusive and illusory. Like a mirage in the desert that looks like water but is just hot air and our eyes tricking us. And Hajra, abandoned with her son, searching frantically for water, her mouth dry and parched, her heart lonely, and heavy with disappointment.

Ultimatum

Memory is a funny thing. It plays tricks on you, makes you remember things that never happened or forget things that did. But it isn't memory that plays these tricks on us. It's us. We play tricks on ourselves and then blame it on memory. The truth, reality, is so unbearable sometimes that we'd rather believe something else. So we often rewrite our pasts, make up stuff, delete things, believe in our own edits, such that they begin to form us, influence our present and future.

Sometimes, we make up temporary stories to suit our purposes, fortify our psychological well-being for the time being, but then we can lose the narrative. With love and support, we can gain the strength to go back and revisit the past, take a second look, undo the edits and try to accept the past as it happened, rather than how we wish it had gone.

I feel this way about my niqab story. Why did I wear it? How did I feel about wearing it? Was I forced to wear it? Did I want to wear it? The answers to these questions have changed for me over the years.

The niqab is a face veil and our cult leader, Dr Israr Ahmed, said that God intended for women to wear it. In general, my parents thought Israr Ahmed's interpretations of the Qur'an were definitive. If he said it, it must be true. Israr Ahmed's wife and daughters, all of whom lived in Pakistan, wore niqab. They were super pious, the most pious. And their piety reflected on him. *His* wife and *his* daughters wore niqab. What a great man.

My mother didn't want to be outdone by their piety. She's a very competitive person and channels her competitiveness through religious fervour. She wanted to be 'the best' at being a cult member, the model female Muslim. But she lived in Canada, and it was far more difficult to wear niqab in Canada than in Pakistan. No one harassed you for wearing niqab in Pakistan. If you were walking on the street wearing a niqab, no one would call you a 'terrorist', no one would tell you to go back to your country. No one wrote opinion pieces in national newspapers, throwing fits about seeing a niqabi on the subway. No one said that wearing the niqab made you inferior, less than, oppressed, stupid, without agency, a non-person – at least, not to your face. But in Canada, all of these things happened. Even before 9/11, before it became politically expedient to equate Islam with terrorism. Even while we were still basking in the afterglow of the Afghan Freedom Fighters visiting the White House.

My mother asked Israr Ahmed what he thought about Muslim women wearing niqab in Canada, where we would be persecuted for wearing it. He said that if our faith was really strong, we'd wear it anyways. And yes, we'd face persecution, but whatever we faced would be nothing compared to what the Sahaba, the Companions of the Prophet, faced for following Muhammad.

Think of Bilal, he said, *lying in the desert, with a huge boulder placed on his chest.* Bilal, the enslaved Ethiopian, tortured by his enslaver for embracing the light of Islam. He persevered, survived, and the Prophet made him the mu'azzin for the community. He called the believers to prayer. What an honour, what a great reward for enduring torture.

But if it is too hard to wear niqab in Canada, Israr Ahmed offered, *God is forgiving.* He would take this into account. Maybe He'd choose to forgive us if we were too weak, too scared to follow His command.

This put my mother in a difficult position. She had the option of accepting that her faith wasn't strong enough to wear niqab in Canada and hope for God's mercy in the Hereafter, when her deeds were being weighed in the scales. The good deeds on the right side, the bad deeds on the left. Which way would the scales tip, deciding her eternal fate? Would she end up in Heaven or Hell? She could gamble on God's mercy or she could demonstrate the strength of her faith by wearing niqab in Canada, an easy physical marker that proved to the world how great her faith was, and accept, submit to whatever discrimination came her way. And remember that at least she had it better than Bilal. The enslaved black Muslim tortured by his Arab master in the desert in the seventh century. And count her blessings, for they were many. Starting with not being enslaved.

My mother really wanted to wear niqab in Canada. But she didn't want to do it by herself; she wanted her daughters to wear it as well. There is strength in numbers. She often said,

ایک اکیلا، دو گیارہ

One is alone, but two is eleven. It works in Urdu.

So she waited for us to grow older so we could all wear niqab together. A family of niqabis. A family ostracised together. My mother dreamed of having an exemplary, legendary Muslim family that would be remembered through the ages for the strength of their faith. How would people know we had such tremendous faith? By our niqabs, of course. They wouldn't see our faces, but they'd see our faith. We'd be known as a Muslim family, a believing family, a family whose women all wore niqabs, even in Canada, in a land of disbelievers. A family that preserved its piety and purity even while surrounded by temptations. I imagine my mother's vision of our perfect family, niqabi women, niqabi daughters and niqabi granddaughters, riding off into the sunset. And my mother, the great matriarch, leading us all.

I wore niqab for ten years, from tenth grade to the end of my master's. Through public high school and two degrees at a public university. I faced a lot of discrimination for wearing niqab. From my teachers, from peers, from strangers. I had to answer a lot of questions about the niqab, so I

needed a clear narrative that responded to the intrusive and persistent queries I fielded, all the time, whether I wanted to or not.

The story of the niqab as told in my family goes like this: my older sister was the one who mustered up the courage to wear niqab to high school. My quiet, shy, but also incredibly strong-willed older sister. I have found that those qualities often go hand in hand. She's the one who decided she didn't want to live a life of *cognitive dissonance*, of *hypocrisy*, of *nifaq*, of believing one thing and doing another. If she believed that God demanded she wear a face veil, well, she would wear it. Come what may. She couldn't square not wearing the niqab for the sake of people who didn't share her values to begin with. Why should she be trying to please them when she meant to please God?

My mother was impressed by her, in awe of her. If her daughter was willing to wear niqab and suffer the consequences – derision, mockery, discrimination, abuse – what was stopping her from wearing it, too? So my mother supported my sister's decision and started wearing it herself.

And when I came of age, in tenth grade, I joined my mother and sister willingly. Why wouldn't I? I shared their beliefs. I wanted to follow Islam. And I lived in a free country. When an old white man at a gas station walked over to me, with great effort, his hands trembling, meaning to speak to me, and I leaned in to listen, out of deference for the elderly, and he said, *Do you know you don't have to wear that in this country?* I replied, *Do you know I'm allowed to wear this in this country?*

No, I'm not being forced to wear niqab! I told people when they asked, *Are you being forced to wear that?* – asking the coded question, a question meant to confirm their racist and bigoted beliefs about Muslims, as backward and oppressive and misogynist.

I didn't want to confirm these beliefs because I knew them to be false. So, what else could I say? I only had one answer available to me, so I said, *I* want *to wear niqab. I believe Muslims are supposed to wear it, so that is why I'm wearing it.*

I even came up with a nice, clean backstory for it. I was in ninth grade and at Jumu'a prayers when I happened upon a cute little copy of the Qur'an in translation. It had gold-leaf edging, and having been published in Saudi, it was practically printed on oil. Its pages were thick and shiny. I had to have it, so I bought it. And then I encountered the verse in the Qur'an that, I would later learn was actually quite vague about what women should wear, but was translated in this cute little fundamentalist Qur'an in clear, precise and unambiguous language.

The verse reads:

يـأيها النبى قل لأزواجك وبناتك ونساء المؤمنين يدنين عليهن من جلبيبهن ذالك أدنى أن يعرفن فلا يؤذين ۞

O Prophet! Tell your wives, and daughters, and the believing women, that they should cast their outer garments over themselves: this is better, so that they may be recognised and not harassed / hurt.

But the Saudi translation read:

O Prophet! Tell your wives and your daughters and the women of the Believers to draw their cloaks (veils) all over their bodies (i.e. screen themselves completely except the eyes or one eye to see the way). That will be better, that they should be known (as free respectable women) so as not to be annoyed.

As a ninth grader, I wasn't yet tuned into the fact that all translation is interpretation, or aware of the politics of religious knowledge production, or how authoritarian regimes rely on patriarchal interpretations of religion to protect their power; so I just assumed that the translation was the Qur'an itself, as if it had not been mediated and tampered with by men. If the Qur'an said that Muslim women should cover everything except their eyes, and if I was a Muslim woman, then it followed that I should wear a niqab. So I wore it. It was as simple as that.

It was hard to wear niqab in Canada, but that was because of racism, not Islam. If people just left me alone, stopped being cruel and mean, then I'd be just fine. It wouldn't be so hard.

My niqab was a mirror of sorts; people couldn't see my face, but it revealed truths about themselves, like the limits of their tolerance, their willingness to be open, accepting, respectful of values different from their own. Most people recoiled at what they saw in my niqab, but they were only recoiling at the vision of themselves revealed by it. And then they either dug in their heels, or tried to be better. In all cases, they used me as a medium to prove their goodness, their well-meaning intentions, even if those intentions were expressed in vile and ugly words and actions. It was exhausting. Wearing niqab in Canada was fucking exhausting.

Parts of the story I've just told you are true. But there are parts missing. And then there are parts that are just made up. One thing that is made up is that I encountered this verse in ninth grade – in fact, I was raised with a patriarchal interpretation of this verse. Another made-up fact is that I wanted to wear niqab, that I wasn't pressured into wearing it.

The pressure to wear niqab started for me in middle school. When I was in middle school, I wanted to assimilate into white Canadian culture. I was wearing hijab and trying to get my mother to sew me dresses and long skirts, Anne of Green Gables-style. I wanted to belong, so I figured that if I dressed like white people in the early 1900s, when they still had a modicum of shame and modesty, then maybe people wouldn't notice my hijab first. Maybe they'd just see me as normal, wearing dresses and skirts, i.e. *Western* clothing, even if it was a bit more covering than what my classmates were wearing. I was restricted to skirts and dresses, even in my imagination, because pants were not an option. No matter how loose. Even the suggestion of legs, or my ass, was too sexy to bear.

As my middle school graduation approached, I was excited. I loved the idea of having my name called out, walking alone on to that stage, everyone watching me. That kind of attention was so thrilling to me, it made me ill with excitement. I trembled with anticipation as graduation approached.

In the meantime, my mother and older sister began a campaign to get me to wear niqab once I started high school. I was upset by this. I did not want to wear niqab, especially when starting high school. Why did I have to wear niqab now that the two of them had started wearing it? I felt persecuted. Doubly so. At school I was too Muslim, even without a niqab. And at home, I wasn't Muslim enough, because I was resisting niqab. My resistance was seen as defective faith, making me the weak link in our family's armour, the one who might be easily pierced, the one who might even invite in the enemy.

The tension between me on one side and my mother and sister on the other mounted throughout eighth grade. I felt like they were ganging up on me. I felt like this was really unfair. I barely had any friends to begin with – who'd be my friend once I wore niqab? I'd be so othered. It was hard enough to wear hijab to school, and the clothes sewed by my mother that always made me feel like an outsider, now I had to wear niqab, too?

The tension came to a head in time for graduation. My mother delivered an ultimatum: wear the niqab to gradua-tion or you cannot go at all. This ultimatum, like all good ultimatums, put me in an impossible position. More than anything, I wanted to attend my graduation, have my moment in the spotlight. But now my mother demanded that I make myself unrecognisable in order to attend. Literally unrecognisable – I mean, no one would recognise me, because they wouldn't be able to see my face. They wouldn't know to associate the niqab with me, because I'd never worn it to school. I was hijabi-Ayesha, not niqabi-Ayesha!

This on top of the fact that I'd have to give up on all my outfit fantasies. Whatever the niqab is, well, at least the way my mother sewed it for us anyways, it is a travesty of fashion. I'm South Asian, and like a 'good' South Asian girl, I love my bling. I had spent countless hours fantasising about what I'd wear to graduation: my sparkling shoes, bangles, lacy dress, the long necklaces that I'd wear over my hijab, how I'd tie my hijab – fashionably, of course! And now it was all ruined. If I wore niqab, none of it would matter. I wouldn't get to be myself at my own graduation.

I was filled with deep angst, angst appropriate to a thirteen-year-old child for whom her eighth-grade graduation meant everything, too much – a thirteen-year-old with little perspective. I cried, I pouted. I was mean and unkind, I had a bad attitude. I tried to be pleasing and win my mother over with sweetness and obedience. I tried to play it cool, like I didn't care about my graduation. I grovelled. None of it worked.

I hoped, desperately, that the ultimatum was a bluff.

That my mother would relent and let me go to graduation without niqab. That she wouldn't follow through with her threat. I fabricated hope.

My mother's love and compassion for me were pitted against her ideals and self-image.

This was a big deal for her. She was worried that I wouldn't wear niqab in high school. She believed that if somehow she managed to make me wear it to my graduation, that would be the perfect way to help me transition from hijab to niqab. That's if she was at all thinking about this constructively and worrying about my well-being and about what would be best for me. It's just as likely she was insecure, threatened by my refusal to wear niqab, even once I got to high school. If I didn't wear niqab, how would that reflect on her? Would she be seen as unsuccessful at raising me with the correct values? Also this: my mother was genuinely worried about my well-being in the Hereafter. She wanted to protect me from any possible punishment for not being a good enough Muslim. She was literally, in her mind, trying to save her daughter's flesh from burning in fire, also known as Hell. Hell is a real thing for those who believe in it. They might do unspeakable things to protect you from it.

My refusal to wear niqab was fucking with her vision of how her family would turn out, the kinds of daughters she had raised and the kind of fate we'd have in the Hereafter.

Or maybe we were just caught in a stubborn to-the-death stand-off that mothers and daughters sometimes find themselves in. No one knows how they got there or how to get out safely.

In the end, we all lost. Everyone always does when an ultimatum is delivered. I couldn't bring myself to wear niqab to graduation, so I didn't go. I felt terrible. The world felt unfair and cruel. My mother lost too, since she didn't get me to wear niqab. I started ninth grade without it. I don't know how my mother felt about denying me my graduation. Did she struggle with it? Did she feel sorry for me, or did she think I got what I deserved for being so stubborn? Did she feel virtuous for following through with her ultimatum? Did she even think about it?

The pressure to wear niqab from my mother and older sister remained relentless. Maybe my sister was embarrassed that her own sister in high school wasn't covering her face. It was bad enough that the other Muslims at school didn't think that the niqab was necessary, or religiously mandated, or even authentically Islamic. It must have been painful and alienating for her, this misrecognition she experienced from other Muslims. I wonder if what she expected to receive from her Muslim peers was admiration, not judgement and a concerted distancing. And then, on top of that, to have a younger sister in the same high school who didn't wear niqab must have further isolated and alienated her, made her Islam feel marginal.

By tenth grade, I had been worn down. I decided to wear niqab to high school. My mother and sister were proud of me. Thrilled. But I felt defeated, and scared. I really didn't want to deal with the social backlash at school, on the bus, in the streets. But I did. And it made me angry that people couldn't just leave me the fuck alone. That I had to keep talking about, explaining, answering questions about it. My younger sister also started wearing niqab in high school. By the time my youngest sister, the one nine years my junior, started high school, I fought my mother on making her wear niqab, even as I continued to wear it myself in university.

She can wear niqab later, I said, *if she really wants to. But she's too young, in ninth grade, to make that decision.*

Thinking about the kinds of hate she'd encounter was heartbreaking to me. I couldn't bear the thought and thankfully my mother relented. By that time, the influence of the cult on my parents was waning anyway. My mother was getting softer. Age seems to do that to people.

When she hit her sixties, my mother started adult education classes for English. She was nervous about going back to school, but exhilarated at the thought of being in a classroom, meeting people and impressing her teachers. She went for a few years and never once wore niqab to class. As she progressed from one grade level to the next, I listened to her breathless stories about her fellow students and teachers.

The small, petty part of me wanted to yell at her, to

shame her, *Where's your niqab? What happened to your faith? You made us wear niqab, suffer through all those years. Now you can't wear niqab to class even for a day? How dare you?!*

Thankfully, a more compassionate part of me prevailed. I said nothing. I should be happy that she was spared the pain of wearing niqab to her classes. So, I am. Happy, that is.

Scripts

When people ask me why I wore niqab or why I took it off, I rarely tell the truth. People are often not interested in the truth anyways; usually they come to the conversation with ideas they are looking to confirm. Sort of like, *Was it hard to wear it? How hard was it? What's the worst thing that happened? Don't you feel so free now? Thank god you live here, right?*

Or maybe, *So, how was it to take it off? Are your parents disappointed? Do you wish you hadn't taken it off? Do you struggle with shame for removing it?*

Or, as one woman hosting a dinner put it plainly, *Shame on you!*

These conversations, when they are conversations, can feel like a kind of non-consensual dance, where I learn what people want to hear and then try my best not to disappoint them and ruin the evening. I am a reluctant participant because this dance demands I tailor the truth of my experience to a garment that is too constricting. In doing so, I am forced to confront the truth of my experience, a truth that is painful, too difficult even to admit to myself, never mind share with strangers. And too complicated besides.

That first day I put niqab on and looked at myself in the mirror before leaving for school, I saw fear. I was terrified of wearing niqab to school. Terrified of other people's reactions to me, terrified of how they would make me feel. I knew people were going to be mean, and I was afraid of being the object of their cruelty, their fear, their insecurity. It's one of the scariest things I've ever done, wearing niqab in Canada. Every day, securing my niqab before leaving the house was like donning armour before going into battle. Because I could be certain that there would be some confrontation every day – whether it was outright hateful, aggressive, angry behaviour, passive-aggressive shit (I was in Canada, after all) or just well-intentioned, offensive ignorance. The niqab evoked strong reactions in everyone I encountered.

One question I was asked over and over again was whether my parents were forcing me to wear 'that'. Immediately, I knew the correct answer:

No! I choose to wear niqab and my parents are supporting my decision.

I was stuck between stereotypes of Muslim women as backward and oppressed and the misguided ideals of my parents. My mother, influenced by South Asian, post-colonial, Pakistani culture, as well as the Saudi-inflected puritanism of the cult she had joined, believed that the more a woman covered, the more pious, pure and 'Muslim' she and her family were. The more invisible a woman, the better.

The cult leader, Israr Ahmed, told the story, oft-repeated by my mother, of a Pakistani family that was so devout that when the women of the family left their house, they not only wore burqas, so that they were covered from head to toe, but additionally, male servants held up sheets around them as they moved from the gate of their house to the covered carriage that awaited them just outside. The sheets were an added layer of security, meant to protect them from the gaze of strangers passing by. We didn't know anything about these women except for how much they covered, and, in the cult's narrative, that's all we needed to know to measure the devotion and piety of the women and, more importantly, their family.

As with most stories we learn as children, I accepted this one wholesale, without questioning. I admired these women and this family. How pious they must have been! When my mother recounted the tale of these women, her voice brimmed with admiration; she wanted her family to be pious like this family. But for that to happen, we'd need to be as pious as those women, and cover up as much as possible. Her dream and our behaviour were inextricably bound; we could, by our actions or inaction, by what we wore, make or break her dreams. It's never a good situation when others have this much power over our dreams. They are bound to disappoint us. It is inevitable. Still, each time my mother recounted the story of these super pious, invisible, nameless women, we absorbed bits of her dream into our minds, into our bodies.

As I grew older, I started wondering about this story. Who were these women? How many were they? What were their names? Were they good people? Were they kind? What was the quality of their lives? Did they go to school? How, exactly, did the whole sheet thing work when they left the house? Who announced that they were exiting? Were the male servants who held up the sheets allowed to see the women with their burqas on? Why them and not strangers passing by? Was it better if only a few, designated, lower-class male servants saw you than random strangers? In this story, we know that a woman's piety resides in her clothing, but does it also increase and decrease in relation to the number of men who see her? How often did these women leave the house, given the to-do associated with leaving: the covering, the calling of the carriage, the positioning of the carriage right outside the gate, the summoning of the male servants, the holding up of the sheets? Were these women even real? I'd never met anyone like them. But I suppose that was the point. Legends thrive as abstractions; they crumble, wither to the touch, as tangible, real people, as people who can say the wrong thing, who can disappoint.

Let's think a little more about the male servants. All societies that cloister segments of their population based on their gender or their wealth must also create a class of people who serve the needs of the cloistered. A lower, servile class. This makes pragmatic sense. If a segment of the population is just going to opt out of, or be prohibited from, full social existence, then others must facilitate, pay for, accommodate, compensate for all the interactions they can afford to forgo. You can insist that the women in your house remain cloistered when you can afford a house where women can wash the laundry inside and have a courtyard in which to hang it to dry; you can keep women inside the house gates when you can afford a house with a gate. Families who want their women concealed as they enter a covered carriage *need* servants.

The script I was raised with at home dictated that the more covered a woman, the more pious. At school, I learned the opposite. The less covered a woman, the more self-assured and independent; and the less covered women in general were, the more progressive, the more free 'we' were as a nation. The script at school cast the covered Muslim woman as oppressed. Muslim women who covered had no control over their lives. They needed saving. This was around the time of the first US incursion into Iraq, and the US government and media were colluding to emphasise the cultural 'otherness' of Muslims. How else could they write off the deaths of hundreds of thousands of innocent civilians as mere 'collateral damage'? Never mind that Iraq's dictator was secular and that Iraq had one of the highest female literacy rates in the world. Those were just irrelevant details. The script at school followed the media's narrative, and dismissed Muslim women who claimed to 'choose' the veil as having 'false consciousness'.

They think they want to wear the veil, but that's only because they're brainwashed!

Only uncovered women could have authentic conscious-ness. Only they had control over their bodies. Only they were free and liberated.

Focusing on superficial things like clothing is a way of covering up the deeper similarities, the shared systemic oppressions, between 'us' and 'them'. It allows us to ignore the fact that in North America women are valued less than men. Literally. Women are paid less than men, our labour is worth less. It allows us to turn a blind eye to the rates of intimate partner violence here, the statistics on rape and sexual assault, the lax repercussions for convicted rapists and the murderers of women. Rather than seeing women's lives as universally devalued differently everywhere – patri-archy is complex, sophisticated and pervasive – this script pitted 'Muslim' women against 'Western' women, casting Muslim women as particularly disadvantaged, as suffering a qualitatively different kind of oppression.

The ironic thing about false consciousness is that there is no way to escape the charge once it is levelled. I mean, if I decided to remove the niqab because of racism and bigotry and sexism, then wouldn't that also be an instance of 'false consciousness'?

In this script, there was no place for me to honestly discuss the circumstances under which I felt pressured to wear niqab; that is, without portraying my mother as a monster and me as a victim, without turning my story into a site for a cosmological battle between 'Islam' and 'the West'. Two categories that don't actually exist outside our minds, categories that do not actually map on to any reality. What is the West? Or Islam? Where do they start, where do they end?

The scripts worked like veils, separating me from myself. They prevented me from seeing myself. Hearing myself. Feeling myself. There was no space for me to just be. I had to protect the very people I felt wronged by as the school script turned the tussle between me and my mother, which was universal and unspecial, into a cosmically significant one; it turned my mother's small and completely mundane tyrannies with a small 't', into Tyranny with a capital 'T'.

These opposing scripts left no room for me to live the life I was actually in, as I was experiencing it. Instead, I had to pick a script, a side. Which one would it be, would I choose the ideal femininity I learned at home, or the one held sacred at school? I picked the cult's script, my mother's script. Because that is where I lived, where I ate my food, where I slept. I came to sincerely believe that I wanted to wear niqab, that it had been my idea, and how sad that I lived in an ignorant society that couldn't make room for any other kind of femininity than the one held sacrosanct by second-wave feminism. I parroted the standard lines of the script that I was taught.

The niqab is liberating, it is a sign of my modesty. It protects me from commodification and sexualisation, which is what women's bodies are reduced to in the West. Degraded and humiliated. The niqab frees others to focus on me, as a person, on my ideas, rather than my body.

I repeated these lines, this script, even as I watched my niqab steal away all their meaning; people rarely heard me once they saw my niqab.

The truth is that once I faced all the hate just for wearing niqab, I could either adopt the niqab as my choice and tell others to fuck off, or take it off altogether. Each choice could easily be labelled 'false consciousness', each could be labelled oppression, and each could be labelled liberation, depending on who was doing the labelling. I chose to believe that wearing a niqab was my choice and came up with a narrative that made this true. Since I was going to wear niqab, I chose to label it an act of liberation, and picked the script in which I was a pious devotee, just trying to live my religion as best I could.

And at some point the niqab *did* become an act of devotion for me. Just because you make yourself believe something doesn't make your belief any less sincere. Belief forms freely, and breaks easily. That's the nature of belief. This is why we have rituals. Rituals, by their very nature, are repetitive. They are meant to remind us of what we believe, lest we forget. They form and re-form our beliefs, so that belief comes to follow action, rather than the other way around. This is true for praying five times a day and standing to sing the national anthem every morning. We are inducted into these rituals before we are old enough to know what they mean, or why we are doing them, but over years of disciplined, persistent repetition, we learn what we are meant to believe.

In my niqab, I knew I'd never fit in in Canada. There was no point in trying. So I started dreaming my parents' dream. The Dream of Return, a return to home. Except that I was born in Canada, so I dreamed of leaving my country of birth, which felt increasingly hostile, in search of a new home, somewhere else. I began dreaming of living in a Muslim country, in a Muslim world, surrounded by Muslims. In a place where I'd be respected and valued. Where I wouldn't be strange, where I wouldn't have to explain myself, endlessly answering the same dumb fucking questions. I dreamed of places I'd read about in books, heard about in stories. Places like Syria, Yemen, Egypt, Jordan. I wanted to go to the 'Muslim world', learn Islam from 'real' Muslims. I was dreaming of a Muslim Homeland.

In so doing, I was marrying, mixing scripts, ones written by Muslims dreaming of the golden age of Islam, and those written by Orientalists – Europeans looking for the exotic other against which to define themselves, measure themselves, orient themselves. These false narratives came together to create a misguided impression in my mind. In my imaginings, the Muslim world was a place in which Islam was still pure, untainted by the West. I imagined

Bedouins riding camels over sand dunes, and men and women spending their free time studying and teaching Islam. These would be the most pious people, free to dress as they pleased, but always choosing the path of utmost modesty. I couldn't wait to join them, to be accepted by them. Maybe they'd marvel at how a girl raised in the clutches of the West could possibly choose to wear a niqab, maybe they would see my choice as strength, maybe they'd be so impressed.

When I finally got the chance to visit my Muslim Homeland, I was surprised and disappointed to find fully functioning cities and Muslims who practised Islam in varied and plural-istic ways. Damascus turned out to be the longest continu-ally inhabited city in the world. It was complex and intri-cate, and there were no sand dunes in sight. Damascene women wore hijabs and jilbabs, and short skirts and T-shirts. The little fundamentalist that I was, I was scandalised by hijab-clad women smoking in restaurants and men hawking racy lingerie in the souk.

Thinking that maybe I'd missed the golden age of Islam in Damascus, I travelled to Yemen seeking a purer Islamic experience. I went to a little town where a community of Muslims aimed to emulate the earliest Muslim community. The women wore niqabs and jilbabs, dressed in black from head to toe. Now I was exactly where I wanted to be, in a town known for its religious devotion, surrounded by women wearing niqab. Finally. I was normative. This was the place I had been looking for all these years.

And I hated it. In this place there was nothing that set me apart; I was just another niqabi, or even worse, just another foreigner looking for an exotic experience. There was nothing to distinguish me from the women of the town in their black jilbabs and niqabs. Suddenly normal and unspecial, I went to my suitcase and pulled out a burgundy jilbab. The burgundy was almost shocking against everyone's black jilbabs, and, just like that, I was strange – special – again. Order was restored.

I realised in layers, over time, how my wearing niqab in Canada, even despite my evolving convictions, was never about Islam alone. It was also about individualism, and agency, and control over my body. Those ideas that white men came up with for themselves, during what they call the 'Enlightenment', when they thought that women were less human than men and that white people were the human-est of them all.

Sometimes we think we're being really clever and original in breaking a standard, boring script only to realise that we've fallen into another one without even knowing it. We can't actually write our own scripts, I think. Scripts are huge, they're bigger than any of us, they're formed by societies and cultures and religions over time.

The men whose ideas formed me to my very core, Muslim and Christian, brown and white, dead long ago

– none of them came up with their ideas with me in mind, a small, South Asian, Canadian, Muslim woman. And yet, their ideas, the scripts they devised, the writings they left behind surrounded me. I had to navigate through the complex web of their thoughts and opinions and feelings, to find a path that might feel free to me, that might allow me to escape the tangled maze they bequeathed us. But try as I might, I kept running into dead ends, retracing my steps, re-evaluating the truth of what I thought I knew. It's hard not to doubt myself, to think that, maybe, there's no way out at all.

Home, Again

People were just getting used to my niqab when I had to switch high schools. My parents moved from one suburb of Mississauga to another, forcing me to switch from a diverse high school to a mostly white high school. I had just spent a full year adjusting myself and others to my niqab, learning which parts of the school to avoid in order to minimise harassment, and then we moved.

My parents bought the four-bedroom house they now live in, on a corner lot. They were super excited and proud to be able to make this purchase. There were enough rooms in the house for their six children. After all those years of living in apartments with too many kids, saving up money and sending it to Pakistan, after trying to move back to Pakistan over and over again, to have finally scrimped and saved up the money to buy a house that their family could fit in, on just my father's blue-collar salary, was a spectacular achievement. The house was brand spanking new, the first to be built in a new development, so that the plots around us were empty and muddy, where, eventually, we would watch tractors dig out basements, mixer trucks pour in cement, churning it like it was ice-cream, and men in hats and over-alls put up two-by-fours that would form the skeletons of the houses before dressing them up in brick. If the owners

were fancy, they might put up some stonework on the facade.
The neighbourhood didn't have complete sidewalks yet –
we'd watch those get poured too. And the trees would be
planted later, once the houses were up. Tiny little saplings.
My young, unbelieving eyes thought it impossible that these
young saplings could grow into full, thick, mature trees. But
they have, for everything that lives ages, fills in and out
before it withers, grows small and dies.

When we moved into our house, the giant lot across the
way was still a landfill piled high with garbage, birds picking
away at it, the smell of rot and general foulness drifting our
way when the wind blew in a certain direction. We'd go
rummaging in the lot adjacent to the landfill, which was full
of short, sometimes brown, sometimes green scrub, searching for rocks. Beautiful, sparkly, multicoloured rocks, rocks
upon which rainbows had made an impression, leaving
behind streaks of pink and red and orange mixing in with
the grey, making even the grey look dazzling. We'd pocket
these rocks and bring them home, playing with them instead
of watching TV or playing video games, because we were
allowed neither. It was a group activity, this collecting of
rocks, rubbing off dirt to inspect them, discovering them,
showing them to each other, sometimes marvelling and
sometimes jealous at what a sibling had found. We'd team
up together when we found a big rock, lugging it home
together, carrying it in turns, maybe one or two or three at
a time, feeling a great sense of accomplishment at bringing
it into our yard. There were free treasures across the street,

just sitting there, waiting to be discovered, and with a little bit of effort they could be ours.

Because the house was new, my parents had some input on its details. They got to pick a floor plan. They agonised over the colour of the brick that would adorn the house, feeling that the decision would make a statement about them as people. Eventually, they settled on a neutral sand. They fretted over the colour of the carpet as well, in the end picking a rose pink. And they chose an off-white paint for the walls, but we repainted them many times together, as a family, over the years. Eventually, each room in the house would have its own colour, lavender purple in my brother's room, blue in my sister's room, floral cut-outs decorating the yellow kitchen. And my father installed long tube lights, like you find in office buildings, in our bedrooms, so we'd have plenty of light and save money on electricity at the same time. Win-win.

The basement of the house was unfinished when we first moved in, but was quickly turned into a living space by my older brother, then an undergraduate. He installed a pantry, a kitchenette, two bedrooms and a living room in the basement. My mother taught Qur'an classes down there and many families in transition lived there over the years, my parents happily offering them the extra space in the house, with pride, grateful to be able to provide this help to those in need. My parents had relied on the kindness of strangers and friends while in transition themselves; they stayed in community members' basements with their children while sorting out their affairs, especially when returning from failed resettlement trips to Pakistan. Now, they were honoured to be able to treat others with the kindness that had sustained them when they were in need.

And they continued receiving generosity from their community too. One summer, when I was an undergraduate at the University of Toronto, I planned a cross-country trip for us. The trip was a consolation of sorts. My older brother was getting married in Pakistan – my mother had arranged the marriage and was present for the wedding. But we couldn't afford a trip to Pakistan for the whole family – we'd just been there last year for my sister's wedding. So, I convinced my father that while my brother was getting married, those of us who couldn't go should take a cross-country road trip instead. My plan was low key and low cost, with us mostly camping in national parks along the way. When we arrived in a city at night, without a national park nearby and in desperate need of a shower, we rented a motel room. My dad would rent one room for himself and we would all sneak in through the back stairs. We did that a few times. But before it came to that, my father would insist on stopping by a phone booth – at that time, phone booths were still a thing – to cold-call people with South Asian and Muslim-sounding names. He'd look through the local phone book in the booth, call the numbers attached to friendly-sounding names, and, if they answered, he'd say, *Assalamu 'alaikum! We're Muslim, in town for the night, can we stay with you?*

We'd be in the car, cringing. But sure enough, the community came through. We spent several nights with total strangers who fed us home-cooked meals and offered us clean beds.

In our own home, there was plenty of room for all of us. My parents got the largest bedroom, with an en-suite bathroom, and the three remaining bedrooms were divided between the six of us. The boys were together in the room above the garage with an en-suite bathroom of their own. This room was closest to the front of the house, the most public; if you opened the curtains, you could be seen from the street. The girls would have been too exposed in that room. So the girls split up the two rooms in the centre of the house, playing musical chairs over the years, changing the algorithm by which rooms were divided as some of us got married and others moved away for school. For most of my time there, the four daughters shared the most central bathroom of the house, the one in the hallway. The wooden wicker basket in that bathroom was procured from a yard sale, and contained the cloth rags for catching our menstrual blood and for cutting into thin strips for waxing off our hair. When we washed and hung the menstrual rags to dry over the shower rod, we didn't have to explain ourselves or be ashamed of our bodies. We spent a lot of time in that bathroom. We'd go in there to talk shit about our parents or each other. We'd leave the water running so we wouldn't be overheard. It was a real communal place, that bathroom.

Now, my parents' bedroom is my mother's. One of the girls' rooms is my father's, and he uses the girls' bathroom.

And the boys' room is a guest suite for whoever – family or friend – might be visiting. And the landfill across the way is a golf course.

Back to high school. Moving from Applewood Heights, where brown people were plentiful enough to form cliques, to Streetsville Secondary, where there were only a handful of brown people scattered across the grade levels, was rough. I had to teach a whole new group of white people how to deal with a niqabi, which is to say, I had to teach them how to treat me as if I were human. I had to teach them that I could speak English, and that a cloth did not get in the way of my words, or my thoughts. Cloth never does.

I didn't have a lot of Muslim friends in school, and there were a few reasons for this. First, there weren't a lot of Muslims to begin with. Second, Muslims didn't like that I wore a niqab; they didn't see it as Islamic and didn't want to be associated with my brand of Islam. Third, I was a bit of a pill. I was an incessant evangelist, preaching to Muslims about how they could be better Muslims – *start wearing hijab, stop wearing Western clothing, read more Qur'an, stop having boyfriends, stop spending time with non-Muslims.* I can hardly blame them for not wanting to be around me.

In both high schools, I was harassed and bullied for wearing niqab. It was much worse at Streetsville than it was at Applewood Heights. And there was a crucial difference between the bullies at the two schools. It was mostly non-Muslim white boys who harassed me at Applewood Heights while the Muslims there gave me a wide berth, but in Streetsville, the white kids were joined in their bullying by a light-skinned Pakistani Muslim boy. He was my most relentless bully and he was everywhere. I couldn't avoid him if I tried. I'd always run into him. He would call me names – *terrorist, ninja, retard* – he'd fake me out pretending to hit me, he'd make faces and stick his tongue out, he'd bang lockers really hard when walking by me, making me jump at the sudden loud sound, which threatened of violence. He could have hit me just as easily. He terrorised me in the school hallways. He really hated me. And he was Muslim and I knew his family – we'd known each other as children – but I didn't know if he knew who I was, or if he knew that I knew who he was, or if he cared either way. I didn't complain about him to my parents because I was afraid that if he got in trouble at home, things would only get worse at school. The physical discipline, which is to say, the physical abuse of children, is quite common. Some families brag about how they keep their children in line with violence, while others are quieter about it. My bully's family was known for using violence to keep their children 'straight'.

And I couldn't bring myself to complain about him at school, because I felt like I'd be betraying Muslims if he got in trouble. So I just lived with it, through all my years at Streetsville. It never got worse, but it never got better either.

A few years out of high school, my bully landed in the hospital after getting stabbed in a knife fight. My brother went to see him soon after. He said to my brother, *I want to apologise to your sister. I made her life hell in high school. I feel really bad about that.*

Turns out he knew me the whole time.

My only Muslim friends in high school were a couple of girls, one Turkish and one Moroccan, both of whom I thought couldn't resist my mix of wisdom and wit, but now realise they were most likely attracted to my intolerant, toxic religiosity powered by guilt and shame. It was compelling for them because they were looking for boundaries. In their own way, each of them was in free fall, and my narrow, restricted but completely predictable, boring and safe rules for life, which disallowed me from doing most things, appealed to them. Imagine if they could be saved from the pain and confusion of their growing, hormone-riddled bodies by just opting out of all experimentation and growth? In reality, I would have switched places with either of them in a heartbeat, but since I couldn't, I settled into the right-eous superiority my lacklustre lifestyle afforded me, happy also to have their company to lighten my loneliness. During lunch breaks, I would teach them to read the Qur'an, start-ing from a primer, going through the Arabic alphabet, teaching them the vowels, and then how to connect letters into words. I'd hold forth on the importance of Islam and the necessity to resist the corrupting influences of the West, parroting whichever VHS tape I'd watched of Mark Hanson, a white man who went by the name Hamza Yusuf, that weekend.

During my entire high school career, I had two white friends, Robert and Noah. Both were male. Both were intrigued by my niqab, the exoticism and mystery of it. Both admired it to some degree, which likely means they had certain conservative and patriarchal leanings. Both enjoyed talking endlessly about religion. I met Noah in English class, and Robert in Calculus. At some point, I had a crush on both.

Noah was Italian and had thick, floppy hair that fell over the side of his face. One time, when I was sitting in class, reading, waiting for class to begin, he came up behind me, peered over my shoulder to see what I was reading and brought his face close enough to mine that his hair touched my temple, just by my eye, where skin was exposed through the slit in my niqab. I remember being thrilled and stunned by this small gesture that likely meant nothing to Noah but too much to me. The intimacy, his hair touching my skin, was exhilarating. So too was his willingness to come close, to treat me like a friend, to not treat me differently because of my niqab, to treat me like a person, a real person. More than two decades later, I still remember the moment vividly. Which, in some ways, makes the memory painful because it makes me see just how alienated and lonely I felt, that a gesture as small as that could mean so much. When I came to school one day and told him that I'd gotten engaged, and that my parents had arranged it, and that I was okay with it, he asked, *Does he know how smart you are?*

I hadn't even spoken to my fiancé yet, so probably not.

Robert was in my thirteenth-grade Calculus class – we had thirteen grades back then. I hated calculus but I liked going to class because Robert was there. He was tall and white and Catholic. I'd chat with him before class while I waited outside the portable for Ms Figuredo to let us into the classroom, holding an embroidery hoop in one hand and a needle in the other, as I cross-stitched little flowers for a cushion. I was trying to keep myself from wasting time, learning some real life skills, like cross-stitching rather than calculus. I'm pretty sure I tried converting Robert to Islam, I know I gave him a copy of Yusuf Ali's translation of the Qur'an. Yusuf Ali was a British-Indian barrister, an Anglophile with two failed marriages to white women, who translated the Qur'an into super snobby British English. Robert didn't convert, but we bonded over our shared conservative values.

I also hung out with the goth kids in high school. They let me hover around them; they smoked whatever they were smoking and I'd just stand around. We'd talk about capitalism and 'the machine'. They grudgingly admired me because I was more countercultural than they were, with my niqab and all. But we didn't have very much in common beyond the fact that we weren't trying to conform to dominant beauty standards. Secretly, I wished I was excelling at conformity, but since I didn't stand a chance in hell at winning at that game, I had to settle with winning at nonconformity. I thought I might have something in common with one of them in particular, a tall, shaggy-haired white guy in a long black trench coat and military boots. We lamented 'society' together, and 'consumer culture' and 'the media'. But then he told me that Jeffery Dahmer was his hero, and I had to stop talking to him.

My siblings and I were discouraged from having non-Muslim friends. They weren't good for our faith because they didn't share it. Procedurally, it was difficult to have non-Muslim friends anyway because we couldn't hang out after school. When we were not doing schoolwork, my mother had us studying the Qur'an, biographies of the Prophet Muhammad, listening to religious lectures and debates, and working our way through a curriculum for Urdu studies. If friends came to visit, they were not allowed to wear shorts, or dresses, or sleeveless shirts. The girls were asked if they'd wear hijab while in the house. We couldn't hang out in our rooms unsupervised. One of my mother's foundational rules was, *There is no privacy in this house.* Privacy was white. We were not white. We did not need privacy.

We were all up in each other's business, we were taught to watch one another, watch over each other and report back if one of us broke the rules. You know, for the good of everyone. This made it tough to have male friends at school, even for the duration of the school day. I couldn't have lunch with a male friend because I always had a sibling in school with me. When I started ninth grade, my older sister was in twelfth grade. After that, my younger brother was always in high school with me. It was reported to my mom when the Muslim kid who lived across the street said *hi* to me a few times on the bus.

She talks to boys, says hi *to Naveed all the time.*

That was the end of that. I had to ignore Naveed and his kind overtures thereafter. And I adapted, making sure that all my conversations with boys happened immediately before, during, or immediately after class, so I wouldn't be seen talking to them.

Was I miserable? Of course I was. I dreamed of killing myself. I tried cutting my wrists with an X-acto knife. It hurt too much and I felt like a coward for not being able to go deeper. I went to see a school therapist about this once. The white woman with short brown hair who examined me was unperturbed and uncaring about my desire to kill myself. She didn't believe me.

If you're not going deep, it probably means you're not suicidal, she declared.

My mother once noticed the cuts on my wrist, which were usually easily hidden by the long sleeves I always wore.

What's that? she asked.

Oh, a paper cut, I answered.

Unbelievable answer that she was quick to accept. She didn't ask how I got multiple paper cuts on my wrists. The one time she shouldn't have respected my privacy, she did.

Like any teenager, my high school years were fraught with angst and existential crises, but they were also full of richness and complexity. Yes, I lived with a difficult set of entirely constructed and unnecessary rules. It would have been hard enough to be a brown, South Asian girl in a primarily white high school in Canada. Adding the layers of fundamentalist Islam and a conservative culture around gender made things exponentially more challenging. But fundamentalist Islam also made me feel like I belonged to something bigger. It staved off my experiences with racism, which I only really fully encountered in all its ugliness once I removed my niqab and hijab, exposing my brown skin to the world. Hyper-performing my identity as a Muslim cushioned me from blatant racism, or at least redirected it to Islamophobia, for a little while. And my Muslim identity was an important part of my self-understanding. I believed Islam was special and I felt lucky to be Muslim. I still do.

I have warm feelings about my life in that house in Mississauga. For a few years, we were all there, in that house, together. The six of us children and our parents. It was a special time. We laughed really hard, watched Ahmed Deedat debates. We played badminton in the backyard, sometimes in the early morning light, right after Fajr, with the wet dew tickling our feet, and other times in the evening, as the sun set. We prayed in the yard, or in the house, together as a family. My mother cooked us parathas for breakfast, the smell of frying butter, or margarine or Crisco filling the house. We would dip the parathas in big bowls of yogurt which my mother or father made in a huge CorningWare donga, wrapped up in a blanket, like a cosy little baby. Store-made yogurt was for stupid people who didn't know they could make better yogurt at home. We were loud and raucous in that house, it was encouraged, a virtue, it was praised as 'ronak'. We would eat ketchup chips, pouring them into a bowl and then sitting in a circle eating them, leaving some at the end for our youngest sister, who was a slow eater. We ate tubs of ice-cream, especially Neapolitan, piling the vanilla and strawberry and chocolate so high in the cones the stack teetered. I could pile ice-cream really high on a cone and so was in great demand at ice-cream time. We engaged in the regular cruelties of children, trying to exclude one or another from our games. Once, my brother and I tied my younger sister to a fence with skipping ropes so we could play on our own. We might have left her there for hours. Forgive me, dear.

When our parents went out for a mosque event or a wedding or a dinner party, we'd beg to be allowed to stay home to do homework. But as soon as they left, we'd rush to their bedroom, which housed the only TV, and watch clandestinely. My parents purchased this TV soon after moving into the house for the purpose of 'knowledge' – which included the news and video lectures of Israr Ahmed, or Mark Hanson, or Ahmed Deedat. When our parents left us alone in the house, we'd watch TV shows in their bedroom, at a low volume, standing close to the TV, making one person a lookout to warn us of the sound of wheels turning into the driveway, signalling our parents' return. At that sound, we'd shout, *They're home!* And we'd scramble to our rooms, make like we'd been reading or writing quietly the whole time. It is like that – secretly, at low volume, standing huddled together – that we watched whatever happened to be on TV at the time. *Invasion of the Body Snatcher*s. Alfred Hitchcock's *The Birds*. *Murphy Brown*. *Friends*.

We had hundreds of people come through the house on Eid, when friends and friends of friends would drop by our 'open house' all day long, unannounced. My mother would cook a huge pot of her famous haleem, which we'd serve with bagels, and I'd make potato salad with macaroni and shredded carrots and several jars of mayonnaise. We raised chickens and roosters in our backyard so we could have meat that was both halal, which is to say slaughtered correctly, and tayyib, as in pure. When the neighbours complained about the racket the roosters made at daybreak, I argued with the weary-looking forty-something city official who came by to tell us to get rid of the birds. When he insisted that we comply, I said, *Well, if I have to change my behaviour for a noise complaint, then you should change your behaviour too. I have a noise complaint about the airplanes that fly over the house every twenty minutes. Change the flight routes, because the noise is disturbing me!*

Already, I was asking, *Whose comfort matters?*

And picking up on the answer, *Not yours!*

We churned butter, old school, with unpasteurised milk my father picked up from a local farm, sitting on a piri, rubbing the wooden handle of the churn between our palms, as the flat wooden head swirled the unpasteurised milk around the clay pot, till we ended up with soft, white, fluffy, buttery cream on top. Then we'd scoop it out, toast a wholewheat slice from an expired but perfectly good loaf of bread, spread the heavenly cream on top, sprinkle it with coarse sugar and eat it with lightly salted, sugary chai as a snack.

I'd be lying if I didn't say that, sometimes, I desperately miss those times.

Extremism

A few years ago I found myself at a meeting, organised by Religious Studies' academics, with representatives from the FBI. Well, I didn't just find myself there. I was invited and I accepted. I felt conflicted about going, and now I know that I probably didn't need to be there. The meeting was held at Harvard University and, unsurprisingly, the majority of the people in the room were white. We had a fancy lunch in an old-timey room, with linen sheets covering circular tables. Academics and FBI agents were sprinkled across the tables. I was the only person of colour at our table. We skipped from topic to topic as we ate. I watched my colleagues pitch themselves to the FBI, *My research could be useful to you because I work on Izlaam*, or some version of that.

The topic of 'extremism' didn't take long to come up, and when it did, my ears perked up. I wondered whether the FBI was taking white supremacist groups seriously when thinking about extremism and, if so, how they were doing that. Several agents said, *Yes, yes, of course we take this seriously*. And then one agent said, *Actually, we take domestic terrorism very seriously, and right now we're noticing a sharp rise in 'Black Identity Extremism'*. I was floored. I had never heard about this before, so I asked some questions, the answers to which clarified that I had not misunderstood. The FBI was worried about the rise of groups like Black Lives Matter that were protesting state institutions and galvanising communities at the grassroots level. The Bureau's position was that those calling for racial justice in the wake of widespread, documented cases of police brutality were taking part in an 'extremist' discourse.

Extremism is one of those words that does a lot of work but is somehow empty of meaning. It is a word that is heavy with moral censure, easily manipulated by opportunistic politics. It is a word that is necessarily vague and hazy; in order for it to have endlessly varied uses, it must resist a fixed meaning. So its meaning is always fluid and subjective, and the way it is used gives us insight into what its user perceives as dangerous or threatening to their own interests. Whenever I hear the word 'extreme' or 'extremist' used to describe an idea or a person, I wonder, *What work is this word doing for you? How are you positioned, in relation to this extremism? How do you benefit from the demonisation of this person, group or idea?*

For much of my life, I have been accused of being an 'extremist' by different people with various bones to pick. On one end of the spectrum, some Muslims and non-Muslims saw my niqab as signalling my extremist tendencies, and on the other end of the spectrum, some Muslims and non-Muslims view my commitment to feminism as extremist. Of course, I do not believe that I am an extremist. I support the right of women to wear whatever they want, without interference from the state, and I believe that humans, regardless of gender, have equal dignity and that their dignity isn't inherently worth more than that of non-human animals and plants. I don't think any of these beliefs make me an extremist. In fact, from my standpoint, you could just as well describe secular fanaticism, unfettered capitalism, intolerance of the niqab, or patriarchy (valuing the lives and worth of non-men less than those of men) as 'extreme'.

'Extreme' is a label we put on behaviours and ideas that deviate from what we consider the 'norm', what is usual, ordinary, customary, what is called 'urf in legal texts, what is considered ma'ruf. But what if the norm is monstrous, oppressive, cruel? What if the norm is genocidal? What if the norm turns lives into commodities, to be bought and sold; what if the norm values, say, money above all else, above the earth herself? Where, then, do we place the extremes?

What I'm saying is, it can be useful to pay attention to how the word 'extreme' is used around you. It is a word that revolves around us all the time, defining the boundaries of acceptable behaviour, threatening dire consequences if we dare step out of line, ask the wrong questions, or just advocate for ourselves.

I often wonder if Tanzeem was an 'extremist' organisation. I think it is fair to call it a fundamentalist group, since Israr Ahmed himself adopted the title 'fundamentalist' with pride. But he didn't consider himself an extremist; though, of course, no one considers themselves to be extremist. Just like no one believes themselves to be racist or sexist; well, almost no one. Israr Ahmed saw 'the West' as extreme, as deviating from the norms set by God. He especially found Western education threatening: universities, he said, were the equivalent of 'training camps', where we were brainwashed by the West. Dr Israr Ahmed believed that he had somehow, miraculously, managed to escape the corrupting influences of 'the West' during his own medical education by engaging with the 'Western' part of the sciences as little as possible, and was now trying to save us from corruption through the tired and highly ineffectual method of abstinence.

Beware the one who seeks to save you on the assumption of his own exceptionalism.

Israr Ahmed preached a vision of the world where 'the West' was the enemy of 'Islam', as though the two were separate and distinct entities. This narrative, commonly known as the 'clash of civilisations' and attributed to Samuel Huntington, was hardly original. Nor is it original that an old idea is now attributed to a living white man. The narrative long predates Huntington; it has existed for centuries, and has been propagated by all sides. It is a simplistic and stupid idea. It is a cop-out. It allows us to point fingers at the 'essential' nature of others and avoid self-critical scrutiny. But, as my mother likes to say, if you point your finger at someone, three of your fingers point back at you. No one has an 'essential' nature, not even a single person. We transform and are created anew by our circumstances all the time. Anytime people start talking about the essential nature of people, you know they're full of shit.

So, I guess the primary ideas of Tanzeem – the clash of civilisations narrative, the aspirations for a khilafa, the patriarchy of it all – taken together might sound extreme. But Tanzeem was avowedly anti-violence. It took seriously the Qur'anic command, *kuffu aydiyakum*, 'tie your hands', even in the face of violence, not even allowing its members to fight back in self-defence. If someone has extreme views but isn't a violent threat, do we consider them extremists? What is the difference between an extremist and an idealist? Is the difference violence? Or the threat of violence? Do we only label people extremists when we're scared of them and their ideas?

By the time I got to university, I had bought into the clash of civilisations narrative hook, line and sinker; especially so because it was validated for me by the white man himself. The white man, in this case, was an American convert to Islam who became a popular Muslim preacher. His name was, well, let's just call him John Doe. Whatever his birth name, when he converted to Islam, Doe took Arabic first and last names. One of those names was 'Yusuf'. Yusuf is the Arabic name for the prophet Joseph, who is known in Islam as the most beautiful man to have ever existed. When the women of Egypt whispered judgemental gossip about the noblewoman Zulaykha trying to seduce Yusuf, who was her servant at the time, her defence was simply to let them see him. She knew that once they saw him, the women would understand that they would have done the same, given the opportunity. To set the scene, she invited the women over, set tables piled high with fruit and gave each of them a knife, supposedly for cutting the fruit. Then she asked Yusuf to walk through the room, you know, super casual. When they saw him, the women were so taken by his beauty, they cut their own hands instead of the fruit; so distracted were they by his gorgeousness, they didn't feel the knives cutting into their own flesh, spilling their own blood. 'Yusuf' is a remarkably popular name among white male converts who adopt an Arabic name to signify their conversion to Islam, turning their conversion into a kind of birth. It is one thing for a mother to look at her newborn child and think, *You are so beautiful, I will name you Yusuf.* It's quite another for a grown man to think, *I am so hot, I must be a Yusuf.*

To emphasise his authority and transformation, John Doe appropriated an 'Islamic' identity to go with his new name. Doe understood 'Muslim' as 'Arab' and dressed himself like the Arabs of his imagination, wearing long, flowing white robes and an imama wrapped around his head. He even spoke with a hint of an Arab accent, and peppered his sentences with over-pronounced Arabic words, really playing up the *'ayn*s and *qaf*s and *kha*s. His performance of 'Muslimness' worked, because he was one of the few people allowed into our home, which is how my parents thought of TV. Watching people on TV, through videos or DVDs or regular programming, was like inviting them into your living room. My parents were extremely selective about whose lectures we could listen to, and Doe made the cut, mostly because his views aligned with the ideology of Tanzeem. His message wasn't threatening; in fact, he confirmed almost everything Israr Ahmed preached.

There were a lot of similarities between Doe and Israr Ahmed. Israr Ahmed was trained as a medical doctor, and Doe was trained as a nurse. Like Israr Ahmed, Doe considered himself an Islamic scholar without having formal seminary training. Also like Israr Ahmed, Doe believed that he had somehow, miraculously, managed to escape the corrupting influences of 'the West', despite being a white man born, raised and educated in this very same 'West'. In line with Tanzeemi ideology, Doe endorsed the clash of civilisations narrative, casting 'the West' and 'Islam' as enemies of each other, and himself as the enlightened émigré, the one who crossed over, saw it all, saw the truth, as the one who adopted the light of Islam and rejected the darknesses of the West, the one who had somehow escaped and expunged 'the West' from his white male self. And now, he warned rooms full of mostly brown and black Muslims of the perils of 'the 'West', its philosophy, its education, its general moral depravity.

Beware the one who seeks to save you on the assumption of his own exceptionalism.

Doe espoused a patriarchal version of Islam as the only authentic Islam. A patriarchal Islam is appealing to a good deal of conservative white men. It offers them religious sanction and a righteous platform from which to spew toxic patriarchal rhetoric; rhetoric that is inescapably misogynistic, homophobic, and promotes hierarchies in which they are the chosen ones. Doe ferociously defended patriarchal Islam, often responding with anger and derisiveness to anything or anyone, real or imagined, who challenged him. He jumped from topic to topic, without rhyme or reason, yelling about one thing or another. He made Israr Ahmed look like a rational, organised thinker. As a teenager, I thrilled at his self-righteous incoherence, mistaking his anger for passion, his verbosity for intelligence, his rants for lectures.

It is difficult to describe his 'philosophy' per se. My memories of his talks are impressionistic. I remember specific things that upset him. Doe found homosexuality disgusting and it angered him that homosexuals might have legal rights. He was obsessed with pornography. He saw it as an urgently pressing problem and warned against its damaging physiological effects; apparently it causes impotence. He blamed immigrants for their experiences of racism in North America and Europe, originally, before 9/11, blaming them for trying too hard to be white and Western when they'd obviously never be accepted. Then later, after 9/11, he blamed immigrants for failing to properly assimilate and for hanging on to their cultural baggage. Following a long American tradition, he blamed racial inequality in the United States on the breakdown of the 'black family'. When it was brought to his attention that this was a racist claim that blamed the victims of structural inequality for suffering in a system designed to oppress them, he leaned on classic white tactics to defend himself; he cried, and then claimed he couldn't be racist because his mother once had a black boyfriend.

Unsurprisingly, given his commitment to a patriarchal Islam, Doe detested Muslim feminists. Muslim feminists challenged the very legitimacy of patriarchal Islam, which jeopardised Doe; they threatened to rip from him the mantle of his tenuously crafted authority. Given that a great deal of Muslim feminist scholarship is produced in universities, Doe described universities as institutions of higher brainwashing. In general, he confirmed all the things I had learned from Israr Ahmed. His lectures were just angrier and more visceral, which made them more fun to watch.

Not all religious conversions are cultural appropriations, but there are some that definitely feel like they are. I'm wary of white converts who become 'experts' on Islam, make money off their conversions, who quickly and easily take positions of leadership as though a 1,400-year-old community was just waiting for them to come along and lead us to the promised land. When I think of John Doe, it is difficult for me to not think about Rachel Dolezal. They're both white people trading on their assumed identities – religious and racial – in a way that increases their social capital; their careers are built on their conversion. Who would even know his name if he hadn't converted to Islam?

And I wonder too, did he change his name legally, like on his driver's licence? Is he his Muslim name when he's condescending to us, but John Doe when he gets pulled over by the cops?

Anyways, you get the point. The guy was an embodiment of the colonial legacy, as in a white man who converted to our religion, then claimed expertise on us, then assumed positions of authority over us, and now had the audacity to behave as an arbiter of 'real' and 'cultural' Islam, separating it away from corrupting influences. His preachings aligned with all the fundamentalist ideas I had been raised with, but they were especially potent in him, because in him they were packaged in an imperious white body. White supremacy upon patriarchy. Misogyny and homophobia and racism, each building on the other.

Like the overwhelming darknesses of the deep ocean, where waves cover waves and are covered in turn by clouds. Darknesses one upon the other. When he holds out his hand, he cannot see it. There is no light for the one whom God has made no light.

أو كظلمـت فى بحر لجى يغشه موج من فوقه موج من فوقه سحاب ظلمـت بعضها فوق بعض إذا أخرج يده لم يكد يرها ومن لم يجعل الله له نورا فما له من نور﴿٤٠﴾

Like other South Asians, descendants of a colonised people who have internalised the colonialists' view of whiteness as superior, I found validation and beauty in white people. They were all Yusufs to me. I was obsessed with John Doe. I loved him. I believed the light of God radiated from his face, though that was more likely the camera light reflecting off his forehead. I loved his severity. I was sure that he'd be impressed by me, proud of me, with my niqab and all, resisting assimilation, being Muslim first, spurning 'the West' by not wearing Western clothing. I watched his videos over and over again. Got high off his bitchy zingers.

Doe talked longingly and incessantly about the time he spent learning Islam from 'real' Muslims in the Middle East and Africa. He was never specific about the details of this learning. But he talked all the time about his time among the 'Bedouins' in the desert, the most 'authentic' humans he'd ever met. He exoticised the shit out of these people, painting a perfect Orientalist picture for his followers. I was mesmerised by his tales. I too wanted to learn Islam from 'real' Muslims, Bedouins in the desert. Why would I study science or engineering when I could be studying Islam?

So, when it came time to apply for university, I decided against it. This was the olden days, when your high school provided you with applications for university and college (two different things in Canada) and you filled them out by hand to be submitted by your school. When I didn't turn in any applications, my teacher asked me why.

Oh, I'm not going to university.

Why not? You're bright, you'd do well.

Well, I want to learn Islam and it doesn't make sense to do that at a Western university. Besides, universities are institutions of higher brainwashing.

I'd learned that from Doe. My teacher was bewildered. I mean, what do you say to that?

I guess some of my teachers discussed my decision among themselves, because another teacher, Ms Figuredo, confronted me shortly thereafter. She was Caribbean of South Asian heritage, wore leather boots and knee-length skirts to class, and was married to a white Italian man. Rumour had it she was Muslim and her husband was not. Steeped as I was in a patriarchal version of Islam, I found this news to be morally and ethically troubling. See, according to a patriarchal Islam (and may I remind you, there is a strong and thriving egalitarian Islam), Muslim men are allowed to marry Christian and Jewish women, but Muslim women are restricted to Muslim men. The assumption here is that children will take the religion of the dominant parent, which, big surprise, is presumed to be the father. Ms Figuredo's marriage posed a challenge for me. Did she not worry that her marriage was invalid? Wasn't she worried about her children's faith? I adored her and wanted to save her. What if she didn't know of the metaphysical danger she was in? I'd never met a secular Muslim before, or I was in denial about having met any, so I couldn't fathom that perhaps Ms Figuredo did not care about my Islamic perspective on her marriage.

While I was trying to build up the courage to save Ms Figuredo, she saved me. She cornered me in the hallway between classes, *I heard you're not going to apply to university.*

Yeah, I said and parroted the lines I'd said to the other teacher, about learning Islam from 'real' Muslims and the bit about universities being a form of 'higher brainwashing'. In retrospect, I don't even know what that means. I must have sounded high – *Dude, I wanna learn Islam from, like, you know, real Muslims.*

Well, she bargained, *could you do me a favour? Please just apply? You don't have to go if you get in.*

Sure, I said.

That sounded reasonable enough. It couldn't hurt to apply. Then she narrowed her eyes at me, *And if you don't go, you're a waste of brains.*

Before I could respond, she spun around and walked off. I stood there for a few seconds, in my rose pink niqab, absorbing what she had just said.

I applied to three universities – Toronto, Queens and Waterloo. I got into all three. I was in Pakistan when I heard. We were there for my sister's wedding. My dad, who had returned to Canada immediately after the wedding, mailed the acceptance letters and the course catalogues to Pakistan.

I remember sitting with the course catalogues in my mother's childhood home, once owned by her father, and now by her brothers. I sat in the courtyard, on a chaar-pai, in the same courtyard and perhaps the same chaar-pai that supported my grandfather's dead body. I sat in that courtyard, in a house that had belonged to our family for only one generation, having been claimed when they fled from India, leaving behind their own haveli, their own interconnected homes, their land, their animals. They claimed this house, a house that belonged to another Punjabi family, a Hindu or a Sikh family.

I pulled out the course catalogues and felt their weight in my hands. I flipped despondently through them, uninterested in their contents. I wanted to go to Queens, but only because the name appealed to me as a good colonial subject. I decided to go to the University of Toronto – my older siblings had gone there, and I could commute from home. In truth, there wasn't much of a choice, since I wasn't going to be allowed to live away from home anyway.

I signed up to be a student at the University of Toronto's Victoria College – again, because I was drawn to the name, chained to my history. It's funny; I was worried about being brainwashed at university, but I registered at Victoria College because I liked the sound of the Queen's name. *Too late*, I think now, looking back, *you were already brainwashed, kiddo!* I 'liked' the sound of the name of a woman who colonised my homeland, stole its resources, pitted my ancestors one against the other, so that the homeland would be split asunder, so that my parents' families would have to flee the homes they had lived in for generations, the land they'd lived and died on for centuries, thus displacing my parents not just once, from India to Pakistan but a second time, from Pakistan to Canada: Canada, another country of which she

made herself the Queen, colonised by her emissaries, a
country where the Indigenous population would fare worse
than my own because the settler colonialists would never
leave. And despite all this, when registering for university
and looking at the list of colleges I could choose from – New
College, St Michael's College, Woodsworth College – I
chose Victoria because it sounded romantic and whimsical
and idyllic, rather than murderous and ruthless and cursed.
My 'liking' the name, that was the sign, the tell of a brain
already thoroughly washed. I 'liked' that name, while sitting
in the courtyard of a house I was only in because of the
fucking Queen and her sense of entitlement.

If extremism is a feeling of superiority, a sense of exceptionalism so complete that you imagine you have the right to
dominate everyone and everything around you, and you are
willing to destroy the earth, poison the land and kill human
and non-human animals to achieve your goals, then Queen
Victoria was most definitely an extremist.

But I didn't understand all of that back then. I thought of
my brain not so much washed as pure, and to keep it
that way while in university I decided to start out part-time
and take only two classes my first year: Arabic, since I
figured you couldn't get brainwashed in a language class,
and 'Global Politics', taught by the famed political scientist
Janice Stein, in which I would be on high alert for brainwashing. My parents weren't really involved in any of these
decisions. When my older brother went to university, his
course selection was a family affair, my mother poring over

the course catalogue with him, my parents debating which courses would be best. With me, they didn't worry so much. I'd be married soon anyway, I didn't really need the education.

Though it is worth noting that I didn't have to fight for an education either. My parents supported my education, they considered it a perfectly acceptable pursuit while I waited to get married, they even paid for my undergraduate degree. I got scholarships for the master's and doctoral degrees. And when it came time for my doctoral studies at New York University, even though my parents were not happy about me moving to New York City by myself, my older sister drove me down to my new apartment, with her two kids in tow, the van full of my belongings. What I'm saying is, it wasn't just me against the world.

Still, I made all these decisions on a whim, sitting alone in a courtyard in Gujranwala, in the same house in which, just a few decades earlier, my grandfather decided it was more important for my mother to care for her own grandfather than it was for her to get an education – just outside the room where she *cried without end* for the opportunity she lost, the things she would never learn and the future she would never have.

I attended the downtown campus of the University of Toronto – a massive, sprawling city within a city. I would commute in from Mississauga on a big yellow school bus operated by the university just for its suburban students. The bus sped along Mississauga Road, which is where the wealthiest people in Mississauga lived. Unsurprisingly, it was also one of the whitest parts of town. It was lined with expensive and gaudy, mostly enormous houses in all differ-ent styles, old and new, some with elaborate golden gates, or high impenetrable hedges, or long driveways with multiple fancy cars. Sometimes there were grand houses set back on sprawling lawns, as if this were the English countryside rather than the suburbs of Toronto. The bus would rumble down Mississauga Road, take the on-ramp to the Queen Elizabeth Highway, and then merge on to the Gardiner Expressway, racing past the new buildings going up, the glass and steel construction that teased the city with the promise of lofts and hipsters, flying by the two old brown buildings that marked a dip in the road that made our stom-achs fall whenever we drove by in my parents' car, but some-how not on the bus. The route went along Lake Ontario, where I always searched eagerly for crashing waves. There were rarely any, this being a lake and not an ocean, but on cold and windy days the water could get pretty choppy.

The bus exited the Expressway on to Spadina Avenue, and headed in the direction of the Sky Dome. One year, all the Muslim communities in Toronto pooled their resources to rent it out and celebrate Eid. That's the only time I've been to the Sky Dome. As always, the organisers figured out a way to separate the men and women, even in such an enormous stadium. I stood near the entrance with my family, handing out flyers protesting the arrest and subsequent mistreatment of Shaykh Omar Abdur-Rahman – 'the Blind Sheikh', as he was called in the media. We were told he was being tortured in prison, and, specifically, that he had been raped with a broom. We were shocked at how apathetic Muslims were; many wouldn't even take the pamphlets we were distributing, brushing right past our outstretched hands as if we weren't there at all. The bus rolled past the Sky Dome, where the Blue Jays also played, and eventually pulled into the St George Campus, letting us out at the circle – we had a circle rather than a quad – right in front of the medical sciences building.

The entire trip from home to campus and back was cocooned, sheltered, safe. My dad drove me to the bus stop every morning and then picked me up from the same place when I returned in the evenings. That way, I avoided all public transportation. This was as much about safety as it was about control. Public transportation is terribly frightening if you're not used to taking it, if you're not exposed to it, and if you look different. Extremisms abound in all forms in the public space, including racist and Islamophobic ones.

I loved my time at the University of Toronto. I delighted in the buzz of the place, the grand stone buildings, the chapels, the arches, the well-worn wooden bannisters, the cosy and numerous libraries. Victoria Park, in the centre of campus, was magical on winter nights, blanketed in soft, pillowy snow that fell gently, illuminated in the glow of the globe lamps. I loved the vines that climbed the walls of New College, the green turning into the most vibrant reds and yellows and oranges in the fall. I loved the little adolescent maple tree in front of Sidney Smith that in the October sun burned a red so bright it looked like it might catch fire. It made me feel like Moses approaching the burning bush. I loved the tiny carrels in Robarts Library. In the six years I was there – four for undergrad and two for my master's – I rarely left campus to walk on Bloor Street or Yonge Street, or anywhere else. I would only discover Toronto years later, with Rumee, after first telling him there was nothing to do downtown.

I want to linger on this point. I took a bus downtown almost every day for six years and never discovered the city beyond the university campus. I explored the campus itself, had wonderful extended conversations about the meaning of life and religion with Menka, and Sarah, and Jacob, and James. I knew almost every tree on that campus, but I never left the university grounds. Why? Simply put, I never considered it. It never really occurred to me to do so, and if anyone asked to leave campus with me, I acted like I didn't want to. But it wasn't that. Or rather, maybe it was, but I interpreted my fear of leaving campus as not wanting to leave. What was I afraid of? I was afraid of being in the real world, unprotected, with my niqab. On campus, I was still

sheltered. If someone was bigoted or racist, I could technically report them, though of course I never reported anyone.
But at least there was a mechanism in place. Off campus, I
was vulnerable, exposed, without a safety net. Who would I
complain to there? Who would care? So, for all my talk
about the niqab not limiting my options, in the end, it did.

Some things were just more difficult with the niqab, like
eating most foods. You could eat small dry foods easily, like
nuts. But messy foods, even chips, if they touched the inside
of the niqab, would leave a residue, a smell, a stain that
would touch your face for the rest of the day. Drinking was
cumbersome too. It's not easy, though doable, to stick a cup
of coffee under your niqab. This had health and social
consequences. I avoided eating all day while at university.
So, if I was at school from nine till six, I just wouldn't eat.
This made it easy for me to fast, not just during Ramadan,
but throughout the year. The Prophet is said to have fasted
every Monday and Thursday and on the thirteenth, four-
teenth and fifteenth of every month in the Islamic calendar.
And during the first ten days of Dhul Hijja. And those first
days in Shawwal. So I fasted all those fasts, too. It wasn't
much of a deviation from my normal eating patterns
anyway. My brother once said, *You shouldn't get any sawab
(merit points) for fasting because you don't like eating!*

Extremist tendencies can manifest themselves in our
eating habits. When I got to New York University for my
PhD, I was diagnosed with clinical anorexia and I had to see
a nutritionist to learn how to eat, regularly, in a balanced

way. Certainly, not eating food was a way for me to feel a sense of control over my life. But it was also just more convenient.

All of this meant that I never went out for meals with friends. The logistics were too complicated. It wasn't worth the hassle. It was also difficult, though not impossible, to work out in niqab. I took an 'Active Healthy Living' class for a science requirement, in which we learned to use the full offerings of the gym. A Korean classmate partnered up with me, and we did all the activities required of us together. I was so grateful for her because I would have never had the confidence to even walk into the gym without her. She was totally unfazed by my niqab. She didn't even really acknowledge it. With her at my side, I learned to use the weight machines, played a little squash, took a tai-chi class, all while wearing niqab. It wasn't ideal, and though I loved working out, I didn't take it up until I stopped wearing it. Bottom line, it's hard to work out in niqab. It seems like an obvious point. Still, I know because I tried.

What's interesting to me about not leaving campus to explore downtown is that it demonstrates just how much fear can limit our horizons, our imaginative and our experiential horizons. I mean, the moment I got on the bus in the morning, and certainly once I got to campus, I was alone and unsupervised. I could have watched movies in theatres within walking distance, I could have explored the parks, I could have eaten great food, I could have even removed my niqab and walked around incognito. I could have done so much, but none of it ever occurred to me. It's not that I was resisting temptation, so much as that there were no temptations to begin with. I *believed*. Like really, truly believed – in what exactly? I'm not sure. My belief wasn't about the specifics, it was more about the broad strokes of who I wasn't and who I was. I wasn't Western, I was Muslim. Even though I now know those categories, 'Muslim' and 'Western' are meaningless – the more you try to pin them down the more elusive they get – back then, they really meant something to me. I lived in a world of black and white. There was no grey.

Doesn't this black-and-white thinking lead to extremism? a friend once asked me.

Extremism is relative, I retorted. *Besides, life is black and white. When you die, you go to Heaven or Hell. There's no in between. Muslims don't believe in Purgatory.*

Most Muslims in the Muslim Students' Association at the University of Toronto were too grey for me. I rarely attended their events. The fact that their events were not fully gender segregated troubled me. Yet, I attended a co-ed university and spent countless hours in conversation with a couple of male friends I met in class. Somehow that didn't stop me from judging Muslims for falling short on gender segregation. I did attend Friday prayers in Hart House even though there wasn't a barrier between the men and women. You still gotta pray.

One Friday at Jumuʿa, there was a reporter visiting from the *Toronto Star*. She interviewed some Muslims, including me, for a piece she was working on, while a photographer took pictures. That weekend, there was a large photo of me on the front page of the 'Life and Style' section, in a dark green jilbab with gold buttons and a black niqab. I remember my family and community members were so proud of me. I was proud of me. The white female reporter, with curly blonde hair, asked me near the end of our interview, *If you had a daughter, would you make her wear niqab?*

I knew the correct liberal answer to that question, *No, of course not! I would let her choose! I'd let her wear whatever she wanted. It would be her choice.*

I would let her choose. As if we live in vacuums and don't influence our daughters with pink hats and dolls and dresses and heels and tanning beds and Botox. As though my daughter would be born into a void where she could 'freely' choose what to do with her body, free from external pressures, free from social conditioning, free to shape her desire as she wills, free to choose between covering her face or injecting it with chemicals. If those are her choices, isn't she already trapped?

In all honesty, though, it did break my heart to think of my daughter not wearing niqab. Why wouldn't she? The reporter must have picked up on the emptiness of my answer from my tone or my eyes – she didn't have much else to go on.

Yes, but you'd advise her to wear niqab? You'd be disappointed if she didn't?

She assumed that I wanted to be a mother, that I would want a heteronormative family, that I'd have children, that one of my children would be a daughter, that I'd see my values reflected in her clothing, that I'd be disappointed if she fell short. We shared all of these assumptions. We had more in common than either of us thought.

Perhaps the most seductive siren call of extremism I have encountered is white feminism. I have found that white feminists are really good at pumping you up, making you feel like *we're all in this together*, we're fighting for *women*, and if you're a woman you're failing ALL women if you don't join in and do your part. But then, when push comes to shove, when resources are scarce, or privilege is close at hand, and you're a woman of colour, they will hold your head under water to keep themselves afloat. It took real betrayal and heartbreak for me to finally learn this lesson, that, like Islam, there are different kinds of feminism, and some are white supremacist while others are genuinely egalitarian. Just like patriarchal Islam assumes the male as its normative subject, white feminism assumes white women as its normative subject. Like patriarchal Muslims who go on about equality but support laws that discriminate against women, white feminists prattle on about equality for all, but cast their votes for white supremacists. I learned this lesson in stages and my education started early.

By the time I started my second year of university, I was in love with the place and attending full time. I was especially enjoying my Philosophy classes. I joined study groups whenever possible; they were fun and a great way to ensure a good grade. You could exchange notes, ask each other to explain an idea and rely on one another to do an extra reading or recap a missed class. In one Philosophy class, a beautiful girl named Ariana organised our study group. Ariana and I became fast friends. We started emailing each other outside of class, we'd sit next to each other, passing notes, rolling our eyes when the white male professor made yet another sexist comment. I started looking forward to Tuesday and Thursday mornings at eleven when I'd walk into the auditorium where the Philosophy class was held. Thick red velvet seat covers and red carpeting made it a cosy space despite the large classroom size. I'd look for Ariana, who'd watch for me and wave me over, usually keeping a seat free for me next to her. I felt close to her in body and spirit. We talked endlessly, but more importantly, we laughed together. We didn't agree about everything, but that was okay. In her presence, I felt seen.

Then one day, a few weeks before the end of the semester, I opened my email and saw a message from Ariana. Excitedly, I clicked on it, saw that it was kind of long, and settled in to read. But as I read, I was filled with sadness, and shame, and finally anger. Ariana wrote to say that she couldn't keep quiet any longer. She felt compelled to speak up. She didn't understand how someone as intelligent and articulate and funny as me could freely choose to live a life of subjugation and oppression while living in a country like Canada, where I could be free, and where no one would persecute me for being independent and liberated. She was hoping that all the hours and weeks she spent getting to know me would give her some insight, help her understand, or help her turn me, unveil me, so to speak, but it had only made her angry and confused. She hated that I chose to wear niqab and that I insisted that I wasn't oppressed – this offended her. How could I see myself as free when clearly I was caged, erased, faceless, serving a patriarchal religion? So, even as she promised me that I lived in a country where I wouldn't be persecuted for expressing my independence by wearing whatever I wanted, she found my choices intolerable. And she just had to tell me all this because she respected me and cared about me. Classic abusive words. *I'm hurting you because I love you.*

I read her email with ringing ears, wind sweeping my mind, which was suddenly a desert, with brown balls of tumbleweed flying about, flimsy, unmoored and directionless. My mouth ran dry. My heart broke again and again as I read and reread Ariana's message. In disbelief. In pain.

This whole time I'd thought we were friends, but in fact, she had been trying to figure out if I was fully human. All she saw was a shadow of me, a flat two-dimensional image, a representation of ideas rather than a delightful, complex, full person. Which is to say, she didn't see me at all. And she saw herself as apart from, as different, as special, as free, because she wore different clothes than me. She thought that she could see, but that I was blind; like she had clarity and perspective while I was chained to ignorance. She wanted to save a person who was not looking to be saved. And that pissed her off.

Beware the one who seeks to save you on the assumption of her own exceptionalism.

Ariana couldn't see me as a full human, as someone who might relate to the world differently than she did, who might make different choices. This angered me; what difference did it make to her what I wore? Why did my clothing choice affect our relationship so profoundly and fundamentally? How dare she decide what I needed to wear in order to be 'free'? What kind of feminism was this?

White feminism.

In his allegory of the cave, Plato describes a people who live shackled in a cave and see the world only through shadows cast on the walls. They mistake these shadows for the real world. But there are some people, some exceptional people, who break their shackles, leave the cave and see the world beyond the shadows, as it truly is, and thus they are able to see the shadows for what they truly are. These special people try to tell the cave-dwellers about the world beyond the cave, they want to free them from their shackles by telling them about a world bathed in light. But the cave-dwellers are at once restricted by and invested in the shadows, because that is the only world they know, the world they see, the world they understand, the world they can imagine. A universe beyond the shadows is unbelievable to them, it is frightening, it is threatening. And though it seems impossible that anything might exist beyond the shadows, an entire colourful, textured universe awaits them, if only they would permit themselves to step outside, traverse a few yards and just *see*, let their eyes be open and behold. Once they see the world, it will become clear to them that they've been living in shadows their entire lives. And the shadows will never be enough again.

I loved this allegory when I first learned it in my university Philosophy classes, when extremism was still appealing to me. But now I get its destructive power, how it justifies the elevation of some over others by gliding over some really important questions. Like, why are there people shackled in the cave? Who put them there? Who are these special people who have escaped? How have they escaped? What makes them so special? And who has the power to 'unshackle' the shackled? What is the price of the unshackling? The allegory of the cave cultivates a class of special, saved, exceptional people, people who are better than everyone else and thus in a position to save others, even when they might not want to be saved. When you read more about Plato, you realise this was exactly his intention.

Beware the one who seeks to save you on the assumption of their own exceptionalism.

The very idea of some people being exceptional, being saved, being special, is delusional, because it requires everyone else to be unexceptional, unspecial, even shackled. Toni Morrison once said, *If you can only be tall because someone else is on their knees, then you have a serious problem.* This principle holds true for any kind of exceptionalism; if you need people to be shackled so you can feel free, then you're not free. You're just an extremist.

The FBI, Queen Victoria, Israr Ahmed, the colonialists, John Doe, Ariana, and me too, we were all participating in extremist discourses, presuming ourselves exceptional, as the ones able to see the truth of the world as it was, as bringing the light to those in shadows, to those we imagined shackled in a cave, content in their own ignorance. But we were the ignorant ones, the ones with narrow imaginations, the ones who could not see, the ones who hurt others while claiming to help them. The principles and beliefs of extremists, their positions even, can vary wildly, but they come to them in the same exclusionary, intolerant way, confident in their own superiority and exceptionalism, certain that they are privy to knowledge no one else has, that they are uniquely positioned to rectify others, show them the way, save them.

You don't have to adhere to a formal religion to be a zealot. Extremism comes in many forms. In all of its forms, it is shallow and cruel.

Jet Skiing on the Mediterranean

The first summer that I was in Syria, I spent most of my time in Damascus, where I befriended a South Asian woman, who, like me, was in her early twenties. She came from a wealthy family in the United States. She was worldly and cool. She got me to consider bending the rules of my highly disciplined and meticulously organised life. We'd stay up late, talking into the night, we'd smoke sheesha, miss Fajr and skip classes at the University of Damascus to explore the Old City. She got me to see young Muslim couples holding hands, being affectionate with each other, as adorable rather than disgusting. She taught me that public displays of affection were cute, sweet even. We spent that summer acting like death was impossible and like we had all the time in the world. Which is to say, we were reckless.

At one point, we decided to visit the Mediterranean so that we could say we went. We got on a bus from Damascus to the coastal town of Latakia. We arrived in the dead of night. When we got off the bus, some guy offered us a ride to our hotel, and we readily accepted, seeing this as a generosity. At one point, he turned on to a mud road that wound through a field. It was dark and we couldn't see the road ahead of us, we didn't know exactly where we were going; we were filled with fear and thrill, as we realised just how dangerous this situation was. No one knew where we were. Anything could happen. Thankfully, the man was upstanding and delivered us to our hotel.

The next afternoon, on a bright sunny day, we frolicked in the water, me wearing tights, a T-shirt, a jilbab and niqab. Of course, no one there knew me or would care if I didn't wear a jilbab or niqab, but it didn't occur to me to wear anything different. I was more comfortable in it than without it.

In the distance, we saw people on jet skis.

C'mon! Let's jet ski! my friend said. She had ridden jet skis before, but I hadn't. *It'll be fun!*

In the back of my mind, I knew that all of these experiences – the late-night trip to a seaside town, the playing on the beach, the jet skiing – would be useful back in Canada. One of the ways that I managed people's emotions about my niqab was to trick them away from their fear, or shock, or disgust and engage them in lively conversation, tell them something they didn't expect to hear, like that I had gone jet skiing on the Mediterranean. I brought this up as evidence of the complexity of niqabi women, of my own complexity. In other words, I brought it up as evidence of my humanity.

See? You don't know anything about the experience of niqabi women! When you see a niqabi, you just see the fabric, not the woman wearing it!

When I was younger, I used to think that this was a brilliant move. Now I realise that Islamophobic ideas are so entrenched that even people who make their living off of examining complex ideas have trouble seeing niqabi women as complex humans.

Recently, I shared an essay from this book, 'Assimilation', with a group of mostly white academics at a prestigious university in the United States. The essay was written to highlight the many overlapping reasons why Muslim women may or may not cover. In the Q&A, a white woman said that it infuriated her, made her angry, that *they made their women cover so much over there*. In her comment, 'they' and 'over there' could have referred to Pakistanis and Pakistan, or Muslims and anywhere Muslims exist.

The 'they' and the 'over there' were figments of her imagination, rather than any real people or places on Earth. Yet her imagination and her sentiments dominated the discussion for the next hour. Even though the central point of my essay is that racism led my parents to embrace fundamentalist Islam in Canada, somehow the discussion devolved into the problem with Islam and Muslims, rather than racism and liberal intolerance. I fielded question after question about Pakistani culture and Islam; I watched my esteemed colleagues indulge in righteous rage against a religion that might oppress Pakistani Muslim women, even as they steadily ignored the danger posed to those very same Pakistani Muslim women by drone warfare waged by the country in which we were all present. In their self-righteous imagination, veils were more outrageous than bombs.

Not long ago, I was at a mostly white party in Canada, where a white gay man living in India – where he ran a business and made his livelihood off of Indians – in the first thirty seconds of meeting me, uttered this sentence: *When I see women in niqab, I just want to rip it off their faces!*

He made a snatching motion with his hand when he said 'rip'. The fact that he said 'rip', a word that denotes violence, indicates he did not give a fuck about the women in niqab. He was moved to violence and felt justified about it. Virtuous even. Brazen.

That level of dehumanisation is widespread; you hear it in the righteous indignation of liberal elites in Western nations under the guise of gender equality, and you hear it from conservative governments and clerics who compel women to cover under the guise of morality. You hear it in official decrees, and in academic venues, and in casual discourse, where women in burqas are referred to as 'walking tents'. It's not the burqa dehumanising those women, it is the people who see a walking tent where a woman walks.

This reductive way of thinking, measuring liberation or oppression through the length of fabric, erases the women wearing the cloth. They are two sides of the same coin; the people who are so obsessed with the veil that they'll force women to wear it and those who cannot abide the women who do; neither is interested in the humanity of the women doing the covering or uncovering.

Get over yourselves! I sometimes want to scream at these people. *You are not the most important person in this conversation. Maybe try listening instead of speaking first.*

So, to get people to listen, one of the things I repeated, over and over again, as I sought to shatter stereotypes of niqabi women, was that I'd travelled by myself to the Middle East, that I'd climbed Mount Sinai in the middle of the night to watch sunrise, that I'd jet skied on the Mediterranean, all while wearing niqab.

The niqab doesn't stop me from anything! I would say.

Somehow, I thought that listing these activities, holding them out as proofs, as evidence of my humanity, would help people see that I was human – a person who did things, beheld beauty, enjoyed life. But it was a degrading and dehumanising enterprise, with me saying, *Lookit what I did, I'm human!* And them saying, in the best-case scenario, *Wow, I had no idea you were human!*

What did these conversations cost me, the human always trying to prove her humanity? It cost me the ability to process the experience of being in my body, to be honest about what happened to my body, how I really felt about it. The politicised nature of the veil made me feel that I couldn't speak about my actual experiences with any depth or complexity, without worrying about how it would look to others. Would my experiences, my stories, confirm or challenge what people thought about Muslims, or the veil? Would my experiences be generalised as 'Muslim' or 'South Asian'? I knew my experiences would never be generalised as 'Canadian', so how would they be generalised?

There is little room for honesty, for truth, in this space. And if there was a chance that my experiences might confirm the worst suspicions of racists and misogynists and Islamophobes, then memories, events, experiences, happenings, truths – they got forgotten, suppressed, erased, disappeared. As if they hadn't happened. As if the whole of my life experience was simple, uncomplicated. As simple and uncomplicated as the boxes people wanted to put me in, the person they expected, even needed me to be. But really, the person I wasn't and could never be. Because there is no simple, uncomplicated person. No one fits in a box. Ever. Humans, by their very definition, are leaky. We cannot be contained.

There was no official place to rent jet skis, so my friend and I approached a couple of guys who had a jet ski of their own and asked if they'd rent it out to us. After some negotiation, we agreed on a price. But one of the guys insisted that my friend and I couldn't go out together on our own, that he'd have to take each of us separately. You know, for safety. One of us would sit up front and 'drive' while he sat behind us, making sure we didn't get hurt. In case you're wondering, no, we didn't have life vests, and no, I did not know how to swim.

My friend went first. I waited on the shore with the other guy. We watched silently as the two of them sped off into the distance, getting tinier and tinier and then larger and larger as they returned. Then it was my turn. The afternoon was turning to evening by now, the sun beginning to descend behind the mountains in the distance. It was getting cloudier and colder. I suddenly was no longer crazy about going out on a jet ski and getting wet again. And yet, when the young man gestured me forward, I got on. I didn't know yet that I could just change my mind. That I was entitled to do so. That I could do the opposite of what I'd just said because now I felt differently. That feeling differently was a good enough reason to not go through with a plan. I got on that jet ski for all the haters out there, so I could say I'd done yet another thing as a niqabi.

As we set out, the guy showed me how to steer, how to turn the throttle to speed up. Once I got the hang of it, it was thrilling. The speed at which you could move, the danger, the flirting with death. At some level, I knew this was insanely reckless behaviour. Again, I didn't know how to swim.

My jilbab was hiked up around my waist so I could straddle the jet ski, and my legs, clad in black tights, were exposed.

At some point, while I was caught up in the fun, the fear, the excitement of the jet ski, I felt hands on my thighs. I looked down and saw the guy's hands. The nail of the pinky finger of his right hand was very long. And the hands were moving. They started caressing my inner thighs and moved up into my crotch. I was stunned. I couldn't speak. I couldn't say, *Stop! Stop doing that!*

I was at this guy's mercy, on the fucking Mediterranean, on a jet ski, without a life vest, unable to swim. I knew, in my core, that the balance of power was in his favour. He could do what he damn well pleased. Joy and thrill curdled into sickening shame in the pit of my stomach. I felt dirty. And damaged. And sick. And dirty. Like *I* was doing something wrong. I hated myself there, on that jet ski. I hated myself for being so stupid as to find myself in this situation, for being so cowardly as to not speak up, to not say *no, stop!*, for not slapping his hands away.

Eventually, we turned around. As we got closer to shore, he pulled his hands away. I jumped off quickly, avoiding eye contact. Though I remember his hands clearly, I do not remember his face. I wouldn't recognise him if I saw him today. That is, if Assad's bombings have not killed him, if he hasn't drowned in the Mediterranean trying to escape the hell that Syria has become. He might be in a refugee camp in Turkey, or he might have joined ISIS. If he is still alive, that is.

My friend and I walked back quietly. The mood turned from light-hearted and adventurous to heavy silence. It was dark enough by now that we couldn't see each other's faces.

Did that guy touch you on the jet ski? my friend asked.

No!

The word was out of my mouth before I could catch it. I lied to cover my shame. As if the lie were a garment, and a garment might actually cover my shame. Like Adam and Eve, I figured, if I could just cover myself with something, even something flimsy, like a lie, like a leaf, it would be enough.

He felt up my breasts, she confessed.

Then why did you let me get on the jet ski with him?! I wanted to scream.

And also this: I was shocked by her confession. I couldn't believe that she would admit to such a thing, say it out loud, like it didn't taint her, like she carried no blame. Her lack of shame stunned me. *I* was ashamed. So ashamed, I lied to a friend. So ashamed, the shame spilled out of me and enveloped her. Rather than confess to the groping I too experienced, I left her stranded, alone, isolated. I offered her no solace, just silence. What I offered myself might have been worse: denial.

At least she had spoken her truth, out loud, without shame. Even if she spoke it too late to save me.

The ones we love are keepers of our shame. They can reinforce it or they can help untangle us from it, help us be free of it. Shame is nurtured in community, it gathers its strength in hushed tones, in whispers and secrets, until it becomes so loud as to be deafening. Shame wants to spread. Others must buy into it or it dissipates. Like the fog that can be so thick as to blot out entire mountains, that can press down, close in and feel suffocating, feel eternal; fog that resists mightily the light of the sun, standing its ground, retreating a bit and then returning with vigour. But that same fog can evaporate under the light and disappear so completely as to leave no trace of itself, barely even a memory.

I suppressed what happened out there on the Mediterranean. Silenced it, wrapped it up in fog, because there was no place for it. This wasn't supposed to happen to niqabi women – that's what I'd been told my whole life.

The hijab protects you! Even more so the niqab!

By the time I returned to Canada at the end of that summer, I was trotting out the line about jet skiing on the Mediterranean in niqab as yet another item that proved my humanity. *That's just how badass she is*, I wanted others to think. I unremembered what happened to me out there, on the Mediterranean. I lived in fog.

More than a decade later, when the fog lifted and I re-remembered, my heart broke for my friend, and also for that young niqabi girl. I feel compassion for her naïveté. She didn't understand yet that the horror and the sorrow of patriarchy is that all of its truths are lies. That none of the things it tells us will save us can save us. And worse still, when we learn that the lies of patriarchy are what they are

– lies – we are forced to cover for it, manufacture shame, blame ourselves for the failures of patriarchy, lie to ourselves and others to protect patriarchy. But the shame and the lies, they are fog, they obscure the truth, prevent us from seeing what lies before us.

Now I know better. I know that patriarchy hates women and that it nurtures shame in us to compensate for its own failures, that shame makes lying necessary. I know now that shame hurts everything it touches. Shame makes it difficult to have compassion, to help a friend in need, to accept help. Makes it difficult to come together, to care for one another, to love each other. Love is the light that takes away the fog of shame.

The fact is, there is no cool story that will get people to see me as human if all they see is a 'walking tent'. Just like no amount of clothing can keep me from being assaulted when people see a sexual object where a human stands. To see a human where one sees a 'walking tent', you have to be able to love the person before you, on her own terms. To see the humanity of someone who decides not to cover in the way you think best, you have to love her. Again, on her own terms.

But to love others on their own terms, we must first love ourselves. I see now that I've always misunderstood the commandment to love one's neighbour as oneself. I thought it meant we were supposed to love for our neighbours what we loved for ourselves. But that's just another way of universalising our desires and imposing them on others. There's nothing noble or loving about that. Instead of assuming that we love ourselves already and challenging us to love others in the same way, the commandment asks us to love ourselves fully, even – especially – the parts of ourselves we'd rather not look at, the parts we are ashamed of, so that we can love others fully, too. Loving like this is hard. It takes practice, it is best cultivated in community. We cannot offer others love, kindness, compassion that we do not first feel for ourselves.

After all, فاقد الشيئ لا يعطيه

The one who does not have something cannot give it.

Hair Diaries

I spent a few years as a fellow at two Institutes for Advanced Study, and in that time, I've had many sustained conversations with mathematicians. Mathematicians, I have found, like to talk about beauty in an abstract, non-political way. Beauty as symmetry, beauty as patterns, repetitions and rhythms, rather than beauty as socially constructed, as subjective, as gendered, as racial. Many of the ones I have been in conversation with cannot even imagine the political, the contested, the subjective, the weaponised nature of beauty. And if they can, they don't see it as relevant to their discussions of beauty. They see themselves as adherents of a different religion – one that reveres a purer, higher, cleaner form of beauty, beauty untainted by human subjectivity. Objective beauty. Beauty that is at once free of human frailty yet somehow recognisable to the human eye, independent of human bias and yet somehow captured by the human mind. They can't see that there is no such thing, that there can be no beauty detached from human complexity and variety and subjectivity. Once human senses, the mind, is involved, nothing is objective. It is all argument. It is all contested. It is all political.

'Aesthetic' is a relative to 'beauty'. As in, *Oh, I love this aesthetic!* or, *This aesthetic doesn't speak to me.* Aesthetic is subjective too, like beauty. It is gendered and racial. It creates a hierarchy, which is to say an argument for what is better and what is less than. Monotone or colourful clothing. Minimalist or ornate interiors. Small or large women. Glass or brick buildings. Black or blond hair. Pigmented or pink skin. Bald or hairy heads. Bald or hairy legs. Bald or hairy armpits. Bald or hairy faces.

Beauty is always a moral argument, because it simultaneously makes claims about what is ugly. 'Fair', as in *the fair-skinned girl* is an excellent example of a word that makes an argument for beauty that is both moral and racial. 'Fair' means pretty and beautiful. 'Fair' means light-skinned, white or whiter. 'Fair' means just, equitable, upright, trustworthy, honourable. 'Fair' does not mean ugly, it does not mean partial, biased, prejudiced, unjust. 'Fair' does not mean dark-skinned. Fair is good. The opposite of fair is bad.

Arguments about beauty are arguments about the good. Code words are used to fool us into missing the arguments that are being made about beauty, to avoid scrutiny, to escape critique. Clean is a common code word for beauty. What is clean is assumed to be beautiful and vice versa. An unclean body is ugly. A clean body is good. A dirty body is bad. You must be ashamed of a dirty body.

I have spent my life trying to be beautiful, to be clean, to be good.

1959

Some of the most bitter fights I have had with my mother were over my hair. Of course there was the drama with covering the hair on my head. When could I start covering it? When must I always cover it? Discussions about hijab are discussions about hair. Still, there's so much more to my hair than its covering. Of course there is.

According to my mother, 'good' girls always had their hair well oiled, parted down the middle in two braids. This was her dream for her daughters. She's the youngest daughter in a family of over a dozen children. Her sisters were all older, much older, maybe by a decade or so. She has vivid memories of her sisters oiling and braiding her hair, threading it with parandas, which are like extensions. Parandas are usually made of cotton, sometimes they are black or brown, to match the colour of most South Asian hair. Other times, they are bright and colourful, like the feathers of a peacock: sky blue, royal purple, hot pink, bright yellow or multicoloured. Frequently, there is some gold threaded through, or wrapped around the ends. A paranda comes joined at the head with three strands, you can weave it into your own braid, to make the hair look longer, thicker, more colourful, more beautiful. If your hair is too short, a paranda will fall out after a few hours.

When she was an itty-bitty girl, my mother loved having parandas braided through her hair, which, at the time, was short and thick. She especially wanted, demanded them when she went to school. It made her feel like an adult, and special, to have a paranda hanging down her back, bouncing against her bum. But the problem was that her hair was short and thick, so the paranda was likely to slip out before she returned home from school. Her older sisters, who oiled and braided her hair, thought that parandas were superfluous, wasted even, on my mother, because she was bound to lose them. But my mother wouldn't have any of it. She told us, with sparkling eyes and an easy laugh, lost in the memory of this happy time, that she'd throw a fit when her sisters refused to braid her hair with a paranda. She'd throw a tantrum so her father would hear her, and then he'd take her side, chiding her sisters for not giving her what she wanted.

What's it to you? he'd scold them. *Just braid her hair with a paranda!*

But Abba-ji, parandas are not free, and she's just going to lose it!

You're not paying for it, I am! he'd retort.

And her sisters would fume, they'd be seething as they pulled her hair unnecessarily hard, yanked her head while twisting her braid. They'd weave in a paranda and threaten to beat her with scissors if she came home without it.

And sure enough, every afternoon, my mother returned home with her hair in disarray, the paranda nowhere to be found.

1985

These memories of childhood hair braiding were formative for my mother, because despite all the drama-bazi, the yanked hair, the case for and against the paranda, the screaming, the confrontation between her father and her sisters, these times spent braiding hair were moments of closeness, care, love between sisters. They were sites of intimacy. My khalas would touch my mother, caress her hair as they oiled it, parted it in the middle, braided it. She'd be sitting at their feet, between their legs, they'd be on a chaarpai maybe, or a piri. My mother wanted to recreate these loving, intimate moments with her daughters. I'm sure she'd imagined it many times, since she didn't have a younger sister herself to boss around, whose hair she could oil and braid, whom she could chide and forgive for losing a paranda. Now she had daughters of her own. Who'd stand in her way?

I would! I didn't want my hair oiled at all. The oil smelled strong, which I interpreted as 'bad', it looked oily. In Pakistan, shiny, braided hair might be beautiful, but in Canada, oily, braided hair isn't exactly high fashion. I didn't want my hair parted down the middle, I wanted it parted off to the side, a little askew, like a hat at a jaunty angle. And I certainly didn't want my hair braided; I wanted to let it hang loose, flowing, so I could flick it back over my shoulder, maybe as I laughed, maybe as I stood around with a group of friends, maybe as I delivered a well-timed joke. I wanted to be like the girls at school, who were mostly white, none of whom had oiled or braided hair. I knew that oily, tightly braided hair was 'old-fashioned' and 'fob-y' at school, 'dirty' even, but at home, loose-flowing hair was 'modern' and 'Western'. Women with loose hair might be loose in other ways, too.

As always, there were pragmatic reasons for my mother's strict rules around hair. It is difficult to wear loose hair under a hijab and under a dupatta. It makes the dupatta slip off easily, and with a hijab, well, it's just a mess. It becomes jumbled, it wraps around your neck, strands inevitably begin to poke out, insisting on being seen even as you keep pushing them back under the hijab. Besides, with four South Asian, Punjabi daughters with hair as thick as ours, I'm sure that braids helped with cleanliness. In my carpet-less apartment, I'm acutely aware of just how much hair I shed on a daily basis. Imagine my hair multiplied by five – that's a lot of hair to clean up. Recently, I went to buy a Dyson vacuum cleaner, and the salesman recommended the model designed to pick up animal hair. When I said that I don't have any pets, he nodded toward my head.

Are you calling me an animal? I asked indignantly.

No! But you do have a lot of hair! he protested, his face flushed red.

My mother mostly got her way with my hair while I lived at home, right through grade school and high school. By the time I was in university, my mother was getting softer on the issue; now, when she occasionally oiled and braided my hair,

I appreciated it for the loving and intimate act it had become. I have nostalgic memories of sitting at my mother's feet as she pours oil into the middle of my scalp, as I feel it trickle down my head, as she rubs it in with the base of her palm, a wonderfully relaxing head massage thrown in as part of the package. She massages my temples and my neck too, sometimes hitting my head gently, with quick strikes from the side of her hand, poised as if to deliver a karate chop. It feels so deeply comforting to be tended to in this way, tenderly, to be at her mercy like this, to be her child.

But when I was younger, especially in grade school, I saw the oiling and the braiding of my hair as a unique act of oppression and tyranny. I hated the funky smell of the oils my mother used, Johnson & Johnson baby oil mixed with sticky mustard oil, or olive oil, and sometimes pungent green Amla oil. I'd be at her feet, she'd sit on a chair or on the edge of the bathtub or a bed. Fat tears would roll down my face. I'd weep as my mother oiled and braided my hair. When I looked at myself in the mirror after my mother had finished, I only ever saw ugliness.

And on top of these hair wars, there was the covering of hair, with a hijab when I was out, and with a dupatta or chador when I was at home.

بال ڈھکو! *Cover your hair!* – an oft-repeated command.

بال نظر آرہے ہیں! *Your hair is showing!* – a common rebuke.

2004

It probably comes as no surprise that my mother cut our hair herself. We never went to a salon. When you have six children, salons are expensive, even the lower-end ones. That means that my mother and I fought over the length of my hair, too. Sometimes my mother cut my hair too short when I wanted it longer, other times she barely trimmed it when I wanted it shorter. A few times, when I was in grade school, she got so sick and overwhelmed by my hair, she just sheared it all off. Without any prior warning. That was a new kind of nakedness, being shorn like that, unexpectedly, like a lamb. I was relieved I wore a hijab back then, because at least I didn't have to suffer public ridicule on top of this violation.

I was disappointed by every single haircut my mother gave me, mostly because I wanted to be beautiful. And beautiful, in my head, was Anne of Green Gables. So the only haircut that could have pleased me was one that replaced me with a freckled, white-skinned, red-haired girl, turning me into someone I was not, erasing me. My poor mother didn't stand a chance.

I started visiting hair salons once I was living on my own. At first I searched for salons with female stylists who agreed to cut my hair after hours, when the salon was closed, ensuring that no man would accidentally walk in and see me without my hijab. When that became a nuisance, I started getting my hair cut during normal hours, regardless of male presence. I'd arrive at the salon with my hair covered, get my hair cut and then leave with my hijab back on my head, ruining the blow-out. Once I stopped wearing hijab, a few of my stylists were male. That felt really scandalous and I had to breathe my way through those haircuts, reminding myself that I wasn't doing anything wrong.

In my thirties, I came to love my brown skin and black hair. I love my hair's thickness, its lusciousness. But first, I tried to destroy it. For a few years, I highlighted it with blond streaks. My passport picture, taken long ago, captures the damage I did in those years. When border agents look at the picture, they glance back at me, then back down at the picture, then back at me. If they are people of colour, I joke, apologetically, *I thought I was white back then.* They laugh knowingly.

Now that I'm more comfortable in my South Asian body, I only colour my hair to its original colour – black #3. I'm not yet fully comfortable in my human body, or with time, or with mortality, so I'm not ready to accept my white hair. Hair dye has ammonia in it, which is a toxic chemical. You know something is dangerous when the people advocating it start playing semantic games.

Is ammonia harmful? I ask.

'Harmful' is a tricky word, they reply.

My stylists warn me that non-ammonia hair dye is less effective.

But isn't ammonia dangerous? I ask them, hoping they'll say, *No, not at all!*

Instead they say, *Yeah, girl! But you pee it right out!*

Another says, *No pain, no gain, right?* as she slathers the dye into my hair, my scalp, my body. My body absorbs this toxicity, so that I might be beautiful. And I bury my head in the sand and wish and wish and wish away all side effects, all cancer, all possible negative results from the mutilations I put my body through, this good and beautiful body . . . for who? For beauty. Beauty for whom?

I hate it when stylists say, *Whoa! You have A LOT of hair!* like it's a judgement, or a challenge, or an abnormality. Or when they say, *You have THICK hair!*

I've finally started saying, *A lot of hair compared to who? Thick hair compared to who?* Because my hair is not thick for South Asian hair, it's normal for South Asian hair.

When I first started going to salons, the white stylists would thin out my hair, because they thought it was a problem that I had so much of it. Now, I look for hair stylists who are themselves people of colour. They don't comment on the volume of my hair, except to appreciate it, and they have never tried to thin it out.

You have such beautiful hair! they tell me, as they run their fingers through it, lovingly.

It's nice when we get cues from others that help us accept, even love ourselves – when others make us feel beautiful, good – rather than cues that make us hate ourselves, afraid of ourselves, like there is something abnormal, wrong, ugly about us. Cues that encourage us to embrace, celebrate, reveal ourselves, rather than police, suppress and erase ourselves.

1999

As a Punjabi woman, I have far more hair on my body than just the hair on my head. My people have a lot of hair. Many of us think we have too much hair. ALL of this hair has been the subject of too much attention, too much discussion, scrutiny and worry. When I hit puberty, my hair came in thick and strong. It was everywhere. Coiled and coarse, my pubic hair held on to pungent odours. My armpits filled with dense hair that smelled strongly and became slippery from sweat. My arms and legs and hands and toes were covered with long, thick hair. And then there was the hair on my face, on my upper lip, on my cheeks, on my chin. It felt like an abomination, a curse, a scourge.

The hair on our head was attractive, beautiful, good but needed to be controlled and covered as much as possible. All the other hair on my body was unattractive, ugly, bad and needed to be either removed entirely or trimmed. There was a fundamental contradiction here. On the one hand, we covered our heads, our faces, our bodies, even our hands – with pretty silk ballgown gloves purchased from the Bay, to protect ourselves from the desirous male gaze. Men were expected to have an uncontrollable desire for the female body. Ontologically. Which means, that's just how they were made, in their essence. Which means they had no control over their desire, over themselves. Which means they couldn't possibly be held accountable for their behaviour when overcome by desire.

I remember one religious preacher, a dentist by training and a cleric by presumption, describing male sexual desire as ravenous, untamed. He said, *Men are like wolves. Asking men to control their sexual desire is like asking us not to be men. Men are sexual wolves. Predatory. Aggressive. That's how God made us, we can't help it. Sometimes we feel hungry. Sometimes we feel thirsty. Sometimes we feel sexy.*

On the other hand, even as we wore clothing to thwart the male gaze, an abstract and desirous male gaze filtered into our most private, intimate lives, defined our relationship to our bodies, dictated our relationship to our hair, to ourselves. Our grooming practices, even those in areas men would never see, catered to the male gaze. The mythic male gaze, because in this strictly segregated heteronormative world, no male actually told me which hair to keep and which to remove, what was attractive and what wasn't. We just knew we had to be desirable, both in terms of our bodies and our character. As for our character, any strength that approached independence and resistance was meant to be reformulated, reshaped into strength that was patient, yielding, long-suffering. And as for our bodies, hair had to be changed, altered, controlled.

Hair on our head was beautiful. Long hair was best, we couldn't cut our hair short. That was too modern. Too Western, too unfeminine; which is to say, too masculine. What is normal, even attractive on men, became unappealing, unsightly, ugly on women.

As for the hair that grew naturally on the rest of our bodies, suddenly that became 'unnatural'. This hair had to be removed, trimmed, controlled. The Prophet said, as related to me by my mother, pubic hair and armpit hair was to be trimmed to no longer than one-third of your finger. It's possible that this demand to trim pubic and armpit hair had hygienic roots. But hygiene has always been connected to ideas about purity and virtue. These grooming prescriptions might also have emerged from a place of deep loathing for the human body, so that it must be transformed, 'cleaned', in order to be desirable, in order to be holy. In this vision, the prepubescent body is the ideal body type, and the healthy, natural growth of hair on an adult female body must be removed for it to be clean and desirable. A female body with all its hair intact is shameful, undesirable and unclean. There is a close connection between cleanliness and shame. The Prophet said:

Haya [shame] is a branch of iman [faith].

And also that, صفائ آدھا ایمان ہے *Cleanliness is half of faith.*

So basically, if you have shame and are clean, you're more than halfway home.

1993

The onset of puberty heralded an endless obsession with hair removal. We started out with waxing. First at the hands of expert women, whom we paid to remove our hair. My mother never spent her hard-earned and carefully counted money getting our hair cut, but she spent it to have our hair removed from our bodies. We got our hair removed by South Asian and Arab immigrants, women who ran beauty parlours out of their living rooms and dens. They charged $20 to wax your face.

They'd boil down sugar until it turned into a beautiful golden wax with plenty of elasticity. This made it possible for them to apply a thick coat of it on to your skin while still hot – not so hot as to burn your skin but hot enough to spread evenly on to your legs, or arms, or armpits, or face. This part was pleasant. It felt nice. Then they'd take a strip of cloth and place it on top of the wax, using their hands to rub the strips into the skin, making sure it adhered. This, too, felt nice, almost loving. Next, they'd grab the strip from one end and rip it off your skin, pulling the thick black hair out. If it was a clean swipe, if the wax had been boiled to the correct consistency, and if the cotton strip had adhered strongly to the wax, then the hair would be pulled out by the roots, lying mostly flat against the golden wax except for the roots themselves, which curled gently upward. Rows upon rows of perfectly round white heads looking up at you.

However, if the wax was poorly made, under- or over-cooked, the hair would enjoy a momentary victory. The wax might peel your skin off along with the hair, or tug at your hair but not hard enough to pull it out by its roots. There would be a whole lot of pain for no reward, just a mess. Hair coated in sugary, syrupy goop, sore follicles. Then you'd try again. Even when it worked perfectly, in those teenage years, the follicles would often bleed, because the roots were thick and strong. You'd be left with red, stinging skin and tiny droplets of blood where hair grew just seconds before. The hair did not want to be pulled out. It punished you for removing it.

I remember my mother taking me to an Iraqi woman's place to remove the hair from my armpit. The woman lived in a condo in Mississauga. She wore a jilbab in her own home. Not out of modesty; it's easier to wear a jilbab at home when guests or clients visit. It takes the pressure off what you're wearing, of thinking about wearing the right outfit. This woman had small children, at least two, watching us with their big brown eyes and curly blond hair. One was on her hip, the other was by the door. When the woman saw my armpit hair, thick and long and dense, she recoiled. Like she had seen something hideous. That's the first time I realised that my normal, natural body might be repulsive to others.

My skin would turn red and it would sting from the waxing but soon after it felt soft and tender and clean. When it was freshly waxed, my skin got very hot. I guess all the blood rushed to the surface, from the trauma of waxing. I liked it. I caressed it. It felt good. Desirable.

To whom?

To the abstract male gaze. To the man who might love me. And touch me. And not be repulsed by me.

The man I married was really a boy because we were both twenty-three years old. Children, really, when I think back on it. Neither he nor I had been with anyone else, and he was surprised to learn that I did not have hair on my legs. His mom had told him that Muslim girls didn't shave; waxing wasn't even something he could conceive of, and he was shocked, but excited, that I waxed my legs for him. I realise now that he might have loved the hair on my legs, if I'd had any, because he loved everything about me, just as I was. He didn't know yet, precisely, the cost – physical, financial, emotional, psychological – of hair removal. The lengths to which I was willing to go for it. How much I had to hate my body to suffer so deeply to alter it, to make it beautiful. To make it clean. To make it good.

2007

Hair removal has been a central fixture in my life. When Rumee and I visited Yemen together, alongside studying legal texts and reading manuscripts in archives, I found time to get waxed. We were graduate students at the time, without much money. Our big weekly splurge was a $30 buffet brunch that was offered between eleven o'clock and three o'clock each Sunday at the Mövenpick Hotel. We would show up at 10:55A.M. with a bunch of other graduate students, place a timer in the centre of the table and fill our bellies at a steady pace for four hours. Every few weeks, I would follow up brunch with a trip to the hotel spa, where I would spend $50 to get my body waxed – my face, my arms, my legs, my armpits.

I never summoned the courage for a Brazilian wax, though I considered it from time to time. I used to shave and now I trim my hair down there, as per my mother's Islamic prescriptions. It's funny, when you think about it, which aspects of religion stay with you, and which are easily shed.

Valuable and scarce financial resources were often channelled toward the removal of unwanted hair. My dear mother taught kids Qur'an recitation five days a week, for two hours per day. She charged her students $20 per week. That's $5 per day, $2.50 per hour. Fridays were free. And she used some of this money to take me to a laser hair removal studio, paying $150 every six weeks to remove hair from my face, to erase the moustache and beard that grew strong and persistent and fierce, that horrified me when I looked in the mirror, that filled me with shame, that made me feel ugly. My mother would look at me with worry-filled eyes, furrowing her brow, tsk-ing tsk-ing, as she turned my face one way and then the other, as she made a threat assessment and confirmed the importance of spending her hard-earned and carefully saved money on laser treatments. Laser treatments that might finally turn the tide and permanently remove the insurgent hair that persistently grew back, maybe even thicker, despite years of waxing and threading.

Back then, laser technology was rudimentary. Like photography and videography, laser technology was made first for white skin. This meant that the technology was less effective for brown and black skin. Another reason to curse the colour of my skin and wish it fair. The woman who administered the treatments was Pakistani. She'd bought a machine and installed it in a poorly heated strip mall storefront in Mississauga. I remember going there, all bundled up in the winter, driving through treacherous snow, on grey winter days. I'd sit in a cold waiting room or a hallway with other South Asian women, all of us hoping to rid ourselves of our unwanted hair, turn our fortunes even, if we could finally be beautiful. All of us subjecting ourselves to painful and potentially dangerous technology in order to remove hair that we believed made us look ugly, undesirable, unfuckable.

Hair that indeed did all of the things we thought it did. We weren't crazy. This was just self-preservation. We were making a calculated decision, giving ourselves the best chance for upward mobility, a good suitor. Well, at least that was true in my case. I don't know the calculations of the others. But I do know it had to do with standards of beauty in our overlapping communities, each one of which found female bodily hair so reprehensible that we were willing to pay a high price, both financially and physically – we didn't know or care about the long-term effects of the treatment – to remove this naturally growing hair.

The laser had to be turned up really high to zap the hair on our non-white skin. As the laser machine warmed up, the technician would shave my face with a razor. This was painless. Then she'd run the laser over it, zapping the hair, making a crackling sound, leaving behind the smell of burnt hair, and red, hot, angry skin. Little bumps would pop up all over my face. I'd have to cool it for *days* with an ice pack. It was one of the few times I was grateful to wear niqab. Because if I thought that facial hair was conspicuous, imagine a swollen red face, little bumps where each and every hair follicle had been fried, hopefully killed, rendered forever inactive, dead.

Years later, when I'd get laser treatments in New York City and Vancouver, with all the new lasers that were meant to do better on dark skin, all promising hair eradication in only six treatments, the experience was just a slightly milder version of those earlier times. There was still the sting of the hair follicle being fried, the smell of burnt hair, the sound of a pop or a crackle, the reddened and swollen face that needed an icepack, the gratitude for the cooling function on the laser to settle the skin. But the redness that looked like a rash didn't last for days anymore, and the skin didn't burn or hyper pigment as much because the lasers were more sophisticated.

Eventually, I was paying for my own treatments. So the financial burden transferred from my dear mother to me, which lightened our relationship, for which I am grateful. My mother saw her spending on my laser treatments as self-sacrifice, as an act of love that I ought to recognise and for which I ought to be grateful and indebted. I want to convey this in a way that isn't only manipulative. Really, it came from a woman raised and living in patriarchal societies. As a woman in a patriarchal state, Canada, my mother didn't have access to many professional development services, such as English language classes, available to male immigrants, because the government of Canada assumed that immigrant women were dependent on their husbands. The government figured that, for at least the first decade after immigrating to Canada, immigrant women would rely on their men to take care of the manly business of learning the language and acquiring skills, and that such services would be redundant for women.

And as a woman in a patriarchal relationship with her husband, my mother could only access power through subversive means. This is how you secured your future. Your children are your security, your insurance. Lord knows you won't have the financial means to care for yourself if you don't work or speak the language. You're dependent on the kindness of a generous husband – if you have one – and your children, if you have them. Children must be reminded to be grateful and indebted; this is important for your survival. Your children's guilt, their sense of indebtedness, that's your insurance.

And I am grateful. Indebted. Guilty.

Love comes in all forms.

1997

In university I met a Pakistani couple that had started moving toward a more conservative version of Islam, an Islam that they were beginning to see as more 'Islamic' than the Islam they were raised with in Pakistan. The wife was from a wealthy Pakistani family, and had never worn hijab before coming to Canada, but now started wearing it and was screwing up the courage to wear niqab as well. Her husband was a PhD student at the University of Toronto. He used to play guitar when he was in Pakistan, but as he became 'more religious', he put the guitar away and grew out his beard. This couple loved my parents, whom they visited often, starting with dinner, and then they'd spend the night. My parents loved them too, they cooked them elaborate meals, inviting them over and insisting that they spend the night. On Wednesdays my Economics 101 class finished at 9:00P.M., and I often spent the night in their graduate student apartment on Charles Street, sleeping on their couch. I convinced my parents that it was safer for me to do this than take the university bus home so late at night. The husband knew I loved bagels so he'd pick one up for me from Tim Hortons in the mornings. And his wife introduced me to a technology that changed my life. For a decade or so.

The Silk-épil. A battery-operated depilatory machine that removes hair by means of small metal clamps on a rotating circular tube. The horizontal tube turns as the clamps open and close. These clamps catch any hair, or skin, they encounter, and the circular motion of the tube tugs on the hair, pulling it out by its roots. I loved this machine because it meant that I could remove my body hair wherever and whenever I wanted, by myself, and in small sections.

Waxing required assistance and a ton of prep, so much so that it almost demanded you remove as much hair as possible in one go. If you were going to go through the trouble of making the wax, ensuring the right consistency by cooking it just right, applying it correctly, getting all sticky, then you might as well wax as much as possible in one shot. Waxing was best administered by someone else. Threading was done by a technician who magically turned threads into scissors, pulling hair out by its root, and sometimes accidentally cutting skin. *Ow!* you might yell suddenly, eliciting an *Oh sorry!* as the aesthetician rubbed your skin lightly and continued. Lasering required, well, a laser. Electrolysis required a whole different machine. One with a gold needle. The technician would slide the needle into each pore on your face, as if sliding a hand into a pocket, and then fry individual hair follicles.

The Silk-épil took all the prep out of the process. It removed the need for assistance entirely. All other methods of hair removal required someone else's help; they required a community of sorts. The Silk-épil inverted this model; it was easier if you were alone. Also, you didn't have to wait for the hair to be a certain length before you pulled it out. You didn't have to become ugly before you could be beautiful again. You could keep up with your hair growth, removing hair in sections, from hands, forearms, calves, armpits, thighs. But what you gained in ease of use, you lost in anxious repetition. The longer your hair got, the more painful it was to remove. You needed to be on top of Silk-épiling, making sure to depilate every few days, blocking off time no matter where you were or what you were doing, knowing that each delay brought with it the promise of greater pain.

'Silk-épil' was always on my to-do list. As I'd rattle off my plan for the day to Rumee I'd often say, . . . *and I need to Silk-épil!*

And though I was made weary by the endless and eternal nature of this task, much like Sisyphus pushing a rock up the hill, I engaged in it with religious regularity.

2015

We are all inheritors. We inherit traditions, religions, cultures and social customs. We inherit ideas of beauty and ugliness. Of morality and virtue. Of good and bad. Of what is civilised and what is barbaric. Of what is sophisticated and what is primitive. It is all intertwined, entangled, wrapped up together in our art, in our curriculum and in our markets. We make our way in the world by negotiating our inheritance. Cherishing some parts, abandoning others, reshaping parts that don't quite fit but that we want to keep anyway. Our relationship with our inheritance changes over time. We might reject an inheritance at first but then come to love it. And the other way around, too. What we inherit is both abstract and tangible. We inherit physical bodies, traits, proclivities, diseases. And also mannerisms, beliefs, memories, skills, traumas and joys.

One of the things Rumee inherited from his family is male pattern baldness. And also, a fear of balding and a sorrow for it. At some point, usually in their thirties, males in his family begin to lose their hair. This particular inheritance is a gift from Rumee's maternal grandfather. It was passed down to Rumee's mother, and then from mother to son. Rumee lived his life in fear of this inevitability. He did not want to lose his hair. Since we became friends and lovers, in our early twenties, male pattern baldness has been an ever-present, underlying anxiety. Rumee's hair was beautiful and thick, and he grew it out long, so that it fell around his face in pretty locks. It was wavy and luscious. He loved his hair. Likely more so because of its impending loss.

And I loved his hair too, and felt his pain, and dreaded, with him, the loss of his hair.

What will I do? he'd wonder.

What will you do? I'd wonder.

Rumee fully expected science and the medical profession to come through for him, to help him avoid the fate of the rest of the men in his family, his ancestors, to escape this plague in his genealogy. So when his hair began to thin, we began visiting doctors. We considered invasive procedures, like hair implants, taking hair from one part of his body and implanting it on to his head. He was pretty serious about it. We met for a consultation with a famous doctor from New York, who also had a practice in Vancouver. It was all going well, the doctor was talking up the procedure, until he learned of Rumee's keloids, which are spontaneous fatty deposits that sometimes appear on his skin, looking like scars left over from a knife fight. The doctor said that the hair implant procedure was not good for someone with keloids, so he wouldn't do it.

Rumee was dejected. He really wanted the procedure to save his hair. He felt his body was conspiring against him, when it was actually trying to save him. Because, of course, there is nothing objectively wrong with losing one's hair. It is not a disease, it is not a deficiency, it is not a plague. It doesn't hurt, it is not painful. The only reason that hair loss is undesirable is aesthetic. Rumee had been taught, by society, by family, by movies, that bald men are aesthetically less pleasing, less beautiful, less virile, less manly. And the fact that none of this is true is beside the point.

The New York doctor in Vancouver told Rumee he couldn't help him with hair implants, but he did encourage him to take Propecia pills to help slow down the hair loss, and maybe even stop it altogether. Rumee was worried about side effects. He didn't want to become sick trying to save his hair. The doctor was dismissive. He waved his hand, quickly, swatting away legitimate concerns as if they were flies in his face, and said, *MILLIONS of men are on Propecia. If it was harmful, we'd know about it.*

He also recommended Rogaine, a topical solution that could work in tandem with the oral medication, to save his hair. Rumee bought boxes of Rogaine, and he'd carefully apply it to his head every morning and every night, with desperate hopes and prayers for a miracle, a reversal of hair loss, the preservation of hair. Pretty soon, the skin on his ears started to peel, and his scalp became itchy and red – he said it felt as if it was on fire. Turns out this is a possible side effect of Rogaine. Apparently, it might help you keep your hair, but in return, you'd be miserable in your skin. What a bargain! Rumee stuck with it for a few months, despite the burning of his scalp and ears, taking a chance at fulfilling a particular vision of beauty in his mind while feeling more and more at dis-ease in his skin. Finally, he could not bear it anymore.

Fuck it, he told me, *I'm not doing this Rogaine shit anymore. God knows what else it is doing to my body.*

Yes, stop! I worried with him, for him.

But he kept up with the Propecia. It wasn't having immediately visible side effects. Months passed and Rumee descended into a deep depression. He became moody and withdrawn. He used to be full of a lightness, an easy joy. Now, he was unhappy, discontent. He said he couldn't keep a thought straight in his head. I had trouble recognising him. It can be difficult to spot depression when you're in it, or if you are too close to someone in it. I knew that

Rumee was acting differently, but I didn't know that he was depressed. I remember spending a picture-perfect day on the beach with him and my sister. We had the day to ourselves, the sun was shining and the water was a glorious blue-green, the waves were majestic. Normally, Rumee would have been ecstatic. He's the one who taught me to love a day like this. But today, he was sitting away from us. At one point I looked over at him and saw that he had a towel on his head to shield him from the sun. When I called to him he looked up, skin deeply tanned, a bright white towel on his head and a face full of such misery that it closed in on itself. Instead of opening his face to accept the kisses of the sun, he was turning away, from love, from light.

We stumbled through the darkness of his depression together, me trying imperfectly and inadequately to hold him up, to pull him along. It didn't occur to me that he was clinically depressed. At some point, he figured it out himself. He knew something was very wrong. He looked up the side effects of Propecia and there it was, in tiny print on the back of a small strip of paper found stuck to the inside of the box: *Side effects may include depression and suicidal ideation.* And then he told me that he had been fantasising about killing himself, about jumping off our balcony. And other horrific thoughts. Graphic fantasies of suicide. He said it had become almost an obsession, an itch that he worried he would not be able to resist. He was so certain he might commit suicide that he wrote up all the passwords for various accounts and put

them in our safety deposit box at the bank for me to find
after he had passed. So I wouldn't suffer the hardship of not
being able to get into our accounts.

I was shocked to learn this. Terrified.

*Don't you think that your death would be a far greater hardship for
me than not having access to our accounts?!* I asked, at once angry
and scared of the answer.

He stopped taking the fucking Propecia and the depression dissolved, slowly, over the next few weeks and months.
Sizzling out, leaving behind a lingering scent, a trail, a
reminder of the horrors that could have been.

On his thirty-fifth birthday, we were in Los Angeles. We
went for a lovely hike off the Pacific Coast Highway, climb-
ing hills that overlooked the ocean. Huge waves crashed on
to the beach below as the clouds rose and lifted around us,
thinning out in places and showing us the ocean, then thick-
ening around us, enveloping us completely. The brown
shrubbery, with the bright purple and orange flowers,
changed dramatically against the ocean and blue sky or
white grey clouds. The same place looked different, smelled
different, felt different, within a matter of seconds. It was as
if the earth was reminding us, teaching us, that we are
always changing, from moment to moment. Change is part
of us. It is essential to us. It is the only constant in life.
Nothing stands still.

When we finished the hike and returned to the city, we
went straight to a salon and Rumee had his head shaved.
We both watched him in the mirror as his hair fell off in

clumps, as his perfectly shaped skull emerged from beneath his hair.

It looks kind of badass, he said, shyly, tentatively, trying out the words.

Yes! You do *look badass!* I agreed enthusiastically.

Over time, the pale skin on his head tanned to a golden brown, matching his face and neck. He has a particular look when his head is freshly shaved, and then it changes on day one and day two and week one and week two of growth. Each look feels different under my hand, rough little bumps of hair that grow to be soft and fuzzy, moving from a gentle scratch to a caress when, in the mornings, he curls into my arms, snuggling into my neck.

We have come to love, truly love, his shaved head.

I almost lost him because he was trying to save his hair. Because he was trying his best to avoid what we now love. Because he was trying to be beautiful, when he already was.

962 BCE

Depilatory methods are ancient.

Human hair is natural, our bodies evolved in this way. It is what is animal about us. It reminds us of our kinship with non-human animals. And it is a uniquely human trait to try to distance ourselves from this kinship, by erasing, rearranging, altering our hair, using increasingly sophisticated methods. Our relationship with the hair on our heads, on our faces, on our genitals, on our limbs, changes with time and place. Sometimes facial hair for men is 'masculine', other times it is not manly enough; sometimes it is read as extremist and other times it is read as hipster. Same with hair on the head – sometimes it is a sign of virility, other times it is a sign of weakness. A hairstyle can be beautiful and uncouth at the same time, depending on context. In the United States, black girls are expelled from schools for sporting natural hairstyles. They are punished for just letting their hair be, which is to say for just being. In France, women are expelled from public spaces for covering their hair. In Iran, women are prosecuted for uncovering their hair. Hair is heavily policed. Hair is political.

Sulayman (King Solomon) was outraged when he learned, from the hoopoe bird, that the land of Sheba was ruled over by a queen. The very existence of an independent kingdom made him insecure, but then to find out that this competing, thriving, flourishing kingdom was ruled by a woman proved too much to bear. It boggled his mind that this Queen was not monotheistic, that she worshipped the sun, which nourished the earth, created food and showed up every morning, rather than an abstract and invisible god whom Sulayman said had personally chosen him to be Prophet and King. So Sulayman set about trying to subdue the Queen, to gain dominance over her. In the end he was able to dominate her, but the story behind that domination is puzzling.

He started by demanding that the Queen submit herself to his rule. The Queen responded by sending Sulayman gifts and good wishes, which were rebuffed and returned with threats of war. To stave off war, the Queen visited Sulayman in the hopes of resolving their conflict through diplomacy. But when she arrived at his palace, she made a critical mistake. As she entered his court, she mistook the smooth, polished glass floor for water and raised her skirt to avoid getting wet; in raising her skirt, she exposed her shins. Rather than a small, laughable misunderstanding, this turned out to be a grave error, because when Sulayman corrected her, explaining that she stood on polished glass rather than water, she said,

My Lord, indeed I have zalamtu nafsi [transgressed against myself]! I submit with Sulayman to Allah, Lord of the worlds.

She became a monotheist. Traded the sun for the invisible god. Why? What was so egregious about her mistaking glass for water that she had to cede her political authority on the spot?

The Qur'an doesn't tell us, but medieval Muslim scholars pondered over it and came up with a theory. They borrowed heavily from their Jewish counterparts, who inherited a very similar story, and said that the Queen's error was not that she mistook glass for water, but that when she raised her skirt, she exposed her shins, and in doing so inadvertently revealed that she had hairy legs. They said that the hair on her legs compromised her beauty – it was a monstrosity, an ugliness, a weakness. It was unfeminine, like the fact of her rule to begin with. Women were not supposed to be rulers, they said. Her very rule upset the patriarchal, monotheistic worldview that medieval scholars took for granted. God didn't choose women to be rulers, He chose men. He was a 'he', and so men, being male, were de facto closer to the divine, more God-like by virtue of their maleness. A queen, a ruler with a vagina and a womb and lacking a penis, upset the order of the universe. Her hairy legs confirmed what everyone already knew, and broadcast to the court that, *There is something wrong here.*

Her hairy legs exposed her unnatural masculinity, her unruliness, her ugliness. Some of these men, these medieval Muslim and Jewish scholars reflecting on the story, went even further. They had such a low opinion of women that they didn't believe that any woman, not even a manly one, could ever be a successful ruler of a thriving empire. So they made up stories about her being a half-demon, that she was the spawn of a beautiful woman and a demon having fucked, upsetting the 'natural' order of the universe further. Her hairy legs proved this, for though she inherited her face from her mother, her legs were her father's. Her hairy legs were demonic.

So great was the power of a woman's hairy legs in the minds of these men that it extinguished her political power in one fell swoop. And these men believed that it was after this moment that women began depilating their hair, having seen how deeply compromising it was. The towering Queen of Sheba, a woman who ruled over a flourishing empire so magnificent that it threatened Sulayman, was thus reduced to the Queen of Depilation.

2010

I know the feminist literature on shaving, on removing hair, on how doing so fulfils specific racialised and gendered constructions of beauty. It's the part of the literature I find myself ignoring. I respect women who don't shave. But I've thoroughly absorbed, internalised, the idea that I am only beautiful when I am hairless, that I am beautiful and clean and good when I've made my skin hairless and smooth. I feel better, to the touch, to *me*. I smell better to *me*. The hair in my armpit holds on to odour that I'm free of when I've removed it. I can smell the difference on myself. I 'look' better to *myself*. I think Rumee finds me more attractive when I remove my bodily hair, though he denies it, says he'd love me just the same if I didn't. But I believe he's as weighed down by this inheritance as I am.

The hijab and niqab did not protect me from the pressures of society's aesthetic preferences, from the beauty standards set for women. I remember an NYU professor's surprise at learning that I was anorexic. He said, *I thought that with your hijab, you would have escaped the demands of beauty standards.*

I wanted to, but didn't say, *Why would you think that? I'm still a person in the world, I see the same billboards and magazine covers as everyone else!*

I know how people see me. I know how people would look at me if I walked into a swimming pool or a sauna, or down the street or into a restaurant in shorts and a T-shirt with all my hair intact, natural. People would be disgusted, they would cringe, they would wrinkle their noses, look away. They might even say something, who knows? But they wouldn't have to. We communicate with our bodies, first and foremost. Much less so with our words.

All my life, I have confronted the repulsed human gaze. The gaze that looks away in pity, in disgust, in horror, in anger. When I wore hijab and niqab, I encountered this gaze on a daily basis. I always assumed that when I stopped wearing them, I would stop facing social ostracism for how I carried my body. For how I presented it and how I covered it. And now, as I imagine walking around with my hairy legs and arms and face, I can see the same looks of pity, and horror, and disgust, and anger focused on me.

In the end, it is as simple as this: instead of being repulsive, I want to be desired, to be desirable. I live in this world. In this world, hairy women aren't desirable. Well, that's not true. Men and women and gender non-binary people do find women in their natural state, with their hair intact, desirable. But we hardly ever hear about it. The narrative of the hairless female body as beautiful is so strong, it erases all other desires, pushes them to the margins, makes them almost unbelievable.

2016

A few years ago, I switched to bleaching the hair on my face, on my upper neck and under my chin. I had less hair there than I used to, so bleaching sort of did the job. The golden hair blended in with my skin tone better than the black hair so that you wouldn't notice it unless you looked closely. I met a friend for lunch one afternoon, and was telling him about my day. As I listed the things I'd done that day, I said, . . . *and then I bleached my face, and then* . . .

He's African American, and it matters for this story, because for a couple of beats, he stared at me, alarmed and confused. I quickly specified, *Oh no, I didn't bleach the* skin *on my face, I bleached the* hair *on my face!* We laughed raucously at the misunderstanding. Soon after, I wondered if we had been laughing at different things: me at his thinking I was bleaching the skin on my face instead of the hair, him at my thinking there was a qualitative difference between the two.

The conversation left me unsettled. Could I be wrong about all this? Dare I imagine that I might be beautiful, desirable, lovable, good, just as I am, in my natural state, without any alterations, without the hair removed from my legs and arms and hands and armpits, my pubic hair shaved or trimmed, my facial hair bleached, the hair on my head dyed black #3? I'm not sure I dare imagine it.

2018

Turns out imagination is important. Vital. If you cannot imagine a thing, it cannot be. And so it is with my hair. I could not imagine it as beautiful in its natural form, though I tried. Not anywhere. Not on my head, and not on my body. For six months, I grew out the hair all over my body. All of it. I didn't colour the hair on my head, nor did I trim or remove hair from anywhere. I let it all grow out. And I could not see myself as beautiful. I only saw ugliness.

White hair sprouted on my head, right in the centre, thick and coarse, ageing me, making me look far older than I wanted. I tried to cover it by parting my hair farther and farther to the left, so that the black hair would cover the white hair, but it would always slip. When I looked in the mirror, I'd be reminded of my age, of my mortality, of my degenerating body. And I'd look away, avoiding my own reflection. I wonder, if I didn't see my reflection, would my hair bother me less? Would I have less trouble letting it grow natural?

And the hair on my body, well, it grew out and was as unseemly as I remembered it. Even though it had thinned out somewhat over the years, there was still too much of it. It covered my thighs and shins and toes and forearms. Rumee assured me that he found me beautiful and attractive with all my hair. I believed him this time.

But I carried an abstract social gaze, a constructed aesthetic within me; this gaze spoke to me, in my head, in my body, it whispered over and over and over again that the hair on my body was unattractive. God speaks to us loudly and clearly, but Satan whispers, he speaks in waswasa. The waswasa of Shaytan is sneaky; to avoid accountability, it hides itself from us, even as it buries itself deep inside us. Now, I heard the waswasa and I covered myself. For whom? Why did I care? I avoided wearing shorts and dresses, afraid to break a social code about hair on the female form. I noticed all the women around me who were hairless.

I saw a little girl playing in the water fountain in New York City's Washington Square Park on a sunny and hot afternoon. Her mother changed her clothes in the park, removing them all before putting on new ones. She must have been about three. As I watched, I realised I hated that little girl's body. Her shamelessness exposed my shame. And I knew in that moment that, despite all my efforts to love myself, I hated my body.

When I got back to Vancouver, I got the hair on my head coloured, and I made an appointment at a laser hair removal centre. This is the most professional place I've been to so far for hair removal; it has a medical aesthetic rather than a spa aesthetic. The white technician who administered my first treatment walked me through the process. She told me that because I was dark-skinned, they would have to use the highest setting on a laser that they called 'the mean machine'.

It will be painful, she warned me. *Basically, the laser goes through three layers of skin and burns the root of each hair follicle. Normally, this would happen only if all three layers of skin were burned off. So, your body is going to think that that is what is happening, and*

it will freak out. But the pain you will feel is just imaginary, because
that is not happening. So, you have to remember that, okay? Your pain
is not real. It is mental, it is in your head.

She recommended that I apply two tubes of Emla, a
topical anaesthetic to my legs and armpits and face in preparation for the treatment. I chose not to do so the first time.
I didn't want the extra poison, even though I was willing to
be lasered. The folly of this bargain is not lost on me.

Rumee felt very conflicted about my decision to remove
my hair permanently. He didn't want me to do it, but he
also acknowledged that he didn't know what it felt like to be
a woman whose hair was considered repulsive, revolting to
others. So, he wanted to get over himself to support me. He
offered to come with me to the appointment. I agreed, glad
for his support, as yet unaware of how much I would need
him.

We entered the little room where the treatment would
take place. There was a large exhaust pipe over the table to
catch the smell of burnt hair and smoke. The technician
gave me two stress balls, one for each hand. And glasses to
protect my eyes. And then the treatment began. Over 2,500
laser zaps on my legs and armpits and face. It hurt more
than anything I have ever experienced. My body shuddered
and quaked. Rumee held my upper arms, which were
stretched over my head. I asked him to pinch me, hurt me
on my arms to distract me from the liquid fire pouring over
my legs. My arms were getting bruised and I needed him to
bruise me more in order to withstand the pain.

Rumee tried to joke, *You could walk right out of here and into a police station, and report me for abuse.*

Yeah, but I'm still a woman. There's a one in five chance they'd dismiss my claim, I shot back.

The technician talked throughout the two-hour treatment. She told me to direct my anger toward my hair.

Die, motherfuckers, die! she screamed. *Don't come back!*

And then, *As far as I know, Islam is the only religion founded by a warlord.*

What the fuck?! I yelled, exasperated, depleted of all patience for bullshit.

She told me she learned that in a course on world religions at the University of British Columbia a few years ago, when she went back to finish her degree. Some of what we inherit is just trash.

I sweated on that table, I writhed in pain. Afterwards, I was quiet, exhausted, cleansed. I told my therapist about my experience, *Honestly, I feel like it cleansed me, like I was purified.*

Oh, I'm sure it did, she responded, *but there are better ways to purify yourself than torture.*

My skin was hot for days after the treatment. It was tender for weeks. Little round circles the shape of the laser strikes lingered on my skin. The next three times I went back for the treatment, I had another, kinder, gentler technician. This white woman did not denigrate my religion, but she did insist that the pain was all in my head. And I applied the topical anaesthetic, which made the treatments slightly more bearable. But it was still so painful as to be torturous. The technician warned me not to use more than two bottles of topical anaesthetic because it could be dangerous.

Did you hear the story of the girl who used four bottles before her treatment? She died in the cab on the way to the clinic.

They gave me an Atavan to calm my nerves. And a Motrin to help with the pain. And I found a place deep inside myself where, for several moments at a time, I could actually escape the pain. Rumee came with me to all the treatments, and massaged my feet.

He and the technician talked, and I moved in and out of myself, hearing only snippets of their conversation. She told us about her husband, who used to be her music teacher between ninth and twelfth grade. She told us about her in-laws. And she asked me, *Do you like your bum hair?* as she zapped a few hairs there.

The last time I saw her, I said, *I know this is fucked up, that I'm doing this. Removing hair that grows naturally. I've internalised the perverse message that I'm only beautiful when I'm hairless.*

But it also feels really nice, she said, *when you've removed the hair and can feel the skin. It feels clean.*

She told me about how she found a sex manual from the sixties in her parents' home when she was young, and the women in the images all had hair where she had none. And it made her worried, because she didn't have as much hair as the women. She thought something was wrong with her. It made me wonder if all representations of humans are harmful, because they can never represent everyone. Will every representation of humans marginalise some people who do not see themselves reflected in the image? Are all representations bad? Maybe Islam was on to something with its wariness around representational art.

At the end of each treatment, my body shivered, my teeth chattered, my legs twitched involuntarily, my toes sweated. I was cold. I was hot. Rumee rubbed aloe vera on the freshly lasered, red-hot skin. My skin was bruised for weeks. And still, I returned.

Here's the thing about inheritance. You might disown it but it can still claim you.

And also this: just because you know better doesn't mean you do better.

2020

I don't laser anymore, or Silk-épil, or thread, or wax, or bleach my hair. I'm even growing out the white hair on my head. Or, rather, I'm letting my hair be. Sometimes I shave the hair on my arms, but not very often. When I look at my almost hairless legs and armpits, I feel an unexpected sorrow. I should be happy that I prevailed over my hair, that I finally

killed the follicles it grew from so I don't have to keep removing it. But instead, I feel a sense of loss. Like I broke something inside me. Finally, and too late, I wonder, was that a
good idea, to make it so my hair doesn't grow? After all, hair
grows on living bodies. It doesn't grow on dead ones.

I succeeded at this endless, repetitive task by paying the
price for imposing order on my body, so it could be clean
and beautiful. And yet. This success feels like failure. And it
makes me think, why do mathematicians call patterns and
order beautiful? What if beauty is in the chaos, in the
unstructured, in the untidy, in the unclean?

God says, وإن تعدوا نعمة الله لا تحصوها

*If you try to count the blessings of God, you will never be able to
enumerate them.*

I always thought this meant that God's blessings were so
many that human numbers could never encompass them.
But what if it really means that we are unable to count the
blessings of God because they are uncountable, they defy
enumeration? Applying a number to a blessing reduces it,
so maybe numbers can never help us reckon with the blessings of God. And further still, what if as soon as we enumerate them, they stop being blessings? Because as soon we
enumerate them, we possess them in a kind of way, and
God's blessings can never be possessed, only enjoyed. What
if the problem is with the counting to begin with? Accepting

the blessings of God means accepting them as they are, as perfect in their natural form, uncounted and uncountable, unaltered. In which case, perfection comes not from our mind imposing our ideas of perfection outside of itself, but rather from submitting to the perfections all around us. What if the only way we know we've encountered beauty is when we know, when we can finally rest in the knowledge, that we no longer need to count, and correct, and measure, and align, and straighten, and civilise, and clean? What if the only way to be clean is knowing we are already clean? When we can finally hear God's voice ringing loud and clear:

لا تبديل لخلق الله

Let there be no change in God's creation.

Children

Rumee and I decided not to have children. The decision sort of emerged for us slowly over the years, in stages, some unplanned. We took it one step at a time, went with the flow, so that now, in our forties and almost twenty years into our partnership, we know that we will not have children. Biological or adopted.

When we were younger and people learned that we didn't plan on having children, their responses were rather dramatic.

Oh no! Why?! they wanted to know.

Your poor parents! they'd worry.

But your children would be SO beautiful!

They'd have SUCH great hair!

YOU'RE the kind of people who NEED to have kids!

But your kids would be SO smart!

The presumptuousness of these comments might make you think that these people were close friends. But to the contrary, we'd only just met. They didn't know much about us, they certainly had no clue as to what kind of parents we'd be, because, well, they didn't know us.

These days the reactions we get are far less dramatic. Probably because we are older. People are less sad about us not having children and we're less defensive. Now, the conversation goes like this:

Do you have children?
No.
Huh.

I was always struck by the invasive, overly familiar nature of the questions I received, and occasionally still receive, for not having children. Apart from being annoying, they're weird. Why is everyone expected to have kids? Why are we all expected to love child rearing? And why aren't there licensing requirements for having a kid, like mandatory parenting classes, the way we have for driving a car? When I asked these questions out loud, a friend worried about the racial and class implications of obtaining licences for having children. He makes a fair point. And I don't want to create yet another way to systemically discriminate against those who are marginalised. But if there were a way to circumvent discrimination – I know, I know, but *if* there were – then there could be a basic curriculum for child rearing, with modules like 'Don't torture your children: Ten ways to break the trauma cycle'. What I'm saying is, in my experience, good parenting is not intuitive. I've seen some truly shit parents in my life who would have benefitted from at least some amount of training. You know what I'm talking about.

I'm genuinely intrigued by the people who pity us, who use passive-aggressive comments to shame us for not having children.

Oh, poor you! You'll never know what it feels like to love someone so completely.

I'm so sad you won't have this experience. Children are amazing! You learn so much from them.

There's a special connection between moms and their kids!

Parenting gives me such a unique and special perspective.

Oh, you wouldn't get it, it's a mom thing!

And then, some time later, usually in the same conversation, a switch flips and the same people, the very same people, might say:

Oh my god! What a smart idea to not have kids! You don't know how hard it is. I don't have a life anymore. I forgot what it feels like to sleep five hours straight.

No wonder you're so happy! It must be nice. It's so hard to do anything with kids. I can't even pee in peace anymore. Or take a shower.

My children are trying to destroy us. We never have sex anymore.

Childbirth changed my body. Nothing is where it used to be, nobody told me that would happen. Everything moved!

Really? Wow. If I had to go back in time, I don't know that I'd do it again. I mean, don't get me wrong, I love my kids, but if I went back in time . . .

Their voices trail off as they get a vacant look in their eyes.

It's that flip that fascinates me, because, presumably, these people know that they have misgivings about having children before the conversation begins. Their laments are fine on their own, and I sympathise, except that they are preceded by a concerted, perhaps even desperate attempt to convince me otherwise. Why the need to hide one's regrets? Why not lead with them, or at least discuss parenthood in a more complex way?

I understand there is a special bond between mothers and their children. This is a bond I will never understand from a mother's perspective given that I am not a mother, though of course I do understand this bond from a child's perspective given that I have a mother. It's also true that couples who have children will never know what it feels like to be in a long-term partnership, where you get to sleep for eight to ten hours on most nights, and have long, uninterrupted conversations. That's a pretty amazing bond, too. And one that would simply not exist, that we would have missed out on, if we'd had children. But being childless is not for everyone. Just like having children isn't for everyone.

Ultimately, I think, conversations about children are actually conversations about loneliness, and mortality, and the meaning of life. Do I like myself enough to be alone with myself? What if I am alone and lonely when I grow old? Who will remember me when I die? What is the purpose of my life? Is there any point to my ever having been here? At some point, every one of us has to confront these questions, grapple with them, answer them for ourselves, come to terms with our choices in the face of them. But most of us try to find a way around these questions, we avoid them for as long as possible; we will go to great lengths to avoid asking and answering these questions for ourselves. Sometimes we produce whole human beings to distract us from these questions. We treat the questions like they are fire, like they will burn us and leave nothing behind. But there is no way around the fire, only through it. And though fire can be destructive, it can also be purifying. It can clear way for new life, it can preserve what is already standing, it can reveal the core of a thing. Fire is a teacher. One of the things the fire has taught me is that what we consider nightmarish can become a source of deep peace and comfort. Loneliness is terrifying until being alone is a solace. And the insignificance of our lives is scary until we see how this truth sets us free.

I always thought I would have children. I was raised to believe it was my purpose in life. Israr Ahmed, for all his disagreements with Maulana Maududi about democracy, was in full agreement with him about the purpose of women: they were *baby-making machines*. I knew what I was supposed to do, what I was meant to do.

When I was a teenager, I couldn't wait to get married and have kids. I remember being impatient for the married and motherhood part of my life to just start already. It's what grown-ups did. They got married and had kids. And I wanted to be a grown-up.

Then I went to university and learned about individualism, autonomy, free will, the rights of the individual versus the rights of the community, feminism, women's rights over their bodies – all the basic tenets of liberalism, taught and promoted as unadulterated goods. My imaginative horizons began to expand. I imagined a future where I went to graduate school and earned a PhD and became a professor. Suddenly, marriage and children went from being the only option, to being obstacles in the path of this new future. In my teens and early twenties, I was engaged three times, to three separate men. Another story for another time. All three men saw my dreams of a PhD and a career as obstacles to their own dreams of marriage and children. One ex-fiancé asked, *Why do you need to study Islam with the kuffar anyways? What are you going to learn from them? And when you're away studying and working, what about my needs? I have needs!*

Well, I was never able to attend to any of his needs, because we never got married.

When Rumee and I started courting, we were pretty fundamentalist, so we made sure to be clear – with each other and with ourselves – that we were engaging in conversation solely for the purpose of determining whether we should get married, and this made space for us to talk frankly about what kind of marriage we envisioned for ourselves. Still, it was a difficult conversation to have because we barely knew each other. We were shy and ashamed, uncomfortable talking about procreation, which is to say, sex. The legal principle, *la haya fi-l-islam* (*there is no shame in Islam*) gave us the courage to have the conversation anyways. So we talked about sex. We would use birth control. I would have control over my body. I would get a veto over my uterus. I would decide whether to have kids or not – though, of course, we would make the decision in a consultative manner. But if we were ever at an impasse, we agreed that my desire to not have children would override Rumee's desire to have them.

Six months after our wedding, my nephew died. I loved him. I still love him. A lot. There was nothing wrong with him. He wasn't ill. His heart just stopped. His death rattled me. You could do everything right. Have a baby in a modern hospital with all the latest technology. When he gets sick, take him to a modern hospital with all the latest technology. And he could still die. The experience of losing someone I loved so much was harrowing and I went into a deep depression.

I was newly married, living in a new city, with no friends or family close by, with in-laws who had disowned Rumee for marrying me. In-laws who did not like me. People comforted us by saying that they'd come around once we had kids.

Just wait and see. They're gonna want to see their grandkids!

IF we have kids, we'd say.

Oh, you'll have kids!

But I didn't want to have children just to make Rumee's parents accept him, accept me. I mean, how fucked up would that be? Create a whole new human being just so that parents who were, at the time, parenting poorly, would start speaking to their son again. Didn't really make a lot of sense to me.

A few years passed. I was on birth control. Yasmin and then Yaz. Both had terrible side effects and became the subject of multiple class action lawsuits. I was insanely hormonal on the pill. My breasts, which I always believed were too large to begin with as B cups, grew to double Ds. I hated them. I had dramatic mood swings. Rumee worried about all the hormones I was putting in my body every day. Then, six years into our marriage, while we were in Los Angeles for the summer, Rumee found a 'vasectomist to the stars' and booked an appointment. His insurance covered the elective surgery, so he paid only $250 for it. The insurance didn't cover my birth control, nor would it cover abortions or the surgery for getting my tubes tied. But it covered vasectomies. It's good to be a man. Not just in Islam.

Given that Rumee and I usually discuss major decisions ad nauseam before taking any steps, it came as a surprise to both of us that, when we tried to talk about his vasectomy, we had very little to say. He'd bring it up, *So, I'm thinking of getting a vasectomy. I don't like all the hormones you're taking. And since we're unlikely to have kids . . .*

Sure, makes sense . . . Are you sure you want a vasectomy? What if we change our minds?

Will we, though?

Probably not.

By this time, I was pretty sure I wasn't interested in producing a child with my body. Nothing about pregnancy or childbirth appealed to me. Not the growing belly, not the waddling, not the difficulty in finding a comfortable sleeping position, not the pain, trauma and suffering of childbirth, the ripping apart of the body, the shitting in front of everyone during the delivery. I hate needles and any medical contact. So, no, I wasn't planning on producing and delivering a baby with my body. We were still open to adoption, in case I got 'egg-y', which everyone kept promising would happen. It never did. Shows how much everyone knows.

Rumee went to the doctor for his consultation. By his telling, it was a pretty straightforward procedure. It would take about fifteen minutes. And though it was technically reversible, it really wasn't. The doctor was going to cut his vas deferens, cauterise the ends and clamp them shut with titanium.

Better not do this unless you're a hundred per cent sure, the doctor advised Rumee.

And then he asked to meet with me to make sure I consented to this procedure. That was when I really understood just how wrong it was for someone to have that kind of power over someone else's body. Sure, it made me feel powerful to provide consent for Rumee to do something with his own body, but it also felt deeply wrong. People should make their own decisions about whether they want to have children or not. No one else's consent should be necessary.

Rumee said the procedure went smoothly. He barely felt anything. I was in the pharmacy on the ground floor of the outpatient facility searching for a 'Happy Vasectomy!' card when he walked up behind me. I was surprised at how quickly it went. Actually fifteen minutes, as advertised. He was sore for weeks after, walking slowly, waddling up and down Abbot Kinney Boulevard. Mostly, he sat in our studio, looked out at the ocean and wrote his first book. I took up yoga that summer and have practised it since. It's been over a decade since the vasectomy and we haven't regretted it yet.

Some people have told me, *It's selfish not to have children.*

As if having children isn't selfish. People have children because they want them. So what's wrong with not having them if you don't want them? Why is one more selfish than the other? People have children to replicate their genes, leave a legacy, pass on their wealth. People have children to keep them company, to stave off loneliness; they have them because they're looking for a project, a hobby, a diversion. People have children as an insurance plan, so someone will care for them and about them in their old age. I've been asked, *Don't you worry about getting old and not having children? Who will care for you, visit you in the nursing home, pay for the nursing home?*

Yes, I worry about that, but I also know that children are a bad insurance policy. Many children leave their parents to fend for themselves, abdicating any and all responsibility. And to create a whole human being to be your caretaker? That sounds quite selfish to me. And then there's the unequal distribution of wealth and consumption and the carbon footprint of children in middle and upper class families – it's impossible to pretend that having a middle or upper class child in Canada or the United States is some kind of gift to humanity. If *I wanted children* is reason enough, then *I didn't want them* should be reason enough, too.

In the end, I did not have children for many reasons. Some of them are only becoming clear to me now. Here are some.

1. I enjoy the company of kids. I love spending time with my nieces and nephews and godchildren. But I also like giving them back.
2. I don't want to worry about them for the rest of my life. Especially with climate change. I mean, my god, what world will they inherit? A world I am afraid to see.
3. Ethically, I feel virtuous about not burdening the earth with another person.
4. It exhausts me to think of the work that goes into responsibly raising a child.
5. Children are expensive.
6. I'm afraid – no, I am certain, that I would fuck them up.
7. Long ago, I read a story about a woman in her forties who said there wasn't room in her parents' relationship

for her, an only child. I wonder if our child would feel this way.

8. I love my body too much. I don't want to put it through pregnancy and childbirth.

9. I hate my body enough to not want to experience it, confront it in this way, through pregnancy and childbirth.

10. My relationship with my mother. It makes me think that I would have a difficult relationship with my daughter. It feels inevitable. My mother and I, we love each other, and we talk, but never about what is most important, most dear to us.

11. My father. Watching him, I have learned that surviving is not the same as thriving. The horrors, the sorrows of the past never leave your body. They lie in wait, gathering strength, biding their time, as you move through the world, doing and making work, creating children and then working, toiling to feed them, provide for them. The horrors, the sorrows, they play along, let you pretend, pretend along with you, that they've been resolved, that time has healed them, that they happened so long ago, so far in the past, how could they possibly hurt with any kind of freshness? But the horrors, the sorrows have all the time in the world, to visit and revisit you, to remind you, to become your present. Occasionally, over the years, they signal their presence, remind you that they are still there, still lurking around, in a dream maybe, from which you wake making a

sound like drowning – not the finely tuned voice of human speech, but a much earlier, primordial sound, a sound of terror, a sound that knows the animal, the animal fear, in us. And then, when you finally have a moment's pause, a respite from the work, the labour of surviving, of feeding, of providing, when you finally have time to rest and do not need to wake in the dark hours for work, when your body can rest from the toil on an oil rig, or in a nuclear power plant, when the days and nights are finally yours, and you live in a house that is yours, and your children are grown, the horrors, the sorrows rise up within you, show you their home inside of you, they undo your work, they unmap you. They take, they bring you back, erase your memories starting from the last ones, so now the present becomes the past and the past is the present and you are a little boy whose brother was murdered, you are a little boy running with his family, jumping on trains, chaos around him, living in makeshift, spontaneous refugee camps, fleeing with his family, fleeing the violence, searching, searching, searching for home, for a place where he can be safe.

12. Sometimes they die.

If you decide not to have children, you might spend so much time defending your decision to your loved ones and to strangers and to yourself that you may forget that you deserve to mourn the loss that comes with not having children. To have made a decision, the right decision for you, maybe, but even in the best of circumstances, a decision that is marked by absence. The absence of the social construct of a 'complete family', of following a normative social script, of your own childhood dreams for yourself. Even if you now believe that the construct of the family, especially the nuclear family, is a myth, you still have to, at some point, contend with its loss, the death of the myth, which is the death of a dream: an attractive, unbelievable, fantastical, simple and perfect dream.

You also have to contend with the failure, if you have a uterus, of your body fulfilling its own dream, its own planning for the future. Month after month, my body lines my uterus, makes a snug, welcoming home for a little one that never arrives; and month after month, she lays waste to that cosy and safe home, throwing it all away, wiping the slate clean. Sometimes, I can feel her disappointment, pulling and pushing me at once, into the earth. But still, she doesn't give up. She keeps trying, month after month, for decades on end, to coax my child into existence. Our bodies mourn, so we must mourn too. Mourn the children that never were. The children that could have been, but aren't. And yet, here they are, because they've been conjured, over and over again, by our bodies, by our minds, by our hearts. They might have names and personalities, a particular laugh, you may have conversations with them, disagreements even.

My children are fine-boned, beautiful little rascals. They are brown. Their names are Rumana Smith and Musa Jones. And Rahma, the one who came first and helped me conjure her siblings. She has big hair, a cackling laugh, and eyes that glint with budmashi.

Perhaps it is better that they are never born into this world, that they remain safe and happy, laughing in the wombs of our imaginations.

The bird is in
your hands, Daddy said, *How you live*
your life can be the child you never had
　　　　　—Nikky Finney, 'Linea Nigra'

PART III

'Please Water Me'

They are important, the rituals we devise around burials, around returning the body to the earth. They have a purpose; they are supposed to help the living confront and deal with mortality. They are meant to help us channel our loss and sorrow. They are conduits for our grief.

Grief. Which is a fast-moving river, a raging, tumultuous, foaming river, which my therapist describes as *love, where the object of love is cut off*. Humans grieve all sorts of losses in a lifetime: parents, siblings, children, friends, lovers. We cannot live without love, so we must live with grief.

Death is ubiquitous, mundane, utterly unspecial. Everyone and everything dies. Death arrives as a package deal with life. And yet, like birth, death is special. Love makes it special. When you love someone, you celebrate their birth and you mourn their death.

The death of a loved one is devastating. Its pain is so great, it can debilitate us physically, emotionally, mentally. It makes our stomachs churn. Our grief can make us unstable; it makes us engage in fantastical thinking, trying to will time itself to turn back, to return to when we were holding our love, so that we can smile instead of frown, forgive easily rather than sulk petulantly. But time does not turn back. The dead do not return.

Burial rituals are supposed to acknowledge and hold our pain. They are supposed to comfort us at a time when comfort seems impossible. They are supposed to help us feel less alone, care for our tender hearts as we drown in the endless depths of our grief, frantically trying to surface for air. If grief is water, then burial rituals are meant to be air. We need them to breathe before we submerge back into the water, over and over again. So that we don't drown. So that we are saved.

Muslims around the world have various, culturally specific religious rituals to comfort the grieving. In South Asia, some mourn for forty days. People bring food to the house of the grieving. They recite the Qur'an together, taking turns, so that they recite the entire Qur'an for the deceased in what is called a 'khatm', a completion. Men and women are often, though not always, segregated. Women sit huddled on the floor, or on a hard wooden bed known as a 'takht-posh', covered in chadors and dupattas, reciting the Qur'an, their voices cracking as they both recite and cry at once, breaking their recitation to weep. They hug each other, dab their tears with their chadors, and then return to the Qur'an recitation.

Usually, there are stacks of siparas – the Qur'an printed in thirty sections – piled in the middle of the room. These little booklets of the Qur'an are gorgeous, covered in floral or geometric patterns, brimming with bright and festive colours, gold and silver and red and green. Friends, family, neighbours move through the house of the grieving. Visitors pick up a sipara and read a bit, then rotate off, passing it on to another person who continues reading where the last person left off, and in this way the entire Qur'an is recited in community. This recitation of the Qur'an is like a benediction; it is for the deceased, it is dedicated to them, it is even recited on their behalf. This recitation is a kind of loophole that cheats death; once we die, we can no longer accrue good or bad deeds because, well, we're dead. But when the Qur'an is recited like this, on behalf of the deceased, the dead are rewarded for that recitation as if they had recited the Qur'an themselves. Like this, the deceased is kept alive, for a little longer. The dead are brought back as the sound of Qur'an recitation in community, they live through this recitation.

Often, there are two piles of almonds in the middle of the room. Visitors chant prayers over an almond in the first pile, and then place the blessed almond into the second, reciting prayers hundreds or thousands of times. The recitations, the prayers, the sounds, the tears, the little Qur'ans, and the almonds, all become vehicles for carrying and expressing grief.

In most of the world, mourners do not know the meaning of the Arabic words they are uttering in their prayers and recitations, and this is a good thing. This makes the prayers and recitations effective conduits for grief. Without content, they become canvases, absorbing the colour of each person's grief. The foreign words allow us to give voice to our grief without shaping it, or defining it, or predetermining how we should think about or relate to our grief. We do not have to choose our words, and this frees us to think, to remember, to process, to mourn. The words anchor us as we swim in the incoherence of grief. The words offer us a way to voice our grief with our mouths, to make sounds that express our grief without having to say anything. The words are love, and through them we voice love – love for the one we have just now lost, love for all the ones we've lost, love for the living, love for ourselves.

And we cook, and feed our bodies, which is an act of love that feels like betrayal. But is, in fact, the earth nourishing herself.

Happiness and sadness, celebration and mourning heighten our sense of loneliness and so are best done in community. We need communities to rejoice and mourn with us, we need communities to heal. Even though it can feel that our joy and our grief are ours alone to carry, still somehow, miraculously, community can help lighten our loneliness, help carry our grief. But communities also police our joy and our grief, so while they can help us, they have tremendous power to hurt us. A community's power is at its most terrifying when it surrenders its sensibilities to the puritans among us. The puritans among us are external manifestations of the puritans within each of us.

Puritanism wears many masks, it has many disguises, and its best disguise is us. It resides within each of us and so can be invisible. It is rooted in our self-hate, but expresses itself as righteousness and virtue. Puritanism is tricky because it hates us and it *is* us. It tries to make a moral argument against us, asking us to transcend ourselves. It hates our bodies, our desires, our passions, it hates our indulgence in pleasure, it hates our excretions, it wants to reduce us to the most sterile version of ourselves. It seeks to suppress what is complicated, messy, dirty, leaky about us. But are we even human if we are not these things?

Puritanism tends toward totalitarianism. It demands control of the state, the market, the mosque, the city square. It seeps into our views of religion, nationality, economics, gender, race and class. All expressions of puritanism are inhuman. Because puritanism hates what is human about us. It demands we transcend our own humanity.

One of the ugliest things about a puritan version of religion is that it treats our humanity as an impediment to approaching God. It fashions a god defined by His utter otherness to us. In the face of this god, our humanity becomes profane, unworthy, it is rejected as sullied and sullying. In denying us our humanity, puritan religion denies us love. And so it denies us grief, which is a kind of love. *Love, where the object of love is cut off*.

Puritan religion claims to transcend our humanity, and yet is imagined, concocted by the human mind. So, actually, it is a trap we create for ourselves. It demands we submit, flatten our vast complexities to a stern, unapproachable, unkind, masculine god. In puritan religion, humans are to God what women are to men: weak, dirty, unapproachable unless cleaned and sanctified, polluted and polluting when we are at our most human, and especially at our most female. Its strictest rules, harshest expressions are saved for when we eat, fuck, bleed and die. Puritanism strips away all the layers of human culture that soften and humanise religion, instead making religion rigid and harsh, turning it into something else, a weapon, with razor-sharp edges, so that human flesh cannot approach it without getting cut, without bleeding, without hurting.

Puritan Islam is no exception to this kind of cutting religiosity. Puritan Islam rears its ugly head most prominently and most devastatingly at the major markers of a human life – birth, marriage, death. Puritan Islam strips away all tenderness and kindness from the rituals around death so that they become sterile, unfulfilling. More than that, they become terrifying, they do violence to our humanity, they hurt us in ways from which it is difficult to recover.

The underlying philosophy of funeral rites in puritan Islam is this: life is ephemeral and its ephemerality makes it at once meaningless and eternally meaningful. On the one hand, the connections we make on Earth, the pleasures we enjoy, the sorrows we feel, are all ephemeral. So, they say, don't get caught up in life, don't let it distract you from your *din*. It's not worth it. Any attachment is weakness, a folly. Any hardship you experience from these attachments is your own fault, and a sign of weakness in your faith. On the other hand, there are angels sitting on our shoulders, writing down all our deeds, good and bad, and we will have to account for each and every single one of them in the Hereafter. We will be shackled by what we do or don't do, the choices we make, maybe even the thoughts we entertain, for an eternity. Our actions have eternal impact.

Imams at pulpits preaching a puritan Islam will say that the Prophet asked us to be in the world like the traveller. They will linger on this analogy. We're just making a pit stop, visiting this life on our way to an eternal life, to our home. Imagine if you were on a trip, they say, you wouldn't want to get too attached to anything or anyone. It's best to travel light. But if we stay with this analogy longer, their explanation doesn't add up. First of all, the Prophet didn't say to be in the world like a traveller, but rather to be in the world like a 'gharib', a stranger or a wanderer. Gharib can also mean impoverished, poor. This word for 'stranger', as a cousin to 'impoverished', cues us into the discomfort, the lack of privileges, the vulnerabilities that go with being a stranger. The Prophet tells us to be in the world like the stranger, the one who doesn't belong, the one who is vulnerable, in need of kindness, to experience the world as others do, as new, and frightening, and exciting; as strange.

The Hadith in question continues, with a Companion of the Prophet, Ibn Umar, commenting on it by saying, *When you find evening, do not wait for the morning and when you wake in the morning, do not wait for the evening. Seize your health before you become sick and your life before you die.*

In other words, *live*, now, here, where you are, when you are. Not tomorrow, and not in the Hereafter. The Prophet tried many times to drive home this message, like when he said, *If the end times come upon you while you have in your hand a sapling, plant it.* Even, *especially*, when you think it is pointless, fruitless, to plant the sapling, when you think there isn't any time, plant it then. Because that is when you most need hope.

When the end is nigh, plant a seed.

Islamic funeral rites complete a cycle of prayer that starts at birth. The shape of this ritual is a circle. To understand how it works, you need to know a little about how congregational prayer works.

First, there is the adhan, the call to prayer that is called out from the minarets of mosques.

Allahu akbar, allahu akbar . . . And then, *hayya 'ala l-salat, hayya 'ala l-falah*, calls the mu'azzin, voice like a foghorn, words floating through the streets, travelling, wandering into the marketplace, the houses, the schools, the government buildings. Sometimes the sound is loud, interrupting your train of thought, and sometimes it glides softly, lazily, as you stir in your sleep or carry on a conversation.

Those who intend to pray, when they hear the adhan, hurry to finish the task at hand so they can prepare for prayer. You might quicken your pace if you're making a delivery, clean your plate if you're eating, read a little faster so you can finish a chapter, intensify your negotiations so you can pause at an appropriate place to pray. The adhan announces, *It's time for prayer, c'mon! Come to prayer, come to success!*

Then, just before the congregational prayer is about to begin, there is an iqama, a shorter, less dramatic call that announces, *Get in lines, we're about to pray, yalla!*

qad qamati l-salat, qad qamati l-salat!

Then the prayer begins.

Allahu akbar! God is great! And the imam takes the congregation through all the cycles of prayer, starting in a standing position, hands folded across the chest, then bowing down halfway, bent at the waist, then prostrated, the forehead pressed to the earth, whispering prayers to the ground, and finally ending by sitting on one's calves, legs folded beneath, the body like an accordion, hands placed on top of thighs, turning the face right and left – *assalamu 'alaikum wa rahmatullah!* – to the angels on our shoulders, one on the right, one on the left, a personal surveillance system, CCTVs for God.

When Muslims are born, three things happen to the baby almost immediately. The adhan is called in the baby's right ear. The iqama is called in the baby's left ear. And the baby's mouth is sweetened with dates, usually by the parent chewing a date and sharing some of its juice with the baby, using their finger, dipping it in their own mouth and then into the baby's mouth. The purpose of the adhan and the iqama is to commence a prayer that is completed only at death, when a congregational prayer will be performed for the baby, the child, the young adult, the elder – however long the baby lives. At that final congregational prayer, there is no adhan, there is no iqama. It's already been called at birth. And more, there is no folding of the body, no bowing, no prostration, no loud Qur'an recitation. Just the community standing in rows. The imam calls out, *allahu akbar!* and then, *assalamu 'alaikum wa rahmatullah!*

And then it's over. The congregational prayer and the life. Now, the body can be buried.

God has many names. Two of Her favourite names are 'Rahman' and 'Rahim'. Linguistically, both are conjugations of the root r-h-m, and carry valences of meaning related to the mercy and compassion of the womb. One of the most beautiful things about Arabic is that almost all words come from a three-letter root. And because they all come from these roots, each word is coloured by, carries the meaning of its root; each word is connected, kin, of all the other words, the children, birthed by each root.

The womb is called a 'rahm' in Arabic, and mercy is 'rahma'. This teaches us that the womb and mercy are relatives; they're from the same family, they share some essential characteristics. The words for kinship, sympathy, relationship, love, respect, sparing someone, showing mercy are all derived from the same root, r-h-m. God's names Rahman and Rahim are both derived from the root r-h-m too, and their meanings as the Merciful, the Compassionate, reflect this relationship. If God Herself is mercy, then it makes sense that Her Prophet too would be mercy, rahma.

وما أرسلناك إلا رحمة للعلمين

We have not sent you except as a mercy to the worlds.

The funeral ritual is supposed to complete a circle started at birth. The circle of life, the circle of prayer; the emergence from a womb, the rahm, and the return to the womb of the Rahman and the Rahim. The earth births us, through our mothers' wombs, then it envelops us into its own womb. Like a birth in reverse. We enter into a womb rather than emerging from one. That this emergence and return is marked by a single prayer is beautiful and profound; the prayer is ushered in by our arrival and it is completed with our return.

In this prayer, the length of human life is the short span of time – the gap, the pause – between the iqama and the beginning of the prayer. This pause usually goes unnoticed, it is gone before we are even aware of it. Like the human life, it is ephemeral, short, fleeting. The place we might overlook as insignificant is where living happens, where life is lived. The rituals of birth and death call our attention to the pause, to the life: pay attention, be mindful. Live where you are, now. *Seize your health before you become sick and your life before you die.*

Key to the ritual of life, of birth and of death, is the sweetening of the baby's mouth with a date. A date first chewed in the mouth of an adult, softened with saliva, and then shared with the baby. The sweetness of the fruit and the human body, both gifts from the earth, mingled together and offered to a baby emerging from a womb. Life can be bitter and sad, but let's start with its sweet. Sweetness calls to pleasure, to indulgence, to love. It says, *I know you're upset about leaving the womb, but there are pleasures to be had here. Look, taste this – you'd never taste this sweetness in the womb. You must leave the womb, leave your place of comfort, you must wander and encounter the strange, be a stranger, and when you find the sweet, indulge in it, take joy in it, pleasure in it.*

When a person dies, there is urgency to bury their body. We emerge reluctantly from the womb, kicking and screaming. And then, like a kid at the end of summer camp, we sometimes end up loving life so much that we don't want to leave. And so we might depart just as we arrived, kicking and screaming. But the body craves its return to the womb of the earth, and so it deteriorates, returning itself to the earth on its own so that we have to hurry up to keep pace with it, and return it to its resting place.

First, the body is gently, lovingly washed. Then it is wrapped in unsewn white cotton sheets so as to have as little barrier between the body and the earth. A silent prayer, a janaza, is performed in congregation for the deceased. There are no words uttered aloud, because words are inadequate in the face of such tremendous grief. There is no movement because what movement could do justice to this loss? The absence of uttered words and movement create space for a community to stand together in grief as they are, in their bodies, without any expectations, without demanding them to say this or that, to move this way or that way. Come as you are. Be as you are. Mercy.

The quiet prayer without movement, the janaza, completes the ritual of life, which started with the adhan and iqama at birth, called tenderly in celebration and excitement, and ending now with a silent prayer marking our loss. Then the body is placed in the earth and the mourners leave. Slowly, we return to our bodies, to our lives, before our time is also up, and others come to mourn for us.

Puritan Islam misses the point about the ephemerality of life, demanding abstinence rather than indulgence. The 'real' life is the next life, it says, and the body must be returned to the earth urgently, immediately, as soon as possible. And so God is transformed from a lover anxiously awaiting the return of her beloved, to a loan shark demanding the return of his investment.

The burial of the body in unsewn white sheets can be beautiful in its simplicity, like lovers rushing to remove the layers between them when they reunite after a long time away. But puritan Islam sees the simple shroud, made of two unsewn sheets as a gesture of humility, arriving before God unadorned, shedding all earthly pretensions. Instead of asking, *How best do I prepare to reunite with my love?* puritan Islam asks, *How best do I avoid coming across as arrogant when I appear before the ultimate judge?*

Puritan Islam insists that Muslims be buried in Muslim-only cemeteries. Some people like to segregate themselves even in death. There can be no markers or beautification of gravesites in their version of the religion. Women are prohibited from participating or even being present when the body is buried. They are emotional, they are loud, they cry too much. They'll distract the men from the serious, manly business of burial. There is almost an obsession with forgetting and denying love, and the pain that comes with love, all viewed as signs of human frailty. Love is a promise of pain; that is the nature of love. The rules in the cemeteries of puritan Islam say, *There is nothing special about your love or your pain. Everyone is born, everyone dies. Get over it.*

Of course, Muslims the world over bury their loved ones beautifully, they honour them by gently bathing their bodies, carefully placing them in kaffans, tenderly lowering them into the earth. They plant trees and flowers at graves, they place elegant headstones. They recite the Qur'an for their loved ones. Comfort each other, hold each other, remember and honour the pain of the grieving by reciting the Qur'an communally on the death anniversary of their loved ones. This recitation, like the one performed at death is also called a 'khatm'. A completion. The circle of love and grief are intertwined and the khatm tries again and again to close the circle. Sits at the place where one ends and the other begins. Sits at the mouth of the river, where the ocean of love spills into the river of grief, and the river of grief flows into the ocean of love.

But puritan Islam scorns all these ways that Muslims love each other. It sees the khatm as a violation of its sterile funeral rites, an aberration, an innovation in the religion, a bid'a, a path away from God, a path toward the fire. It sees its own insipid ritual as simple, clean, in service of its demanding god rather than humans and their frailties.

The great tragedy of Sibghatullah's life is that it was so short. A mere four and a half years. Little baby. This beautiful, brilliant life, snuffed out so suddenly. So unexpectedly. And the great wrong that was done to us was that he was buried according to the rituals of puritan Islam. Which is to say, his funeral honoured neither him nor the pain his sudden departure caused, the grief of a love suddenly without its object, in free fall, in a chasm that feels like eternity. This great, expansive love, an ocean of love, shared by so many, suddenly without direction, heaving, frantic, searching, bereft. *Love without its object.*

There is nothing simple or straightforward about a funeral. There can't be. Humans are not simple. Our love is not simple. Our deaths are not simple. Trying to simplify a life at death is a cruel violence. How sacred is life if it should not be mourned?

If God isn't there to comfort us, what is the point of God?

I am sitting curled on the floor of our Baltimore apartment, reading a book on liberation theology in Islam, drinking hot chocolate, all warm and toasty and dry after a workout and a run in the rain when my cell phone rings, blinking its red light. The number is unfamiliar, so I answer with a tentative,

Hello?

No words on the other side. Just the wild wailing sound of a wounded animal, a creature in anguish. The sound of my sister, it turns out. Though I did not, at first, recognise that sound as her.

As I try to figure out where the call came from – an unknown number, I hope it was an accidental call, a wrong number, a mistake – a part of me, it seems, did recognise the sound, and knew that it brought with it incomprehensible pain. I did not want to be so close to the source of such pain.

And soon after, another call. Another sister. This one from Canada, from a number I recognise. This time I answer, *Hey . . .*

I have to tell you something. Her voice is low, serious, grave.

What? I ask, with trepidation.

Sibghatullah. Sibghatullah just died.

Disbelief.

What?! What do you mean he died? Are you sure? Always, in these cases, you want to be sure.

Yes.

There has to be some mistake.

There is no mistake. He is dead.

The initial grief is like wet cement. Heavy, thick, hard to move through. Rumee and I, married for just six months, pack our bags, place them in the trunk of our car, and begin the drive to Worcester, Massachusetts, where my sister is visiting her in-laws. It's a seven-hour drive. Seven hours of bewildering darkness. The drive is punctured by periodic calls from my sister, my sister with the now dead son.

I want my baby back! she wails, screaming, crying. I am crying with her, my nose stuffed, my face wet.

I know, dear. I know.

Utter helplessness. There is nothing I can do. Once you're dead, you're dead.

We arrive at the house that holds my sister at 7:00a.m. The night has passed into day, but it doesn't brighten anything. There might as well be no light, no sunshine. It's probably a beautiful June morning, but there is no room for beauty in my heart.

We park across the street from the house sitting in this suburban neighbourhood. The house is quiet. No movement. I don't know what I expected, but not this. I would rather the house be a ball of fire to reflect the hell that has just been unleashed on its inhabitants. The pain, the anguish, the loss is so intense, so dramatic, it is shocking to see that there are no reverberations, no signs of this on the house, which stands silent, sleepy, like any other house on the block. Like nothing catastrophic has just happened.

The front door is unlocked, and I walk right in. There are stairs in front of the doorway, leading up, covered in cream-coloured carpet. Somehow, I know she's upstairs. Maybe someone tells me. Maybe I just know. I don't wait for permission. My heart will jump out of my body to my sister if I don't move fast enough to keep up with it. I run up the stairs. There is a door on the left, slightly ajar. The sound of crying, my sister's cries, are coming from that room. I open the door fully and stand in the doorway, looking in. The room is flooded with light. There is a bed in the room, which looks huge compared to my sister, who is sitting in a corner of the bed, leaning against the headboard, looking at me. Sheets are crumpled all around her. For a second, there is a pause in the grief, a brief, ever so quick movement, where we both look at each other and I wonder,

Now that we are both here, is Sibghatullah still dead?

Just the question, the possibility of it, lets in a tiny sliver of hope that is swiftly and mercilessly crushed. Yes. Yes, he is still dead.

I rush to embrace her, we hug and cry. The first thing she says, when she can finally speak, gather enough breath to utter words, is:

I'm going to bury my son.

A look of defiance flashes across her face. I understand. She wants to be at the cemetery when her son is buried. When his body is handed over to the earth. She knows that my parents are enamoured with puritan Islam, and according to puritan Islam, women are strictly forbidden from being present at the burial of the body. Until this moment, none of the women in my family has ever been to a cemetery for a burial, and this is a point of pride for my parents. It is proof of the strength of their faith. My parents, we know, will resist my sister's presence at her own son's burial. This will not be easy. In telling me *I'm going to bury my son*, my sister is instructing me,

Figure it out. Make it happen.

I look at her. *Okay. Of course. Of course, you'll bury your son.*

I explain the situation to Rumee. He doesn't understand why my parents might resist. I explain that puritan Islam treats a moment like this – a death, a birth, a wedding – as a test of faith. It's like an exam. If you don't follow its rules now, in a moment such as this, it means you have no faith.

We need to take the lead on the funeral arrangements, I say, *so we can be in control of the logistics.*

Though I say 'we' need to take a lead on the funeral arrangements, essentially I mean *he* has to take the lead on them, because I'm a fucking mess. Rumee, a twenty-four-year-old, steps into the shoes of an adult, calling cemeteries and funeral homes. Trying to figure out how to organise a funeral. Learning what our society does with its dead.

My sister is weeping in her room. Her older son runs in and out, constantly in motion. He's six and a half years old, we're not sure he understands what has happened. My sister has Sibghatullah's clothes in a Ziploc bag, light brown shalwar kameez, with delicate embroidery on the kameez. These were the last clothes he was wearing when she took him to the hospital. She keeps opening the bag to smell them. They still smell like him. She's desperate to see him again. But she can't. The hospital will release his body to the funeral home after conducting an autopsy, and only then can we see him, wash his body and prepare him for burial. We're learning this slowly, step by step.

A few hours later, my parents arrive with my sisters and brother. They drove all night too, from Toronto, through a night of grief, in a green van.

Where's Sibghatullah? Can we go see him?

I walk everyone through the steps. *We can't go see Sibghatullah yet because he's still at the hospital and the hospital will release him to the funeral home.*

Why can't we go pick him up ourselves? my father asks.

They don't release the body to the family, only to the funeral home.

Well, why do they still have him, why haven't they released him yet? What are they doing with him?

They're going to do an autopsy on him first, to find out the cause of death.

No, no, no, no, no! We don't want an autopsy! He's already dead, what difference will it make to know why he died? He'll still be dead! We don't want him cut up like that! Both my parents are near hysterical at the idea of an autopsy.

Rumee explains that he asked the hospital if we could opt out. *They said 'no', that especially in the case of young children who die unexpectedly, they require autopsies. They advised me that it was in our interest to do the autopsy, in order to rule out child abuse, at the very least. So that child services won't be involved.*

We look at each other, confused and anxious. Why would child services be involved? Obviously no one wants child services involved. We can't even think this through.

Once the body is at the funeral home, we will go there and see Sibghatullah. We can wash him there. Then we will take him to the cemetery, pray the janaza there and bury him.

My parents look even more confused. My mother is getting increasingly upset.

Where will the women go when the men are burying him? she asks.

Well, we'll be at the cemetery, so we will pray there and then bury him immediately afterwards.

No, no, no. Women are not allowed at the cemetery! my mother says. She is starting to shake with righteous indignation, her body filling up with air as she prepares to launch into a lecture about why women can't go to the cemetery, why it is especially important to follow the rules at this moment. I cut her off.

Your daughter wants to bury her son. And since it is her son that died, that is what we are going to do.

My father acquiesces. My mother does too. But whereas my father is resigned, hurting too much to make an issue of this, my mother is seething, hurting too, but quiet only because she sees she won't win this one just now.

We stumble our way through the preparations.

Rumee calls cemeteries, desperately trying to find one that will give us a plot on short notice, which turns out to be more difficult than we expected, especially given that this is a holiday weekend. Eventually, he finds a Muslim cemetery with an available plot, where they are willing to let us bury Sibghatullah the next day. It is about an hour's drive away, the next state over, in a small New England town. The volunteer funeral director is away, but agrees to let us conduct the funeral in his absence, understanding the importance of a quick burial. He gives Rumee a list of rules that we must abide by and asks him to sign it. The list is long, and upsetting.

You agree not to raise any headstones or monuments marking the grave.

No one will pray at the gravesite or make any comments other than reciting the Qur'an.

Women are prohibited from being present at the burial.

The list is two pages long, and it is exceedingly strict, even for a Muslim-only cemetery. But the same puritanism that informed the list is permitting us to bury our Sibghatullah right away. Rumee looks through the list, and reluctantly signs.

But, we're not going to follow these rules . . . I worry.

Whatever. He's not going to be there, Rumee tries to reassure me. *We'll just go and do our thing.*

As Rumee is working on the funeral arrangements, the rest of us go to see the body, Sibghatullah's body. When we see him, it is shocking. He doesn't look like Sibghatullah. I mean, he does and he doesn't. Death and the autopsy have changed his shape. His torso has been cut open in a Y, starting at his shoulders, connecting at his chest, then going down to his navel. And it has been sewn back together with thick, coarse thread. It shocks us, how his body has been handled. Crudely, like he was dead. Not gently or tenderly, like he was our precious little baby. Now I understand my parents' resistance to the autopsy. They have seen what it does to a body.

When we see Sibghatullah, we weep. We touch his hair, caress and kiss his face, and hands, and feet. My mother washes his body. We watch and help. She has experience with this. She washes the bodies of the dead women and children in our community, and I am grateful for her service so she can lead us here. This is the first dead body I have seen since my grandfather's, when I was five years old, as he lay on a bed made of rope above a chunk of ice the size of a coffin, in the sehan of a house in Gujranwala.

Once we've washed Sibghatullah, we shroud him in two unsewn white sheets. I'm not sure where we got those sheets from. Did my mother bring them with her from Canada? Our tradition would have him buried like this, simply and without a coffin, but we're having trouble bearing it. How can we leave his body unprotected like this? Turns out it is against state law to bury someone without a coffin anyways, so the funeral home offers us one made of cardboard, for a 'simple' burial. We see the box and balk. We cannot bury him like this, not in a cardboard box.

Since it is too late to buy a proper coffin, and we are feeling the pressure for a quick burial, my two brothers, Rumee and my father go to Lowe's and purchase the necessary materials to build a coffin out of pinewood. My older brother leads them, using the woodworking skills he developed years ago, while building a suite in the basement of our Mississauga home, the first home Sibghatullah arrived in when he was born. They borrow equipment from the store, buy the wood there. They build a box, a home, a final resting place for Sibghatullah's body, in the Lowe's parking lot. They measure and cut the wood, nail together a coffin with love, tears and prayers. Building the coffin gives them something to do. A way to express their love, their grief, their pain for a child, a lovely, beautiful and beloved child. Building the coffin is prayer.

They return to the funeral home, where we are in the company of Sibghatullah's body, and we are relieved to see the coffin, that simple box, not quite a Western coffin, not lined with cloth, but also not made of cardboard. We place Sibghatullah's body in the box crafted by his family, gently, making sure not to hurt his head, tenderly, so as to protect his body – for *us*, so we can feel we are still doing something for him. Because, although we are utterly helpless in the face of his death, soon there will be nothing left to do for him at all. He will require nothing from us. The emptiness to come will be greater than the emptiness that envelops us now.

The drive to the cemetery is long. It is late afternoon by the time we get there. The cemetery looks small, plain, ugly and inadequate to me. We pray the janaza – completing the ritual started four and a half years ago in a room in Credit Valley Hospital in Mississauga, when my mother called the adhan and iqama in Sibghatullah's ears on a snowy night in December. Now, four and a half years later, on a June evening, we are all gathered unexpectedly at a Muslim cemetery in rural New England, about to bury this same child. Who could have imagined this? The women pray behind the men. There is little ceremony, by design. The prayer is silent and quick. It feels like drowning. The light recedes, nightfall approaches.

A machine has removed soil from the ground, making a rectangular hole in the earth. The men place a lid on the coffin, nailing it shut. It hurts when they nail that box shut, another new and foreign pain, as it sinks in that this box, this coffin, will never be opened again. Now we carry the coffin to the hole. My brothers jump down into the grave to receive the coffin, handling it gingerly, as if Sibghatullah is alive but just resting, and moving the coffin quickly will wake him, as if he might feel the movement. And then they come up, they are helped up, grabbing hands that pull them up and out. The living emerge from the grave, leaving the dead behind. We each throw handfuls of soil into the hole. It hurts. We throw some roses down there, the red mixing with the brown-black earth, against the pine-coloured coffin beneath. Sibghatullah's brother uses a shovel to throw in the soil, which makes a hollow thudding sound as it hits the coffin.

We are all crying, weeping, hugging each other. I turn to embrace my mother and she whispers in my ear, in between sobs, through the tears and the pain, *You broke God's law today by bringing us to the cemetery. You will have to answer for this.*

I pull away, recoiling from her words. How can she hurt me now, at this time, like this, when we are both in so much pain? This is the tyranny of puritan Islam. It centres itself so all of our pain is secondary to its demands. Nothing, absolutely nothing, supersedes it. It is merciless. Without rahma, bay raham.

The drive back to the Worcester house where we are staying is long and silent. When we get to the house, my sister collapses on the front steps, refusing to cross the threshold to sleep in the comfort of a bed, under a roof, while her son lies unprotected, exposed to the elements, cold, alone, vulnerable. My brothers carry her in. We are exhausted and worn out. The funeral, as imperfect as it was, is over. We will spend the next decade trying to forgive ourselves for it. A decade healing from this funeral of puritan Islam. A funeral that did not care for our grief. Did not hold and comfort us. A funeral that gave us no path toward healing. More than a decade after the funeral, on my way to visit Sibghatullah's grave, I will voice my regrets about the funeral to a friend, wishing we'd done better. My dear friend, who is driving us, will say, *Weren't you, like, twenty-four years old when you organised the funeral? How could you have done better?*

And I will realise, *Oh! That's true!* We were kids ourselves, we did the best we could. Even if it wasn't good enough, not then, not now, not for Sibghatullah, not for us, it was still our best. And that's worth something. We cannot be held responsible for the impoverishment of puritan Islam, which restricted our imaginations and our choices.

If we'd been raised with another, richer, more colourful Islam, the entire experience could have been different. Our pain and grief and sorrow would all still be there, but looking back at the funeral, we might have more healing memories, memories of tender expressions of love, both in words and in gestures. The funeral might have started a process of healing, rather than another violence that cut us so deeply it took me a decade to even contemplate it again. To look at it and see it for what it was, and not just push memories of it away. The funeral could have been a ceremony for the living, a way to honour Sibghatullah, to remember him. The service, instead of mirroring our grief, reflecting back its darkness shrouded in white, could have offered colour, hope, a path forward. A path awaiting us in the days and years to come, when we were ready to move, take a step, pack up our grief and carry it along.

I don't remember much about the immediate days, weeks, months after Sibghoo's death. I cried a lot. I slept a lot. I was filled with anxiety. I had trouble sleeping. The first experience of relief I had from the crushing sorrow that threatened to obliterate me was a few weeks later – or was it months? I had a dream. In the dream, I had just taken Sibghatullah to a public bathroom, and now we were emerging from the bathroom stall. The bathroom was covered in black marble, polished and shining. The stalls and the counters were black, too. The sinks that dotted the long marble countertop were stainless steel. There was recessed lighting, bright, shiny bulbs beaming down on us. We were at some fancy place. I touched him. He was wearing grey shalwar kameez, with a little white, crocheted kufi. His curly brown-blond hair ringed his kufi, making him look so cute as to be delicious. His clothes were soft under my fingers. His skin was smooth and plump. I took his pudgy little hands and washed them. It felt so good. To see him alive. To touch him. To do something for him. To love him. It was a relief. When I woke, it took me a few minutes to remember that he was dead. But the memory of that dream, how it made me feel, stayed with me. It comforted me, even in my waking hours. He came back, to offer me comfort, to offer me respite from my grief. To let me love him.

When Cain kills Abel, he doesn't know what to do with his dead brother's body. He's sitting with it, trying to figure out what to do next, when he sees a crow nearby standing next to the dead body of another crow. The living crow digs a hole in the earth, then places the dead crow in the hole and covers up the body. In this way, the crow teaches Cain, the murderer, how to bury his brother.

One snowy afternoon, when we were living in rural New York, Rumee and I heard a loud thud, something hitting the side of our house. It jolted us out of our seats, at the desk and the couch, where we were working. What was that sound? In the living room, there were large windows that ran the length of one wall. Outside these windows, lying on the ground, we saw a dead hawk. It had flown straight into the bank of windows and broken its neck. We stared at the dead hawk. What were we supposed to do with it? We couldn't quite bury it; it lay atop at least two feet of snow, and the ground beneath was frozen hard. So we left it there, its body lying peacefully, majestically, on the pristine snow. Then, over the next few days, we watched in horror as squirrels and birds and other creatures feasted upon its body, spreading its carcass, its feathers, bones, red bits of flesh, throughout the yard, turning the snow into a canvas for painting the cycle of life.

We live, we eat, we die, we are eaten. We feed on others; then we feed others. We are birthed by the earth for the earth.

And in this way, we can see our lives as short, meaningless, ephemeral, or eternal, beautiful, meaningful. We are so much bigger than ourselves. We live forever in the earth, being nourished by her and then nourishing her. We are the birds, the squirrels, the trees.

The purpose of the funeral is not just to bury a body. A murderer can do that. The purpose of the funeral is to create meaning, to offer a way to think about death that is not hopeless. Its purpose is to comfort us, bring us closer together, to articulate our fears and sorrows, to make us see how and why our lives are meaningful despite, or even because of, our mortality.

Know this: the funeral is for the living.

It is unsurprising that, given the impoverishment of the funeral ceremony for our darling Sibghoo, it wasn't enough. We tried to make it right again and again, each in our own way, sometimes together, but mostly in isolation. Rumee had signed documentation promising we wouldn't place any markers on the grave, but when we went to bury Sibghoo we saw that, actually, many graves in the cemetery were marked, some with headstones, others with trees, and others still with elaborate stonework. My sister wanted to place a polished granite rectangle around Sibghatullah's grave, marking the place her son was buried. She bought four polished granite blocks and a few weeks after his burial, we returned to his grave. Under the hot July sun, we toiled, digging four feet into his grave, using shovels and pickaxes. When we got to four feet, we were just above his coffin. Just above him. My younger brother kind of collapsed there, sitting in the grave, looking up at us with sad, empty eyes.

He's right here, he said, pointing down.

We mixed and poured cement over long pieces of rebar to create a foundation for the four polished granite blocks that would frame the grave. Then we replaced the earth. We were hurting so much. Our eyes and faces filled with sadness.

My sister was completing a graduate degree when her son passed, and her advisor organised a memorial for Sibghoo on her campus. They printed out a huge photo of Sibghoo and placed it on a stand; people read poems, said nice things. The grounds crew planted two dogwood trees for him because Sibghoo loved dogwoods. This was a few months after the burial, in the fall, so the whole family couldn't be there. We didn't even tell my parents, for fear they would disapprove.

A few years later, my sister moved away from New England. Before leaving, she planted a dogwood tree at Sibghoo's grave, inside the granite boundary. She watered and tended it for months, then placed a laminated sign around the tender, young sapling that read:

Please water me.

When Rumee and I visited Sibghoo's grave shortly after her move, we were horrified to see that someone had chopped down the tree. The little stub of the trunk was still there, decapitated. The sign still hung around the stump:

Please water me.

Motherfuckers! I was so angry and hurt. Disgusted at the kind of inhumanity it takes to chop down a tree with a sign that politely asks for water.

Who cut down that tree? I don't know. It could have been the puritan Muslims running the cemetery, or it could have been someone from town. The mostly white town, where everyone looks at us suspiciously when we drive through to the cemetery and stop off at the Big Y to buy flowers. Racist white people are puritans, too. Puritanism transgresses religious and racial boundaries. It can be a shared value.

The cost of puritanism is mercy. I couldn't bring myself to tell my sister that the tree she so lovingly planted for a son buried too soon was cut down by some heartless piece of shit.

The god of rage is the god of sorrow with both eyes torn out.
—the poet Ross Gay, misremembering
a poem by the poet Patrick Rosal

Sibghatullah's death unleashed a fury in me. My rage was a sharp blade; it focused my vision and showed me the essence of things, allowed me to cut off the fat and leave the meat behind. I burned with righteous outrage at patriarchy, at racism, at social inequality, at capitalism, at how we keep on destroying the earth, even though we know better. In this way, my rage did important work. Often, especially when I was in the throes of grief, my rage felt like mercy. But it didn't stop there.

I burned hot and feverish with rage. I trembled and pulsed with it. It hummed and buzzed in me. I was angry at the useless hospital where Sibghoo died, at the doctors who didn't save him, at the funeral home director who acted like death was normal, at the cemeteries that closed over the long weekend, at the rules of the cemetery that was open, at the ugliness of the earth, at the heartlessness of mortality, at the horror of death, at the pain that brought us to our knees, at how pathetic our pain made us look, at seeing how helpless and vulnerable we were, at the fact that he'd died at all. I was angry at a God who'd clearly fucked up, at a religion that was full of promise but now felt like an empty husk. I was angry at my mother, at my father. I was angry at my sisters, at my brother-in-law, at my brothers, at Rumee, at the third-floor apartment where you had to carry every freaking item up three flights of stairs when you moved in, at the boxes and boxes of books, at my cell phone, at how big the earth was, at how long it took to get from one place to another, at laughter, at the two white women at a park who called the police on my father and Sibghoo's six-year-old brother for looking 'suspicious', at the police who showed up to check if indeed they were 'suspicious', at Worcester, a place with a name that wasted letters by not pronouncing them. I was angry at myself.

The rage was a hardening. It was meant to shield me from the softness in me that sorrow had exposed, a softness that alarmed me. The sorrow made me feel helpless, while the rage gave me a sense of control; the sorrow demanded submission while the rage promised to carry my pain. The rage was just a facade, though, a way to hide the sorrow. And there was so much sorrow.

Sorrow for little Sibghoo. Sorrow for my sister. Sorrow for her loss, sorrow for her sorrows. Sorrow for the colonialism and Partition that displaced my grandparents, rendering impossible countless futures. Sorrow for the sorrows my parents inherited from them and passed on to us, for all that they lost – their lives, their friends, their families, their connection to the land, their faith in humanity for the horrors they witnessed. Sorrow for my parents who spent less than twenty years in Pakistan and then were somehow 'from' Pakistan for the rest of their lives. Sorrow for us, their children, watching our parents spend their lives trying to belong to a place they were barely from. Sorrow for watching our parents unsuccessfully but persistently, god bless them, try to make us belong to that dream place they imagined they were from. Sorrow for watching our parents see the dream place for the real place it was each time they moved back with us, the crushing disappointment, the sting of betrayal, the shamefaced embarrassment. Sorrow for hearing my parents' tense voices as they tried to figure out how to make ends meet when my father was fired by the foreman at his job for praying Jumu'a, for the worry in their eyes as they balanced their principles against the need for a paycheck. Sorrow for seeing my parents pump each other up to ask his brother for a loan of five thousand dollars and the desert their eyes became when he refused – maybe because he didn't have the money himself, maybe because he didn't want to lend it. Sorrow for witnessing, over the years, white people in uniforms – cops, TSA, customs and border agents, doctors, store managers – talk down to, deride, yell, bark at my parents, our gods humiliated and disrespected so. And my parents, trying to maintain their dignity, covering up their shame with rage. Sorrow for seeing our parents through the eyes of white people, seeing their class, their foreignness, their lack of education, their suddenly accented English in the face of whiteness, how the rules of this new country confused them so they looked more like lost children than adults who knew the way. Sorrow for my parents' losing their family members in Pakistan, one by one – parents, a brother, a sister, a niece, a nephew – learning the news written on thin blue airmail envelopes in difficult-to-read scrawl, or on a frantic call with a poor connection in the middle of the night, absorbing the sorrow of lonely mourning in a foreign land, setting their jaws and eating their daal chawal, setting their shoulders and cleaning the dishes, because what else could they do?

Hai, there are so many sorrows. Sorrow for how we were raised, as sacrificial offerings at the altar of an ideology. Sorrow for how little we played and how much we studied. Sorrow for how shame was one of our primary teachers. Sorrow for how the shame is a partition that separates us from each other, disconnects us from ourselves, turning us into islands. Sorrow for how difficult it is to admit the truth of our experiences even to ourselves, and more so, to speak our truths without hurting each other, causing more pain, creating more sorrow. Sorrow for how we repeat the mistakes of our parents. Sorrow for trying to belong to places we are barely from. Sorrow for the multitudes of violences such desperate belonging, such settling, always makes necessary, starting with the pretension that we have the right to be where we are, that we deserve what we have, that we don't owe each other anything, when we are from each other, we have only each other. Sorrow for the weight of failed dreams, dreams of a utopia, of a paradisiacal place which is always a garden full of flowers, now withered and faded and turned to dust. Sorrow for who we were supposed to be, for who we will never be, and for who we turned out to be.

A few years ago, in a rare moment of complete honesty, my mother confided sadly to Rumee, *I ruined my children's bachpan. I sacrificed their childhoods to Tanzeem.*

The puritan in us often expresses herself as the god of rage, but somewhere, deep down inside, she knows that she is actually the god of sorrow. But she cannot see. Her eyes are torn out.

For several years I couldn't bring myself to return to Sibghoo's grave, feeling guilty every time I had the chance but didn't go. Then, in 2015, I got a fellowship at Radcliffe, so I moved to Boston for a year and was able to visit Sibghoo's grave a few times. I made a new friend who was also mourning the death of loved ones. We walked the path of grief together, holding hands, leaning on each other. I was grateful for his company. He helped me see myself and my grief in a new light. He helped me see that the cemetery wasn't as ugly as I had always believed it to be. There was beauty there, like an autumn olive tree, and black raspberry bushes. Together, we lovingly picked out lilies and lilies of the valley from a local nursery in Boston and buried, planted them at Sibghoo's grave. He listened to me talk endlessly about Sibghoo, about his life, his death and his burial. Importantly, he helped me think about where Sibghoo is now. As we knelt at Sibghoo's grave, burying, planting the bulbs of colourful flowers to come, he asked me, *Where do you think Sibghoo is now?*

You mean, where is he, according to Islam? I replied with a question.

No. Where do you think he is now?

I don't know . . .

I was surprised to learn that I couldn't answer his question. Until he asked, I thought I knew the answer.

We were quiet for a while. Planting. Burying.

And then suddenly, I could see him all around me, in the green cemetery, under the bright blue New England sky. He was in the grass, and the bushes, and the trees. He wasn't alone. He was surrounded by beauty. He was, he *is* beauty.

Later still, I took Rumee back to the cemetery.

Look, look dear! Look at the black raspberries growing right next to Sibghoo's grave. Look at the little green lily shoots pushing up through the rich, delicious soil, promising flowers, promising colour and beauty.

We picked off the black raspberries, cute, tender, tiny and juicy and we popped them in our mouths. They were sweet. *Sweet too where sorrow is.* Sweet too where sorrow is.

إنا لله وإنا إليه راجعون

We are God's, and to God we return.

Acknowledgements

اقرأ باسم ربك الذى خلق ۞
خلق الإنسن من علق ۞
اقرأ وربك الأكرم ۞
الذى علم بالقلم ۞
علم الإنسن ما لم يعلم ۞
كلا إن الإنسن ليطغى ۞
أن رءاه استغنى ۞

Recite in the name of your Lord who created
Created humans from a clinging clot of blood
Read and your Lord is most generous
The One who taught with the pen
Taught humans what they know not

Certainly, humans transgress
When they imagine themselves independent, self-sufficient.

All books are written in community and this book was especially nurtured, cultivated in community – in several communities. There are so many eyes, ears, hearts and hands that have cared for this book and for me throughout the years, so much enduring love that has guided and supported what this book and I have become.

Although writing can feel cerebral and lonely, it is fundamentally a metabolising of experiences and a reaching out, a reaching toward; a deep awareness, when we are alone, that we desire to commune, speak to others, offer ideas, write beautiful sentences, share ourselves with others. Writing is about listening deeply and speaking to those who are not before us, who might have passed, who are elsewhere, who have yet to arrive. *Writing*, Robin Wall Kimmerer teaches us, *is an act of reciprocity.*

Those who know me know that I love to share, to be in conversation, so almost as soon as I wrote the sentences in the first draft of this book, and every draft thereafter, I was sharing them, reading them aloud, talking about them with my loves, with my friends, with my family. Reading and listening, reading and watching, trying to understand how the words were landing and how I needed to change them to carry the meanings I meant to convey. Thank you, to everyone who listened.

I owe my deepest gratitude to Rumee, whose brilliance illuminates my world and without whom this book would simply not be. Thank you for the walks, the listening, the sharing, the caring, the nurturing, the reading, the editing, the deep thinking and, most of all, for the loving – for loving all the versions and forms of me; for always, always so willingly doing with me, so lovingly, the work of love.

I am deeply and happily indebted to bbbg. Thank you

for your light, your laughter, your dancing, your tenderness, your ears and sunflower eyes and dil on this book; for pointing out smells and sounds, for showing me beauty tucked away or in plain sight on a well-worn path; for eyes that make the old new again.

I am grateful to all who read this book in its entirety, believed in it, encouraged it, provided me with careful feedback chapter-by-chapter, whose eyes made it better. Rumee (*I mean, goddamn!*); Anver (*take out that scene!*); Joyce (*I screamed when I read that*), Ross (*show us how you get from rage to resolution*), Daniel (*too much is a way of saying not enough*), Samira (*this is a love letter*), Lauren (*the things we are dogmatic about are the things we are willing to sacrifice love for*), Lynette (*we come of age at different ages*).

In 2018, I organised a three-day workshop around an earlier version of this book and I am grateful to the participants who shared so generously of their time, their energy, their insights, who showed me the work the book was already doing in their lives – Sadaf, Iman, Shehnaz, Maysa, Waged, Sadaf, Noor, Samira, Homayra.

I am indebted to all those who listened to or read excerpts of the book over the years, who engaged with it thoughtfully, nourished and nurtured me and my writing, feeding my heart, my body, my soul, and my mind. Thank you to Renisa, Riaz, Sayeed and Lialah (pound cakes and making space for us on your apocalypse raft); Tara, Sebastian, Asmani and Gaia (seed bars, spelt loaves, freshly squeezed juice & huggles); Rosily and Dick (feeding us the garden);

Shakeela and Shehnoor (kebabs and clams and bike rides); Bill and Susan (our adventures, our transformations); Nadia (sharing your story to hold space for mine); Amal (making Vancouver home); Noor and Youssef (hiring committee!); Meher Aunty (impromptu meet-ups); Adel and Nihal (asking me to read more); Minelle (interviews and affirmations); Tamir, Nina and Salma (picnics and plums); Daniel and Kent (pizzas, the blanket and your home); Ben, Lisa, Sophia and Theo (flatbreads and walks); Letina and Solomon (the injera); Naveena and Hassan (newborn daal); Janice and Mary (counsel, coffee walks and dumplings); Allyssa (*it's okay to cry at work*); Candis (exploring freedom); Kim (living openly); Malinda (step counts); Talia and Blair (culinary adventures); Jamie and Ashley (witnessing and dreaming); Vivette and Katherine (trusting me); Iman and Waleed (*Cardi B is Lebanese!*); Azza (insisting on religion); Alia (inviting me to your farm); Tania (the blessing of a dastarkhwan); Doug and Barney (Persian stew); Anna (the bread and the bag); Max (for always helping me celebrate); my sagacious and sorely missed therapist Tracy (*now is the only forever because it is always now*); my brilliant therapist Mercedes (*if love is weakness, then let us all fall to our knees*).

I am thankful to The Rainbow Coalition at Radcliffe, which was one of the sites where this book was birthed. Our care and witnessing of each other was essential for this project – thank you, Joyce (for catching me); Ross (gifting the best reading lists); Sarah (that dumpling dinner); Tiana (encouraging me to stay and look at Mars); Laurence (no party is complete without an online poll); Kris (yoga and knowing when to walk out); Alyssa (teaching us to trust ourselves); Reiko (instructing us through silence). At Radcliffe also, thank you, Michael (reminding me about curiosity, and caring about and for this book); Valerie (*you're a writer, no, I mean, a real writer*); Elliott (catching me too, and for writing Rumee); Peter (encouraging this book).

There are people in Islamic Studies and Religious Studies whose support has been essential in getting me to where I am. I am indebted to you, Leila, Anver, Diana, Farid, Rahuldeep, Niloofar, Steven, Ziba, Mahan, Ebrahim, Erik, Kristian, Yossef, Andrew, Sa'diyya, Amina. Thank you to anyone who has written a letter for me, unbeknownst to me, who has supported me when they have had power; thank you to everyone who has opened the gate.

I have the great fortune of working in a unit, the Social Justice Institute at the University of British Columbia, that is supportive and kind and generous. Thank you especially to Denise, for your wise leadership over the years, and Janice, for your wonderful turn as acting director. I am grateful to each of my colleagues for brilliant, thoughtful exchanges, and always for your generosity. I am indebted to my students, for taking a leap of faith with me, for practising freedom together, for teaching me that freedom is only ever practised in community.

I was supported by several fellowships that made this work possible, most especially by giving me the gift of time. My gratitude to the Radcliffe Institute for Advanced Study, the Canada

Research Chair Program, the Peter Wall Institute for Advanced Study, and the Pierre Elliott Trudeau Foundation.

I am grateful to the writers and artists whose work has made mine possible. It is impossible to count them all but I was deeply formed in the writing of this book by the voices, the wisdom, the wit of Chimamanda Ngozi Adichie, Riz Ahmed, Rumee Ahmed, Hilton Als, Elizabeth Alexander, Aziz Ansari, James Baldwin, Asma Barlas, Leroy Little Bear, Joyce Bell, Lucille Clifton, Ta-Nehisi Coates, Kimberlé Crenshaw, Barbara T. Christian, Michaela Coel, Angela Davis, Assia Djebar, Toi Derricotte, Ava Duvernay, Anver Emon, Nikky Finney, Ross Gay, Aracelis Girmay, Donald Glover, Saidiya Hartman, Ziba Mir-Hosseini, Daniel Heath Justice, Tayari Jones, Kristiana Kahakauwila, Mindy Kaling, Robin D. G. Kelly, Laurence Ralph, Robin Wall Kimmerer, Sarah Koenig, Jhumpa Lahiri, Kiese Laymon, Audré Lorde, Kris Manjapra, Renisa Mawani, Hasan Minhaj, Wesley Morris, Toni Morrison, Fred Moten, Mira Nair, Zarqa Nawaz, Issa Rae, Claudia Rankine, Patrick Rosal, Arundhati Roy, Amy Tan, Sonia Sanchez, Sa'diyya Shaikh, Gyatri Spivak, Malinda Smith, Zadie Smith, Kim TallBear, Amina Wadud, Jenna Wortham, and Laurie Zoloth.

A book like this would never see the light of day, no matter the loving care it is nurtured with, unless someone is willing to take a chance on it, which is to say, to take a risk. Thank you, Simran Jeet Singh, for supporting my writing after hearing me talk on an academic panel and introducing me to your amazing agent. Thank you to my agent, Tanusri Prasanna, for reading my manuscript in two days and being exuberant in your love for it; for saying *I don't think I could rest until this book is out everywhere.* I am grateful for your generosity and care throughout this process. Thank you, Anver Emon, for letting this book into your heart and for introducing me to your friend, the publisher. Thank you, Novin Doostdar, for understanding this book and betting on it. Thank you to Vanessa Kerr and Anna Carmichael at Abner Stein. Thank you, Cecilia Stein, my publishing editor, for taking this book on and for believing in it. Thank you to the team at Oneworld, thank you, Ben Summers, for the cover design; Paul Nash and the production team; the communication and marketing teams; everyone who has helped bring this book forth, and will help it yet, thank you.

My debt, my gratitude to and for my family is boundless. Thank you, dear parents, for teaching me to dream, and for bringing me along on yours. Thank you, Mommy, for teaching me the art of telling a story for a moral purpose. Thank you, Deddy, for teaching me to listen and really feel. Thank you, my siblings and your life partners, for all the ways you cared and continue to care for me along this journey, all the little and big kindnesses, countless generosities – staying up late, past midnight, tenderly helping me with a ninth-grade project after yet another fainting episode; moving me, driving me, to New York City, in a van full of stuff, and two beautiful children; taking me flying; oh, that beautiful gift of art on a door, which is a door, always will be a door; and my darling, for the hugs that speak more than words ever could, for holding space for the fullness of our truths. Thank you to my beloved nieces and nephews and godchildren, for the lights that you are in the world. May you tread lightly upon the earth. Thank you, my darling Sibghoo, for all the titlys that you are.

I live and write on stolen land, land of which the xʷməθkʷəy̓əm, səl̓ilwətaʔɬ, and Coast Salish Peoples are the rightful custodians. I am an uninvited settler here. Yet, I am treated with kindness and generosity. I am indebted and I am grateful. Thank you.

And readers, it was fun imagining you as I wrote! Thank you!

Writing is an act of reciprocity with the world; it is what I can give back in return for everything that has been given to me. And now there's another added layer of responsibility, writing on a thin sheet of tree and hoping the words are worth it. Such a thought could make a person set down her pen . . . What would it be like, I wondered, to live a life of heightened sensitivity to the lives given for ours? . . . And just in that moment, I can hear John Pigeon say, 'Slow down — it's thirty years of a tree's life you've got in your hands there. Don't you owe it a few minutes to think about what you'll do with it?'

Robin Wall Kimmerer, *Braiding Sweetgrass*

THE THRONE OF CAESAR

THE THRONE
OF CAESAR

STEVEN SAYLOR

MINOTAUR BOOKS
NEW YORK

THE THRONE OF CAESAR. Copyright © 2018 by Steven Saylor. All rights reserved. Printed in the United States of America. For information, address St. Martin's Press, 175 Fifth Avenue, New York, N.Y. 10010.

www.minotaurbooks.com

The Library of Congress has cataloged the hardcover edition as follows:

Names: Saylor, Steven, 1956– author.
Title: The throne of Caesar : a mystery of ancient Rome / Steven Saylor.
Description: First edition. | New York : Minotaur Books, 2018.
Identifiers: LCCN 2017041306 | ISBN 9781250087126 (hardcover) |
    ISBN 9781250087133 (ebook)
Subjects: LCSH: Gordianus, the Finder (Fictitious character), 110 B.C.—Fiction. |
    Caesar, Julius—Fiction. | Rome—History—Empire, 30 B.C.–284 A.D.—Fiction. |
    GSAFD: Historical fiction. | Mystery fiction.
Classification: LCC PS3569.A96 T48 2018 | DDC 813/.54—dc23
LC record available at https://lccn.loc.gov/2017041306

ISBN 978-1-250-20903-0 (trade paperback)

Our books may be purchased in bulk for promotional, educational, or business use. Please contact your local bookseller or the Macmillan Corporate and Premium Sales Department at 1-800-221-7945, extension 5442, or by email at MacmillanSpecialMarkets@macmillan.com.

First Minotaur Books Paperback Edition: June 2019

10 9 8 7 6 5 4 3 2 1

To Rick,
there from the beginning

The primary and the most beautiful quality of Nature is motion, that agitates Her without ceasing—but this motion is simply a perpetual sequence of crimes, perpetuated by means of crimes alone; the person who most resembles Her—and therefore the most perfect being—necessarily will be the one whose most active agitation will become the cause of many crimes . . .

—DONATIEN ALPHONSE FRANÇOIS, MARQUIS DE SADE
Justine, ou les Malheurs de la vertu

A world without people in it would be better.

—LAWRENCE DURRELL
Sappho: A Play in Verse

DAY ONE: MARCH 10

I

Once upon a time, a young slave came to fetch me on a warm spring morning. That was the first time I met Tiro.

Many years later, he came to fetch me again. But now he was a freedman, no longer a slave. The month was Martius, and the morning was quite chilly. And we were both much older.

Just how old was Tiro? My head was muddled by last night's wine, but not so muddled that I couldn't do the math. Tiro was seven years younger than I. That made him . . . fifty-nine. Tiro—nearly sixty! How was that possible? Could thirty-six years have passed since the first time he came to my door?

On that occasion, Tiro was still a slave, though a very well-educated one. He was the private secretary and right-hand man of his master, an obscure young advocate by the name of Cicero who was just starting his career in Rome. All these years later, everyone in Rome knew of Cicero. He was as famous as Cato or Pompey (and still alive, which they were not). Cicero was almost as famous as our esteemed dictator. Almost, I say, because no one could ever be as famous as Caesar. Or as powerful. Or as rich.

"There was a dictator ruling Rome on that occasion, too," I muttered to myself.

"What's that, Gordianus?" asked Tiro, who had followed me through the atrium, down a dim hallway, and into the garden at the center of the house. Nothing was blooming yet, but patches of greenery shimmered in the morning sunlight. Crouching by the small fishpond, Bast—the latest in a long line of cats to bear that name—stared up at a bird that sang a pleasant song from a safe perch on a roof tile. I felt the faintest breath of spring in the chilly morning air.

I wrapped my cloak around me, sat on a wooden bench that caught the morning sunlight, and leaned back against one of the columns of the peristyle. Tiro sat on a bench nearby, facing me. I took a good look at him. He had been a handsome youth. He was still handsome, despite his years. Now, as then, his eyes were his most arresting feature. They were an unusual color, a pale shade of lavender, made all the more striking by the frame of his meticulously barbered white curls.

"I was just saying, Tiro . . ." I rubbed my temples, trying to soothe the stabbing pain in my head. "There was a dictator ruling Rome on that occasion, too. How old were you then?"

"When?"

"The first time I met you."

"Oh, let me think. I must have been . . . twenty-three? Yes, that's right. Cicero was twenty-six."

"And I was thirty. I was recalling that occasion. It wasn't at this house, of course. I was still living in that ramshackle place I inherited from my father, over on the Esquiline Hill, not here on the Palatine. And it was a warm day—the month was Maius, wasn't it? Then, as now, I answered the knock at the door myself—something my wife insists I should never do, since we have a slave for just that purpose. And . . . seeing you today at my front door . . . I had that feeling . . ."

"A feeling?"

"Oh, you know—we all feel it now and again—that uncanny sensation that one has experienced something before. A shivery feeling."

"Ah, yes, I know the phenomenon."

"One experiences it less as one grows older. I wonder why that is? And I wonder why we have no word for it in Latin. Perhaps you or Cicero should invent one. 'Already-seen,' or some other compound. Or borrow a word from some other language. The Etruscans had a word for it, I think."

"Did they?" Tiro raised an eyebrow. There was a mischievous glint in his lavender eyes.

"Yes, it will come to me. Or was it the Carthaginians? A pity we made Punic a dead language before plundering all the useful words. Oh, but my head is such a muddle this morning."

"Because you drank too much last night."

I looked at him askance. "Why do you say that?"

"The way you look, the way you walk. The way you sat down and leaned back against that column so gingerly, as if that thing on your shoulders were an egg that might crack."

It was true. My temples rolled with thunder. Spidery traces of lightning flashed and vanished just beyond the corners of my eyes. Last night's wine was to blame.

Tiro laughed. "You had a hangover on *that* morning, all those many years ago."

"Did I?"

"Oh, yes. I remember, because you taught me the cure for a hangover."

"I did? What was it? I could use it now."

"You must remember."

"I'm an old man, Tiro. I forget things."

"But you've been doing it ever since I got here. Asking questions. Trying to think of a word. *Thinking*—that's the cure."

"Ah, yes. I seem to have a vague recollection . . ."

"You had a very elegant explanation. I remember, because later I wrote it down, thinking Cicero might be able to use it in a speech or a treatise someday. I quote: 'Thought, according to some physicians, takes place in the brain, lubricated by the secretion of phlegm. When the phlegm becomes polluted or hardened, the result is a headache. But the actual activity of thought produces fresh phlegm to soften and disperse the old. So the more intently one thinks, the greater the production of phlegm. Therefore, intense concentration will speed along the natural recovery from a hangover by flushing the humors from the inflamed tissue and restoring the lubrication of the membranes.'"

"By Hercules, what a memory you have!" Tiro was famous for it. Cicero could dictate a letter, and a year later Tiro could quote it back to him verbatim. "And by Hercules, what a lot of rubbish I used to talk." I shook my head.

"And still do."

"What!" Had Tiro still been a slave, such a remark would have been impertinent. He had acquired a sharp tongue to match his sharp wits.

"I call your bluff, Gordianus."

"What bluff?"

"About that Etruscan word, the one that just happens to escape you. I don't believe any such word exists. I wish I had a denarius for every time I've heard someone say, 'The Etruscans had a word for it.' Or that the Etruscans invented this or that old saying, or this or that odd custom. Such assertions are almost invariably nonsense. Things Etruscan are old and quaint, and hardly anyone speaks the language anymore except the haruspices who perform the fatidic rites, a few villagers in the middle of nowhere, and a handful of crusty old dabblers in forgotten lore. Etruscan customs and words are therefore mysterious, and exert a certain mystique. But it's intellectually lazy to impute a saying or custom to the Etruscans when there's no evidence whatsoever for such an assertion."

"Even so, I'm pretty sure the Etruscans had a word—"

"Then I challenge you, Gordianus, to come up with that word by the last day of Martius—no, sooner, by the day you turn sixty-six. That's on the twenty-third day of the month, yes?"

"Now you're showing off, Tiro. But as for this word, I suspect it will come to me before you leave my house—and if you continue to vex me so, that may be sooner rather than later." I said this with a smile, for I was actually quite glad to see him. I had always been fond of Tiro, if not of his erstwhile master—on whose behalf, almost surely, Tiro had come to see me. Lightning again flashed in my temples, causing me to wince. "This 'cure' seems not to be working as well as it did when I was younger—perhaps because my wits are not as sharp as they used to be."

"Whose are?" asked Tiro with a sigh.

"Or perhaps I'm drinking more than I used to. Too many long winter nights at the Salacious Tavern spent in dubious company—to the dreaded displeasure of my wife and daughter. Ah, wait! I remember now—not that elusive Etruscan word, but the little game of mental gymnastics I played with you the first time we met, which not only cured my hangover but quite impressed you with my powers of deduction."

"That's right, Gordianus. You correctly deduced the exact reason I had come to see you."

"And I can do the same thing today."

Tiro folded his arms across his chest and gave me a challenging look. He was about to speak when he was interrupted by Diana, who stepped from the shadows of the portico into the sunlight.

"I can do likewise," said my daughter.

Tiro looked a bit flustered as he stood to greet the newcomer. He cocked his head. "Now *I'm* the one who's having that feeling—that eerie sensation we need a word for. Because on the morning we first met, Gordianus, surely this very same ravishing female appeared from nowhere and took my breath away. But how can that be? Truly, it's as if I've stepped back in time."

I smiled. "*That* was Bethesda, who joined us that morning. *This* is her daughter—our daughter—Diana."

Diana accepted Tiro's compliment without comment. And why not? She *was* ravishing—breathtaking, in fact—just as her mother had been, with thick, shimmering black hair, bright eyes, and a shapely figure that even her matronly stola did little to conceal.

She raised an eyebrow and gave me a disapproving glance. "Did you answer the door yourself, Papa? You know we have a slave for that."

"You *sound* like your mother, too!" I laughed. "But you were just saying that you could deduce the reason for Tiro's visit. Do proceed."

"Very well. First, who sent Tiro?" She peered at him so intently that he blushed. Tiro had always been shy around beautiful women. "Well, that's easy. Marcus Tullius Cicero, of course."

"Who says that anyone sent me?" objected Tiro. "I'm a free citizen."

"Yes, you could have come to visit my father on your own initiative—but you never do, though he invariably enjoys your company. You contact him only when Cicero asks you to."

Tiro blushed again. A red-faced youth is charming. A red-faced man nearing sixty looks rather alarming. But his laugh reassured me. "As a matter of fact, you're right. I came here at Cicero's behest."

Diana nodded. "And why has Cicero sent you? Well, almost certainly it has something to do with the Dictator."

"Why do you say that?" asked Tiro.

"Because anything and everything that happens nowadays has something to do with Julius Caesar."

"You are correct," conceded Tiro. "But you'll have to be more specific if you want to impress me."

"Or if you want to impress *me*," I added. Diana was always seeking to demonstrate to me her powers of ratiocination. This was part of her ongoing campaign to convince me that she should be allowed to carry on the family profession—my father and I had both been called 'the Finder' in our respective generations—to which my invariable response was that a twenty-five-year-old Roman matron with two children to raise, no matter how clever she might be, had no business sorting out clues and solving crimes and otherwise sticking her nose into dangerous people's business. "Go on, daughter. Tell us, if you can, why Cicero sent Tiro to fetch me this morning."

Diana shut her eyes and pressed her fingertips to her temples, elbows akimbo, as if channeling some mystic source of knowledge. "The first time you met my father was in the second year of Sulla's dictatorship. You came to ask for the Finder's assistance to help Cicero uncover the truth behind a shocking crime—an unholy crime. Vile. Unspeakable. The murder of a father by his own son. Parricide!"

Tiro made a scoffing sound, but in fact he looked a bit unnerved by Diana's mystic pose. "Well, it's no secret that the defense of Sextus

Roscius was Cicero's first major trial, remembered by everyone who was in Rome at the time. Obviously, your father has told you about his own role in the investigation—"

"No, Tiro, let her go on," I said, captivated despite myself by Diana's performance.

Her eyelids flickered and her voice dropped in pitch. "Now you come again to ask for my father's help, in this, the fifth year of Caesar's dictatorship. Again, it's about a crime, but a crime that has yet to be committed. A crime even more shocking than the murder of Sextus Roscius—and even more unholy. Vile. Unspeakable. The murder of another father by his children—"

"No, no, no," said Tiro, shaking his head a bit too insistently.

"Oh, yes!" declared Diana, her eyes still flickering. "For hasn't the intended victim been named Father of the Fatherland—so that any Roman who dared to kill him would be a parricide? And hasn't every senator taken a vow to protect this man's life with his very own—so that any senator who raised a hand against him would be committing sacrilege?"

Tiro opened his mouth, dumbfounded.

"Isn't this the reason you've come here today, Tiro?" said Diana, opening her eyes and staring into his. "You want the Finder to come to Cicero and reveal to him whatever he may know, or be able to discover, regarding the plot to murder the Dictator, the Father of the Fatherland—the conspiracy to assassinate Gaius Julius Caesar."

II

Tiro looked from Diana to me and back again. "But how could either of you possibly . . . ? Has someone been spying on Cicero and me? And what is this plot you speak of? What do you know about—"

Diana threw back her head and laughed, delighted by his reaction.

I clicked my tongue. "Really, daughter, it's unkind of you to disconcert our guest."

"Is there a plot against Caesar, or isn't there?" said Tiro. His worldly, commanding presence fell away and I had a glimpse of him as I had first seen him all those many years ago, bright and eager but easily alarmed, easily impressed.

I sighed. "I'm afraid my daughter has seen her father pull such tricks on visitors too many times over the years, and she cannot resist doing so herself. No, Tiro, there is no plot to murder Caesar—at least none that I know of. And Diana certainly knows no more than I do. Or do you, Diana?"

"Of course I don't, Papa. How could I possibly know more than you do about what's going on out there in the big, bad world?" She batted her eyes and put on a blank expression. Many times over the years I have been made aware that women, despite the constraints of their sheltered

existence, do in fact have ways of discovering things that remain unknown and mysterious even to the fathers and husbands who rule over
them. I could never be sure exactly what Diana knew, or how she came
to know it.

I cleared my throat. "I suspect that my daughter simply followed a
line of reasoning—taking her cues from your reactions, which are as easy
to read now as when you were a youth. Add to her capacity for deduction a certain degree of intuition—inherited from her mother—and you
begin to see how Diana was able, essentially, to read your mind."

Tiro frowned. "Even so—I never said a word about . . . any sort of . . .
conspiracy."

"You never had to. We had already established that your visit had
something to do with the Dictator. Now what could that be, and why
come to me? To be sure, I have a link to Caesar—my son Meto is quite
close to him. Over the years, he's helped the Dictator write his memoirs. Meto will continue to do so when he leaves Rome before the end of
the month, when the Dictator heads off to conquer Parthia. Could it be
that Cicero is so eager to know when the next volume of Caesar's memoirs will be published that he would call me to his house to ask me? I
think not. And as for anything to do with Caesar or the Parthian campaign that isn't already common knowledge—well, Cicero knows that I
would never let slip anything Meto might have told me in confidence.

"So, what is this concern of Cicero's, having to do with Caesar, and
why summon me? Most likely it's something to do with crime or
conspiracy—those are the areas where my skills and his interests have
intersected in the past. But what crime? What conspiracy?

"If this were ten years ago, or even five, I'd presume that Cicero was
mounting a defense for an upcoming trial. But there are no trials any
longer, not in the old-fashioned sense. All courts are under the jurisdic-
tion of the Dictator. And everyone knows that poor Cicero's voice has
grown rusty, with no speeches to give in the Senate or orations to deliver at a trial. They say he spends his time reading obscure old texts and
writing yet more texts for lovers of abstruse lore to pore over in the distant future. What is Cicero working on now, Tiro?"

"He's very nearly finished with his treatise on divination. It's going to be the standard text for any—"

"Ha! No wonder you're up on your Etruscan vocabulary, if you've been helping Cicero translate texts on haruspicy. Well, I doubt that Cicero wants to pick my brain about such matters, since I know no more about divination than the average Roman."

"Actually, Papa, I suspect you know more than you realize," said Diana.

"Kind words, daughter. Nevertheless, I think we're back to crime or conspiracy. Who has *not* heard the rumors flitting about Rome the last couple of months—rumors that someone intends to kill Caesar? But how credible are such rumors? Certainly, after so many years of bloodshed and civil war, there must be quite a few citizens who would like to see our dictator dead. But who are they? How many are out there? Is it only a disgruntled senator or two, or is Rome full of such men? Do they have the will and the capacity to act? Do they have *time* to act? Because once Caesar leaves for Parthia, each day will take him farther and farther from Rome—a general on campaign, surrounded by handpicked officers every minute of the day, virtually impossible to kill.

"Is there or is there not a plot afoot to kill Caesar? That's a question Cicero must have on his mind these days. It's on my mind as well. After so much suffering in the past few years, we all wonder what the future might hold—and no Roman can imagine the future now without taking Caesar into account, one way or another. The death of Caesar—well, it's almost unthinkable. Or . . . is it?"

Tiro made no answer. He was looking across the pond at Bast, staring at the unmoving cat that crouched and stared at a twittering bird on a roof tile.

"Or," I continued, struck by a terrible thought, "I suppose it could be that Cicero is part of such a conspiracy—and he thinks he might be able to recruit me."

"Certainly not!" protested Tiro. He gave such a start that the bird flitted off and the cat bolted away, its claws scraping the paving stones. "Cicero is most certainly not involved in any plot to harm the Dictator," he said, so distinctly it was almost as if he feared some spy might be listening to us.

"But he nevertheless thinks that *I* might know something in this regard," I said. "I suppose that makes sense. My son Meto might have let slip some detail arising from Caesar's own network of informers. But I would never share such privileged intelligence with Cicero, or with anyone else."

Tiro sighed. "Even so, Gordianus, Cicero very much wants to talk to you. Won't you come—as a favor to me, if not to him?"

Diana took a step closer. "Perhaps we should go, Papa."

"We? Oh, no, you won't be coming along, dear daughter. Though I suppose I should take that hulking husband of yours for a bodyguard. Would you fetch Davus for me, Diana?"

"But Papa—"

As if to illustrate where her priorities should lie, her two children suddenly joined us. Aulus hurtled straight toward me. Little Beth toddled after him. I gathered my arms around them and sat one on each knee, groaning at the weight. Beth was still tiny, but at the age of seven Aulus was getting bigger every day. Perhaps he would grow to be as big as his father.

The children's nursemaid appeared, a look of chagrin on her wrinkled face. "Apologies, Mistress! Apologies, Master! I don't seem to have enough hands to hold the two of them when they're determined to run to their grandfather."

"It's no bother, Makris," I said. "You would need as many arms as the hydra has heads to hold these two in check."

I glanced at Tiro and saw a wistful look on his face. Whatever else the Fates had given him—a good master, then freedom, then a considerable degree of prestige and the respect of his fellow citizens—they had not given him progeny.

"But Papa, surely we should offer refreshments to your guest," said Diana.

"Morning refreshment will be supplied, but by Cicero, not by me. Quit stalling, daughter, and fetch Davus."

"It's such a short walk," said Tiro, standing up. "My own bodyguard is waiting for us outside. Later, he can walk you home—"

"Then how would Davus report to Diana all he sees and hears? Yes, daughter, I know you dream that the two of you should someday work as a team—you the brains, him the brawn."

Diana made a grunt of exasperation, then went to find her husband.

"I trust that Cicero *will* supply refreshment?" I said to Tiro as I gently ejected the children from my knees, one at a time. "I have cause for celebration."

"What's that?"

"My hangover is cured!"

III

When first we met, I had lived on the Esquiline Hill and Cicero near the Capitoline Hill. To visit him I had to traverse both the Subura (Rome's roughest neighborhood) and much of the Forum (the heart of Rome, with its splendid temples and magnificent public spaces). Since then we had both moved up in the world. My house and his were both on the Palatine Hill, Rome's most exclusive area. We were practically neighbors.

At one point during the short walk, I had a clear view of the top of the Capitoline Hill to the north, crowned by the Temple of Jupiter, one of the most imposing structures on earth. In a prominent place before the temple stood a bronze statue. Though the features were indistinct at such a great distance, I knew the statue well, having seen it unveiled on the day of Caesar's Gallic Triumph. Standing atop a map of the world, striking a victorious pose and looking down on the Roman Forum below, stood not a mere mortal but a demigod—so declared the inscription on the pedestal, which listed Caesar's many titles, ending with the declaration, DESCENDANT OF VENUS, DEMIGOD. The statue was visible from virtually every part of the city.

"And who would dare to kill a demigod?" I muttered.

"What's that?" said Tiro.

"Nothing. Talking to myself again. Something I seem to do quite often these days."

As we approached Cicero's house, I saw a brutish-looking guard standing outside the front door, a man with a face that could frighten small children to tears. My son-in-law nudged me and indicated another watchman pacing the roof. He and Davus acknowledged each other with small nods, as neutral bodyguards do. The guard at the door nodded to Tiro, kicked the door with his heel, and stepped aside. Not a word was spoken, yet the door opened for us the moment Tiro set foot on the stone threshold. There was yet another guard in the vestibule. The slave who had opened the door and closed it behind us remained out of sight, as if invisible.

Cicero had developed a mania for security over the years. Who could blame him? At the peak of his political career the tide had turned so viciously against him that he was driven into exile. His previous house on the Palatine had been burned to the ground. Eventually his exile was rescinded by the Senate and he was welcomed back. He moved into another house on the Palatine—and then was forced to flee the city when Caesar crossed the Rubicon and headed for Rome with an army. I vividly remembered visiting him the day he frantically packed his most precious scrolls and valuables, lost in a haze of despair. Now Cicero was back in Rome, pardoned by the Dictator, but clearly uncertain of the future and braced for any new reversal of fortune.

I spared a glance at the wax masks of Cicero's ancestors in the niches of the vestibule, which unblinkingly watched everyone who came and went. They were a stern-looking bunch, and not very handsome. Some of them exhibited the chickpea-like cleft nose that had earned the family its distinctive cognomen.

Leaving his own bodyguard behind in the vestibule, Tiro led Davus and me past the shallow pool of the atrium and down a hallway to Cicero's library. Tiro entered the room first. Cicero, seated and clutching a metal stylus and a wax tablet, hardly looked up. He appeared not to notice that Davus and I had also entered the room.

"Tiro! Thank Jupiter you're back! I've been struggling with this passage ever since you left. Here, tell me what you think: 'Why, the very word "Fate" is full of superstition and old women's credulity. For if all things happen by Fate, it does us no good to be warned to be on our guard, since that which *is* to happen *will* happen, regardless of what we do. But if that which is to be *can* be turned aside, there is no such thing as Fate. So, too, there can be no such thing as divination—since divination deals with things that are going to happen.' There. Is it clear enough?"

"Even I can understand it," I said.

"Gordianus!" Cicero finally noticed me and flashed a broad smile. "And . . ." He frowned as he tried to think of the name. "Davus, isn't it? By Hercules, you're a strapping fellow, aren't you?"

Davus grunted, at a loss for words, as he often was.

"You needn't say anything, son-in-law," I said. "That's called a rhetorical question and requires no reply."

Cicero laughed and put down his stylus and tablet. "Teaching him rhetoric, are you? Alas, too late, since there's no use for it anymore. Please, all of you, take a seat!" A pair of young slaves produced chairs from various corners of the cluttered space, and then, at a signal from their master, left the room.

"You seem to be in a good mood," I said, genuinely surprised. When I had last seen him, Cicero had the consolation of a teenage bride to distract him from the sorry state of the Republic, but that marriage had ended in divorce. Another blow had occurred at about the same time, when the light of his life, his beloved daughter Tullia, died in childbirth. On this Martius morning he seemed unaccountably cheerful.

"And why not?" he said. "Spring is almost here. Can't you feel it in the air? And at long last I have the time and resources to do what I've wanted to do all my life: write books."

"You've always written."

"Oh, a trifle here and there, speeches and such, but I mean *real* books—long philosophic tracts and discourses, books that will stand the test of time. There was never opportunity for that kind of writing when I was busy in the law courts and the Senate, and certainly not when

I was away from Rome, slogging from camp to camp, marching with Pompey to save the Republic. Alas, alas!" He sighed, then reached for another tablet. There were a great many of these stacked on small tables and tucked amid the shelves that housed the hundreds of scrolls that made up Cicero's library. Apparently he jotted down any idea that occurred to him, and he needed many tablets. Grudgingly, I had to admire his ability to stay busy and find purpose after all the disappointments and disasters that had befallen him.

"Here, speaking of Pompey, listen to this." He read aloud. " 'Even if we could foretell the future, would we wish to do so? Would Pompey have found joy in his three consulships, his three triumphs, and the fame of his transcendent deeds if he had known that he would be driven from Rome, lose his army, and then be slain like a dog in an Egyptian desert, and that following his death those terrible events would occur of which I cannot speak without tears?' " His voice quivered as he read the final words, but he smiled with satisfaction as he looked up.

"Not 'like a dog,' " said Tiro. "Too harsh."

"Oh? Should I remove it?" Cicero peered at the tablet. "Yes, of course, you're right, Tiro, as you invariably are." He scratched out the words with his stylus. "Pompey was a true believer in portents and omens, you know. He placed great reliance on divination by those Etruscan haruspices who poke about entrails, looking for odd spots or growths on this organ or that. A lot of good it did him. And you, Gordianus? Do you consort with haruspices?"

"I've known a haruspex or two in my time. There was one particularly favored by Caesar's wife—"

"Which wife?" quipped Cicero. "His ex-wife, his current wife, or his Egyptian whore across the Tiber?" This last remark referred to Queen Cleopatra, who was making her second state visit to Rome and residing at Caesar's lavish garden estate outside the city.

"As far as I know, Caesar has only one wife: Calpurnia. I was somewhat acquainted with her favorite haruspex, Porsenna—"

"Ah, that unfortunate fellow! Reading entrails didn't save him from his sorry end, did it? More irony! Perhaps I should add his example to my discourse. She has another one now, you know."

"I beg your pardon?"

"Calpurnia. She has another haruspex hanging about her house, telling her which days are safe for Caesar to be out and about, especially since he stopped using his bodyguards. Not that Caesar himself pays any attention to Spurinna, but he did make the fellow a senator, if you can believe it. An Etruscan diviner, in the Roman Senate! What would our forefathers make of that?" Cicero shook his head. "At least Spurinna comes from an old and distinguished Etruscan family. It's those other new members of the Senate who gall me—the Gauls, I mean. Outrageous!"

With so many of the leading men of Rome killed in the civil war, the ranks of the Senate had been greatly depleted. To fill the chamber, Caesar had appointed hundreds of new senators, rewarding his supporters and allies, and not just men of Roman blood. With roughly half of the eight hundred or so senators appointed by Caesar, many of the older members complained that Caesar had rigged the odds, making sure that any vote in the Senate would be in his favor, now and for the foreseeable future. "How better to avoid another civil war?" Meto had said to me, defending the man who was his commander and mentor, and now everyone's dictator.

"So you're not a believer in divination?" I asked.

"Gordianus, how long have you known me? Second sight, soothsaying, mind-reading, fortune-telling, seers and portents and oracles—you know I have no faith whatsoever in such things."

"So your discourse debunks divination?"

"Ruthlessly. Of course, at the end I have to express some support for it, as a tool of political expediency, in order that we may have a state religion. How did we decide to put it, Tiro?"

Tiro quoted: "'However, out of respect for the opinion of the masses and because of the great service to the state, we maintain the augural practices, discipline, religious rites and laws, as well as the authority of the augural college.' Of course, that refers to Roman rites of divination, not the Etruscan rites."

That was Cicero, I thought, always slippery with words, whether arguing in the law courts or writing a scholarly treatise. He had been the same when choosing between Caesar and Pompey, waiting until the last possible moment, and then joining the losing side. That mistake had made him more cautious than ever. What did he really want from me? The moment had not yet come to press him about that. "Perhaps we might have refreshment?"

"Of course! What am I thinking, making you sit there with empty hands and empty stomachs! Tiro, can you see to that?"

Tiro nodded and slipped out of the room.

"Ah, yes, Pompey and his superstitions," said Cicero. "Cato was quite the opposite. Cato thought that haruspices were downright disreputable, and also ridiculous, especially with those conical caps on their heads . . ."

I supplied Cato's well-known quote: " 'When one haruspex passes another in the street, it's a wonder that either one of them can keep a straight face.' "

Cicero smiled wistfully. "Alas, poor Cato, he fared no better than Pompey in the end, cornered by Caesar's troops in Africa like some beast of prey and driven to a messy suicide. By Hercules, I must include Cato's words somewhere in the treatise." He reached for his stylus and tablet, then put them down. "Ah, but I've neglected one of my principal reasons for wanting to see you, Gordianus—to congratulate you."

"For what?" It seemed to me I had been doing very little lately, other than sitting in my wintry garden and making an occasional excursion to the Salacious Tavern and back.

"Please, Gordianus, you needn't be modest. I refer to the change in your status as a citizen—your elevation to the Equestrian class."

"How in Hades do you know about that?"

"From the postings in the Forum. You know I dispatch a slave every day to peruse the lists—notifications of deaths and funerals, marriage announcements, and so on. When I was told that your name had appeared on the roster of new Equestrians, I was delighted for you. I won't ask how you managed to accumulate that much wealth in the last year or two—"

"Entirely by honest means, I assure you."

"Ah, well, there are plenty of men in Rome who got there by other ways."

This was true. Many fortunes had been made, as well as lost, in the chaos of the civil war, often by shadowy means or outright crime. I had in fact come out of the war years better off than when they started, thanks to a particularly generous remuneration from none other than Calpurnia, for my hard work and discretion involving a matter that I had no intention of explaining to Cicero. Among Caesar's tools for restoring order was a canvassing of wealth. My good fortune had not gone unrecorded; hence my registration in the Equestrian class traditionally made up of wealthy merchants and landowners. When formally dressed in a toga, I had the right to wear underneath it a tunic with a narrow red stripe over the shoulder not covered by the toga. By this visible red stripe all men would know me as an Equestrian. I had not yet bothered to obtain this garment. Members of the Roman Senate, a class defined more by power than wealth, wore a tunic with a broad red stripe, not a narrow one—a subtle but significant distinction.

"You should be very proud, Gordianus. When one thinks of how far you've come from your beginnings—"

"I'm no better a man than my father was," I said brusquely. In fact, my father would have been delighted at my elevation in status, something he could never have dreamed of. "As far as I can see, the honor has only drawbacks. I'll be made to pay more taxes, and serve on committees, and maybe even on juries, if the legal system ever returns to normal."

"Have you thought of that word yet?" said Tiro, stepping back into the room. Two young female slaves followed him, one carrying a tray with pitchers of water and wine and cups, and the other carrying a tray of delicacies in silver bowls. I saw olives of many hues, dried dates and figs, and little honey cakes. Next to me I heard Davus's stomach growl.

"What word?" I asked. "Oh, you mean that elusive Etruscan word for the universal sensation of having experienced this very moment at some previous time."

"A universal sensation?" asked Cicero.

"Yes. Everyone experiences it."

"Not me."

"No?"

"I've no idea what you're talking about."

"Ah, well. Then you'll be of no help in coming up with that Etruscan word for it. So perhaps we should move on to the reason you wanted to see me—other than congratulations on my dubious rise in the world."

"And what would that be?" asked Cicero, raising an eyebrow and glancing at Tiro, who raised an eyebrow back at him.

"I didn't tell him," said Tiro. "He guessed."

"Actually, it was Diana," said Davus, speaking up to make sure his wife received due credit.

"Yes, Cicero," I said, "shall we talk about the assassination of Julius Caesar?"

Cicero blanched at hearing the words spoken so openly. Was it that expression on his face, or the light in the room, or the disposition of the many-colored olives in their silver bowl, or something else altogether that caused me, in that very moment, to experience the sensation I had just been talking about? Even as those brash words left my lips, some memory of the past—or premonition of the future—caused me to shiver and feel an icy chill down my spine.

IV

Cicero took a deep breath. "If you already know so very much, Gordianus, perhaps you also know about the warning that Spurinna the haruspex delivered to Caesar less than a month ago."

"I've heard the story," I said. In fact, my son Meto had told me, scoffing at every detail. It was on the first day the Dictator appeared in public wearing purple robes and a laurel crown, seated on an ornately gilded chair. He had been voted these unprecedented honors by the Senate. No man had worn purple and sat on a throne in the Forum since the last of the hated kings was driven out and Rome became a republic, more than four hundred years ago. The Dictator's regal trappings overshadowed the actual event, a religious rite at which an ox was sacrificed on the altar. The newly appointed senator Spurinna, as presiding haruspex, examined the entrails and other organs. He was unable to find the heart. A sacrifice without a heart boded ill, he said. The very heart of the Roman state, Caesar, was in danger, and would be so for the next thirty days.

"Spurinna warned Caesar to be on his guard until the Ides of March," I said.

"Yes," said Cicero, "the omen foretold a month of danger—a period that will end just before Caesar leaves Rome for the Parthian campaign.

Well, that only makes sense. The greatest dangers to Caesar must be here in the city, where his surviving foes have all come home, now that the civil war is over. Once he leaves for Parthia with his devoted companions, he leaves behind anyone who might wish him harm."

"Yes, I noticed the specific time period of the warning," I said. "Perhaps Spurinna wants to be taken along on the expedition. He can deliver a new omen every thirty days, and make himself invaluable to Caesar in perpetuity, rolling ever forward like the new calendar Caesar gave us."

"Are you implying that the soothsayer manufactured the omen to augment his own importance?" said Cicero. "Yes, that's certainly possible. On the other hand, it could be that Spurinna actually knows something, or thinks he knows something, about an actual plot to harm our dictator."

"Then why not tell Caesar outright what he knows or suspects?"

"Yes, why be so devious? But that's the way with some people, especially those unskilled in rhetoric, who must use whatever means of persuasion they can. Or . . . could it be that Spurinna, though in every way an ally, even a creature, of Caesar, was taken aback when he saw the Dictator's purple robes and golden chair? Perhaps Spurinna, as a friend of Caesar, nonetheless thought the man needed to be taken down a peg—and to do so, the haruspex tried to humble him with a warning, thus to turn away the Evil Eye of the envious."

"Like that fellow who stands behind a Roman general in his chariot when there's a triumph," said Davus, "reminding him that he's as mortal as every other man."

I looked sidelong at my son-in-law, who every now and then could be quite astute. I shook my head. "Your mind is too subtle for the likes of me, Cicero. What does all this matter, anyway? It's my understanding that Caesar paid no attention to the omen. He still wears purple. He still sits in that golden chair when it suits him. He goes wherever he pleases all over the city, no longer bothering to take along his famous band of bodyguards from Spain. I should think Caesar knows better than Spurinna who wishes him ill and if they're dangerous, and nonetheless he chooses to walk about unguarded."

"But what if Spurinna was motivated to speak because he knows of some real danger?"

I shrugged. "Perhaps *you* have some secret knowledge of a threat to Caesar," I said.

Cicero jumped up from his chair. "That's exactly the problem! I *don't* know what's going on! Caesar hardly speaks to me. When he does, he shares nothing of importance. His friends and allies snub me. Some, like Antony, openly despise me. As for what remains of the opposition—fine, upstanding Romans, men of honor and good pedigree, brave young men—they no longer include me in their deliberations. Oh, they make a show of respecting me. They address me as Consul, to honor my past service to the state. They invite me to dinner. They ask me to read from my latest treatise, and laugh in all the right places. But I'm always the first to go home from those dinners. The host bids me farewell, and the rest of the guests linger behind. I see the looks they give one another, as if to say, 'Thank goodness the old fellow is finally leaving! Now we can let down our guard and talk about what's really on our minds.'"

"Surely not," I said. "What dinner host would ever want to see the back of Marcus Tullius Cicero?" I kept a straight face, but Tiro shot me a reprimanding look. "Who are these men, anyway?"

Cicero bit his lower lip. "I'm talking about men much younger than myself, in their twenties and thirties, or barely into their forties. They survived the civil war with their lives intact, if not their fortunes. They still harbor certain ambitions that were instilled in them from boyhood—to win elections, to lead armies by appointment of the Senate, perhaps even to be elected consul. Thwarted ambitions—since only one man now decides who will command the legions or serve as magistrates. They smile and nod to the Dictator. They feign gratitude for the crumbs he gives them. They pretend to be satisfied, but they're not. How could they be?"

"What are these younger men to you, Cicero? And what are you to them?"

He sighed. "They are the upstart new generation, and I am the wise elder—by Hercules, how did I ever grow old enough for that to happen?"

He cocked his head a certain way, with a bemused expression, and for just a moment I saw him as he had been when I first met him—an ambitious young advocate, more sure of himself than he had any reason to be, brimming with enthusiasm, on fire to make the world sit up and take notice of him. Then the moment passed and I saw him as he was now. A spark of that youthful flame yet remained in his eyes, but dampened by bitterness and regret.

"The civil war was very hard on our generation, Cicero. There aren't many of us 'wise elders' left. You and I are lucky to still be alive."

"All the more reason you might think these younger men would be eager to seek my advice and take advantage of my experience."

"Yet you sense that something is going on behind your back. Is it that you think there's a plot against Caesar, and you feel left out?" I said.

"Of course not!" He spoke a bit too quickly.

"Or is it that you suspect such a plot, and you wish to stop it?"

He began to answer, then caught himself and exchanged a guarded look with Tiro. He spoke slowly and carefully. "If there were such a plot, one might wish to thwart it not just to save Caesar but also to save the conspirators from themselves. That is, if one believed that the murder of Caesar would serve only to open yet another Pandora's box of chaos."

"And is that what you believe, Cicero? That Rome is better off with Caesar alive than with Caesar dead?"

He spoke even more cautiously. "Caesar has been voted dictator for the duration of his lifetime—"

"By a Roman Senate packed with men chosen by Caesar himself."

"In a matter of days he'll meet with the Senate to make some final appointments and ratify some last bits of pending legislation, and then he'll join his troops and head for Parthia. Perhaps he'll rendezvous with Queen Cleopatra in Egypt on the way; Caesar will need the grain of the Nile to feed his army. And then . . . but who knows what will happen to Caesar in the months and years to come? Crassus staged the last Roman invasion of Parthia. His legions were annihilated and his head ended up as a stage prop for a king. Of course, Caesar is ten times—no, a hundred times—the military leader Crassus was. No one doubts that he'll have his way with the Parthians. But once he's conquered Parthia, repeating the success of Alexander the Great, like Alexander he may find it necessary to stay in that part of the world to govern it. Caesar may never come back to Rome."

"Alexander might have returned to Macedon had he not died suddenly, so far from home."

"Caesar, too, someday will die."

"Is that the counsel you'd give to any hotheads who'd like to see Caesar dead and out of the way? To patiently await their turn, because every man dies sooner or later? No wonder the youngbloods see you off to bed before they get down to business!"

This was so harsh that even Davus furrowed his brow and frowned at me. If I spoke out of turn, it was because Cicero had touched a nerve. Where Caesar went, so too would Meto go. If Caesar never came back, I might never see my son again.

"Apologies, Cicero. You're absolutely right that the younger generation of senators should be looking to you for insight and inspiration. You're a survivor, if nothing else."

"Cicero is much more than that," said Tiro, rising to his old master's defense. "He saved the state once, when he was consul and put down Catilina's insurrection. He may just save the state again, if given the chance."

I drew a deep breath. So that was it—Cicero thought he might yet become the savior of the Roman Republic. The puttering, even pathetic old scholar was just a pose. Cicero aspired to write the next chapter of Roman history, and thought himself capable of doing so—if only other Romans would look to him for leadership.

"What is it you want from me?" I said quietly.

"Only this, Gordianus: that you put your ear to the ground, and share with me, through Tiro, any rumblings you might hear. You're so good at that sort of thing—making sense of rumors, knowing whom and what to ask, seeing what others fail to see. Think of the occasions when you and I worked together over the years—remember our first collaboration, when we tweaked the nose of the dictator Sulla! If those memories mean anything to you, all I ask is that you share with me any information you come across regarding any plot to do away with the Dictator. What I do with that information will be my own business, leaving you blameless . . . if I should take a misstep. Once Caesar leaves Rome, the situation will change completely, and I'll ask no more of you after that."

"We're talking about a matter of days, Gordianus," said Tiro.

"Why you think *I* might know anything of importance . . ." I shook my head.

"You have a way of acquiring other people's secrets without even trying," said Cicero, "rather like the iron of Magnesia that attracts other bits of metal to itself."

"Exactly so!" agreed Tiro, who reached for a stylus and tablet to jot down the comparison. Would it be filed with other items about me, for inclusion in the memoirs Cicero planned to write someday?

I looked at Davus, seeking silent solace in his bovine features, but he seemed to think my glance required a comment. He cleared his throat. "They're right, you know. Some days, whether you like it or not, you're covered all over, from head to feet, with other people's secrets."

I tried to picture such an image, and failed—what, after all, do secrets look like?—but I knew exactly what the three of them meant. Sometimes I sought out secrets, but at other times, very often, they came to me unbidden.

"Such was the blessing the gods gave me," I said quietly. "Sometimes, the curse."

V

I took my leave of Cicero with no agreement to see him again, much less report to him. Probably he thought otherwise, having endless faith in his powers of persuasion. It was hard for Cicero to hear the word "no."

As Davus and I strolled toward my house, a thought struck me: Might Cicero himself be part of some plot against Caesar? If that were the case, his questioning of me might have been aimed at discovering what Caesar himself knew or suspected, information I might have learned from Meto. That Cicero could be so conniving I had no doubt, but that he was part of a plot to kill Caesar I could not credit. To murder in cold blood was not Cicero's way. This was not to say he was squeamish. When he was consul, he had put Catilina's supporters to death without blinking an eye, and even boasted of it—behavior that led to his temporary exile. But those had been executions carried out by the state. Legality made all the difference to Cicero, who lived and breathed Roman law. If Caesar could be put on trial and condemned to exile or death by legal means, then Cicero might enthusiastically take part. Any number of Caesar's actions since crossing the Rubicon might be construed as capital offenses against the state. But to kill the man without legal sanction— no, I couldn't see Cicero taking part in any clandestine scheme.

That meant he was genuinely in the dark about such activity, if in fact it was happening. He didn't like feeling uncertain and excluded, and to inform himself he had called on me. Cicero wasn't merely curious, he was alarmed. His political instincts had become unreliable in recent years, but they still counted for something. If Cicero was alarmed, should I be also? And should I convey the details of our encounter to Meto, who might then convey them to Caesar?

Davus and I rounded a corner, and my house came into view. An expensive-looking litter with expensive-looking bearers was stationed in front of my door. Expensive but not ostentatious. The wooden poles were beautifully carved with a leafy pattern, but not painted or gilded, and while the curtains appeared to be of silk, they were a somber grayish-green color, without tassels or other gewgaws. They were also drawn back, so that I could see that the compartment, strewn with silk cushions of the same somber color, was empty. The visitor must be inside my house.

I had already received one unexpected caller that morning. I was not looking forward to another. "An old man deserves a bit of peace and quiet," I muttered to myself. Davus overheard and nodded in agreement.

The bearers were dressed in identical loose-fitting tunics of a color similar to the curtains, but made of linen, not silk. The one in charge glanced at me as I approached my front door, appraised my status, then lowered his eyes. They were all big fellows, bigger even than Davus, and looked quite capable of acting as bodyguards as well as bearers. The fact that their leader took careful notice of an approaching citizen and then averted his gaze meant that they were exceptionally well trained. How many surly, ill-tempered bodyguards owned by other men had I endured over the years, even though I was a citizen and they were slaves?

I knocked at the door. The slave whose job it was to peek at visitors through a narrow opening did so, then hurriedly allowed me in. Diana appeared in the atrium, looking radiant under the slanting column of sunshine from the skylight above.

"Papa! You'll never guess who's here!"

"I had no idea until this moment, but from the look on your face I think it must be Meto."

"Right you are, Papa." Meto stepped into the sunshine beside his sister. Though they shared no kinship by blood, to my eyes they looked much alike, and equally beautiful. Meto, not quite thirty-five, still had a boyish smile. He was dressed not in military garb but in a toga. While I gave him a warm embrace, I saw from the corner of my eye that Diana was greeting Davus with a kiss that was anything but perfunctory.

"How curious that you should pay us a visit," I said to Meto. "I was just thinking about you."

"Good thoughts, I hope."

"Better thoughts than most I've had this morning."

"Diana says Tiro called on you and dragged you off to Cicero's house."

"Yes."

"What can that broken stylus want from you?"

"Oh, you might be surprised."

"Or not," said Diana, speaking from Davus's encircling arms. "Oh, Papa, the look on your face! Don't worry, I kept my mouth shut. I know it's your business, not mine, to inform Meto about your dealings. I told him where you'd gone and said no more. You men are so touchy about such things."

"So true, daughter," said another voice, a bit deeper than Diana's but of the same timbre. "A woman must never spoil a bit of gossip before a man can deliver it himself."

"Good morning, wife," I said, stepping to Bethesda and giving her a kiss more modest than that exchanged by Davus and my daughter. "I let you sleep late. You look all the lovelier for it."

She squared her shoulders, ran her fingers through her silver and black tresses, and made a quiet snort. "You thought I was asleep when you came home last night and when you rose this morning, but I wasn't. You came home inebriated and you woke with a terrible headache. I heard you groaning."

"Bethesda, must you reprimand me in front of my children?"

"If I don't do it, who will?"

I sighed. "Shouldn't you be in the kitchen, wife, telling the cook what to fix for our midday meal? We'll need an extra portion for Meto.

Perhaps a double portion," I said, looking at him. It seemed to me that he was at the very peak of manhood, bursting with vitality—an ideal warrior to head off to Parthia with Caesar. The thought filled me with both pride and dread.

"I'm afraid I can't stay to eat," he said. "Nor can you, Papa."

"Why not?" Even as I spoke, I knew the answer. Meto would never have arrived in a litter like the one outside my door if he had simply come to pay a visit. It was the sort of conveyance, comfortable yet discreet, that a powerful man like the Dictator would send to bring someone to his presence. Meto saw the comprehension on my face and nodded.

"What in Hades can Caesar want with *me*?" I shook my head. "Cicero and Caesar in one day—and while recovering from a vicious hangover! I don't think I can manage it."

Bethesda pursed her lips. "The hangover is entirely your own fault. And you will certainly *not* decline an invitation to see the Dictator."

Since my elevation to Equestrian status, my wife had become increasingly conscious of her own new social rank and that of our children. She and Diana seemed always busy with preparations for some festival, mingling with other matrons of their newly achieved class. I was rather surprised—and pleased—at how readily the other Roman matrons seemed to accept Bethesda, considering that she had been born a slave (and abroad, in Egypt), and had become a free woman only through marriage with me, a Roman of humble origins. But many things in Rome surprised me these days. Times had changed. Many who had been at the pinnacle had fallen into the abyss, and many, like my wife, who had begun life at the very bottom, now found themselves, if not at the top, then allowed on occasion to rub elbows with those who were.

"Don't you have some function to go to today?" I said irritably.

"As a matter of fact, Mother," said Diana, "don't forget that we have a meeting at the Temple of Vesta, to talk about planning for the festival of Anna Perenna on the Ides. Oh, and there's a gathering right after that, at Fulvia's house, to talk about the Liberalia. So much is happening in the next few days."

"You're going to Marc Antony's house?" I said. Though our meetings over the years had been amicable, I had not seen the Dictator's right-hand man in many months—not since he'd abandoned his scandalous affair with the actress Cytheris and married the most ambitious widow in Rome. The joke went that the only reason Fulvia hadn't married Caesar was that he already had one wife too many—meaning both Calpurnia and Queen Cleopatra. Fulvia, twice the widow of rising politicians struck down in their prime, had now settled on Antony. I smiled. "If you think your husband drinks too much, imagine being married to Antony."

"On the contrary," said Bethesda, "Fulvia has pulled him into shape quite nicely. He hardly drinks at all, takes vigorous exercise every day, stays out of trouble, and is firmly back in Caesar's good graces."

"If only women could be generals, then Antony could stay at home while his wife goes out to conquer something."

"You joke, husband, but Fulvia is a marvel at organizing things. There's no task too challenging. No detail, large or small, escapes her. Truly, the woman is a wonder. Marc Antony is very lucky to have finally found a wife who appreciates his talents and is determined to see him make the most of them. . . ."

As she continued to extol the virtues of Fulvia, my thoughts wandered. Might it be that Caesar wanted to see me for the same reason as had Cicero—to find out if I knew anything, or could discover anything, about any danger that might loom in the remaining days before he left Rome? What sort of predicament might arise should I find myself pulled between them? How simpler my life would be if other men would leave me alone.

"What *does* Caesar want?" I asked Meto.

"A golden throne," he said with a straight face. "Oh, you mean with you, Papa? Quite honestly, I don't know, though I have a suspicion."

"Share it, then."

"I'd rather not, in case I'm wrong."

"Oh, come now, Meto. Speak."

"Papa, really, I'd rather not." A shadow flitted across his smiling face, and I was reminded, as perhaps he was, of a time in the past when we had been sadly estranged. His loyalty to Caesar had come between us—at least, that was my way of explaining the trouble. Whatever the cause, I never wanted such a gulf to open between us again.

"Very well, then, I shall go to see the Dictator and find out for myself what he wants from me. You'll be coming, too, I hope?"

"Of course, Papa. We can talk on the way and catch up on family news. I'd love to know how Eco and his brood have been faring since they moved down to Neapolis. Is it true that he and Menenia are living in a villa twice the size of this house?"

Paid for, I thought, *by a small portion of the same windfall that landed me in the Equestrian class.* "Their house is quite modest compared to all the luxurious estates surrounding them on the Cup," I said, using the name locals preferred for the Bay of Neapolis. "Your brother is doing very well. Plenty of work for a Finder, he says. Adultery and murder and backstabbing among the old rich, or what's left of them. Even worse behavior among the new rich who've moved into all those villas left vacant by senators who died in the war."

"And Eco took Rupa with him?" Mute Rupa, a blond Sarmatian, was the youngest of my three adopted sons, and the brawniest.

"Well, we didn't need two such big fellows here in Rome, did we?" I nodded toward my son-in-law. "I could hardly afford to feed both! Rupa serves as a bodyguard for Eco, as Davus does for me."

"If only Caesar was as concerned about bodyguards," said Meto. "And Mopsus and Androcles—they're down in Neapolis as well?"

"Those two! Too loud and rowdy for the household of an old fellow with delicate nerves like myself," I said, though in fact I often missed the two slave boys. "They serve as Eco's messengers and errand runners, as they once served me. As I say, he's very busy. The Cup practically brims with crime."

"Not like Rome, then," said Meto. "With Caesar in charge, there's much less crime than there used to be, don't you think?"

"Less crime of the sort perpetrated by one rich man against another, yes. With Caesar watching, the powerful mind their manners. But there's more crime of the petty sort, I think, crimes of the poor against the poor.

The war left a lot of broken men in Rome, maimed in body or mind or both. Broken women, too. Desperate people resort to desperate measures—thievery, threats, violence, murder. That's what I hear, anyway, during my evenings down at the Salacious Tavern."

Meto frowned. "Mother tells me you're down there quite often these days, drinking more than you used to."

"It passes the time. But the Dictator awaits. Should I take Davus with me?"

"No need. Caesar's litter-bearers will see you safely home."

"Then as soon as I can change into my toga, let's be off."

VI

Mistakenly, I had assumed that the litter-bearers would take us to Caesar's official residence in the city where he lived with Calpurnia, called the Regia, only a short trip from my house. When the bearers turned in the opposite direction, I shot a questioning look at Meto seated on the cushions opposite me.

"We're headed out of the city, to the garden estate across the Tiber," he explained. "The trip will give us plenty of time to talk. You've been there before, haven't you?"

"As a matter of fact, I dropped in on the queen when she was last here in Rome, when Caesar was staging his four triumphs."

"Ah, yes. And now Cleopatra is in residence there once again."

"With her son, I hear. Or should I say *their* son?"

Meto smiled. "As you well know, Papa, there is reality, and then there is official reality."

"And to which category does Caesar's paternity of Caesarion belong?"

"That matter," he said carefully, "may be in flux."

"How vexing it must be, having to deal with two realities. Navigating one is challenging enough for me. I didn't think you much cared for the Egyptian queen."

"My feelings toward her have mellowed. As have hers toward me, I think."

"The boy must be about four years old now. Speaking much?"

"Oh, yes. He inherited his mother's gift for languages. She has him reciting nursery rhymes in both Greek and Latin. Probably in Egyptian as well."

"And how does the little boy address Caesar? As 'Dictator'?"

"Papa, you're incorrigible. In private, he addresses Caesar as I address you."

"But not in public."

"I don't think Caesar and Caesarion have ever been seen together in public, at least not in Rome. Perhaps, when we visit Egypt on the way to Parthia, to work out supply lines for the legions, that might change."

"The queen has some public ceremony in mind? There's a rumor that Caesar intends to marry her, make himself king of Egypt, and name Caesarion as his royal heir."

"I can't speak for the queen on that matter. Nor for Caesar."

"But Caesar is residing at the garden estate along with Cleopatra?"

"Certainly not! That would set endless tongues wagging. Caesar visits the estate only during the day. He spends his nights with Calpurnia at the Regia."

There's plenty that can be done by daylight that could cause tongues to wag, I thought.

I looked at Meto and realized how glad I was for this unexpected little journey, which allowed me to spend some precious, rare time alone with him. Soon he would be leaving Rome again, off to war. What a worry he was to me, my warrior son! How many more chances would I have to see him? I had long feared for his life, but now I feared another mortality—my own. Whichever of us was to die first, the passing of time made it more and more likely that every moment spent together might be our last.

We descended the Palatine and passed though the Roman Forum, where a religious procession of some sort interrupted our progress. Then the bearers skillfully threaded their way through the bustling marketplace in the Forum Boarium. We crossed the nearby bridge and found ourselves at once in the countryside, or at least a well-tended version of it. We passed by the Grove of the Furies and then by the public meadows along the riverbank, where a handful of strollers were enjoying the lukewarm Martius sunshine.

A bit farther on, the road veered away from the river and then ran parallel to it, giving access to the sumptuous private estates that fronted the most desirable stretch of the Tiber. Here the wealthy of Rome had their second homes outside the city, where they could relax in lavish gardens, pursue fashionable hobbies like beekeeping, and in summer go boating and swimming in the river. From the road, almost nothing could be seen of these estates. They were hidden behind high walls that were themselves obscured by lush vines and other greenery.

We came to a gate in one of the walls. It opened to allow the litter to pass through. I never saw a guard, though there must have been several. Cleopatra, if not Caesar, would insist on stringent security. The queen had managed to eliminate most, but not all, of her close relatives. As long as any of them remained alive, there was always a chance they might make an attempt on her life, or that of Caesarion. That was the way of the Ptolemies.

I saw the house and its many terraces only in glimpses, through breaks in the greenery. We came to a stop, and Meto and I stepped from the litter into a garden with a view of the sun-spangled river. It was the same formally laid-out garden where I had visited Cleopatra before, with manicured shrubs, gravel paths, and carefully pruned rosebushes not yet in bloom. Tucked amid the shrubbery were exquisite pieces of Greek statuary. I recognized many, such as the young boy absorbed in pulling a thorn from his foot. But at least two of the sculptures were new to me—one of winged Cupid playing with a lioness, and another, quite large, of two centaurs making off with two captured nymphs. This piece was so stunning I had to stop and stare at it.

"Remarkable, isn't it?"

I knew the voice but was still a bit startled to turn and face Caesar.

He was dressed as if for some formal occasion, in the purple robes that he alone was allowed to wear.

"Dictator," I said. I almost bowed my head, as one is expected to do for royalty, but stifled the reflex.

"Gordianus, welcome. And thank you, Meto, for bringing your father so promptly."

"We were a bit slow getting across the Forum," said Meto.

"No matter. I saw you gazing at the centaurs and nymphs. Truly, a remarkable piece. It creates a tremendous tension in the viewer, I think, whether he realizes it or not. One smiles, seeing the joyous lechery of the grinning centaurs—and then one quails, seeing the sheer terror on the sweet faces of the nymphs. I feel that tension, between the power of lust and the love of innocence, each time I look at it. By Arcesilaus, as I'm sure you can tell—you with your fine eye for details, Gordianus."

"Yes, I noticed his stamp on one of the centaur's hooves."

"Ever since Arcesilaus did such an outstanding job sculpting the goddess for my new Temple of Venus, I've been collecting his work. I've just about filled the garden. Calpurnia complains that if I buy any more, we'll have to purchase a whole new estate to make room for them. Ah well, I have no more time for such concerns. Though inevitably, in my coming travels, I'll discover many works of art that I simply must bring back— so that I can share them with the people of Rome, of course."

"Of course."

A cloud obscured the sun. Caesar looked up, then at the Tiber, no longer lit with sparkles like hammered silver, but dull gray, the color of lead. "I'd thought we might talk here in the garden, but without sunshine it's a bit chilly, don't you think? Follow me. I'll conduct you across Little Egypt and into the house. If the queen will permit us passage, that is." He flashed a knowing smile at Meto.

Caesar led us though the garden. Each area was separated from the others by hedges, as rooms are separated by walls. There were yet more sculptural marvels, but Caesar's brisk pace allowed me only passing glances. We arrived at length in a section of the garden with a shallow pond at the center, hedged all around by nodding stalks of papyrus. The pond was strewn with lily pads with bright purple flowers. Dominating the garden was a statue of Isis in one corner. The goddess was shown as the mother of Horus. She was seated, wearing a long dress that left bare her breasts, one of which she held in her hand, offering it to the suckling child on her lap. On her head was a nemes, the striped headdress worn by pharaohs, and surmounting that, reaching high in the air, was a crown of the Hathor type, a solar disk embraced by two upright cow horns and circled by a rearing cobra. The statue was of marble and brightly painted.

The image of Isis in the heart of Caesar's estate was all the more striking because her worship in Rome, always controversial, had been banned by the Senate before the outbreak of the civil war, and her temple in the city had been demolished.

So completely was I absorbed by the statue of Isis that only when I heard the squeal of a child did I realize the garden was occupied. I turned to see Cleopatra seated on a wooden bench in the opposite corner, attended by a pair of handmaidens. She wore a gown of pleated linen. Her dark hair was pulled back into a bun. She wore a necklace and bracelets made of silver and adorned with jewels of smoky topaz and black chalcedony.

"*It!*" cried the little boy as he rushed toward Caesar. He was twice as old as when I had last seen him in this garden, and almost twice as big, but still a bit small for a four-year-old, I thought. Perhaps it was his parents who had taught him to use an Egyptian word for "father"—*it*—instead of the Latin or Greek, as if this kept the relationship at some unofficial level, especially here in Rome, where the idea that an Egyptian prince might be heir to Caesar's throne was so loathsome to the citizens of the Republic.

"Caesarion!" said Caesar, scooping the boy up in his arms, then loudly groaning as men of his age do when picking up a small child. He swung the boy about, then set him on the ground. One of the handmaidens quickly took Caesarion's hand and led the child to one side.

"Permission to pass though Little Egypt, Your Majesty?" said Caesar, casting an arch glance at the queen.

"Permission granted," she said, and from the playful look on her face I thought she might spring up and give him a kiss. Perhaps she would have, had not a visitor been present. She turned her eyes to me and held my gaze until, almost against my will, I made the requisite nod of obeisance. She was a visiting head of state, and I a Roman citizen of Equestrian status. It seemed only proper.

"I remember you, Gordianus-called-Finder." The queen gave me a look almost as bewitching as the one she had cast at Caesar. Cleopatra was not a great beauty, if statues of Venus were the standard—her nose and chin were too prominent, almost manly—but she exuded a charm that was impossible to deny. This charm seemed only stronger now that she was in her middle twenties, with a voluptuous figure shown to great advantage by the moss-colored linen gown that hugged her snugly in all the right places.

"And I remember you, Your Majesty."

She laughed as if I had said something quite absurd. Could anyone meet Cleopatra and forget the experience?

"Little Egypt?" I said, mostly to myself. I gazed around me, suddenly realizing that it was quite impossible for papyri to be flourishing and lily pads to be blooming in Rome in the month of Martius. I touched one of the papyri stalks and realized it was made of wood, carved and painted to look like the Egyptian plant. Now that I looked more closely, I saw that the lily pads were also replicas, as were most of the other Nilotic specimens in this Egyptian garden. Caesar saw the look on my face and laughed.

"To make the queen feel at home during her stay, I had this garden made for her," he explained. "But I think the thing she likes best is the one she brought herself—this splendid statue of Isis, a gift to the people of Rome."

"And I thank you, Caesar, for creating this space so congenial to the goddess—though I hope to see her officially installed in a newly dedicated temple, if not during this visit, then the next time I come to Rome." She turned her gaze to me. "Caesar tells me that the people of the city never stopped loving the goddess, despite the opposition of some of your senators. With a new temple, the Roman people will benefit greatly from the blessings she will bestow."

"Between Caesar's wish to share great art with the people, and your desire to reacquaint us with Isis, we Romans are very fortunate," I said. This elicited a small grimace of disapproval from Meto, but neither the Dictator nor the queen perceived any irony in my words. Indeed, Caesar was pleased.

"Beautifully stated, Gordianus. I would almost think that Meto inherited his gift for words from you, never mind that he's adopted."

"Speaking of gifts . . ." said Cleopatra. "Hammonius!"

At her summons, a man appeared from a break in the false papyri, dressed as I had seen palace officials in Alexandria, in a long linen gown with a broad leather belt. Behind him, wearing a metal collar and led on a tether as if he were some exotic beast, was a young man of very dark complexion, naked except for a scrap of cloth around his loins. The slave was a skinny fellow with a plain face, and there were curious scars, like ornamental markings, on his arms and chest, difficult to make out against his dark skin. Since he appeared neither especially beautiful nor strong, it was hard to see what made him a suitable gift, especially for a man who already possessed virtually everything a man could own. Perhaps he was a singer, I thought, or an acrobat; but his talent was of another sort.

"I asked and was told you don't own one of these," said Cleopatra. "I thought he might be useful to you in your travels. Or even here in Rome."

"What is the fellow?" Caesar looked at the slave and cocked his head. "Those scars look familiar. Wavy lines . . ."

"They're snakes," said Meto. "Or symbols that stand for snakes. Don't you remember? We saw such scars on a local tribe, when we cornered Cato's forces in Africa."

"Ah, yes," Caesar said, then recited a line of poetry: "'As a Punic Psyllus by touch charms a sleep-inducing asp . . .'"

"Very apt!" said Meto. The quotation was unknown to me.

Cleopatra laughed, and her son, seeing her delight, likewise laughed. "I own a few of these fellows," she said, "but I'm told this one is the best."

"The best at what?" I asked.

"The Psylli are snake handlers," said Meto.

"Oh, they're much more than that," said Cleopatra. "They're immune to snakebites. In fact, if a snake bites a Psyllus, it's the snake that dies. But more than that, the most talented of them, like this fellow, can suck the venom from a snakebite and tell exactly what sort of serpent it came from, and what sort of remedy may cure it. They practice a sort of magic that gives relief from other poisons as well. A taster can keep you from eating poison in the first place, but a Psyllus can save you afterward."

"What a thoughtful gift," said Caesar. "If you're sure you can spare the fellow . . ."

"Of course. I have my own Psyllus here in Rome. I never travel without one. Nor should you, Caesar."

Hammonius bowed deeply, then led the Psyllus away.

"My gratitude again, Your Majesty," said Caesar. "Time spent with you is always a pleasure, but now I must confer with this citizen." He nodded in my direction. "Will you excuse us, Your Majesties?" By using the plural he included the little prince, at whom he winked.

"You are excused," said Cleopatra, giving him that look again. Caesar seemed trapped by it for a moment, then with a blink and a shiver he broke from her gaze and led us toward the house.

VII

We ascended a series of steps that ended at a wide terrace with a view of the gardens below and the Tiber in the distance. Off the terrace, heated by burning braziers, was a dining room with couches pulled into a square to face each other. Caesar indicated that I should take one and Meto another. He reclined on one elbow on the couch between us, which faced the terrace. The couches were upholstered with blue fabric, except for Caesar's, which was purple, like his robe, and bordered with gold embroidery. Even his dining couch had been made to resemble a throne.

"Are you hungry, Gordianus?" he said. "Of course you are. You've been to Egypt and back this morning!"

I didn't think I was hungry until I smelled the delicacies making their way toward us on silver platters carried by a trio of young male slaves. Bits of tender whitefish and dried figs had been glazed with olive oil and honey and roasted on skewers. Wine was also offered, mixed with cold springwater and sweetened with dollops of honey. Presumably it had all been tasted already, for Caesar's protection. Or had he dispensed with that precaution, just as he had given up his Spanish bodyguards?

As we drank and ate and commented on the food, I took a closer look at Caesar. Despite his ebullient mood, it seemed to me that he appeared a bit thin and haggard, especially for a man about to set out on an expedition to the far side of the world.

"Remind me, Meto, that I must bring a gift for Cleopatra the next time I visit," said Caesar. "What do you think, a pair of gladiators, perhaps? I own so many, and they're something of a novelty in Egypt."

"I'm sure the queen would find some use for them," said Meto.

Turning to me, Caesar explained, "The queen and I always exchange gifts or perform some other ceremonial act of state when I come to the garden villa. That way, no one can say that I visit the queen for any reason other than in my role as Dictator, conducting the business of the Senate and People of Rome. As for the gifts themselves . . . sometimes we swap them back and forth. The queen knows I'm fond of gladiators, and with all the intrigue that surrounds her, Cleopatra surely has more need of that poison detector than I do!"

"Such intrigues do not surround the Dictator?" I said.

"Interesting that you should ask," said Caesar. "What do you think, Gordianus? Is there some danger hanging over me?"

I should like to have said, *What a coincidence. Your old friend and enemy Cicero was just asking me that same question.* Instead I said, "Are you worried about the omen delivered by Spurinna a month ago?"

"Not quite a month has passed since then," said Caesar. "But no; Spurinna's divination is not on my mind. I think you know that I give no credit to such things. Concrete information is another matter. As long as I have you here, I'll ask you outright: Have you any knowledge of any intended threat to my person?"

The question was framed in such a way as to imply that he had actually summoned me for some other purpose and was asking only to take advantage of my presence. I should like to have asked him, outright, to tell me the reason I was there, but it would have been impertinent for a citizen to answer a direct question from the Dictator with another question. "No, Caesar. I have no knowledge whatsoever of any plot to do you harm. But my value as a source of such intelligence is very small. It was different once upon a time, perhaps, but nowadays I'm like the sleeper in the Etruscan fable who dozes through one calamity after another and wakes only after all the trouble is over."

"Oh, I think you underestimate yourself, Finder," said Caesar.

"He's right, Papa," said Meto. "You always know more than you give yourself credit for."

"In any case, should you think of some bit of hearsay you've forgotten, or come by some useful information, if you would convey the details to me as quickly as possible I would be grateful, as would the Senate and People of Rome—and my wife."

"Your wife, Caesar?"

He flashed a crooked smile. "To be honest, Calpurnia suggested that I should seek you out expressly for this purpose. 'It is the way of wives to wait and to worry,' as Ennius says, and my wife worries more than most. For some reason she has a great deal of faith in you."

Because she hired me herself a couple of years ago, behind your back, I thought, *and my efforts on that occasion saved your life—a fact that Calpurnia made me vow never to reveal to you.* Now she was sending Caesar to me directly. Was the threat this time as real as it had been before, or just the conjecture of a worried wife and an overly zealous haruspex?

"Keep your ears to the ground," Caesar went on. "Perhaps you might actively seek out such information, using whatever channels are available to you. Make a few discreet inquiries in that establishment you frequent."

"Establishment?"

"The Salacious Tavern, I mean."

How in Hades did Caesar know where I spent my idle hours? Not from Meto, who only an hour earlier had been informed about my drinking habits by Bethesda and Diana. Who had been talking about me behind my back? Was Caesar actually bothering to spy on me?

"See if any of your drinking companions have any thoughts on the matter."

"My drinking companions?" I had an image of old graybeards like myself, drunk on wine, singing bawdy songs and pinching barmaids, and was quite sure I didn't fit the description. The Salacious Tavern these days was a quiet, sad place where many of the patrons drank alone, not the thriving den of vice it had been in its heyday, when the poet Catullus and his circle frequented the tavern. "I hardly think, Caesar—"

"Nonetheless, do this favor for me." His tone put an end to the discussion.

"Of course, Caesar."

"In fact, it occurs to me that you might drop in on certain men, discreetly. Find some pretense for your visit. You know how to do that sort of thing. And while you're there, ask a subtle question or two, and keep your eyes and ears open for any bit of useful information. Use that power of yours to draw the truth out of men even when they try to hide it from you. I see the ambivalent look on your face, Finder! But don't you understand, it's that very attitude of yours, your doggedly diffident approach to politics and matters of state, that makes you the perfect hound for catching the hare? Men known to be loyal to me—like your son—are useless for ferreting out such secrets. No enemy would confide in them. And men not so loyal to me . . . well, those are the ones I'm worried about. I'll make up a short list of the men I'd like you to visit, and in a few days you can convey your impressions to me."

"But, Caesar," I said, "didn't every senator take an oath to protect you, with his own life if necessary? All the senators who survived the war, whatever side they fought for, took the oath, did they not? And all those new senators you've appointed have done so as well."

"True. The oath must be taken before the Senate on the day a New Man wears his senatorial toga in public for the first time. As you will soon discover."

His last words somehow escaped my attention. Nor did I take much notice of the smile that appeared on Meto's face.

Caesar also smiled. "What does Parthenius say? 'A spoken oath is only air passing the lips. True loyalty need never be spoken aloud.' Well, then, I'll make sure that list of names is in your hand before you leave."

The word "list" sent a chill through me. In my experience, any time a dictator had made a list, heads ended up on stakes, never mind Caesar's much-vaunted propensity for mercy. I sighed. How had it come about that in a matter of hours both Cicero and Caesar had drawn me into conducting an investigation for which I had no appetite whatsoever? If only Eco had not moved down to the Cup, I would have passed the burden to him.

"Oh, and in the unlikely event that you should cross paths with Calpurnia, say absolutely nothing about this matter. She worries enough as it is."

"First you ask me to discover secrets. Now you ask me to keep one." I shook my head, but I understood Caesar's concern. Spouses sometimes felt compelled to protect one another from the ugly parts of life.

I could hardly refuse a commission from the Dictator. A happy thought occurred to me: Surely I would report anything I should discover, significant or not, to Meto—and so I would have more precious chances to see my son before he left Rome.

A final course was served, of mushroom caps stewed in vinegar, to cleanse the palette. Our cups were filled again with wine and springwater. Caesar looked bemused.

"Let me ask you something, Finder—because you're older than I, and there aren't many such men left alive in Rome. . . ."

Thanks to you, I thought. Caesar gave me a sharp look. Was my face so easy for him to read?

He went on. "At least, there are not many older men left whose opinion I would ask. Tell me, have you yet experienced in your long life a moment when you thought, *This is it. This is the apex, the zenith. I have arrived. After this, everything else will be downhill?*" Caesar paused for a moment, more to compose his thoughts than to await a reply. "For me, such a moment came during my first triumph, the one that celebrated the conquest of Gaul. I was in the chariot, wearing the laurel wreath, holding the scepter and the laurel bough, surrounded by the cheering multitudes. And I thought, *I have reached the peak, the very summit of human affairs, from which I can gaze down on every land and sea. Only a god could stand higher.* That feeling has never quite left me. It sustains me from day to day, like the air I breathe, like the water I drink. But after that moment—more triumphs. More war—that messy operation in Spain—and yet another triumph. Moments of satisfaction, of antici-pation, even of exaltation—but never . . . never quite the same . . ."

"But now, Caesar, the Parthian campaign," said Meto, with a look of concern. I took it that Caesar seldom spoke in such a way, even with his intimates. "It's all we've thought about or talked about for days. Planning, poring over maps, looking ahead. Another campaign. Another triumph!"

"Ah, yes, now Parthia." Caesar sighed. "Of course, before I even begin that campaign, we'll have to stop in Damascus to fix the current mess in Syria."

"Syria is in a mess?" I said.

"Isn't it always?" Caesar suddenly laughed and shook his head. "Great Venus, here sits the master of the world feeling sorry for himself! How absurd I must look. I do believe there is some truth to those rumors about your power to draw secrets from others."

"Is it a secret that Caesar has moments of uncertainty? Surely every man does."

"And I am as mortal as all the rest—as those fellows behind me in my triumphal chariots kept reminding me. But where was I? What was I talking about?" Caesar looked genuinely perplexed, and Meto again looked concerned. "Oh, yes! Answer the question, Finder. Have you yet experienced the apogee of your rather long life?"

"I'm not sure. I've never really thought about it. There have been cer-tain moments. . . ." I remembered the day Meto, born a slave, had reached manhood and put on the toga of a Roman citizen. Had that been the proudest moment of my life? Perhaps . . .

"Well, good citizen, you may very soon have cause to feel that you've reached the summit. Before I leave Rome, I'll attend one final session of the Senate, on the Ides. There are some important items on the agenda—including the addition of one more member to the ranks of the Senate, my final appointment. Have you any idea whom that last senator will be—Gordianus?"

I shook my head, then looked at Meto. He had a broad smile on his face. So euphoric was his expression that I was almost alarmed by it.

Caesar gave me a cunning look. "Must I repeat the words I just said? 'That last senator will be—*Gordianus.*'"

It was a not a question this time. It was a statement.

I looked from Caesar to Meto, who was wiping tears of joy from his eyes, and then back to Caesar. I was too stunned to speak.

VIII

"Well, Finder, what do you say?" Caesar's smile was almost cruel, as if he enjoyed my befuddlement.

"Yes, Papa, speak!" said Meto

"I . . ."

Caesar laughed. "Well, that's a start. Of course, I'd never have considered such an appointment had you not been added to the Equestrian roster. I've been quite generous with my appointments—innovative, some would say—but there *are* limits to just how far I'll push the old-timers in the Senate. Not a few of them would balk, I suspect, at welcoming Gordianus the Finder into their ranks, but they can hardly object to Gordianus of the Equestrian class, a man of wealth and accomplishment. I must admit, I was surprised to see your name when it appeared on the list. I had no idea you'd accumulated such a fortune. I asked Meto if you'd received an inheritance, and he said you hadn't. How did you make all that money, Finder? Bit by bit, or by a sudden windfall? Well, I won't pry into the matter."

"I assure you, Caesar, the sudden increase in my wealth came from strictly legal means—"

"No, no! Say no more." Caesar waved one hand at me and with the other raised his cup to his lips. He took a long sip. "With whom a Roman citizen sleeps, which gods he worships, and how he makes his money should be no one's business but his own, don't you think?"

I blinked and slowly nodded.

Caesar leaned back on one elbow and peered at me. "I've seen other men become speechless when I've given them this news, but every one of them eventually managed to say, 'Thank you.'"

"And I do, Caesar. Of course I do . . ." I had been made an Equestrian whether I liked it or not. But was it possible to turn down an appointment to the Senate? Why was I even thinking such a thought? But how could I not think it? I, who had shunned politics all my life, was to be thrust into the very center of what remained of republican government in Rome. "Indeed, Caesar. Thank you."

Caesar sighed. "You might muster at least a modicum of enthusiasm."

"My father has a tendency to overthink," said Meto. "Things that are simple he makes needlessly complicated. He's doing it right now. I can see the cogs and wheels spinning behind his eyes." Meto smiled as he pointed a gyrating finger at me, but I could hear the strain in his voice. He was embarrassed by his father's peculiar, even perverse reaction.

"It's only that . . ." A blunt refusal was out of the question. What argument could I make against myself? "Gauls and haruspices are one thing, but I fear that your appointment of a fellow such as myself would rouse more controversy than you anticipate. A man of my lowly origins—"

"Lowly? You were born a Roman citizen, were you not? As was your father before you, and his father, I presume. There is nothing lowly about that."

My eyes were on Meto. He was a citizen now, having become a freedman when I adopted him, but he had been born a slave. Did I see a shadow cross Meto's face as Caesar spoke?

"What will Cicero say?" I murmured, thinking aloud.

"Cicero? Ha! To be sure, I would like to see his face when he finds out," said Caesar. "But you must know, though I continue to show him respect in public, for the sake of decorum, Cicero's time has passed. No one cares about his opinion anymore. And didn't Cicero once call you 'the last honest man in Rome'? If he dares to object to your appointment, here's a chance for you to out-Cicero Cicero: Throw his own words back in his face, as he's so famous for doing to others in the courts and on the floor of the Senate."

A chill ran down my spine. "Might that happen? Might I be called on to debate Cicero? To defend myself before the Senate?" The idea made me light-headed.

"Certainly not," said Caesar. "Once I announce your appointment, your approval by the Senate is a mere formality. You deserve to join their ranks as much as any other man I've named. Have you not been a hard-working, honest, and loyal citizen of Rome all your life, and have you not rendered valuable services to some of the most powerful men in Rome, including myself, always with an eye toward what was best for the Republic? Well, then, there you have it. Five days from now, on the Ides of March, you shall become a senator of Rome."

Caesar sat upright on his dining couch and leaned forward. I thought he was about to reach out and give me a reassuring touch, but he leaned the other way and did so to Meto, grasping his shoulder firmly and giving him a look so intimate and tender that I suddenly felt an intruder. For many years now there had been a special bond between them. On long military campaigns they had shared the same tent. Back in Rome, by lamplight, they had spent long hours collaborating on Caesar's memoirs. Now the two of them were about to set out on yet another campaign that might take them to the ends of the earth and beyond, together.

As they looked into each other's eyes, I realized that my elevation to the Senate was a gift not to me, but to Meto. Having been born a slave, my son could never be considered for such an honor. I was to become a senator in his stead. No matter what I thought of the matter, for Meto's sake I had to accept, and do so as graciously as I could.

The same litter and bearers that had delivered me to the garden estate were summoned to take me home. Meto joined me but said he would accompany me only part of the way, as he had business in the Forum.

I was stunned by what had happened, but Meto was ebullient. His smile and glittering eyes made him look like a child again, the high-spirited slave boy I had encountered long ago in Crassus's villa on the Cup. How much had happened since then! No one could have foreseen the twists of fortune that lay ahead. Crassus, the richest man in the world, had been killed campaigning against the Parthians. Now his death was to be avenged by Caesar—accompanied by Meto, who had been the slave of Crassus. And I was to be a senator, like Crassus, like Cicero, like Caesar, and so many others I had dealt with over the years.

"You look dazed, Papa."

"And you look overjoyed."

"I am!"

"Then I'm happy for us both. Even though . . ." *Even though this is madness,* I was about to say, and then was struck by a chilling thought. What if the idea to make me a senator had come literally from a man not in his right mind?

"You've known Caesar a long time," I said. "You've seen him in many situations. Does he seem entirely normal to you?"

Meto's smile faded. "What do you mean?"

"I thought he seemed a bit confused at times. And melancholy. Or changeable, I should say. Melancholy one moment, happy the next. Does he still suffer headaches? And bouts of falling sickness?"

Meto didn't answer.

"I understand, if it's something you can't talk about. I respect the confidence he places in you, and the confidentiality he expects."

Meto nodded slowly.

"Of course, he has a great deal on his mind," I said. "So much business to finish here in Rome. So many preparations for the upcoming campaign. Really, it boggles the mind of a simple fellow like myself, all the logistics. I can't imagine how Caesar does it."

"He's a truly remarkable man," said Meto. "Although . . ."

I waited for him to gather his thoughts.

"There *is* something in what you say, Papa. By Hercules, you're a keen observer. You noticed what many haven't, not even men who see Caesar every day. There's a . . . a slight haze about him sometimes, a dullness. I might put it down to the fact that he's just getting older—except that I've never seen such a dullness about you, Papa, and you're ten years his senior. I tell myself it's as you suggest, his mind is simply overburdened with too many thoughts, more than any man could reasonably handle. But then, as you know, there's the falling sickness. It went away for years, but just lately . . ." He shook his head. "I shouldn't talk about it."

"I understand."

Meto smiled. "But the old fellow's not so mad that he's making you a senator by mistake!" He laughed, and I was so glad to see the shadow leave his face that I said no more about Caesar's state of mind.

The litter crossed the Tiber. We passed through the riverside markets, not as crowded as before, and came to the Forum, where Meto called for the bearers to stop.

"I'll leave you here," he said, nimbly leaping from the compartment. "The bearers will see you safely home." He rearranged the folds of his toga, then stepped closer to me. He looked very serious. His voice trembled. "Papa, I'm so proud of you!"

Tears came to my eyes. I nodded, unable to speak. Meto at last stepped back and gave a signal to the chief litter-bearer. With a slight jolt I was carried forward. Meto waved to me, then was lost to view, swallowed up by the crowds of men in togas going about their business in the Forum.

Days are short in the month of Martius. Already the light was beginning to fade. It would be the dinner hour soon, but I felt a bit thirsty.

I called to the litter-bearers to stop. The leader stepped to the compartment. He gave me a quizzical look but didn't speak. He had probably been trained never to speak first.

"What's your name?" I said.

"Hipparchus."

"Tell me, Hipparchus, do you know a place called the Salacious Tavern?"

He looked at me shrewdly. He shook his head to say no. His expression said otherwise.

"Take me there," I said.

"My orders were to take you home."

"And *my* orders are to take me to the tavern."

He looked unsure.

"By Hercules, Hipparchus, I'm soon to be a member of the Roman Senate, believe it or not. If that's worth anything at all, it should at least convince you to do as I say. Otherwise, I'll get out and walk."

"No, don't do that. We'll take you to the tavern. But then we'll wait outside and take you home when you're ready."

"But then you'll certainly get into trouble with Caesar, taking so long to return to him. No, just take me to the tavern and leave me there."

Hipparchus looked dubious, but resumed his position and called to the others to follow his directions. We turned around and headed back the way we had come, left the Forum and entered the markets, then came to a cluttered area of workshops and warehouses. Little pillars were inscribed with the names of shops and businesses. Past the ninth signpost we came to a pillar that bore no name. Atop it stood an upright marble phallus. A lamp hanging from the post, not yet lit, was in the same suggestive shape. Crudely drawn graffiti on the walls were likewise mostly phallic in nature. The place exuded an odor of stale wine, cheap perfumes, and the various human excretions and odors meant to be hidden by the perfumes.

By fading daylight, the tavern presented a shabby appearance, more decrepit than lascivious. There were cracks in the plaster walls, and the wooden door looked a bit rotted in places. I stepped from the litter and rapped at the door.

A little trapdoor opened and a bloodshot eye peered at me. I had no need to speak; I was known to the management. The door opened and the keeper of the door stepped back to let me in.

I looked over my shoulder at Hipparchus. "You may go now. I've arrived at my destination."

"We'll stay here," he said, "until you're ready for us to take you home."

"What, in the street? With every citizen who comes by taking a second look and thinking, 'Doesn't that litter belong to the Dictator? Is the master of the world inside, drinking and gambling and whoring?' No, no, I insist that you move on. Go now. Move! Off with you!" I waved my hand for emphasis.

Hipparchus looked unhappy, but at last he called to the others to set off. I watched them disappear around a corner, then stepped inside the Salacious Tavern.

IX

Salacious Tavern was not the real name of the place. As far as I knew, it had no name. The colorful epithet had been coined by a famous poet no longer among the living, who in his verses had celebrated this lowly establishment. Probably most people thought the poet was describing a fictitious tavern, but those who had known Catullus—and had been inside the Salacious Tavern with the poet himself, as I had—knew the place was only too real. We would never call it anything else.

Perpetual twilight reigned inside the tavern. By night it was dimly lit by lamps and candles. By day the only light came from dusty shafts of sunlight that pierced the ill-fitting shutters on the windows. The place wasn't crowded—only a handful of whores, gamblers, and drinkers were present—but as I stepped inside all eyes turned to me. I realized it was because I was wearing my toga, which I had put on so as to be presentable to the Dictator. I had never set foot in the tavern dressed so formally. The preferred outfit was something dark and shabby, to hide any wine stains. My white toga was as conspicuous in this setting as the purple robe of Caesar would be in the Senate House.

It occurred to me that a toga would also make me a bit conspicuous when it came time to walk to home alone. It would mark me as a man of means, out without a bodyguard, and especially vulnerable were I to be a bit drunk, which was not unlikely. Ah, well, I would worry about that later. The nagging voice of reason in my head fell silent. There was something about setting foot in the Salacious Tavern that made a man put aside caution. Breathing in the stale wine fumes, I felt my cares fall away.

I was not the only man in the place formally dressed. Across the dimly lit room, seated in a corner by himself, was another man in a toga. I knew him. In fact, he had become, over the last few months, my regular drinking companion in this establishment, though usually at a later hour and not so formally dressed.

Gaius Helvius Cinna was in his midforties, strikingly handsome, and vain about his appearance. His curly black hair, just beginning to show some gray, was always clean and freshly cut and lightly dressed with expensive aromatic oils; as I crossed the room toward him I caught the scent of sandalwood. The same barber who cared so lovingly for his master's hair also kept him perfectly clean shaven. Cinna had a strong chin, worth showing off. All his features were strong, including his broad nose and wide mouth and piercing gray eyes, but together they achieved a harmony that would please the eye of the most discriminating Greek sculptor. He could have posed for a statue of Mars.

He wore a plain white toga, suitable for a tribune, the office to which the Dictator had appointed him along with nine others. Cinna was only a few months into his year-long term, but he had already achieved considerable notoriety by taking legal action against two fellow tribunes. Those two had removed a diadem that someone had placed on one of Caesar's statues, and they had also arrested a group of men who publicly hailed Caesar as king. Cinna charged the two tribunes with offending the dignity of the Dictator, and they had been driven out of Rome. Cinna had thus established himself very openly as a dedicated, even fanatical, partisan of the Dictator.

Cinna had a full cup of wine in his hand and raised it at my approach.

"Hail, Gordianus! If you *are* Gordianus. I hardly recognized you, dressed up in that toga."

"Yet I recognized you at once—handsome fellow that you are—though I could hardly believe my eyes. A tribune, with so many important duties, indulging in undiluted wine in the middle of the afternoon?"

"Hardly the middle. It'll be sundown soon enough. Besides, I'm here not as a tribune but as a poet."

"And what has drinking to do with poetry?"

"Everything! The nectar of Bacchus unleashes eloquence."

"Does it? I know that being drunk can make a man *think* he's eloquent."

"Oh, Gordianus, you're such a naysayer! That's why I treasure you. I spend most of my time with sycophants of one stripe or another—a household of slaves who cater to my every whim, an adoring daughter, citizens begging for favors from a tribune, admirers who want to tell me how simply divine they find my *Zmyrna*."

"Your what? Is something stuck in your throat, Tribune?"

"There you go again, bringing me down to earth. You know perfectly well the name of my most famous poem, though I think you must be the only literate man in Rome who's never read my *Zmyrna*."

"Alas, Cinna, I don't know a single line of this poem, which you insist is more famous than the *Iliad*." This was true. I knew nothing about his *Zmyrna,* except that the poem was named for its Greek heroine. The myth it recounted was obscure, at least to me. Modern poets like Cinna made a great show of retrieving forgotten lore and spinning it into immortal Latin verse. This was certainly safer than lampooning living politicians, as Catullus had done, and more fashionable, at the moment, than celebrating scandalous ladies and their sparrows or tragic warriors and their wrath. "So why, as a poet, are you skulking in such a dark hole at this hour?"

"Skulking? Hardly. Any hour is a good hour to spend at the Salacious Tavern. And now I have someone to talk to. Clearly, the Fates have conspired to bring us together on this fine Martius afternoon."

"The Fates have played all sorts of tricks on me today."

"Have they? Well you must sit down, acquire a cup of this very fine

Falernian at my expense—I insist—and tell me about your day." He snapped his fingers at a buxom barmaid passing by and pointed at his empty cup and at me.

"Falernian? Do you have something to celebrate?"

"As a matter of fact, I do. The new poem is about to be born."

"But that's marvelous! Share a line with me."

"*About* to be born, I said. Not yet ready for the eyes and ears of the world at large."

"Too bad. Well, then, you could always recite a bit of the *Zmyrna* for me, if you like. I wouldn't stop you."

"Never! Your utter ignorance of my poetry, however much it indicates a serious flaw in your character, is precisely what makes you the perfect drinking companion. I come here to escape my notoriety and to forget my muse for a while."

"You just said wine inspires you, and that you're here as a poet."

"That part about inspiration was a lie. You had it right: Drunkenness only makes men *think* they're clever. But I *am* here as a poet—a poet who drinks to forget the tremendous pressure being put upon him to share with the world his next great work."

"But it's finished, you said. Or nearly so."

"No poem is ever truly finished. It is merely at some point published—trapped like a fly in amber, or slain like a tiger that's skinned and made into a trophy. Publication kills the poem, in fact, but how else can it be made to lie perfectly still, and stop changing, so that others can examine it at their leisure? To read a published poem is like examining the corpse of a beautiful woman. She may still be beautiful, but how much more beautiful she must have been with flashing eyes and smiling lips, living and breathing and loving and ever-changing—like a poem while it's still alive in the mind of its author, before it's been made stiff and rigid on the pages of a scroll?"

"I could listen to you talk like that all night, Cinna." This was true, even though—or precisely because—I could hardly understand a word of what he was saying. As coming to the tavern and conversing with an ignorant, uncultured, and undemanding fellow like myself was an escape for Cinna, so his erudite babbling, the more abstruse the better, was a wonderful escape for me, a man who had spent his life listening closely to every word he heard, constantly seeking hidden meanings, coded secrets, unspeakable truths.

"Perhaps, Cinna, this new poem will be so extraordinary it will make people forget your *Zmyrna*. Then you can have her back to yourself, so to speak."

"That can never happen. It took almost ten years to make her—almost as long as the Trojan War, or the wanderings of Odysseus!—and since then another ten years have passed. At twenty, my beloved *Zmyrna* is too old for me now." He laughed and shook his head. "No, my fear is that the new poem will *not* be thought as good as the *Zmyrna*, even though in every way it's a greater work—longer, bolder, more complex, more elevated and elegant, expounding a far greater theme. You see, my new poem combines—for the first time ever, I think—two very different stories known to everyone—except perhaps to you, Gordianus—and shows that neither story can be fully understood without coupling it to the other."

"Now you've completely lost me."

He sighed. "Even you, Gordianus, must know how Orpheus died."

"I think so."

"And how Pentheus the king of Thebes died, after offending Bacchus?"

"I know the play by Euripides."

"Name-dropping Euripides—you, who pretend to be such an ignoramus! But of course, they're both murder stories, aren't they—the horrible end of Orpheus and the even more horrible end of Pentheus? And murders, at least once upon a time, provided your livelihood."

"But no longer. I'm retired now. No more murders for me."

"Except in verse, perhaps? Yes, Gordianus, now is the time of your life to tend a garden, take long walks, and acquire a taste for poetry."

"Yet here I sit, drinking wine in a tavern while the sun's still up, listening to a poet complain. Go ahead. Share a verse or two of this new masterwork."

"But I can't. I never recite my work before it's published, while it's in progress—still alive and breathing."

"So no one has yet heard it or read it?"

"Actually, the scroll—the only one in existence, written in my own hand—is now in the possession of its first reader. I tremble, awaiting his judgment."

"Then the new poem *is* finished. And you *are* here to celebrate. No wonder Falernian," I said, and took a sip of the most famous of Italian wines.

"To celebrate? Not exactly. I'm here in this godsforsaken place trying to forget that *he* might be reading my verses at this very moment. Is he marveling at my masterwork—or is he shaking his head and grumbling under his breath, wondering how I could have wasted ten years on such drivel?"

"Who is this lucky reader whose opinion you esteem so highly?"

"Just . . . a man who owes me a favor. Or two. Otherwise he'd never have found time."

"A busy fellow, then?"

"No one in Rome is busier."

"Some high magistrate? A politician—and yet you trust his judgment about your verses. Who could that be?"

"I thought you were retired from this business of teasing out secrets, Gordianus."

"Old habits die hard."

"But you'll never guess. I shall dedicate the poem to him—provided he likes it—since he was instrumental in getting me to finally finish the poem."

"How so?"

"In a matter of days he's to leave Rome, and will likely be gone for months if not years. For him to read the poem and give me his thoughts,

I had to finish the blasted thing. Only yesterday I wrote the very last line—in my own hand, mind you, as I never trust any scribe to properly take my dictation."

"Someone who's leaving Rome with Caesar, then? Am I getting closer?"

"Oh, no, Gordianus, you shall draw me out no further! Let's change the subject. Just what are *you* doing in this place at such an hour? I can come anytime I wish, being a widower with no wife to nag me, but your lovely Egyptian wife keeps a rather tight leash on you."

"You've never even met Bethesda."

"Yet the picture you've drawn of her is quite vivid in my head. She won't like it that you're here, drinking wine at my expense, instead of sitting quietly at home in your garden while she pesters the kitchen slaves to fix a dinner worthy of their master. I think you have a reason for being here. Not a tragedy, as you don't look sad. *You're* the one who's come here to celebrate."

I grunted and drank more wine. What would Cinna make of my elevation to the Senate? I was not ready to share the news. But just as Gordianus the Finder was said to have an uncanny power to draw secrets from others, so Cinna the poet was somehow able to draw out my secrets.

"That's why you're wearing your toga. Something big has happened. But what? It's no use resisting me, Gordianus. 'As a Punic Psyllus by touch charms a sleep-inducing asp—' "

I gave a start. "What's that? That verse you just quoted?"

"That, Gordianus, was a line from my *Zmyrna*. You've practically been begging me to recite a bit of it ever since you arrived—"

"But I heard it earlier today, when I was at . . ." I stopped myself, for if I revealed I had been to visit Caesar, Cinna might somehow deduce the reason. In our friendly guessing game I would avoid giving him any clues if I could.

I had a sudden realization and drew a sharp breath. "*That's* who's reading your new poem! That's why he quoted you earlier today, because you and your work are on his mind. . . ."

Now it was Cinna who drew a sharp breath. "Then the man you were visiting was . . ."

"And the man reading your poem is . . ."

"Caesar!" we said in unison.

"I should have known," I said. "Who but the world's greatest man could pressure the world's greatest poet to finish his new masterpiece?"

Cinna laughed. "Your flattery will not deflect me, Gordianus. Yes, it's in Caesar's hands that my new poem resides, awaiting his judgment. And it's from Caesar that you've just come, dressed up in your toga. The Dictator must have summoned you for a private interview. Not to hire you; you're adamant that you've retired. For some personal reason, then. But what? Let me think. . . ."

I was busy with my own thoughts. "*You're* the one who's been talking about me to Caesar. It's from *you* that he knows I frequent this establishment. Confess, Cinna! You've been gossiping about me."

"Only to Caesar. To no one else. No one else is much interested in you these days, Gordianus. Yes, when I delivered the new poem to Caesar, and we talked of this and that, for some reason he mentioned your name, and I did happen to say that occasionally I see you here and share a cup of wine with you. I thought nothing of it at the time—the poem was the only thing on my mind—but now I wonder why your name came up at all, unless Caesar had some very specific reason for inquiring about you. When I mentioned seeing you here at the Salacious Tavern, he asked me if you had become a drunkard, and I assured you hadn't. He's had enough of drunkards—all the trouble he had with Antony, when Antony was carousing every night with that actress. I promise, I gave a sterling account of your character—that's what he seemed to be interested in, your good character. But why should Caesar care? Unless . . ."

By the look on his face, I knew that Cinna was drawing close to the truth. Was this how my own face looked when on the verge of a realization? For an instant I seemed to glimpse myself in Cinna's handsome face and sparkling gray eyes.

He put down his cup, laughed and slapped both thighs. "By Jupiter, Neptune, and Pluto! It can't be true! But it is. The Dictator has gone and made you a senator, hasn't he?"

I shook my head in wonder and drank more wine. From this man I had no secrets.

X

"Will marvels never cease? Since Caesar became dictator, it's as if the world's been turned upside down. Anything can happen. Anything!" Cinna stared at me for a long moment, then snapped his fingers for more wine.

"But . . . how did you guess?" I asked.

"There's a typical pattern of events. First, Caesar takes it into his head to make some fellow a senator or a magistrate. Next, Caesar makes a few discreet inquiries. If no alarming secrets come to light, Caesar invites the candidate for a private chat and springs the good news, impressing the delighted new senator with his boundless largesse. It was the same with me, when Caesar put me forward for tribune. I could hardly believe my good fortune. But *your* good fortune is even harder to credit." He furrowed his brow. "Almost impossible!"

"I can't tell if you're being serious, Cinna."

"As serious as I ever am."

"Then I suppose I should be . . . insulted." My voice trailed off, for I was as amazed as Cinna. The more I thought about it, the more incredible it seemed. Of all the ways I might live out my final years, to do so as a Roman senator had never occurred to me, not even in my wildest dreams. "I'm as appalled by the news as you are, Cinna. I don't suppose one can *refuse* an appointment to the Senate?"

"Not if you want to keep in the good graces of the Dictator. Don't be ridiculous!"

"It seems I'm ridiculous if I accept Caesar's offer, and ridiculous if I don't. . . ."

We were momentarily distracted by an argument that broke out across the room, where several men were huddled together, tossing dice on the floor. One of them accused another of cheating and the usual war of words ensued, brought to an end when the burly tavernkeeper outshouted them all and threatened to throw them out.

The tavern fell quiet for a long moment, until the rattling of dice on the floor broke the silence.

"Venus Throw!" one of the gamblers cried, exulting in his triumph.

"Was Cleopatra there?" asked Cinna. "At the garden estate? I presume that's where you met with Caesar."

"As a matter of fact, she was."

"Did you see her?"

"I did."

"She was nowhere to be seen the day I delivered the new poem to Caesar. I have yet to lay eyes on her." Cinna swirled the wine in his cup. "You have some history with the queen, don't you?"

"A bit. I happened to be in Alexandria with my son Meto and with Caesar on the day she introduced herself to him."

"What! You were present when Cleopatra was smuggled into the palace and unrolled from that carpet before his astonished eyes?"

"I, too, was astonished."

"No! You're making this up."

I shrugged. "Think what you wish."

Cinna gave me a sulky look. "How do I know this isn't just another of your tall tales?" This had become a standard refrain in our conversations, especially when I happened to reminisce about my travels or the adventures of my youth. The farther back in time the story, or the farther from Rome, the more likely was Cinna to scoff and accuse me of embellishing my tale with stardust. This was merely a method of pulling information from me, as I well knew, having used the trick countless times myself. If you want a man to give you more details, express doubt.

"You know I lived for a while in Alexandria when I was young," I said. "And I was there again only a few years ago, traveling with Bethesda. That's where I had first laid eyes on her, in Egypt. I've seen the Great Pyramid . . . and the Pharos Lighthouse . . . and Cleopatra. And the greatest of all these wonders was . . ."

Cinna peered at me over his wine cup. "Yes?"

"Bethesda!" I laughed, and so did he. "If I dare to say otherwise, I'm likely to find myself in a great deal of trouble."

"Come now, Gordianus. I seriously doubt that your lovely wife has spies here in the Salacious Tavern."

"No? You might be one, for all I know."

"Absurd!"

I shook my head. "Women have ways of gathering information that elude the scrutiny of us men. I speak from many years of experience, dealing with women of all ages, from every station in life, and from many nations. Sometimes I think they read minds."

"A terrifying thought."

"Not for you. You have no wife at present."

"Ah, but I have a teenage daughter. And my daughter has a nursemaid who's been with her from infancy. Come to think of it, sometimes she and old Polyxo do seem to communicate without speaking. But, returning to the subject of *the* woman—I mean the one about whom everyone in Rome is talking—am I to understand that you did in fact see Cleopatra today?"

"I did, briefly, passing through a garden that's been decorated to remind her of Egypt. It was because of her that your poem was quoted. Cleopatra made a gift of a certain slave to Caesar, and he recited that line. How does it go? 'As a puny Psyllus . . . touches a charming . . . wasp?'"

Cinna groaned. "'As a Punic Psyllus by touch charms a sleep-inducing asp.' Well! Caesar himself, quoting me to Egyptian royalty. I'm giddy. I insist we have more Falernian, this time congratulating Cleopatra."

"Congratulating her? Does the queen have something to celebrate?"

"Ah, not yet, Gordianus. Not yet!" He gave me a coy look.

"What's this, Cinna? My head is already spinning. I'm not sure I can stand any more surprises."

"But you must, because I can't keep it secret any longer." He leaned toward me and lowered his voice. "As you know, Cleopatra was only ever married to her own brothers, but she's run out of those. Now she may soon take a new husband."

"A new king for Egypt? What man would Caesar allow her to elevate to the throne? And for whom would she settle, other than Caesar?"

He hardly spoke above a whisper. "They're going to marry each other."

I likewise lowered my voice. "Surely not. Caesar's happily married already, and even if he weren't, Rome would never accept his marriage to a foreigner, especially *that* foreigner, with all the tangle of royal politics that would ensue. Can a dictator of Rome also be king of Egypt?"

Cinna raised an eyebrow. "Why stop with Egypt?"

I looked around. The dice game proceeded. The players paid us no attention. One of the lone drinkers had fallen asleep in a corner. Another was nodding and humming quietly to himself. The women I had taken to be whores were no longer present, having gone upstairs to nap or do business. The busty serving girl was behind the bar, helping the tavernkeeper decant an amphora of wine into smaller vessels.

I returned my gaze to Cinna. "What in Hades are you talking about?"

He bit his lower lip, then let out a giggle and smiled from ear to ear. His gray eyes sparkled with excitement. "You must swear to me, by the shade of your father, that you will repeat to no one—*no one*—what I'm about to tell you. Not until the Ides."

Why the Ides? I thought. That was the date set for Caesar's last full day of business with the Senate, the day I was to be put before that august body by the Dictator himself and accepted as a member. What else would happen on the Ides? There was the annual feast of Anna Perenna, when young couples take food baskets for picnics at a sacred grove north of the city; Cinna's daughter, if I remembered correctly, was perhaps of an age to take part in such a courtship ritual, provided she had a suitor. I also recalled that someone was staging a gladiator exhibition on the Ides, at the Theater of Pompey, in the same rambling complex of buildings where the Senate would meet. Caesar loved such exhibitions, but despite its proximity I doubted he would have time to attend.

"Very well," I said. "I'll tell no one. But why the Ides? What will happen that day?"

"The Senate will meet—as you well know, Senator Gordianus."

This was the first time I had heard the title spoken aloud. I felt a thrill of exhilaration, but also something akin to panic. My heart sped up. "I'm not a senator yet."

"No, but you will be soon enough. And quite possibly the first bit of legislation you'll be called on to consider and to ratify—which of course you shall, as shall all the rest of Caesar's handpicked senators, and any others who care to remain in his favor—will be a legal exemption and special permission drawn up by myself."

"An exemption for whom? Permission to do what?"

"For Caesar, who as Dictator for Life shall be exempted from the constraints of common law regarding marriage, and who shall be permitted, while outside Italy and throughout the duration of his military campaigns, to take in marriage howsoever many wives he wishes, for the express purpose of furthering the diplomatic and strategic interests of Rome and for the propagation of children. Presumably one of those wives will be . . . Cleopatra."

"Which would make Caesar king of Egypt!"

Though I had lowered my voice to a hoarse whisper, Cinna winced and raised a finger to his lips. "Not so loud, Gordianus."

I shook my head. "Cicero will be apoplectic."

"He may not be in attendance. Too busy dictating his deathless thoughts to Tiro."

"If not Cicero, then surely someone will speak against the idea."

"I don't think you understand how business is conducted in the

Senate these days, Gordianus. Debate is severely restricted, especially in the case of emergency legislation, the category into which this bill falls."

"Caesar might wish to bed some barbarian princess, and that qualifies as an emergency?"

Cinna smiled. "The urgency is dictated by the Dictator's impending departure. It's a piece of business that must be tended to before he leaves, which means on the Ides, and quickly, as there will be other equally pressing matters on the agenda."

"You mean Caesar's put this off until the last moment, so that he can get it done in a rush, before there's time for people to react."

"If you must put it so bluntly."

"The Senate may say yes, but what about the People's Assembly? As a tribune, isn't that where you should be introducing this legislation?"

"In due course, I'll put the exemption before the people directly. Unfortunately, that will have to wait until after Caesar departs. But having already been approved by the Senate, the bill will have no trouble being similarly approved by the people. You've never heard me orate, have you? Just as you've never read my poetry! I have a way with words, Gordianus. I can be as persuasive as Cicero, as eloquent as Scipio, as impassioned as the Gracchi brothers."

"Are you sure you want to take the blame for introducing such a measure?"

"Blame? There may be some opposition at the start, and some lingering resentment from old-fashioned republicans like Brutus or Cicero. But the benefits I reap will be much greater."

"Has Caesar promised you some extravagant reward?"

"Of course he has, but I'm talking about my reputation. Think, Gordianus! When Caesar finally comes back to Rome—the greatest conqueror since Alexander, a king many times over, with wives residing in countless foreign capitals, showering the people with untold riches pouring into Rome, handing out lucrative foreign postings to all his favorite senators—no one will care how many wives he's taken or how many princes he's produced, as long as no one here in Rome ever has to address him as king. There will be triumphal processions and games and feasts and rejoicing for months. And for having introduced the legislation that made it all possible, Gaius Helvius Cinna will be hailed as a genius, not just of poetry but also of politics. Not many men can claim such a double distinction. Perhaps none, come to think of it, when you consider those dreadful verses produced by Cicero. Even Caesar stumbled when it came to writing poetry—"

"By Hercules, Cinna, you've just delivered the only news shocking enough to make me forget my own shocking news, and now you're rambling on about poetry again."

"Because in the end it all comes back to poetry, as you would know if you weren't such an ill-read dullard. Politics comes and go. Poetry endures forever."

I put down my cup. "On that note, I'll take my leave."

"No, stay! Can I tempt you with more Falernian?"

"My head is spinning already. Or is it the room?" I blinked.

He smiled. "So, we've each managed to startle the other with a bit of good news. And where else but the Salacious Tavern?" He spread his arms and scanned the room. The gamblers had gone. Two of the whores were back, chatting to each other and comparing their fingernails. The tavernkeeper was carrying a flaming taper from lamp to lamp. Beyond the shutters night had fallen, suddenly, as happens in Martius.

"But remember, Gordianus, you promised to keep my news a secret."

I nodded. Whom would I be tempted to tell? Meto probably knew already. My mind-reading wife and daughter would be harder to keep in the dark, but I would do my best.

I stood.

"Before you go, Gordianus, there's one last thing."

"Yes?"

Cinna flashed a crooked smile. "It's so trivial, I almost forgot. Probably I shouldn't bother to mention it. But—as long as you're here . . ."

XI

Cinna dipped a fingertip into his cup of wine and on the wooden table-top he traced what looked like a Greek letter. He added letters, until a word appeared:

προσοχή

"You know Greek?" he asked.

"Enough." I sat down. "That's the Greek word for 'beware.'"

"Yes. Someone scratched those letters in the sand in front of my door-step."

"When did this happen?"

"A few days ago."

"Is it still there?"

"Certainly not! I erased it with my foot immediately. I didn't want it to be seen by everyone passing by, and certainly not by any visitor to my house."

"Which way did the letters face? I mean, was it written so it was right side up as you stepped out of the house, or as you stepped in?"

"The first."

"So it was addressed to someone in the house, not to someone coming to see you."

"So it would seem."

"Curious that it was written in Greek, not Latin."

"Curious that it was there at all!"

"Were you alarmed by this message?"

Cinna shrugged. "It's not a pleasant word to see as you leave your house."

"I should think not. Do you have any idea who wrote it, or why?"

"Not a clue."

"Have you received any other messages of this sort?"

"Not that I can think of."

"A pity you scratched it out. The way any given person makes Greek letters can be quite distinctive."

Cinna shook his head. "I didn't recognize the handwriting, though I admit I didn't scrutinize it very carefully, or for very long. My impulse was to erase it at once, before my daughter could see it, though I fear she may have. Sappho is a very sensitive girl."

"Sappho?" Though he mentioned her occasionally, this was the very first time I had heard him call her by name. "Is Helvia not pretty enough?" That would be the only name assigned her by law.

"Why shouldn't I bestow on my beloved only child the name of my favorite poet? My favorite in Greek, anyway. Her favorite as well. She knows every line of Sappho by heart. She's even tried to live up to her namesake."

"You daughter writes poetry?"

"A bit. Nothing special. To be honest, she's not very good. Still, better than Cicero."

"For what that's worth." We both laughed. "Do you think this message might have been intended for her?"

Cinna furrowed his brow. "That seems doubtful. Sappho's led a very sheltered life. She knows hardly anyone outside the household. I suppose I've been even more protective than most fathers, having lost my wife at a very young age." He shook his head. "Sappho is such a mild creature, as meek as a sparrow. I can't imagine that anyone would want to harm her."

"Then the warning was for you?"

Cinna shrugged.

"Are you worried, or not?"

"Should I be?"

"Your recent actions as a tribune on behalf of Caesar, contriving a way to expel those two other tribunes who disrespected him—I fear that you deeply offended some of your fellow citizens."

"Granted."

"And this scheme you're about to launch on Caesar's behalf, this permission to marry and propagate as he wishes—that, too, might cause a few people to get angry at you. Very angry."

"As I've told you, that's a secret."

"Nonetheless, someone might have got wind of it."

He shifted about in his seat. " 'Beware.' Awfully vague. Beware what, or whom?"

"Could it be that you interrupted the writer before he finished?"

"I looked up and down the street. I saw no one scurrying off." He squinted and gazed into the middle distance, picturing the scene. "The way the word was positioned, precisely centered in front of the doorstep, makes me think that single word comprised the entire message."

"Puzzling, then, as well as alarming. Perhaps that was the intention—to cause you distress. A political enemy winding you up. Or could it be a fellow poet? Have you offended some rival versifier, slighted some fledgling author?"

"They're all jealous of me, of course. Just as every senator is jealous of Caesar. Greatness inspires envy, always."

"I wouldn't know."

"But I'm not actively feuding with anyone at the moment, if that's what you mean. I haven't picked any literary quarrels lately. I've been too busy trying to finish my new poem! That is, when I haven't been listening to complaints and petitions and pleas from my fellow citizens, in my role as a tribune."

"Your role as a tribune—I think you've put your finger on it. I imagine this word scratched in the sand has something to do with politics. But whether it's a trivial bit of harassment, or a serious warning, who can say?"

"Indeed. Ah, well, I only thought I'd mention it, before I forget about it altogether. I suspect it's of no importance. No importance whatsoever."

"Let's hope so."

"Well, then, off with you. I won't keep you any longer. Fortune be with you until we meet again, Gordianus."

"May fortune be with you as well, Cinna."

I left the stuffy, warm air of the tavern and stepped into the bracing twilight of an early Martius evening. The few patches of the horizon I could see between the jumble of buildings were a dusky blue. Overhead, the black sky twinkled with stars. I drew a deep breath and tried to blow the fumes of wine from my lungs.

I took a few steps and at once regretted having dismissed Caesar's litter. I was a bit drunker than I had thought, and the way home was almost entirely uphill.

I took a few more steps and then froze, for it seemed to me that a figure was approaching from the deep shadows where the narrow, empty street met an intersection. I looked around. There was no one behind me; no one ahead, either, except the hulking silhouette. I took a step backward, for the towering figure was most certainly coming closer.

Where was my son-in-law when I needed him? At home with Diana, I thought, where he belonged. If something unpleasant was about to occur, I couldn't blame Davus, only myself.

Any other man of my wealth, no matter how newly acquired, would have hired a professional bodyguard or two to shadow his every step. I had preferred to spend the money on household slaves for Bethesda and a tutor for my grandchildren. . . .

The figure moved closer. I took another step back, and stumbled. I righted myself and suddenly felt quite sober. The figure made a sniggering noise, as if amused by my awkwardness. In the eerie silence that followed, I heard the booming sound of my own heartbeat.

Why had I so casually dismissed Caesar's litter-bearers? Because I'd had my fill of people demanding my attention, and I wanted to be left alone. I wanted to step into the Salacious Tavern with no one waiting for me outside, a free man, unfettered by worries and cares.

I was worried now.

The shadowy figure spoke in a deep, steady voice. "I haven't frightened you, have I?"

I recognized the voice of Hipparchus, the leader of Caesar's litter-bearers. He moved closer. His face was lit by dim starlight.

I pressed my hand to my chest, trying to muffle the booming of my heartbeat. "What were you thinking, sneaking up on me like that? And what are you still doing here? I sent you back to Caesar."

"Apologies, citizen." He lowered his head. Being so tall, he still looked down on me. "I sent back the litter and the other bearers, but I couldn't leave you here alone. Caesar would never forgive me if something untoward befell a guest on his way home. I decided to wait here, outside the tavern, out of sight, so as to attract no attention."

"You were certainly out of sight until you came lumbering toward me. You might have spoken sooner."

"Apologies, citizen. I've been taught not to speak until spoken to, unless it's absolutely necessary. I kept my mouth shut, until I saw the look on your face—"

"Yes, I understand." What a frightened old man I must have looked, for such a well-mannered slave to snigger at my misstep. I thought of the doddering, panic-stricken old fools who were stock characters in Roman comedies. Is that what I had come to resemble, after so many years of rectitude and striving? I stood stiffly upright and drew the folds of my toga more securely around me. That, too, was a stock character, the put-upon man of affairs in a toga trying not to look a fool.

I stared at Hipparchus. At least he wasn't laughing at me. "I suppose you'll want to accompany me all the way home."

"If you'll allow me, citizen," Hipparchus said, sounding quite respectful.

I took a deep breath. I collected my wits, until I felt myself again. I was Gordianus the Finder, citizen of Rome, world traveler, friend of famous poets and dictators alike, soon to be a senator—no man's fool, surely.

XII

To say that I hoped to skulk unobserved into my own home would do me a disservice. That would cast me as yet another laughable character from Plautus. Nonetheless, when I arrived at my front door, with a watchful Hipparchus striding dutifully beside me, I lifted a finger to my lips to demand his silence and made a very gentle knock. What were the chances I could shush the slave who opened the door before he could say a word, slip quietly inside, and find some hiding place where no one would bother me until I was entirely sober?

My hope was thwarted. Whichever slave was supposed to be minding the front door at that hour—I left it to Bethesda to assign such duties—was either absent or asleep. I knocked a bit louder. Then, with a sigh of exasperation, louder still.

At last the peephole opened and I saw the eyes of my daughter staring back at me.

"Papa! What took you so long? Mother is getting worried."

The peephole was shut, the lock gave a rattle, and the door swung open. Diana stepped to the threshold. Her dark hair was done up in some fashion I'd never seen before, with combs and pins and a slender silver chain holding it all together. There was a new slave in the household, a very expensive eunuch from Egypt, who had been purchased because he was expert at creating such hairstyles.

I turned and gestured to Hipparchus. "As you can see, daughter, and attest to your mother if necessary, I was never alone or in any danger, thanks to the diligence of this fine servant of the Dictator."

"I see," said Diana, appraising Hipparchus a bit more closely than was necessary.

"You may leave me now," I said to Hipparchus. "No, wait." I stepped inside the door and reached for a small bowl in a niche, in which were stored small coins suitable for gratuities to deliverymen and messengers. I pressed a few pieces of copper into Hipparchus's hand. "Your master needn't know that I gave you this."

"Thank you, citizen," he said, but with his eyes on Diana, not me. The two of them seemed to have arrived at some tacit agreement allowing the mutual gratification of their ocular senses. At the risk of playing yet another stock character—the disapproving father—I felt obliged to step between them. The interruption seemed to break some invisible thread of tension, for they simultaneously released very faint noises of regret, one coming in my right ear and the other in my left.

"But," Hipparchus continued, "I could never accept any gratuity, no matter the size, without informing my master."

"Tell Caesar, then, if you wish," I said, thinking that such a small transaction could hardly merit the attention, even for the blink of an eye, of a man with Caesar's responsibilities. But from single stones are built the longest roads, as my father used to say. No detail was too small to escape Caesar's attention. The loyalty of every man, from slave to senator, mattered to him.

With a last stolen glance at my daughter, the slave took his leave. I turned toward Diana, thinking to rebuke her with a raised eyebrow, but found myself face-to-face with my wife. Her hair was combed and piled up in an even bolder fashion than that of my daughter. She couldn't have been that worried about me if she had spent the afternoon with Diana doing up their hair. At least they were putting the new slave to good use.

"Husband, you smell of—" she began, but I pressed a finger to her lips.

"Say nothing, wife, until you've heard my news. Diana, gather everyone in the household, including the slaves. I might as well tell all of you at once, and be done with it. Come, we'll do it in the garden. Light lamps and braziers. I want to see everyone's face when I deliver the news."

Diana rounded them up. There were the two slaves who cooked and ran the kitchen and the three who cleaned the house and kept the garden (and were supposed to take turns minding the front door); there was another who sewed and did shopping, and her small son, who ran errands and took messages, and of course the new one who applied cosmetics to my wife and daughter and dressed their hair; and yet another couple of slaves who surely did something all day—Bethesda must have known their duties, though I did not. There was no point in trying to keep the news from any of them, because household slaves inevitably discover everything of importance that takes place in the house. They might, if they feared or loved or respected me enough, be trusted to keep the knowledge to themselves and not spread it outside the house. I made sure that was the first thing I said—"Say nothing of this to anybody until after the Ides"—looking not only at the slaves but also at Diana and Davus and Bethesda, as well as little Aulus and tiny Beth (for even my grandchildren would know the word "senator" and might repeat it in public unless admonished not to).

"Well, husband, what is it? What have you to tell us?" Bethesda looked at once dubious and quietly excited. A part of her, suspicious as a cat, thought I must be up to no good. Another part thought I must have a good reason to gather them all in one place to make my announcement.

"As you know, Meto dropped in on us earlier today and swept me off to visit the Dictator, at Caesar's request."

"Are you in trouble?" asked Davus. A furrow of concern creased his broad forehead.

"You might say that. You might say that I've been made an offer of the sort no man can refuse."

"An offer?" said Bethesda. "Holy Isis, husband, what are you talking about? Has Caesar offered you work?"

"You might say that as well."

"What can the man possibly want from you, at your age? You're a respectable member of the Equestrian order now. I won't have you digging through people's rubbish and getting yourself into trouble, not even for Caesar!"

Why was I hesitating? I had heard the words spoken—by Caesar, by Meto, and by Cinna—but I myself had not yet said them. Words once spoken can never be called back. It was as if the words themselves contained a sort of magic, like a spell, irrevocable once uttered.

"I . . ."

"Yes, Papa?" said Diana.

"I'm going to be . . . that is, Caesar has appointed me . . . or will appoint me . . . on the Ides . . ."

"Husband!" Bethesda almost shouted. Her lips trembled. There was a look on her face I had never seen before. She had guessed what I was about to say and could hardly contain herself.

Diana looked from one of us to the other, not quite understanding but sensing the enormity of the thing yet to be spoken. Like her mother, she trembled. Davus put his arm around her.

The excitement was contagious. Aulus clutched his father, little Beth her mother, and both let out a scream.

"I am going to be a senator," I said, in a low, hoarse voice so unfamiliar in my ears that I felt compelled to say it again. "I . . . am going to be . . . a senator."

Bethesda rushed into my arms. Diana followed, as did the children. Davus blinked and staggered a bit, as if I had smacked his forehead. The slaves burst into applause. I felt somewhat unsteady, but was in no danger of falling, encircled by so much adoration. Was this what real politicians felt when crowds of cheering well-wishers lifted them on their shoulders? Was this what Caesar felt when senators sprang to their feet and shouted his name as if he were a god?

"We must send word to Eco and Menenia at once!" cried Bethesda, between planting kisses all over my face. She was ecstatic. And why not? She had come the farthest of anyone in that house. She had been born a slave in Egypt but would end her days as the wife of a Roman senator. "Oh, what will Fulvia say?"

"No, no, no, wife! Did you not hear me? No one must be told until it actually happens, on the Ides."

"Don't be ridiculous. You can't keep such a thing secret. For one thing, you'll need to go shopping for a new toga—a senator's toga!"

"She's right, Papa," said Diana. "There can't be more than a handful of tailors who specialize in such an item, and even the most reputable tailors are notorious for spreading gossip. They see everyone stripped naked, so to speak."

"Why would you want to keep it a secret, anyway?" said Davus.

I blinked. "Fear of the Evil Eye?"

Even Roman generals feared the misfortune that might arise from envy. That was why chariots in triumphal processions were fitted with an ancient phallic talisman underneath, to ward off the black magic that might emanate from so many jealous onlookers. That was why mothers put such talismans in the cribs of their newborns, to ward off the malevolent envy of women who were barren or whose babies had died.

"Never fear, mother and I will do all that can be done to propitiate the gods and ward off ill fortune," said Diana. "Mother knows Egyptian spells she's never even shared with me. And we can ask Fulvia. She knows a lot about such things—"

"That Fulvia is a sorceress I don't doubt!" I laughed. "But not the most successful, to judge by her string of dead spouses—"

"Husband! That is just the sort of quip that might attract the Evil Eye. Not to mention the ire of Antony, a man you can hardly afford to offend, since Caesar will be leaving him in charge after he goes, and you're to be . . . you're to be a . . . senator!" Bethesda, too, felt the strange, giddy power of speaking the word aloud. She clapped her hand over her mouth.

. . .

Dinner that night was a celebration. Bethesda called for the best wine in the house. While not in a class with the Falernian I had been drinking with Cinna, it was quite pleasant to the taste, especially accompanying a hearty lamb stew. The cooks outdid themselves.

Every word Bethesda said, every movement she made seemed slightly more calculated than usual, more elegant, more refined. It was as if she were trying on the guise of a Roman senator's wife, which fit a bit snugly but flattered her nonetheless. To see her thus stimulated and gratified was the most compelling reason to accept Caesar's appointment. For Bethesda to be a senator's wife, I had to be a senator. So be it.

Diana, too, seemed quietly content. She wore a heavy-lidded expression like that of a purring cat. Davus, always affable, seemed happy for the rest of us, but surely he too felt a sudden welling of pride. Having attained freedman status by impregnating (secretly) and then marrying (with my blessing) my daughter, he would now be a senator's son-in-law, and his children would also rise in status.

Later, after all the food and drink had been cleared away, and everyone else had gone off to bed—everyone except Bast the cat, whose silhouette prowled the rooftop—I sat alone in the garden under the starlight, huddled close to the last flickering brazier.

"I am a New Man," I whispered to myself, for thus were called those who were the first of their family to rise to the Senate. But was I truly made anew just because Caesar said so? Surely I was the same now as I had been yesterday, and would be so on the Ides of Martius as well, and the day after. New obligations I would have, new expenses, new demands from my wife and daughter, new pressures to take sides in one dispute after another.

I looked up at the stars and sighed.

"Your father would be very proud of you," said a hushed voice. For an uncanny moment I imagined it was my long-dead mother speaking. I had not thought about her voice in a long time. I had forgotten how she sounded but now suddenly remembered, so similar in that moment was the voice of my daughter, who stepped from the shadows into the glow from the brazier.

"You never knew my father," I said.

"No. But you're thinking about him right now."

"Mind reader!"

Diana shrugged. "It was in your sigh."

I nodded. "It was the very first thought that occurred to me when Caesar told me—once my mind settled down enough to have a rational thought. 'What would my father think?'"

"I often think those words, myself. 'What would father think?' Meaning you. Quite often it's the thing that matters to me most of all."

"Only quite often? Not all the time? A Roman father's will should transcend all other concerns, even to matters of life and death."

"I do have a husband to think of, you know. And an Egyptian mother!" Diana laughed. "But you always come first, Papa. I am a good Roman daughter."

"And soon, the daughter of a Roman senator."

She gazed at the crackling flames in the brazier. "Papa, it's incredible." She spoke quietly, but her eyes were very wide.

"I know. And you're right. My father would be very proud of me." I felt a tear slip down my cheek. It must have glittered in the light, for Diana reached out and touched it with a fingertip.

We sat for a long time in silence

"What a day you've had!" she finally said. "Cicero and Caesar in a single day! I know why Caesar wanted to see you, but what did Cicero want?"

"He was eager to hear my thoughts on his new dissertation. 'On Divination' is the title."

She raised a skeptical eyebrow. "You'll have to come up with something better than that."

"Very well, the truth: Cicero thinks there might be a plot afoot to harm Caesar. He wanted me to look into the matter."

"If there were such a plot, I'd think Cicero would be at the heart of it."

"A plot to depose Caesar, perhaps, but not to murder him. That would not be Cicero's way. But he thinks there may be those who feel otherwise, who wouldn't stop at violence. For all I know, he may be right."

"And if you uncovered such a plot, what would Cicero do about it?"

"Lecture the plotters, I imagine! He feels neglected. Left behind. Irrelevant."

"But at this point, who would want Caesar dead? The civil war is over at last, and from what I understand, Caesar has been far more merciful than those who fought the last civil war, men like Marius and Sulla."

"But none of those men made himself Dictator for Life. It's hard for many Romans to stomach. I find it rather distasteful myself."

"Even though the Dictator's now made you a senator?"

"And what does that mean, in a Senate that serves to ratify one man's will?"

The brazier crackled and hissed.

"What if Caesar *were* to die suddenly, Papa? It needn't be murder. He could die from natural causes. What would happen then? What if Caesar died in his sleep this very night?"

"Then there would be no Parthian campaign, no string of conquests from here to India, no fresh sources of plunder to pour riches into Rome."

"That would be bad for Meto."

"Or good, if it means he won't die on some battlefield a thousand miles from home."

"And here in Rome?"

"A mad scramble for power. Chaos. Revenge. Recriminations. Another civil war, almost certainly. Unthinkable!"

"And even more unthinkable—in all the confusion, and without Caesar as your champion—you might not become a senator after all."

"That would be a disaster for your mother."

"Yes, it would. Have you ever seen her so thrilled?"

I shook my head. "What a thought! The death of the world's most powerful man, probably the most powerful man in history, a veritable god—a death that would alter the destiny of the world—might also frustrate the social aspirations of a certain Roman housewife!" I laughed. "We must keep things in perspective."

"But isn't the perspective of every mortal the same, Papa—with the universe circling around, and oneself at the center?"

I stood and yawned, finally weary enough to sleep. "But what are we worrying about? Cicero's fears are exaggerated, I'm sure. I am to be a senator. Meto will go off to Parthia and come back a hero, covered in glory. Caesar will rule the whole world from Spain to India, and outlive me. You and your children will grow up in the richest, most peaceful, most wisely ruled empire the world has ever known."

Diana smiled. "Of course, Papa. It shall be just as you say." She kissed my cheek, and the two of us went to join our slumbering spouses.

DAY TWO: MARCH 11

XIII

My sleep was surprisingly sound, considering the excitement of the day. I was awakened early the next morning, well before dawn, by the amorous advances of my wife.

It had been awhile since we made love. Pent-up desire might partly explain the enthusiasm she showed, but I suspect that waking up next to a soon-to-be senator was the thing that most excited her. We had not coupled with such passion in months, perhaps even years. As our bodies touched and moved against one another, I returned in memory to the young man I once had been, when I was living in Alexandria and I first laid eyes on Bethesda. The pleasure I experienced transcended time. I was at once in the moment and also in all the moments of the many, many occasions we had made love over the years. I felt enfolded by the passage of time, not my enemy but my friend, for had it not delivered me to this present moment of consummate bliss?

Afterward, wide awake and whistling the tune of an old love song from my Alexandria days, I made my way to the garden. I wrapped my cloak around me as I sought the warmth of the brazier that had been glowing all night and now was being stirred into open flames by one of the slaves.

I had in my hand the brief list of names Caesar had given me the previous day. I remembered his words: *Drop in on certain men . . . find some pretense for your visit . . . and while you're there . . . keep your eyes and ears open for any bit of useful information. Use that power of yours to draw the truth out of men . . .*

Ironically, the first name on the list was Cicero—the one man I was certain posed no threat to Caesar. The frustration he had expressed at being left out of any plots had been too genuine even for Cicero to fake. How flattered he would have been to know that his name headed Caesar's list!

As I perused the other names, it occurred to me that Caesar himself had provided a suitable pretext for these visits: I was to become a senator. If the fact could not be kept secret, then I might as well use it to my advantage. As the men on the list were all senators themselves, I could say I was seeking advice, as a New Man soon to join their ranks. Indeed, it might be revealing to see how each man reacted to the news that Caesar was to make Gordianus the Finder a senator.

I decided to start with the man about whom I knew the least and about whom I was most curious: Spurinna, the Etruscan haruspex who had been made a senator by Caesar. It was in his role as a diviner that Spurinna had delivered the warning to Caesar that he would be in danger until the middle of Martius. Meto had told me where Spurinna lived.

Dawn was too early to call on a man of such importance, so I bided my time for an hour or so before I set out, wearing my toga and taking Davus for protection. As I was stepping out the front door, Bethesda appeared, still in dishabille and looking more desirable than any women in Rome half her age. She asked where we were off to.

"Tending to some senatorial business," I told her, not entirely a lie, at which she seized my shoulders and gave me a long kiss that took my breath away.

As we set off down the street, Davus looked at me sidelong and made a low whistle that broke into a knowing grin. "Diana was the same, last night," he confided. "You should become a senator every day!"

Spurinna lived in a rather grand house on the Aventine Hill. An obsequious slave admitted us to an exquisitely furnished reception room, then scurried off to inform his master. The floor was paved with geometric mosaics and the wall panels were alternately red and orange. For decoration there were some very fine pieces of terra-cotta sculpture executed in the old Etruscan style that collectors find so desirable—a smiling man and woman, almost life size, reclining together on a couch as if to dine; a smaller piece that depicted two dancers with open arms looking skyward; and at the center of the room, set atop a black marble pedestal, a small but exquisite statue of a mounted warrior wearing a three-horned helmet.

"Haruspicy must be a profitable business," said Davus, following my gaze.

"Perhaps. But according to Cicero, Spurinna comes from a very old and distinguished Etruscan family. New Man he may be, but there's likely to be an ancestral fortune. These terra-cotta pieces may be family heirlooms."

"So they are," said a reedy voice with the lilting accent common to those who come from the more northerly Etruscan cities, farthest from Rome. "Welcome to my home, Gordianus."

Spurinna was dressed neither in a senatorial toga nor in the costume of a haruspex, but in an elegantly tailored tunic of pale linen cinched at his narrow waist with a thin leather belt. He was completely bald but had a long, very thick beard mingling silver and black. There was something disconcerting about his face. I realized that his dark eyes and eyebrows were not symmetrical, with one side higher than the other, a peculiarity that created odd expressions.

"Thank you," I said. "This is my son-in-law, Davus. I don't think we've met before."

"But I know who you are. Just as you must know who I am."

I nodded. "We have that in common, that each has knowledge of the other. But we have something else in common."

"Do we?"

"Caesar made you a senator, did he not?"

"Yes, to the dismay of some, but to the delight of my family."

"I can say the same. Or rather, I'll be able to say so, a few days from now."

Spurinna gave me a keen look. "Are you saying that Caesar is making you a senator?" Spoken without emotion, the question gave no clue as to what he might feel about the matter.

"Yes. On the Ides."

Spurinna raised an eyebrow, which on his face had an effect opposite that of most people, for it brought his features into alignment and erased any hint of irony. He was a hard man to read. "How interesting. So much is likely to happen on the Ides."

"What do you mean?"

"Come, Gordianus. You will have heard about my warning to Caesar, perhaps from that son of yours, who happened to be present when I conveyed the omen divined from the sacrifice."

"You warned Caesar of a threat hanging over him. You told him to be careful for the next thirty days."

"Exactly. The period of greatest danger will expire just after the Ides."

"What if you're wrong?"

Spurinna looked down a hallway toward a portico where a patch of morning sunlight had appeared. "Come, let's talk in the garden. I think today will be warmer than yesterday."

There were more terra-cotta statues in the garden. We followed him to a pair of benches close to an image of the goddess Turan, said by some to be the same as the Roman Venus, despite the wings that sprouted from her back. Spurinna and I sat, while Davus leaned against a pillar.

"If the Ides should come and go and nothing untoward befalls Caesar," said Spurinna, "I shall be delighted, of course. Haruspicy is not an exact science. Interpreting the divine signs is a tricky business even for the most experienced practitioner, like myself. Or it might be that Caesar will escape the threat precisely because of my warning, no matter that he scoffs at it. Who knows what choices Caesar will have made in light of my divination, knowingly or not—choices that will have steered him away from danger?"

"I see your point. If the warning successfully protects Caesar, then the threat will remain unseen, and there'll be no proof of the divination's accuracy. Perhaps you might explain that conundrum to Cicero. He's writing a treatise on divination."

Spurinna snorted. "And how could he possibly be qualified to do that? Is that why you're here? Did he send you to feel me out about contributing to his impious efforts?"

"No. I wasn't sent by Cicero. I mention him and his work only because I happened to see him yesterday."

"And what does that old crow make of your elevation to the Senate?"

"Actually, he doesn't yet know. Or at least, he didn't know when I saw him. And neither did I."

"So this has only just happened?"

"I was told by Caesar yesterday."

"Ah, that explains why I'm only now learning about it. I'm usually abreast of all developments surrounding the Dictator, even those of little consequence."

That certainly puts me in my place, I thought. "Are you so knowledgeable because of your connection with the Dictator's wife?"

Again I was frustrated when I tried to read his expression, but his voice sounded vaguely amused. "Calpurnia has come to rely on me, yes, and I see her often. In matters of divination she's more devout than her husband. Such is frequently the case. Women are more sensitive, more receptive than are men to divine manifestations."

"Yet only men practice haruspicy."

"Women have their own ways of divining, largely outside the control or the knowledge of the state, or of men in general. Conversely, the divination of men is regulated, with ranks and rules, priesthoods and colleges. There are exceptions. The women who become Vestals are very much part of the state religion. And undoubtedly there are men who in secret practice sorcery, just as many, perhaps most—perhaps all—women do. But you must know all about such things, eh, Finder? Your career must have brought you into contact with many a seer and diviner."

"True. I happened to have met the haruspex who preceded you as Calpurnia's confidant, that fellow Porsenna, not long before he met his untimely end." Did I see a frown on his lopsided face? "I should think the haruspex who dies of violence is probably not the best practitioner of his craft," I added. "Unlike yourself, I'm sure."

"Indeed. My personal divinations indicated that I would have unexpected visitors today. That certainly describes you and your son-in-law, Finder. And though you are most certainly welcome, I'm still unaware of the purpose of your visit."

I wanted to see with my own eyes the man who publicly warned Caesar of a threat hanging over him, I thought. *I wanted to hear you speak, watch you move, observe your dress and the place where you live.* But what I said was: "The reason is quite simple. I need to acquire a new toga to suit my new rank, and I have no idea where to make such a purchase, especially on such short notice. I mentioned this in passing to my son Meto, and he said, 'Why don't you ask Spurinna? He acquired his senatorial toga not that long ago, and everyone knows he's a man of impeccable taste.'" I seldom resorted to outright lying, but this untruth seemed harmless enough, and Spurinna would never doubt it. Men who dressed as elegantly as he did, and furnished their homes with such fine works of art, never question a compliment.

"You must go to Mamercus, of course. His shop is on the so-called Street of the Ironmongers. His family has been in the business for generations. Mention my name and I'm sure he'll treat you very well."

"Excellent! Davus, you'll remember that, won't you?"

"Mamercus the tailor, Street of the Ironmongers," said Davus slowly, as if learning a foreign phrase.

Having been complimented and beseeched for a favor that cost him nothing, Spurinna finally let down his guard. I detected a slight relaxation around his mouth and a more friendly glimmer in his eyes.

I lowered my voice. "But what can you tell me about this threat to Caesar, the one you've foreseen? I can't help but be curious. You are, after all, the foremost haruspex in Rome." Additional flattery relaxed him even more. "Did your divination shed light on the nature of the threat? Did it point to any particular individuals, or even the sort of men who might be involved?"

"I see that you're genuinely worried about our mutual benefactor," said Spurinna, "so I'll tell you what I can." He raised a finger to his bearded chin and furrowed his brow; one side of his face looked more thoughtful than the other. "You presume the threat to Caesar is from other mortals. In fact, it could be from some natural danger. It might even emanate from some divine agency."

"But if that's the case, of what use is a warning? How is Caesar to avert such a nebulous threat?"

"Prudence. The Dictator must avoid every kind of accident that might naturally occur in the course of a day—a fall down stairs, a slip at the baths, a burn from a flaming brazier. He must do nothing to incite the wrath of any deity. He must make every proper sacrifice and observe all rituals necessary to placate the gods. He must ward off witchcraft— Calpurnia can help him with that—for if the threat is indeed human, it might arise not from his rivals or enemies but from their wives . . . or widows."

"And there are so many widows in Rome." I sighed. "Such a wide array of threats!"

"Mortal dangers beset every man, every day, but for Caesar the peril is acute, and will remain so until the thirty days have passed."

"Then may the Ides come and go swiftly."

"Indeed," said Spurinna.

"Indeed!" echoed Davus, with surprising vehemence. When I gave him a curious look, he added, "For after the Ides you'll really be a senator, and think how pleased our wives will be."

Spurinna gave Davus a wry glance. Half of his face looked incredulous and the other half amused. He laughed. "How wise you are, big fellow. In the end, it all comes back to pleasing our wives and mothers, doesn't it? That's so even with Caesar."

It seemed to me unlikely that Caesar's career owed much to pleasing Calpurnia, or Cleopatra, or any other female. Spurinna saw the doubt on my face.

"It's true, Finder. You must know the story of Caesar's dream the night before he forded the Rubicon. To cross that boundary with his army meant that civil war would inevitably commence. And what did he dream the night before? That he slept with his mother."

I nodded. Meto had told me the story. How had Spurinna heard it, from Calpurnia? Did everyone in Rome know?

"And far from putting him off," said Spurinna, "the dream spurred him on to cross the Rubicon and fulfill his destiny—*to please his mother,* don't you see?"

I blinked. "Is that your interpretation?"

"What other is there?"

"I should have thought . . ." I hesitated. "I should have thought that the maker of our dreams was warning Caesar that by marching on Rome he was about to commit an unnatural act."

"Nonsense!" said Spurinna. "That's why I'm a haruspex and you are not."

"True. The work of reading omens would never suit me."

"The role of a senator will suit you much better, I think."

"I have my doubts about that, but it's kind of you to say so."

I decided I rather liked the man, despite our different ways of looking at the world. It also seemed to me that Spurinna posed no threat to Caesar. Nor did he have anything useful to say, if such a threat existed.

XIV

"Shall we go to that tailor the haruspex recommended?" asked Davus as we made our way down the street in front of Spurinna's house. "I remember the name and the location."

"So do I, Davus. But on a matter as weighty as having a toga fitted, surely I should get a second opinion. I think we have time for another visit before midday. If I remember correctly, down that street there is the house where Marcus Junius Brutus lives. I wonder if he might receive an unexpected visitor?"

The house of Brutus was far less ostentatious than that of Spurinna. There was often such a distinction between the old and the new in Rome. Ancient as Spurinna's Etruscan bloodline might be, in Rome he was very much a newcomer and always would be, whereas no one in Rome could claim a pedigree as old and distinguished as that of Brutus, who descended from the Brutus who drove out the last king and founded the Republic more than four hundred years ago. Such a man has no need of decorations and ornaments to proclaim his arrival. He had arrived even before he was born.

So I was not surprised to see that his residence looked, more than anything else, old. Among all the surrounding houses, it looked by far the oldest. The architecture was plain and simple. The clay tiles along the roofline were chipped and weathered. The stone steps leading up to the door had been worn in the middle from countless footsteps.

To those footsteps I added my own and those of Davus. Even the door was old and chipped, especially around the much-used peephole where an eye perused us for a long moment before the door swung open on creaking hinges.

We were led down a long gallery. From niches on both sides the death masks of scores of ancestors gazed sternly. Among them, set in a niche of honor slightly larger than the rest, I recognized the bearded, austere countenance of Lucius Junius Brutus, founder of the Republic.

Once past this intimidating display of ancestry, I found the interior of the house to be no less simple than the exterior. There was not much furniture in the room where we were invited to wait, and the pieces looked exceedingly uncomfortable; it was as if cushions and chairs with backs had not yet been invented. One wall had been painted with some sort of scene, perhaps of a hunt, but the image was so faded I could hardly make it out.

The most striking feature of the room was its terra-cotta statuary. Unlike the splendidly preserved pieces in Spurinna's house, these specimens, displayed on simple pedestals, appeared to be mere fragments— bits of geometric and vegetal decoration, a gigantic horse's head, and remnants of a masculine figure, including a large hand clutching a rein. Like those of Spurinna, these pieces were almost certainly of Etruscan manufacture. Etruscan artisans introduced terra-cotta statuary to Rome, including the giant statue of Jupiter with his chariot and horses atop the original temple of the god on the Capitoline Hill, a structure long ago lost to fire and demolished and rebuilt.

I peered at one of the fragments—a leaflike architectural device the size of my head with chipped edges and much-faded color—and suddenly realized what I was seeing. These pieces called to mind the fabled quadriga of Jupiter atop the temple because they *were* that statue, or what remained of it. The disembodied hand holding a rein was not just any hand, but was the hand of Jupiter himself, and not just any Jupiter, but one of the oldest images of the god ever created for the city of Rome.

I let out a small gasp, just in time for my host to hear. Had I contrived it intentionally, I could have devised no better way to ingratiate myself, for he knew at once the reason for my surprise.

"These aren't actually . . ." I said.

"They most certainly are," said Brutus. He was a handsome man with a long face and keen eyes. He wore a simple white tunic embroidered with a Greek key pattern in blue.

"But that would mean these pieces are even older than the Republic," I said.

"Yes. They date to the reign of King Tarquinius Superbus, when the first Temple of Jupiter was built. The greatest of all Etruscan artisans, a fellow named Vulca, not only designed the temple but also created the statuary. All that remains is what you see here."

"I should think such precious artifacts would be stored in the temple itself."

"Yes, one might think that. But, massive as it is, even the Temple of Jupiter has only so much storage space. All those Sibylline books in the basement, you know. And a great many sacred phalluses, I'm told, some of them quite large, and all very ancient, much older than the temple itself. And who knows what else."

"But how did you acquire these pieces?"

"Well, it wasn't *I* who acquired them. It was my ancestors."

"But how?"

"Who knows? Not I. And if not I, then nobody. Some great-great-grand-somebody-or-other got his hands on them, and here they are. I tell people they've been in the family forever, but literally speaking, that's not true, of course. Even we Bruti haven't existed *forever*. Almost, but not quite. The gods are older!" He produced a barking laugh. "What do you say, Mother?" He turned to a tall woman wearing a simple yellow stola who had just entered the room. "Who's older than us? Some say the Julii, and maybe they are, if it's true they descend from Venus. Venus must be even older than *you*, eh, Mother?" He laughed again, then stepped aside, ceding to his mother the focal point of the room where she could see and be seen by her guests.

"Who are these people?" she said brusquely. Despite her son's jocular tone, Servilia was not a woman to be taken lightly. With her graying hair piled atop her head, her erect bearing, and her chin held high, she was the very picture of a patrician matron. Brutus had joked about her age, but at fifty Servilia was still quite attractive. I could see why Caesar had taken her as a lover when they were both much younger (and much to the consternation of Servilia's brother, Cato). A lingering sentimental attachment might explain why the Dictator was so indulgent and forgiving of Servilia's son, despite his opposition to Caesar in the war.

"This man, Mother, is called Gordianus the Finder. And the younger fellow . . . well, by Hercules, I'm sure the slave told me, but now I've forgotten. Not one of your adopted sons, is he?"

"Not quite. Davus is my son-in-law."

"Ah, yes. That's it. Gordianus the Finder and his son-in-law, Davus."

"Why have you abandoned your other visitor to see this fellow?" said Servilia. "You have important business to attend to."

"How well I know, Mother. But dear old Cicero once told me, should Gordianus the Finder ever come calling, I would do well to see him. 'The fellow can be quite irritating, but he usually has something interesting to say, and he's never frivolous.' Well, from Cicero, that's quite a compliment."

Servilia looked me up and down, as if by sight she could determine the accuracy of Cicero's statement. "Well, then?" she said, sounding impatient. "Say something interesting, Finder. Or prove my son's beloved Cicero a liar."

Before I could answer—and to my relief—another figure entered the room. From the way she carried herself I knew she must be the mistress of the house, Porcia, Brutus's new wife and also his cousin. She was rather plain to look at, but her marriage was said to be a genuine love match: Porcia had been a young widow with a child when Brutus divorced his previous wife to marry her. Certainly Brutus could not have improved his standing with the Dictator by marrying the orphaned daughter of Caesar's bitterest enemy.

Cato—Porcia's father, Servilia's brother, and Brutus's uncle—was dead, but not forgotten. After Cato's messy suicide in Africa, Brutus, a protégé of both Caesar and Cato, had published a eulogy praising his uncle's steadfast Republican virtues. Copies proliferated and were posted all over the city. Caesar felt obliged to publish his own objurgation, a sort of anti-eulogy that denounced the late hero of the opposition as a greedy, lecherous drunkard. Despite this war of words over a dead man's reputation, Caesar had named Brutus urban praetor for the year and had put him in the lists for a consulship a few years hence.

Porcia had inherited more than her plain looks from Cato. Like her father, she was said to be headstrong and demanding—not unlike a younger version of her aunt and now mother-in-law, Servilia. Perhaps that explained her appeal to Brutus. As Spurinna had said, *In the end, it all comes back to pleasing our wives and mothers.*

Servilia stiffened a bit as Porcia entered the room. Brutus smiled and took her by the hand.

"This visitor, my dear . . ." he began, and introduced us again, repeating the line from Cicero. "And now we must all look to Gordianus to say something interesting. And not frivolous."

Three pairs of eyes turned on me. Four, counting Davus.

"You'll think me presumptuous . . ." I began, and felt their scrutiny sharpen. "It was my son Meto, I think . . . yes, most definitely it was Meto . . ."

Servilia and Porcia both looked to Brutus, who explained, "Adopted. Freedman. On Caesar's military staff. Helps with letters and memoirs and such."

"Yes, I said to Meto, 'Now that I have need of such a thing, whom might I ask for advice? Some New Man, perhaps—'"

"Like Spurinna," said Davus, catching on and trying to be helpful.

"Yes, exactly, some New Man, like Spurinna? And Meto said, 'By Hercules, Papa, certainly not! Don't go to the newest member for advice, go to the oldest—oldest by family, at least—and that would be Marcus Junius Brutus. Ask him where to go. Loving Caesar as he does, Brutus will surely want the last of the Dictator's New Men to look his best on the Ides."

All color abruptly drained from Brutus's face. Porcia, too, seemed to blanch, but Servilia merely looked vexed. "What on earth is this fellow talking about? Cicero was half right. Irritating, indeed!"

"I think, Mother . . ." Brutus began, then swallowed, looking a bit queasy. He dropped Porcia's hand so that he could wipe a bead of sweat from his brow. "I think . . . well, I don't know what to think." He stared at me. "Are you saying . . . ?"

"I am to become a senator. On the Ides." It still felt very strange to say those words aloud, especially to such a man, in such a house.

Porcia, the one I least expected to speak first, stamped her foot and clenched her fists. "Oh, *that* is the limit! Husband, why have you even allowed this . . . this . . . *person* . . . into our home?"

Brutus spoke through gritted teeth that gave the false appearance of a smile. "I told you, my love. Cicero vouches for the fellow."

"And who is Cicero but another New Man? A man with no ancestors. A nobody!"

"Well, he's hardly that, my dear." Brutus looked pained.

"We all have ancestors," I said quietly. "Even Cicero. Even me. Else how did I get here?"

Brutus cleared his throat. "But you said something about . . . asking my advice?"

"Yes. I must purchase a new toga. A senator's toga, to wear on the Ides. As you can see, the venerable old toga I'm wearing today is so ancient and threadbare, I doubt the man who sold it to me is still in business. So I have no idea where I should go. You must know the best of the best."

Brutus appeared to stiffen every time I mentioned the Ides. Was the idea of my becoming a senator so appalling that it actually made him flinch? Spurinna had buoyed my confidence. Brutus was demolishing it. But both recommended the same tailor.

"In some families," said Brutus, "it's a tradition for a son to wear one of his father's senatorial togas. But since in this case that isn't . . . possible . . . then I'd say go to Mamercus, in the Street of the Ironmongers. His work is impeccable. Even if you need the order in a hurry, which . . . obviously . . . you do."

"In time for the Ides, yes," I said. "I should probably go there at once."

"Yes, you probably should."

Even as I nodded and turned to leave, a figure wearing the red-bordered toga of a praetor appeared in the doorway. I recognized him only because Meto had pointed him out to me at public gatherings. Gaius Cassius was Brutus's brother-in-law, married to his sister. He was a tall, lean man of forty, beginning to bald a bit, as Caesar had done at that age. Like Brutus, his name was on the list Caesar had given me, but the Dictator must have had some degree of trust in the man's abilities, since he had made Cassius a praetor and appointed him to be governor of Syria in the coming year, a job that would require considerable skills as both diplomat and military man. "The current mess in Syria," as Caesar had called it, would have to be put straight if the Dictator were to march confidently into Parthia, with Syria at his back.

Cassius's manner was very refined, even haughty. When he deigned to look at me, I saw a great deal of his clean-shaven chin. He proceeded to ignore me and spoke to Brutus. "Brother-in-law, I'm afraid I can't stay any longer. I must meet some friends over on the Esquiline. We can continue our discussion later tonight. I'll bring the men I mentioned."

"Yes. Very well. All right, then," said Brutus, who clearly had no intention of introducing me. So much for my prestige as a budding new senator!

To further distract my host, another figure appeared in the opposite doorway, which led to the private areas of the house. He was a red-bearded man of middle age with the rumpled look of a philosopher or private tutor, which in fact he was. It was Porcia who acknowledged him with a nod, giving him permission to speak.

"Apologies, Mistress, but you asked me to let you know as soon as the boy finished his morning lessons."

"Yes, Artemidorus. I've promised him a midday excursion to the Capitoline Hill." She turned to Cassius. "I'm going to introduce him to the statue of Marcus Brutus. Can you believe he's never seen it?" Then to the little boy, who had appeared alongside his tutor: "Not *our* Marcus

Brutus, your stepfather, but the Marcus Brutus who lived long, long ago. And what did he do?"

"He dethroned the king!" the boy cried enthusiastically, stabbing the air with his fists.

Porcia turned to Cassius. "It's time he got to know some of the older members of the family into which he's been adopted." She spoke as if the statue were a living person, not the image of a man dead for hundreds of years. "I think there's a family resemblance between that Marcus Brutus and our own. The statue depicts an older man, of course, and with a beard, but otherwise my husband could have been the model."

"Yes, I've always thought they looked alike," said Cassius. "Handsome but determined. So my little nephew is to have an adventure!" He bent his knees and clapped his hands, and the child went running to him.

The boy sped past me, hesitated at the sight of hulking Davus, who gave him a friendly smile, then ran into the arms of Cassius, who lifted him high in the air.

"Careful, please!" cried the tutor. "If you swing him about as you did last time, he'll have another nosebleed." Looking at Artemidorus's distinctive red beard, and recalling his name, I realized the Greek was not just any teacher but a rather famous rhetorician from the city of Cnidus. His even more famous father, Theopompus, had taught Caesar. To instruct his own adopted son, Brutus had sought out the best of the best.

Just as Artemidorus had feared, flecks of crimson appeared at the boy's nostrils as his uncle swung him around. A few drops of blood flew through the air and spattered Brutus. Brutus looked down at the tiny spots of blood and turned as white as his tunic.

"Oh, Gaius, you're too reckless. Look what you've done!" snapped Porcia, clutching Brutus's tunic, apparently more distressed by the stain on her husband than by her son's bleeding.

Looking chagrined, Cassius set the boy down. Servilia bent and held out her arms in grandmotherly fashion, but it was not to her but to Artemidorus the boy ran. The tutor lifted the hem of his long tunic and pressed it to the boy's bloody nose.

The moment was exquisitely awkward for everyone, including me. I raised my hand to catch my host's attention. Brutus looked at me blankly.

"With your permission . . ." I said, venturing a step backward and taking Davus by the elbow.

"Yes, yes . . . of course," muttered Brutus. No one else in the room was paying the least attention to me. I might have been invisible, or a slave.

Stepping out of the house, slipping a bit on the smoothly worn stone steps, I sucked in a deep breath.

"Such people!" said Davus, shaking his head.

"What do you mean?"

"Such an old family, so respectable, and all that," he said. "But when you gave them your news, not one of them congratulated you."

"Quite the opposite," I said, looking up at the sky. "Midday, or close enough. What do you say to a bite to eat?" *And perhaps a spot of wine, to brace my nerves,* I thought.

"Yes, please." Davus was seldom without an appetite. "Home?"

"I think not."

"Where, then?"

"Follow me, big fellow."

XV

As we neared the Salacious Tavern, Davus grunted to show that he was not surprised at our destination. He had escorted me there and come to escort me home any number of times, and occasionally had whiled away an hour or so sharing a bit of wine with me. ("Learning bad habits from his father-in-law," as Diana put it.) The food at the tavern was only passable, but there was always something on offer. At midday it might not yet be too stale or too spoiled to eat.

The tavern was nearly deserted. Having the pick of locations, I chose a corner with a clear view of the entrance, as my father had long ago taught me to do. From the corner, you can see anyone coming toward you. The position can help defend a man from assassins, to be sure, but is also helpful in less contentious situations, as for example allowing one to compose one's expression accordingly and gain a slight advantage by seeing who has just entered the room before he sees you. So it was, only a few moments after we sat, that I saw Cinna step inside, looking a bit blinded by the change from light to dark. A few blinks later he saw me and flashed a genuine smile of surprise. In the meantime, I had put on a frown of mock-disapproval and shook my head gravely as he approached.

"Tribune Cinna, back at the tavern again so soon? You've hardly had time to sober up from yesterday."

"I could say the same to you, Finder. Senator, I mean."

I silenced him with a forefinger to my lips. Some say this gesture springs from the resemblance of an upraised finger to a phallus, as both may be intended to ward off the Evil Eye. "You mustn't call me that yet. I'm still a mere citizen, thus free to indulge my vices as I wish, owing no explanation to the censor in charge of public morals or to the good citizens of Rome."

"And when you do become a senator, I shall hold you to a higher standard, as you do me!" Cinna laughed. "Besides, I came here to eat, not drink."

"Now that is surely a lie. To eat *and* drink I can believe, since that's what I'm here to do, but not the one without the other. No one comes to the Salacious Tavern just to choke on stale bread or nibble some moldy cheese."

"I hope we can do better than that." He clapped his hands to attract the tavernkeeper's attention. "Wine for all of us, my good man, including this big fellow." Cinna nodded to Davus, with whom he had become acquainted on previous visits. "And bring whatever you have to eat that won't make us ill."

The tavernkeeper looked aggrieved. "We happen to have a bit of grilled fish caught in the Tiber this morning, served with a fine garum and olives on the side, and flatbread hot from the oven."

"Sounds delicious!" declared Cinna. Davus's stomach growled.

"What brings you out on this lovely day, Finder? Making the rounds of your soon to be colleagues?"

"Something like that."

"You might as well ask *him,* too," said Davus.

"Ask me what?" Cinna raised an eyebrow.

I was puzzled for a moment, then realized what Davus meant. "I need to acquire a new toga, of course, and on short notice, so I'm wondering—"

"Wonder no more. The fellow for you is Mamercus, located—"

"On the Street of the Ironmongers," we all three said together.

Cinna smiled. "I see I'm not the first to recommend him."

"I thought senators were supposed to disagree about things. How else can they hold a debate?"

"You're behind the times, Gordianus. 'Consensus' is our watchword now. We have consensus on just about everything, thanks to the Dictator."

"Even on the question of a tailor, apparently."

"Well, Mamercus *is* the best."

"Just as you are the best poet in Rome," I said, reaching for the cup of wine offered by the tavernkeeper. When we all three held cups, Cinna raised his aloft. "Here's to always demanding the best," he said.

"And never settle for less," I added, and at once made a liar of myself by emptying a cup of rather mediocre wine.

"When he was young, my father-in-law was a friend of the best poet in the world," said Davus, endeavoring to say something useful. Cinna stiffened. Davus didn't understand how sensitive poets can be when ranked against other poets, even the dead.

I smiled. "My old tutor, Antipater of Sidon, certainly *thought* he was the best poet in the world, and never hesitated to call himself that, though I'm not sure how many others thought the same. Besides, that was a long, long time ago. Antipater has been gone for . . . well, for almost a lifetime, it seems."

"Ah, yes, you've mentioned this connection to Antipater of Sidon before," said Cinna. "It was he who took you to see the Seven Wonders of the World."

"We traveled together when I was young, yes."

"He was a great poet, there's no disputing that, though his work seems rather quaint nowadays—all those poems about Myron's statue of a cow! I happened to pass by Antipater's gravestone a few days ago and thought of you, so I paused to take a good look at it. Quite extraordinary. And talk about old-fashioned! The images are a sort of rebus, meant for the viewer to decipher. A rooster, a palm branch—I confess I couldn't make it out."

"Yes, and the gravestone would be even more extraordinary if Antipater were actually buried there," I said.

"What?"

"By Hercules, you've done it again, Cinna!" I muttered. "I've let slip a secret, and for no reason other than your presence."

"But you must explain. If the tomb of Antipater of Sidon is empty—why, that's just the sort of thing from which one might fashion a poem."

"Perhaps. But the story is too complicated for me to recount it now."

"Then you'll recount the story in your memoirs, I hope. Along with everything else you can remember about Antipater. Aren't you thinking of writing an account of your life and travels?"

"By Hercules, how drunk was I when I told you that?"

"Very. Which does not negate the idea. In wine, truth. Or tall tales, at least. The readers won't much care which you tell, or if you mix them up together."

I shook my head. "No one writes memoirs these days except politicians hoping to sway voters, or generals trying to secure a place in history."

"Oh, I'd much rather read the life story of Gordianus the Finder than that of Sulla, or even Caesar's war diaries."

I sipped more wine. "To be sure, I have met a great many interesting people. And I've witnessed great events. And the stories I have to tell might differ considerably from the official versions."

"Exactly! Your memoirs would offer a different version of things. As you say, the memoirs of great men are mostly propaganda, entirely self-serving."

"I'm not sure that even the most honest man could give a true reckoning of his time. My daughter said to me only last night that the perspective of every man is different and yet the same, with the universe circling himself at the center. Two men never share exactly the same truth. And the gods are just as self-centered, if we're to believe Homer."

"Antipater, Homer—for a man as ill read as yourself, you do like to drop names. You'll be talking about the good old days with Catullus next."

"Catullus! You know, I never set foot in this place without thinking of him. Poor put-upon poet, lifting a cup here at the Salacious Tavern and longing for his Lesbia." I laughed. "For a while, his poems gave this place quite an infamous reputation. You could hardly get in the door. Then the excitement died down. But you must have known Catullus much better than I did."

"We were close, for a time." Cinna nodded thoughtfully. "Now *there* was a great poet. And a great judge of poetry, as well. Do you know the compliment he paid me? Or rather, the compliment he gave to my *Zmyrna*?"

"No, but I suspect I soon will."

Cinna cleared his throat. "According to Catullus, my *Zmyrna* 'will travel as far as the deep-channeled streams of Satrachus. The centuries will grow gray in long perusal of the *Zmyrna*.' A poem for all the world, and a poem for the ages—so said Catullus."

The fish arrived, served on skewers. There was a bowl of garum for dipping, and another bowl with olives, and a generous piece of flatbread that we tore into three portions.

"Whatever happened to Catullus?" said Cinna. "The last I heard, he was called to Verona on some family business, and he never came back. Then I heard he was dead, but no one seemed to know how or why. Then came the civil war, with death and confusion everywhere, and people forgot about Catullus. Not about his poems. Every literate person knows those by heart. But the man himself, and whatever became of him, is a mystery." He gave me an arch glance. "Now *there's* a puzzle you might investigate, Finder, something to draw you out of retirement. The mystery of the vanished poet!"

"I decline the case. I'm much too busy."

"Doing what?"

"For a start, I need to see that tailor about a toga. But before I do that . . ." I thought of Caesar's list of names.

"Yes?"

"I'm trying to think of an excuse to call on Marc Antony."

"Don't you know him?"

"Our paths have crossed. And my wife seems to be on surprisingly

familiar terms with his wife. But Antony has become such an important fellow. I'm not sure I can trouble a consul with my little question
about a tailor."

"Why not? I shall take you there myself."

"Right now?"

"Right now."

"Without an appointment?"

"I hardly need an appointment to call on my dearest drinking companion in the world, other than you."

"You and Antony?"

"Oh, yes. Before I took up with the likes of you and the other low-
lifes in this establishment, I had the pleasure on countless nights of drinking till dawn with dear old Antony, reciting poetry back and forth, and
challenging the other guests to outdrink us—which they never did. That
was back in the good old days before he married Fulvia, when he was
living with that lovely actress, the divine Cytheris."

"But you're drinking companions no longer?"

"No. Antony is a reformed man, forever striving to please our Dictator on the one hand and his wife on the other. Oh, and also to please
our fickle citizenry, who for some reason frown on having a drunkard
for consul. The two of us are still great friends, and always will be, I hope.
But—I shall put it bluntly—Antony is no fun anymore. No fun at all.
So drink up now, before we go, because we're not likely to be served a
drop of wine at the consul's house!"

XVI

Antony's house was located on the southwestern slope of the Esquiline Hill. To reach it, Cinna, Davus, and I traversed the entire length of the Forum, walking past gleaming temples and across grand ceremonial spaces. For a while, following Caesar's victory, the Forum had become a strangely quiet, dreary place, depopulated by the deaths of so many among Rome's ruling class. Now the Forum was bustling again, as senators and magistrates and priests and bankers crisscrossed the open spaces and gathered to talk on temple steps, attended by little armies of scribes and clerks and citizens seeking favors from them. Some of these senators looked rather foreign, sporting braided hair and long mustaches, and they sounded foreign, too, chattering among themselves in their Gaulish dialects.

Having crossed the Forum, we ascended the Esquiline and at last arrived at the House of the Beaks, so-called because the vast dwelling had once been owned by Pompey the Great, who had decorated the huge vestibule with metal ramming beaks from ships captured during his illustrious campaign to rid the sea of piracy. After Pompey lost his head in Egypt, there had been a mad scramble by Caesar's supporters to lay hands on his many houses and estates. Antony claimed the House of the Beaks.

I had visited the house not long after Antony moved in, when he was living there with Cytheris. Though Cytheris thought them hideous, the ramming beaks had remained in place. Only the choicest of these trophies were displayed; it was said that Pompey had captured over eight hundred ships. I presumed that Antony had disposed of them—who would want to keep a dead man's trophies as decoration to be seen by every visitor?—but to my surprise, the beaks were still there. As the three of us waited for word of our arrival to be conveyed to Antony, we strolled about the huge vestibule, gazing at the beaks. Sometimes one sees ships with crudely fashioned beaks, little more than man-size lumps of bronze with a pointed end, but these were all amazing works of art, fashioned to look like griffins with ferocious beaks or sea monsters with multiple horns.

"Beautiful, aren't they, Finder?" said Cinna.

"Fearsome, I would say."

"Beautiful *and* fearsome," said a voice I knew at once. I had not seen Fulvia in quite some time—not since her marriage to Antony—but her voice, like everything else about her, was distinctively her own, deeper than that of most women. Mannish, some called it, a word often used to describe Fulvia. The passing years had made her voice even deeper, giving it a pleasant huskiness that played upon the ear like silk upon one's fingertips.

Fulvia had risen to prominence thanks to marriages to one powerful, ambitious (and doomed) man after another. Her first husband had been the rabble-rouser Clodius, whose control of the mob gave him the run of the city. Eight years ago Clodius had been murdered on the road his ancestor built, the Appian Way. Fulvia had staged his funeral as a grand political event that turned into a riot and climaxed with the burning of the Senate House. Her second husband, Curio, had been one of Caesar's most promising lieutenants, but Curio died early in the civil war, killed by King Juba of Numidia, who desecrated his corpse and took his head for a trophy. After that humiliation, Fulvia had vanished from public view, reappearing in a seat of honor to view Caesar's African triumph, in which the late King Juba's infant son had been paraded as a victor's trophy. Her second widowhood ended with her marriage to Antony. He was arguably the most promising of her husbands, though it was hard to say how much any man's ambition mattered now that a dictator ruled Rome.

"That one is Antony's favorite." She pointed to one of the beaks, a spike that looked like a giant conical seashell. I looked at Fulvia instead. My association with her went back many years. When I had last seen her, she was still dressed in mourning for Curio; her black mantle had framed a beautiful but brooding face lined with bitterness. Now she had to be in her forties but actually looked younger than before. Strife and strain had been erased from her face, replaced by an expression that was at once happily optimistic and grimly determined. She was dressed in a sleeveless gown suitable for home wear, immodestly showing her shoulders and arms.

"I know that you, Gaius, have a rather soft spot for this one." Fulvia touched a beak cast in the form of a young sea nymph with a smiling face, seaweed for hair, and small, bare breasts.

Cinna smiled. "It's the irony that strikes me. Imagine a crew of sailors being sent to the bottom of the sea after being rammed by such a pretty thing." He touched the cold metal, allowing his fingertips to linger on the girlish breasts.

Fulvia raised an eyebrow. "Greetings, Gaius, and welcome." She offered her cheek, to which Cinna pressed his lips. But the kiss never happened. Fulvia drew back very slightly just as Cinna's lips might have touched her.

"And welcome to you, also, Finder. And to your son-in-law." No cheek was offered to me or Davus.

"I presume the three of you have come to see Antony, not me. You're in luck. He hasn't yet gone out for the afternoon. There's so much pressing business for a consul, every hour of every day. It never stops."

"Keeps Antony out of trouble," said Cinna.

"Most of the time," said Fulvia. "I keep him out of trouble the rest of the time. Follow me. I think he's in the garden."

As we were led through various rooms and hallways, I remembered the last time I had been in the house, and how stripped of furniture and ornaments it had been. Hundreds of items accumulated by Pompey were being put up for auction by Antony, with the proceeds supposedly going to the public treasury. Some said that Antony, and others allied to Caesar, were simply enriching themselves, seizing properties and taking much if not all of the proceeds for their own use. There had been some friction between the Dictator and Antony over the matter, but apparently the rift had been healed, since Caesar had seen fit to make Antony consul. And the house no longer looked empty. The many corners and walls and niches had been redecorated with furniture and paintings and statues, presumably brought in by Antony's new wife. One of the pieces, a small but striking bronze statue of a satyr cavorting with a goat, I recognized from a visit I had paid to Fulvia after the murder of her first husband.

About the matter of confiscated property, Antony and Caesar had been reconciled. Now they were said to be at odds again, this time over Caesar's choice of a consul to replace himself and to serve alongside Antony after Caesar left for the Parthian campaign. Caesar intended to hand over the consulship to Dolabella, whom Antony detested. The question was to be decided at the meeting of the Senate on the Ides. It seemed a relatively small matter to me, but not, apparently, to Caesar, who had put Antony's name on the list he had given me. Perhaps Caesar feared that living in Pompey's house had given Antony ideas about becoming a second Pompey. More likely, it was Fulvia who might goad his ambition to one day be called Antony the Great. I recalled words once spoken to me in confidence by Calpurnia: "Mark my words, Fulvia has her eye on our Antony, and if those two should ever join forces . . . beware!" Perhaps Calpurnia's husband shared her apprehension.

Deep within the house, completely secluded from the street, was an unusually large garden. Pebble-strewn pathways were bordered by small trees and shrubs and decorated with bubbling fountains and elegant statues.

The most prominent of these, because it stood in the garden's center and towered larger than life over everything else, was a bronze statue of

Bacchus. The god of wine and ecstatic release was shown in his youthful guise, wearing long, loose robes. Grapes and vines adorned his long hair and framed his boyish, beardless face. In one hand he held an upright spear twined with ivy, in the other a cluster of grapes. But the most striking details were the silver horns that sprouted from his temples. Statues depicting Bacchus with horns were rare, at least in my experience. He was said to reveal his horns only at the moment his frenzied female worshippers, called Maenads or Bacchantes, were on the brink of the divine madness called bacchanalia.

"That wasn't here the last time I visited," I said to Cinna as we passed before the statue. "It wasn't among Pompey's decorations."

"You're right. The statue arrived with Fulvia. Ironic that she brought with her the god of wine but won't allow Antony himself to play Bacchus."

This was not the only change I noticed. When I had last been in the garden, there had been many dining couches piled with plump cushions set amid the little arbors of myrtle and cypress, elegant accommodations for the famously raucous parties held on warm summer evenings when Cytheris played hostess and Antony quite literally played Bacchus, with ivy wreathing his brow and an endlessly replenished cup of wine in his hand. Those days were over. There was much less furniture now, and what there was looked much less comfortable. The corner where Antony sat, attended by scribes on either side and with a table of scrolls before him, looked more like a magistrate's office than a place for bacchanalia.

Antony was formally dressed in his consul's toga hemmed with a thick red border. He was dictating to one of the scribes but stopped at our approach. His wide, ruggedly handsome face broke into a beaming smile at the sight of Cinna. He rose from his chair and the two embraced. I was struck by the contrast. Cinna was slender and classically handsome. Antony, with his craggy brow and dented nose, was slightly shorter but twice as broad.

"And here, Gordianus, let me embrace you as well!" This came as a surprise, but I awkwardly submitted to a hug that squeezed every bit of air from my lungs. Antony had the build of a boxer and the strength of one as well.

"Congratulations!" he said, releasing me from the hug but then gripping my shoulders as if he intended to crush them. In his enthusiasm he started shaking me. I clenched my teeth to keep them from rattling.

"Congratulations!" he said again, finally stepping back.

"But . . . for what, Consul?"

"Your appointment to the Senate, of course! Ah, Gordianus—always so cagey, even when receiving congratulations. Well, you'd better get used to it. Come the Ides, you will be inundated with words of welcome and praise."

"I will?"

"Most certainly! Think how many men in the Senate owe you a debt of gratitude for getting them out of some scrape or other, or helping them find evidence to destroy some villain in the law courts. You've made many a friend over the years."

"And many an enemy," I said. "But how did you know of my appointment? I was hoping to give you the news myself."

"These days, Gordianus, there's very little that happens in Rome that I don't know about. Part of my wife's bride-gift was the network of spies she's built over the years. Fulvia's eyes and ears are everywhere. Everywhere! She makes the perfect consul's wife."

He reached for Fulvia, pulled her close, and gave her a kiss. She might have succeeded in making Antony a sober, hardworking magistrate, but staid he would never be. She accepted the kiss with an enthusiasm that surprised me, considering that three visitors and two scribes were present. The moment was rather touching, for there could be no doubt that their affection was genuine. Fulvia had finally found the mate she deserved. So, perhaps, had Antony.

The kiss ended, but Antony held Fulvia close. "And congratulations to you as well, my dear Gaius," said Antony.

"My life is so replete with accomplishments, I'm not sure for which of them you congratulate me," said Cinna.

"For completing the new poem, you lout—and just in time for Caesar to read it before leaving for Parthia. Now that's writing to deadline! I have no doubt he shall love it as much as I do."

I looked sidelong at Cinna. "I thought Caesar was the first reader."

"Indeed he is—the first reader of the complete poem," said Antony. "But I've been privileged to hear bits and pieces of it over the years."

I raised an eyebrow. "Cinna told me he never recites from his work before it's published."

Cinna looked a bit chagrined. "Antony is the only exception to the rule."

"And what a lucky man that makes me!" said Antony. "Magnificent stuff, this new poem! The stories of both Orpheus and Pentheus are told, side by side, so to speak. Your description of the beheading of each is the stuff of nightmares. I shiver, remembering those lines. 'Then did his mother lift up the sundered head, and kiss her son upon the mouth, and thought she felt him draw a shuddering breath—the passage of a breeze across the blood-wet emptiness of his severed throat.' By Jupiter, Gaius, it's as if you were actually there to witness such a thing."

I felt a chill down my spine. Once I had seen a man beheaded—Pompey, on the beach in Egypt, at a great distance, to be sure. That moment still haunted my dreams. I glanced at Fulvia, who had by slow degrees withdrawn from her husband's encircling arm, and I saw her turn pale. She, too, must have been thinking of a real beheading, that of her husband Curio at the hands of Juba's soldiers in Africa.

Looking at me and then at Fulvia, Antony realized the impact of his words and drew a sharp breath. "But the poem is about much more than that, of course. . . ."

"Indeed it is," said Cinna quietly. I saw that Fulvia was staring at him with a strange, fixed gaze, as if to accuse Cinna of some impropriety simply for having written such words—words intended, I had no doubt, not merely to shock but also to evoke the terror and pity that Aristotle held to be the highest accomplishment of art.

"I think we must have some wine," said Antony. Fulvia shot him a piercing look. "But we *must,* my love. It isn't every day that a fellow gets made a senator, or finishes an epic, and here we have a chance to celebrate both!"

"Very well." Fulvia clapped to summon a slave and ordered that special cups be brought, along with a pitcher of Falernian. "Your favorite, as I recall," she said to Cinna.

"Indeed it is."

Fulvia turned to me. "I understand from your wife that those two slave boys I gave you are now down on the Cup, pestering your son instead of you." Her interest in the matter was surely slight, I thought, but the question served to change the subject.

"Yes. But Mopsus and Androcles are hardly boys anymore. They've shot up like weeds in the last year or two."

"They must be thriving, then. I'm glad. I do have fond memories of them."

Did she really? It was sometimes easy for me to forget, when dealing with persons of her stature, that Fulvia was a woman like any other, capable of feeling genuine affection for her inferiors—as long as they didn't cross her. Mopsus and Androcles had assisted me when I looked into the matter of Clodius's murder, and afterward Fulvia made a gift of them. Had they remained in her household, I had to think it likely that they would have come to grief, given their penchant for getting into mischief. It was hard to imagine the woman who gave orders to Antony granting leniency to a slave.

The wine arrived and was served in decorated silver cups of extraordinary workmanship. The sculpted metal depicted a riot of drunken Maenads amid leafy foliage, celebrating their love for Bacchus, who appeared on each cup in his youthful guise as the ivy-wreathed giver of wine and lord of abandon. Here, as on the statue, the young god's horns were clearly to be seen amid the grape clusters and vines on his brow.

"Appropriate for the occasion, I thought," said Fulvia, addressing Cinna. "I presume Bacchus must play a role in this new poem of yours, Gaius, since it's Bacchus whom Pentheus offends, for which crime the Maenads, including his mother, tear him apart."

"Why, yes, of course. Though the Maenads on these cups appear to be having just a bit of innocent fun."

"And in a few days," said Fulvia, "after the Ides, Rome will celebrate the festival of Father Liber, who is none other than Bacchus under a very old Roman name. I am honored to be organizing and playing host in this very garden to certain rituals of the Liberalia, those that are the exclusive domain of we plebeian women, as handed down by ancient custom." She turned her gaze to me. "In preparing for the Liberalia, your wife and daughter have been very helpful to me, Finder. How gratified they must be at the great honor the Dictator has granted you."

I nodded.

"And to be sure, Bacchus has always been a favorite of my husband, to whom the god has in turn shown great favor."

I looked at Antony, thinking this was the moment he would offer a ritual toast, but he seemed content to keep silent and let Fulvia do it. She turned her gaze toward the statue of Bacchus at the center of the garden.

"So as we drink, let the god be present among us in all his names and guises—Bacchus, Bromius, Father Liber, Dionysus, Euhan-Euhius-Eleleleus . . ."

With her cup raised to the horned statue, and her eyes half shut, she sounded like a priestess as she invoked the god. This was a side of Fulvia I had not seen before, the pious Roman matron who took care that every occasion in her home, however great or small, should be pleasing to the gods.

I arrived home that afternoon quite exhausted by so much walking, and a bit slow-witted from Antony's Falernian, which had replenished the silver cups of Bacchus more than once.

Bethesda was delighted that Fulvia had mentioned her and appalled that I had not yet visited the tailor.

"Do it now, husband!"

"Now? There's no time."

"The sun is still up."

"Not for long. A fitting at a tailor can take hours."

"All the more reason to get it done right now—"

"Wife, desist! I'm tired and I wish to take a nap before dinner. I'll tend to the toga tomorrow."

I had two slaves carry a sleeping couch and bring a warm coverlet to the garden. Bast the cat joined me, purring loudly as she burrowed between my legs. I drifted off to sleep beset by unsettling thoughts.

When had Roman wives begun to give orders to their husbands? When I was a boy such disrespect for the head of the household was unheard of. Yet here was Fulvia corralling Antony like a tamed bull, and my own wife presuming to tell me what to do. I still found it hard to believe that the half-savage slave girl I purchased in Egypt long ago was now a Roman matron (thanks to the fact that I manumitted and married her) and consorted with the likes of Fulvia, quite possibly, after Calpurnia, the most influential woman in Rome. What could the two of them have in common? Was it possible that my wife and Antony's, when in private and away from masculine ears, ostensibly making plans for some festival, in actuality shared observations and advice regarding the manipulation of their menfolk? Did there exist, unseen but not unfelt by men, a veritable conspiracy of women?

Tomorrow, I promised myself, I would do as Bethesda demanded and take care of the toga. How absurd it seemed, that in the days leading up to the all-important Ides I should be so anxious about a mere piece of wool with a bit of scarlet dye.

DAY THREE: MARCH 12

XVII

I woke the next morning fully intending to visit the tailor as soon as I had washed my face and had a bite to eat. But no sooner had I dressed than a visitor arrived.

"Who is it?" I asked.

The slave, half asleep himself, mumbled the name "Brutus." I told him to take the guest to the small library at one corner of the house, and soon thereafter headed to the room expecting to find Marcus Brutus. I couldn't imagine what he had to say to me. Had my visit to his house ended too abruptly for his liking?

That puzzle evaporated and was replaced by another as soon as I saw the visitor. Marcus Brutus, with his elegant comportment, seemed born to wear senatorial dress. This man, though about the same age as Marcus Brutus, had a very different bearing. He would be more at home in military armor, I thought, than his poorly fitted toga. He wore a neatly trimmed beard, as military men often do, saying they encounter enough dangerous blades in battle. His posture was stiff and in his eyes was a look that proclaimed he had no time for nonsense. Junior officers would be terrified of such a man.

"Do we know each other?" I asked.

"We do not," he answered. "That's why I've come. To meet you. As a courtesy."

This was not very enlightening. "You know my name, I take it. But I don't know yours."

He grunted. "Decimus Junius Brutus Albinus. I did give my name to the man at the door."

"Apparently four names are too many for the poor fellow to remember."

"Then he shouldn't be answering the door." He grunted again, perhaps realizing it was rude for one man to lecture another about household slaves.

"He did remember 'Brutus.' Since I saw Marcus Junius Brutus only yesterday, I thought perhaps—"

"Different branch of the family," he said.

"Yes, as that Albinus at the end would indicate."

"But likewise descended from the founder of the Republic."

I nodded. "As a matter of fact, I think *you* look a bit more like that famous statue than does your cousin Marcus. Especially with the beard."

He touched it. "It helps me to pass as a Gaul."

"Do you do that often?"

"On occasion."

"Ah, yes, I remember. You're the Dictator's handpicked man to govern Gaul. My son says you speak several Gaulish dialects better than the Gauls themselves."

He said something that must have been a Gaulish proverb, for when he saw my incomprehension he translated: "'To rule the henhouse you must think like a rooster.' The Gauls are very proud of their gaming cocks."

"Speaking of Gaul," I said, "you and I were both in the vicinity of Massilia a few years back, when Caesar laid siege to it. I was trapped inside the walls. You commanded the fleet that destroyed the Massilian navy offshore. I saw some of the battle from the walls of the city. Ships aflame. Mangled bodies and blood amid the waves."

"If you thought it looked ghastly from shore, you should have been on the water that day." He flashed an incongruous smile.

"My son Meto does that sometimes, too."

"What's that?"

"Smile, when recalling something horrific."

He shrugged. "It's the excitement. There's horror in the actual moment, but when a man thinks back, it's the excitement he recalls."

"I should have thought it was the other way around."

Decimus Brutus laughed. It was a hearty laugh, devoid of any rancor or irony. "Caesar said you were like that."

"Like what?"

"'A deep one,' he called you. 'Cuts straight to the heart of the matter. Practically a philosopher.'"

"I suppose I'm flattered that the Dictator finds my character worthy of discussion, though I can't imagine why."

"I asked him about you. After he told me we're to dine together. Always nice to know a bit in advance. That's why I dropped by. Just a casual visit. We can talk at greater length when we dine."

"What in Hades are you talking about?"

He raised his eyebrows. "Oh. I see. The invitation hasn't arrived yet. I'd thought—well, obviously I got it wrong. My timing, I mean."

"Make that sort of error on a battlefield and men could die."

He shut his mouth tightly and relaxed only when I smiled. "Did Caesar not warn you that I can be rather perverse, as well? When is this dinner that you speak of?"

"I really should say no more. But it was my understanding that you and I will be attending the same dinner on the day after tomorrow."

"Where?"

"At a location to be decided."

"How mysterious. With whom?"

"With Caesar, of course."

I frowned. "That can't be right. That's the night before the Senate meets. Caesar will have a great deal to do. He won't spend his time dining with me."

"I may have arrived with news ahead of the official invitation, but I didn't get the details wrong." This was said with a military man's conviction. "We are both to dine with Caesar two nights hence. Along with your son Meto."

"That I find less surprising. Meto can at least take notes for the Dictator, but I should be quite useless at such a dinner."

"He's doing it *for* Meto, of course."

"What do you mean?"

"Your son is very important to Caesar. Caesar wishes to honor him, here in Rome, before the departure for the East. And to honor you, as Meto's father."

"I should think that what happens on the Ides will be honor enough."

He gave me a blank look, and for a long moment said nothing. Finally he drew a sharp breath and nodded. "You mean your elevation to the Senate."

"What else?"

"Even so, I think we will soon be dinner companions. Ahead of the occasion, I thought I'd pay a call, to introduce myself."

The man was a diplomat as well as a general, I thought. Both skills would be essential when it came to governing the numerous tribes of Gaul.

"There's the guilty slave," he said, looking past me. I turned to see the slave who was tending the door. Decimus Brutus looked as if he expected me to thrash the miscreant then and there. The slave caught his look and flinched, though no one was near him.

"Another visitor, Master. Your son."

"You hardly need to announce Meto," I said, and a moment later opened my arms to embrace my son as he stepped into the room. The slave scurried out of the way and quickly vanished.

Meto and Decimus Brutus acknowledged one another with curt nods. Neither seemed entirely surprised to see the other. Decimus Brutus no doubt surmised that Meto was the bearer of my dinner invitation, and Meto, with thinly veiled displeasure, surmised that his surprise had been spoiled.

Decimus Brutus said a hasty farewell and left the library, saying he would see himself out.

"He ruined my surprise, didn't he?" said Meto.

"I'm afraid so. It's true, then? Dinner with the Dictator, two nights hence?"

Meto smiled broadly. "I wanted to give you the news, but perhaps it's better that Decimus Brutus got here ahead of me. You don't always enjoy surprises."

"Hardly ever. To an old man, there is no such thing as a friendly shock."

"Are you quoting something?"

"Only the thoughts in my own head."

"But Papa, isn't it wonderful? It's to be a very formal dinner, with lots of courses, and some sort of entertainment or recitation—something very special, Caesar says—but also a very intimate affair. Only six of us."

"Only six! I shall run out of conversation after the appetizer."

"Nonsense. You're the best conversationalist I know. After Caesar, that is."

"You flatter me."

"Not at all. Did Decimus have some other reason to visit you?"

"He said it was a courtesy call, to introduce himself ahead of the dinner. Seems a bit odd, now that I think about it."

"Not really, Papa. It's an old military habit—scouting the terrain ahead of time. Decimus no doubt has his own agenda for the dinner—political favors to ask of Caesar, that sort of thing—and never having met you, he's wondering just what sort of dinner companion you'll be. How much of Caesar's time will you take up, what sort of tone will you introduce? And so forth."

"It's not as if I'm some barbaric Gaulish chieftain."

"Actually, the behavior of a barbarian from Gaul would be easier for Decimus to anticipate. Caesar likes to say that Decimus has 'gone Gaul,' the way some men are said to 'go Greek' when they become too at home with the natives and pick up local customs. I think Decimus feels a bit of an outsider when he's back here in Rome. Dealing with Gauls is easy for him now. Dealing with his fellow Romans requires effort. The more

Roman the Roman, the greater the effort. And there is no Roman more Roman than you, Papa. Except Caesar."

"Again you flatter me!"

He smiled. "Besides telling you about the dinner invitation, I had another reason for calling on you."

"Yes?"

From the way he scanned the little library and then peered down the hallway, making sure we would not be overheard, I knew what he was about to ask.

"You want to know if I've seen or sought out information about any of those men on Caesar's list," I said.

"Yes, Papa."

"As a matter of fact I have. But I have nothing of substance to report."

"Which of them have you seen?"

"Yesterday I paid calls on Brutus—the other one—and Antony. Oh, and I saw Cassius, as well, but only in passing. He was at his brother-in-law's house when I happened to call."

"Anyone else?"

"Only Cinna, who most certainly is *not* on Caesar's list. Oh, and Decimus Brutus, just now, who isn't on the list, either. I suppose Caesar must trust him as much as he does you, since you'll both be at this dinner party."

"Yes, Decimus is the last person Caesar would suspect of treachery. And your impressions?"

I shrugged. "If anything, I'd say the wives pose the biggest danger to Caesar."

Meto snorted.

"I'm quite serious. Let me explain . . ."

XVIII

"It's hard for me to see Brutus as a threat to Caesar," I continued, "except for one thing—the fact that he's now married to Cato's daughter and subject to her influence. If Porcia is anything like her father, she detests the Dictator and everything he stands for, and almost certainly she blames Caesar for her father's suicide. Cato never let go of a grudge. Like father, like daughter?"

"Cato didn't have to die," said Meto. "He could have surrendered. Caesar would have pardoned him."

"Perhaps. But Cato preferred what he considered an honorable death to the dishonor of submitting to a tyrant. Many people respect Cato for that, whether they sided with him or not. As you may recall, when Caesar in his African triumph paraded a gory image of Cato gutting himself with a knife, many people were offended, and not just Cato's supporters."

"There may have been some who thought that picture was in poor taste—"

"I was there, Meto. I heard the booing. Of course, I don't know how greatly Porcia influences her husband. But there's also the fact that Brutus himself is Cato's nephew, and his mother is Cato's sister. Servilia is a formidable woman by any measure. Remember what I said about Cato and grudges? Like brother, like sister?"

Meto frowned. "You make it sound as if Cato poses a threat to Caesar, from beyond the grave."

"That's one way of putting it. The dead do have a habit of taking vengeance on the living. Of course, once Caesar is off to Parthia, the excitement of the new war will supplant the bitterness of the old war. No one will remember dead Cato if Caesar returns with a living Parthian king in chains to be paraded in yet another triumph."

This idea made Meto smile.

"And then there's Fulvia," I said.

"Another woman."

"Yes, and even more formidable, I suspect, than Porcia or Servilia."

"Not even Fulvia could turn Antony against Caesar."

"No? I think she has even more sway over her husband than does Porcia over Brutus. And she's driven by something stronger than any grudge: ambition. I mean the sort of grand, earth-shaking ambition that Caesar himself possesses. Ambition that transcends marriages and military alliances, disappointment and death. Ambition that only grows stronger each time it's thwarted."

"You make Fulvia sound almost supernatural, like a Fury, or some sorceress from the myths, like Medea."

I raised an eyebrow. "I wouldn't be at all surprised if she practices sorcery of some sort. She also has a veritable army of spies, informants she's known and nurtured for years, since her first marriage, to Clodius."

"But could Fulvia turn Antony against Caesar?"

"The two men have had their ups and downs. Antony must be disappointed that he's not accompanying Caesar to Parthia."

"He'll have the honor of governing Rome instead."

"Which he's done before, not entirely to Caesar's liking, which caused the last rift between them. If Antony were to turn against Caesar, Fulvia would make a powerful ally."

Meto looked thoughtful. "You also saw Cassius?"

"Briefly, at Brutus's house, whirling his little nephew in the air. He seemed harmless enough—though he did give the child a nosebleed! And Decimus Brutus, who's not on Caesar's list. And Cinna." I sighed. "Far from posing a threat, Cinna seems disposed to do anything the Dictator asks, no matter how radical. You must know about this legislation he intends to introduce on Caesar's behalf, allowing the Dictator to take as many wives as he wishes."

Meto smiled. "That law is likely to be the first piece of legislation on which Senator Gordianus will be called to vote."

I groaned. "Perhaps I won't be inducted until late in the day, after the law's been voted on."

"I suspect your induction will take place early on, so don't count on missing the vote. Caesar likes to test the loyalty of a new senator as soon as possible."

"And voting in favor of that measure will certainly be a test!"

"But I thought Cinna was your friend."

"Cinna is my drinking companion. Because we share the occasional cup of wine doesn't mean I want to support his political ambitions, whatever they may be. I've never even read the man's poems."

"You haven't?" Meto peered at me in disbelief. "But Papa, how is that possible? Everyone's read the *Zmyrna*."

"No, Meto, not everyone, because I haven't read it."

He leaned back and stared at me, genuinely taken aback. He scanned the shelves around us. "Amid all these scrolls, there's no copy of the *Zmyrna*? People say Cinna is the world's greatest living poet."

"Is that your opinion as well, Meto?" A writer himself, having helped Caesar recount his military campaigns, my son had strong ideas about both poetry and prose.

"With Catullus gone, yes. I know Caesar thinks so."

"I'm surprised the Dictator has time to read. I don't. I still haven't managed to reach the end of Caesar's *Gallic War*." Despite loving Meto, I sometimes found his collaborations with Caesar a bit of a slog, with too much detail about siege engines and trench digging and other minutiae of warfare.

"Then by Hercules, Papa, put aside the *Gallic War* and pick up the *Zmyrna*. Although . . ."

"Yes?"

"You might not like it, after all. Not to your taste, perhaps."

"How so?"

"For one thing, the language. Very ornate and deliberately obscure, loaded with convoluted metaphors and antiquated words. Beautiful to hear but often difficult to comprehend. What was Cicero's critique? 'Certain poets pay more attention to sound than to sense.'"

"So not everyone agrees with you and Caesar about Cinna's greatness?"

"Cicero might not think Cinna great, but he's read him nonetheless. The language is certainly difficult. Also, given your sentiments on certain subjects . . . your deeply felt sense of right and wrong . . ."

"What has that to do with Cinna?"

"Papa, do you have any idea what the *Zmyrna* is about?" Meto's tone was at once exasperated and sad.

"Well, no. To be honest, I haven't a clue."

"Incest."

Now I was taken aback. "What do you mean, incest?"

"Well, in this case, between a father and daughter. You *do* know who Zmyrna was?"

"I've heard of her, of course. There's a Greek city with that name, though I usually see it spelled with a Latin 'S' instead of the Greek 'Z,' and I'm not sure the city has anything to do with the girl. As for her story . . ." I shook my head. "Something to do with myrrh? I seem to recall that the word 'myrrh' is somehow derived from 'Zmyrna' . . ."

"Papa, what a muddle your mind must be." Meto sat back and folded his arms. "The *Zmyrna* isn't unique, or even unusual—the incest theme, I mean. It's part of a whole genre of incest poems—forbidden and usually tragic love between fathers and daughters, mothers and sons, sisters and brothers."

"Tragic?"

"Someone usually ends up dead, or metamorphosed by a god into something not human—as happens in the *Zmyrna*."

"The death or the metamorphosis?"

"Both. But seriously, Papa, have you never read Parthenius? Or Euphorion? Or—"

"Seriously, Meto, I have not. They're merely names to me. I told you, son, I have no time to read modern poetry."

His face brightened. "Well, then—now I know what I must give you for your birthday. It falls on the twenty-third day of this month, doesn't it?"

"I think so. . . ."

"Are you not sure?"

"Is anyone sure of his birthdate anymore, after all that fiddling Caesar did with the calendar? Adding sixty days to the year of his triumphs—which meant my next birthday was postponed for sixty days, and I actually turned sixty-five sixty days *before* the twenty-third day of Martius arrived last year. Thanks to the Dictator, even a man's birthday is no longer his own."

"On the contrary, Papa. By fixing the calendar, Caesar restored each man's birthday to its rightful date and season. Remember how badly the old calendar had fallen behind the actual seasons? The old calendar had *lost* sixty days, so that your birthday was falling in the actual month of Januarius, never mind that the calendar read Martius. But last year, thanks to Caesar, the twenty-third of Martius arrived when it *should.*"

"Still, it seemed quite strange that a man could be, say, thirty years old one day, and twenty-nine the next, if his birthday happened to fall at midnight on the day before Caesar added the extra sixty days."

"Now you're just being nonsensical, Papa. But since you don't trust the new calendar, I won't wait until the twenty-third to give you your present. We shall go and get it right now."

"Go where?"

"Don't you need to shop for your new toga?"

"I'm told I should purchase it from a certain Mamercus and no one else. But you can't buy my toga for me."

"I don't intend to. I know where that shop is located, on a street with a number of other very exclusive establishments—including the most prestigious bookseller in Rome. I shall buy the *Zmyrna* as a gift for you, and you shall read it tonight."

"Nonsense, I can buy it for myself."

"Don't be ungracious, Papa." This came from Diana, who happened to be passing by the doorway and paused to look in. "You're so hard to shop for—the man who wants for nothing because he wants nothing. If Meto knows of a book you might like, by all means, let him have the pleasure of purchasing it for you. What's the title? I'm not sure I heard it correctly."

"*Zmyrna*, a very famous poem by Papa's drinking companion, Cinna. Have you heard of it?"

"With two children and a husband to look after, I have even less time for poetry than father does. Perhaps you can read it aloud to me, Papa."

"Or perhaps not," I said, "considering the subject matter."

"Which is?"

"Never mind. Shall we be off, Meto? We have shopping to do."

XIX

If there had ever been any ironmongers on the Street of the Ironmongers, they had departed long ago, driven out by rising rents. The street was just off the Forum, on the Subura side, the Subura being Rome's most crowded, dirtiest, and most dangerous neighborhood. Some speculator in real estate realized that if one walled off the north end of the street, so that it no longer opened to the Subura, the Street of the Ironmongers could be entered only from the Forum. The wall was erected, and gone now were the petty thieves, drunkards, and beggars who could no longer scuttle off into the wilds of the Subura at a moment's notice. Taking their place were muscle-bound slaves who loitered in the street, trying to look inconspicuous as they kept an eye on the clientele and guarded the expensive goods of their masters.

I had intended to visit the tailor first, to be done with my toga shopping, but Meto was so eager to acquire the *Zmyrna* that I allowed him to lead me straight to a bookseller at the very end of the street, next to the wall.

The shop smelled of ink and papyrus and wood shavings. Pigeonhole shelves along the walls were stuffed with scrolls. Some were merely rolled and tied with ribbons, but others were wound around dowels with handles made of wood or ivory.

"Ivory rollers for books!" I muttered. "Who could afford such a luxury? What words could justify the expense?"

"Ivory handles speak less about the book and more the man purchasing the book," said a wizened little man behind the counter. His keen eyes peered out of a wrinkled face that terminated in a huge beard not quite as gray as my own. I had reached the age where many an elderly fellow I encountered was not yet as elderly as myself.

"I'm Simonides, the proprietor of this shop," he said. "We offer books suitable for every reader and every level of wealth. Books for old or young, books for men of all sorts, and even books for women. As you noted, we supply ivory handles, wooden handles, or no handles at all; bring your own rollers and we'll mount the scroll for you. We also offer the fastest and most accurate copying service in Rome. Small jobs like letters or love poems can be done while you wait." He gestured to an open door behind him, through which I could see a number of scribes bent over small tables. The scratching of styluses across papyrus made a quiet but steady rasping noise.

"We're looking for a particular book," said Meto. "A poem."

"Yes?" said Simonides. "We handle all the finest poets, both Latin and Greek."

"The *Zmyrna* of Helvius Cinna."

"Oh!" exclaimed the little man. "What a wise choice you made when you chose to visit the bookshop of Simonides! This happens to be the *only* place in Rome where discriminating readers can purchase a copy of the *Zmyrna*. We are the exclusive copyists for the works of Helvius Cinna."

"Is that a fact?" I said.

"It is."

"I should have thought a poet would want his words to be distributed as widely as possible, available in every bookshop."

"Some poets, perhaps," the little man said sourly, "and all the politicians, that's for sure—they want everyone everywhere to read every word of their memoirs. Some of those books I can't *give* away."

I glanced at Meto. Before he could ask if the bookseller had a copy of Caesar's *Civil Wars,* I steered the conversation back to Cinna. "But you do have a copy of the *Zmyrna?*"

"I'll have to check," Simonides said thoughtfully. "As I was saying, some poets would hawk their wares on every street corner in the Subura, but Cinna is quite the opposite. His work is so refined, so complex, it's really accessible only to the keenest intellects."

"I've been told that Cicero thinks Cinna makes a lot of sound but not much sense."

"The *sound* of Cinna—well, yes, it's ravishing, isn't it? To hear those words read aloud is to succumb to a kind of music, to a song like the sirens sang. As for making *sense,* before Cicero dares to critique a work by Cinna, he might wish to expand his own vocabulary and reacquaint himself with some of the lesser-known but no less potent myths. Jupiter knows what Cicero will make of Cinna's forthcoming poem."

"There's to be a new poem by Cinna?" I asked, curious to hear what the bookseller knew about it.

"Indeed, there is!" Simonides lowered his voice and gave us a conspiratorial look. "Rumor has it that this new work will eclipse even the *Zmyrna.* The poet drops by this shop from time to time, and has on occasion uttered a line or two from the forthcoming poem, teasing me, as it were—each line sublime in itself, so that one can only imagine the exalted magnitude of the complete poem."

"Something about Orpheus, isn't it? And Pentheus?" I said innocently.

Simonides gave me a blank look. "Is it? Cinna never told me that. He's always very guarded about the subject matter, says he doesn't want some other poet to overhear and steal his idea." He cocked his head. "Who did you say you are?"

"Apologies," said Meto. "We failed to introduce ourselves. This is Gordianus—Senator Gordianus—and I am his son."

The bookseller gave me a reappraising look and, though I was not in senatorial garb, he seemed to accept Meto's word. His eyes glittered.

"But it's the *Zmyrna* you're asking for. As I said, I shall have to check my stock. I don't keep a copy on the shelves for customers to freely peruse—even these days, there's the occasional ignoramus who's likely to pick up the *Zmyrna,* scan a few lines, turn all red and flustered, and then loudly accuse me of selling filth and ruining public morals. You know the sort—country bumpkins who haven't read a book since Sulla's *Memoirs,* who wander in here only because their wives have sent them into town to buy a cookbook." Simonides shuddered. "But let me go and see. . . ."

He disappeared into the back room. Meto and I browsed the scrolls for sale. On one shelf I came across a play by Euripides I had never read or seen performed, *Phaethon.* I was tempted to suggest that Meto should buy it for my gift instead of the *Zmyrna,* which was sounding less appealing to me the more I heard about it.

Meto meanwhile was pleased to find an entire shelf filled with works by Caesar, not only the war memoirs but also a number of his speeches and tracts, including *Against Cato.* There were also some of his youthful works, a poem called *The Praises of Hercules,* and a play about Oedipus in verse.

Simonides returned with a broad smile on his face and in his hands a long, narrow linen pouch. From the drawstring that cinched the pouch dangled a tag on which I could clearly read in red letters ZMYRNA and CINNA.

"Fortuna smiles on you today, my friend. This is my very last copy of the *Zmyrna.* The chief scribe tells me another won't be ready until the Ides of Aprilis."

Meto moved to take the pouch, but I gently deflected him. "Surely, Meto, we shouldn't take this copy. If Simonides is the exclusive seller, and will have no more after this, then for a whole month no one else will be able to purchase the *Zmyrna.* I shouldn't deprive Cinna of a new reader."

"Papa, you *are* the new reader," said Meto. "Don't you see? This scroll was meant for you. The Fates brought us here today."

"As for being out of stock for a while," said Simonides, "Cinna won't mind. He knows that scarcity adds to the book's appeal."

"How so?" I asked.

Cinna is happy for his words to reach only those readers capable of fully appreciating them. If a book as special as the *Zmyrna* is not available on a given day, such a reader will persevere, returning as many times as necessary to lay hands on the unique object of his desire. He will appreciate it all the more for the effort required to obtain it. Rarity and exclusivity only add to the mystique of a work already so rarefied and so exquisite."

"Imagine a beautiful woman, Papa," said Meto. "If she gives herself to every man she meets, is she any less beautiful? No. But less desirable? Almost certainly. Then imagine a beautiful woman for whom you have to wait, and who waits for only you. Is she not more desirable?"

I shook my head. "I suppose I'll never understand great literature."

"Maybe not," said Meto with a laugh. "I'll be curious to see what you make of the *Zmyrna*." He took the scroll from Simonides.

I stepped outside while Meto paid for the book. After all his talk about scarcity and artistry, I feared Simonides would demand a steep price, but Meto looked pleased with himself when he joined me in the street.

"If I told you the first price he named, you'd faint," he said. "But when I explained who I was, and who you are—in relation to Caesar, I mean—he lowered the price considerably."

"Meto! I wouldn't want that fellow to take advantage of you, but on the other hand, I don't like the idea of you bullying shopkeepers by mentioning the Dictator."

"Papa, you misunderstand. Caesar's books bring that fellow a great deal of business. He told me that the latest installment of the memoirs is the largest-selling item he's ever had, and there's no fear of running low on stock, since Caesar's own copyists supply the shop. Simonides makes a very tidy profit on those sales. When I explained that I played a part in creating those books, he quite reasonably gave me a better price—an author's discount, if you like."

"You take favoritism for granted," I said. "I suppose that I, too, will have to get used to the fawning of my inferiors once I really *am* a senator."

I intended mild sarcasm, but Meto slapped me on the back and said, "That's the spirit, Papa. Now let's see how good a bargain we can strike on this new toga of yours."

XX

We crossed the street and stepped into the establishment of Mamercus the tailor. The large vestibule was as sparse as the bookshop had been cluttered. Mamercus dealt in nothing but togas, so there were no women's or children's garments on display, and only a few pristine specimens of the shop's handiwork hung on the walls. The floor was a mosaic of green, white, and black tiles. The geometric pattern was subtle, so as not to distract from the goods on offer, but laid with exquisite craftsmanship. We approached a long tiled counter on which was repeated the geometric pattern of the floor. The quiet shop felt very elegant and fearfully expensive.

The man behind the counter had longish red hair and was dressed in a dark green tunic with long sleeves. He was busy folding something and barely looked up at our approach. His aloofness matched the elegance of his surroundings, but Meto took one look at him and judged him to be a menial, not the proprietor. "We're here to see Mamercus," he said.

The clerk looked at Meto with heavy-lidded eyes. "Do you have an appointment?"

"We do not. But we do have need of the best toga maker in Rome."

"Impossible, without an appointment." The man reached for a large wax tablet on which a calendar of the month had been drawn. "Perhaps you could come back sometime after the Ides. Not on a holiday, of course—"

"No, we have need of Mamercus at once."

I drew Meto aside and spoke in his ear. "Son, I can speak for myself."

"Nonsense, Papa. Do you think Caesar ever deals directly with menials? No, and nor should you. I'm quite used to doing this sort of thing for him. Allow me to do it for you."

Meto spoke just loudly enough for the clerk to overhear. The man took a good look at us, frowned, then turned to push open a thick wooden door and disappear into the back of the establishment. For the brief moment that the door was open, the elegant spell of the vestibule was broken by the smells that issued from the room beyond. They were typical of any tailor's shop—the odors of dyes bubbling in metal pots, the smoke of burning dung and wood, and the mild stench of urine, an essential ingredient in every fuller's formula for cleaning wool to a bright, lustrous white.

A few moments later the clerk reappeared, followed by a tall, clean-shaven man wearing a dark tunic. A necklace and bracelets of silver and lapis marked him as a man of wealth. He had silver hair and looked even haughtier than the clerk.

"How may I help you?" he said.

"A new senator requires a new toga," said Meto, gesturing toward me as if I were something extraordinary to behold.

Mamercus studied me for a long moment. He was clearly unimpressed, but he spoke with caution. "A friend and supporter of the Dictator, I take it."

"You flatter me, tailor," I said. "I am as nothing to Caesar, but he shows favor to me nonetheless."

"When do you need the toga?"

"On the Ides. Or better, the day before."

"Which is the day after tomorrow. No, no, that's quite impossible."

"I realize I've come to you on very short notice," I said. "But everyone I've asked has told me that you can work miracles in speedy fashion. Marcus Brutus . . . Decimus Brutus . . . Antony . . ."

He twitched as I recited each name. At the mention of Antony, he twitched twice. He looked at me glumly, and I could read his face like a book: In such a world, turned upside down by war, how was a man to tell anymore who was important and who was not? Was the nondescript fellow standing before him really the confidant of magistrates and generals? Did the handsome young man with me truly move in the innermost circles of the Dictator himself? How many rude but rich Gauls had barged into his shop in recent months, announcing that they were senators and wanting a toga to match their station—barbarians who had never before worn a toga of any sort in their lives? Mamercus was the latest scion of a long family business, clothiers to generations of upstanding, respectable Romans. Many of those customers were never coming back, and neither were their offspring, exterminated by the catastrophes of war. Mamercus was not yet at ease with the new customers who had taken the place of the old.

"My name is Gordianus," I said. "You don't know me. Nor did you ever know my father, or anyone else in my family. I have never been to this shop. But I am, indeed, about to become a senator, and my induction will take place on the Ides. I must have a senatorial toga. There can be no investiture without proper vestments."

"At least you understand and respect the importance of the toga," said Mamercus quietly. "But it's impossible, nonetheless. Every senator I know intends to be present at that meeting on the Ides, hundreds of them. I've been inundated with togas—togas for mending, togas for washing, togas that need alteration to accommodate a bit of added girth. Those who didn't bring togas to be cleaned or altered came to order brand-new togas, so as to look their best at their last meeting with the Dictator before he leaves Rome. I don't know how I shall make good on all the outstanding orders I have already. I can't possibly accept another."

"But you must have something for my father to wear," said Meto. "Perhaps a toga you acquired secondhand, or one that was never retrieved and deemed abandoned by its owner, or perhaps a toga that failed to meet the owner's specifications—"

"Young man!" snapped Mamercus. "You are asking if I might lower my standards of quality to somehow accommodate your father's needs—and the answer is no. No toga has ever left, or will ever leave, this premises without being perfect in every regard—perfectly fitted, perfectly cleaned, even perfectly folded, wrapped in linen and tied with string to be carried home by the slave who comes to fetch it. No, no, no! You ask too much of me."

I waved my hand to silence them both. "Mamercus, I understand perfectly what you're saying. I regret that it won't be one of your togas that I shall wear on the Ides, for I should like to be clothed in a garment made with such obvious care and pride. But impossible is impossible. If it can't be done . . ."

"I assure you, citizen . . . or, rather, Senator Gordianus . . . I cannot supply a toga for you on that date."

"Then I must find another solution," I said, giving him a parting nod. I gripped Meto's arm to cut short whatever remark was poised on his lips, and walked toward the door, pulling him with me. "I'll somehow make do, with something less than the best—as many a Roman must these days—and in the meantime, I will have the consolations of poetry." I nodded toward the linen-wrapped scroll in Meto's hand. "We leave without a toga, son—but not without the *Zmyrna*."

XXI

"But why *Zmyrna*?" I asked, prolonging slightly the buzz on my lips as I spoke the first letter.

"Because she's the subject of the poem, of course," answered Meto.

We sat in the library of my house, which was lit by a great many lamps. Night had fallen. Dinner had been eaten. Wine had been drunk, a bit more by me than by my son. Bethesda had gone to bed, as had Davus and Diana. Meto and I had retired to the library, where I loosened the drawstring and slipped the scroll from its linen pouch.

"No, Meto. When I say, 'Why *Zmyrna*?' I don't question the meaning of the title but the way it's *spelled*. As far as I know, there is no letter 'Z' in the Latin alphabet. In the Greek alphabet, yes, but not in Latin, not since it was banished many generations ago by our wise ancestors. The great Appius Claudius said about the letter 'Z' that 'the man who makes such a sound produces a facial expression like as that of a grinning skull.' Cicero once said to me, 'Old Appius Claudius achieved many a great thing—the Appian Way, the Appian Aqueduct—but his other achievements pale beside his banishment of the letter that shall not be named.'"

"I'm sure Cicero was joking, Papa."

"Exaggerating, perhaps, but not joking. Cicero takes letters very seriously. But as I was saying, since the poem is in Latin, why did Cinna spell the girl's name in Greek fashion instead of in Latin, with an 'S'—Smyrna? *Zmyrna* seems a bit . . . precious."

Meto laughed. "Oh, Papa, if you start by finding the title pretentious, I fear to imagine what you'll make of the actual verses! But you make a good point. Even before the poem begins, with the very first letter of the title, Cinna announces to his reader that we are about to enter a web of complex and sophisticated language, full of word games and esoteric references. The same announcement is made to the listener who hears the poem recited, since at the very outset the reciter must say that dreaded letter, pulling back the lips and baring the teeth. Cinna very deliberately chose to title his poem *Zmyrna,* and you, Papa, picked up on the significance of that choice right away. I'm impressed."

I was gratified by his praise, even as a part of me dreaded the sesquipedalian word games I was likely to encounter with each turn of the scroll. Could I even get through the poem? And if I did, would I feel a complete dunce by the end?

"Perhaps I should read it on my own, silently, to myself," I suggested.

"Oh, no, Papa. A Latin speaker's first reading of the *Zmyrna* is one of life's richest literary pleasures. I want to share it with you. We can take turns reading aloud to each other."

Was this a pleasure he had shared with Caesar in their tent on long wintry nights up in Gaul, or in stolen moments on the banks of the Nile? I felt a curious stab of jealousy. But here was Meto not merely offering but insisting that we read the poem together. I could hardly refuse.

With all this talk of Zmyrna, the outcome of her story had come back to me: Having offended an Olympian goddess (I couldn't remember which), poor young Zmyrna fled from the lands of the Greeks into the wilds of Arabia. On the point of death, she was transformed into a small, twisted tree. Her tears became the sap of the tree, the precious substance myrrh, a word derived from her name.

I had also remembered that this was not quite the end of the story. Even as Zmyrna became a tree, a child emerged from her woody womb.

That child was Adonis, who would eventually become the beloved of Venus. Did this mean that Zmyrna was pregnant before she fled to Arabia? Who was the father of Adonis? I had no recollection of that part of the myth.

My ignorance was about to be rectified by Cinna's poem.

The story was not recounted in a straightforward fashion. If Cinna's vocabulary was challenging, the structure of his poem was perhaps more so. It jumped about in time and space and shifted points of view yet somehow never lost coherence. Each fragment, complete and perfect in itself, somehow connected with every other fragment, so that the whole was greater than the sum of its parts.

The very cadence of the poem cast a spell, as did the musical quality of the language—sometimes as playful as a flute, sometimes as frantic and unsettling as the rattle of a Maenad's tambourine, sometimes as bewitching as the plaintive notes of a lyre heard by moonlight.

I thought I would prefer those moments when Meto read aloud, for he had a beautiful voice and knew exactly where to place each stress depending on the secret meanings of the words. But I enjoyed just as much the experience of reading the verses aloud myself, letting my lips and tongue play upon the absurdly convoluted edifice of language. Even when I didn't quite understand what I was reading, the words themselves produced music. When I did understand not merely the outermost level of meaning but also the multiple puns and learned references, I felt an added thrill, as if the words that emerged from my mouth were truly something more than air, compounded of some enchanted substance that encircled and gently caressed both Meto and myself.

Enraptured as I was by the spell of the language, it was only gradually that the *story* of the poem crept up on me. From the outset every detail seemed strangely familiar, like a dream forgotten, then experienced again. Had I once known the story of Zmyrna and deliberately forgotten it? A dream—or nightmare—is perhaps the best comparison I can make to my experience of Zmyrna's story that night, sometimes spoken by Meto, sometimes spoken by myself. It seemed at once I slept and yet was awake, that I was an active participant in the story but at the same time a passive, impassive dreamer. The tale of Zmyrna seemed very far away, a figment of a distant past, and yet at the same time terribly near, like an object almost touching one's eyeball—tiny yet unimaginably monstrous.

It was the wine intoxicating me, changing my reality, I thought—then I realized I hadn't touched my cup since our reading began. A slave appeared from time to time to replenish or replace the lamps. This silent, flitting figure seemed like a shadow visitor from some other world.

The poem certainly achieved one goal of such a work, and more profoundly than I had ever before experienced: I forgot completely the cares and distractions of the workaday world. The *Zmyrna* created its own world, which seemed in some impossible way to be more real than the one where I fretted and fussed each day.

A summary of Zmyrna the story cannot possibly convey the power of *Zmyrna* the poem. Those who can read Latin must read it for themselves to understand what I experienced that night, and indeed still experience anytime I happen to pick up that poem and scan even a few verses. But here I will tell her story in bare detail.

The setting of the tale was the island of Cyprus, in the long-ago days when it was ruled by King Cinyras and his queen, Cenchreis. Of all the men in the world in those days, Cinyras was the most handsome, with a beauty to rival that of Achilles or even Apollo. It was more from her father than from her mother that their daughter, Zmyrna, inherited her beauty. Even as a child she was strikingly lovely, and with each year that passed the girl grew yet more alluring. Queen Cenchreis, proud of her daughter's beauty—which far surpassed her own, if not that of her husband—boasted at a public banquet, where all could hear, that Zmyrna was even more beautiful than Venus.

What madness possessed Cenchreis to make such a claim, which could only give offense to the goddess? From high Olympus, hearing her name invoked, Venus pricked up her ears. She overheard the boast. She flew faster than a comet across the sky and stopped above the island of Cyprus to look down at the royal assembly, narrowing her gaze until it fixed on young Zmyrna. The girl was on the very cusp of womanhood, her body still soft and smooth like that of a child yet beginning to show the shapely contours of a woman's hips and breasts. Her face, likewise, was exactly poised between the innocence of a child and the allure of a woman. Her beauty was poignant, seductive, breathtaking, the beauty of all women and yet of none, for no such beauty as that of Zmyrna had ever existed among mere mortals—except in the person of her father.

Venus had expected to find the queen's boast frivolous and hollow. Instead, she was taken aback by what she saw. The goddess was not pleased.

Venus considered how she might avenge herself on the boasting queen and her daughter. She summoned Cupid and whispered in his ear. Grasping his bow and arrow, the winged cherub flitted downward to the island of Cyprus. He took aim not at the beautiful king or the boasting queen, but at their daughter, who let out a gasp as the arrow struck her breast and then, its poison delivered, vanished into thin air. No one at the banquet ever saw the arrow, not even Zmyrna, who clutched her breast and wondered at the sudden pain—a pain she had never felt before, so exquisite it might almost be called a pleasure.

The princess turned her gaze to her father. Everyone called Cinyras the most handsome man on earth, but for the first time Zmyrna understood why this was so. She stared at her father, transfixed, and touched the place where the arrow had pierced her.

The banquet ended with an announcement by the king: His daughter, Zmyrna, had come of age to marry. Any suitors who thought themselves worthy of her were invited to present themselves at the palace in the coming days. Zmyrna heard this decree not with excitement but with dread.

Suitors came from far and wide. To each, Cinyras put two challenges—first a feat of strength or daring, then a riddle seemingly impossible to solve. With these riddles, Cinna took the opportunity to digress into some of the poem's most obscure references. Had the poet been less skillful, this part of the *Zmyrna* might have become tedious. Instead, the language was so ingenious and the startling revelations of forgotten lore so fascinating that I found myself wishing this part of the poem could have been longer.

Some suitors passed the tests, others did not; but to Zmyrna herself the king granted the final say. He loved his daughter too much to force any marriage on her, no matter how suitable the match or outstanding the suitor. Zmyrna rejected one suitor after another; not one of them would she accept. When pressed for a reason by her parents, she dissembled. To tell the truth was unthinkable—that she grew heartsick at the idea that any man but Cinyras should ever have her. The one mortal in the world whom she desired was the one man she could never have.

She hid this passion and tried to forget it, but the longer she concealed it, the deeper it grew. The girl became despondent. She barely spoke and could scarcely eat or sleep. Thinking her ill and desperate to cure her, Cinyras and Cenchreis consulted oracles, called on physicians, and prayed to Asclepius. But Zmyrna grew more fragile day by day, consumed by her shameful secret.

The king and queen each blamed the other for their daughter's decline. They fell to bickering and moved to separate bedchambers.

One night, alone in her room, Zmyrna decided to hang herself. Had she died, her secret would have died with her, and perhaps Venus would have been satisfied with this revenge on Cenchreis. But at the last moment, as the noose was tightening on Zmyrna's throat, the girl's nursemaid discovered her and pulled her free of the rope. The old woman had tended Zmyrna from infancy, loved her dearly, and knew her better than did anyone else. She sensed that the cause of the girl's despair was some forbidden love and demanded that Zmyrna tell her the name of her beloved. Zmyrna refused. The old woman tore open her gown to bare the sunken breasts that had nourished Zmyrna as a baby. At the sight of them, Zmyrna was convulsed with sobbing. Her face wet with tears, barely able to speak, she spoke the name of her beloved: "Cinyras. My father, the king."

The nurse was speechless. She covered her breasts and ran from the room. But the love she felt for Zmyrna was greater than her revulsion. In her thoughts, she sought justification for Zmyrna's passion. She considered all the animals that mate freely with parent or offspring; if nature allows such freedom to the birds and beasts, why not to mortal men and women? Cinna described the nursemaid's thoughts in an uncommonly straightforward manner. I felt a chill as I read the words aloud:

"What nature allows, jealous law forbids. And yet . . .
Somewhere far from here, they say, are lands where mother and son,
Daughter and father mate. Siblings, too, get and beget,
And love is increased by the double bond. If under that sun
My mistress had been born, then, oh! Her passion could be let
Free. Wretched girl, to have been conceived where none
Can even speak of such a love. Like a crushing debt
Her unspent passion weighs upon her. What can be done?"

At length, the old woman returned to the girl and told her that she had devised a plan to save her. The idea was audacious. Zmyrna was at once delighted and appalled. She refused at first, but then, by gradual degrees, she was seduced by the nursemaid's cunning and the power of her own desire.

That night the nursemaid stole into the king's bedchamber after all his attendants had withdrawn. Thinking that only bad news about his daughter would bring the nursemaid to him at such an hour, Cinyras was alarmed. But the nursemaid dispelled his fear with a beguiling smile and told him that she had come on a mission suitable only to such a place and such an hour. She had been approached, she said, by a beautiful girl—so beautiful, indeed, that she must be the most beautiful girl on the island of Cyprus, save for Zmyrna. Smitten by the king's perfect form and face, this girl was in a fever of longing and desperate to give herself to him.

The king was intrigued. Estranged from the queen, he had grown restless and randy. How old was the girl? "The same age as your daughter," said the nursemaid, "and a virgin." The king felt a sharp stirring of lust. From time to time, looking at his budding young daughter, he had felt such a stirring and had always quickly suppressed it. But here was a girl as young as Zmyrna and almost as lovely, ready and eager to give herself to him. He told the nursemaid to bring the girl to him at the same hour the next night.

But there was a condition, the nursemaid explained. The girl wished to give herself in darkness, so that Cinyras would never see her face, and also to give herself in silence, so that he would never hear her voice. She wished to keep her identity a secret, even to the king. Cinyras frowned at this, but the nursemaid told him it was for his own protection. If in the future he happened to confront the girl in some public place, the least glint of recognition might reveal his transgression to the queen. No telltale expression could give him away if he never saw the girl's face or heard her voice. The king agreed, and from that hour onward his every waking thought was bent toward the upcoming assignation.

The next night, the nursemaid bathed Zmyrna, brushed her long hair, anointed her with sweet-smelling oils, and pulled a loose sleeping gown over her shoulders. Quivering with anticipation, Zmyrna allowed the nursemaid to lead her through the dark hallways to her father's bed-chamber. The nursemaid opened the door and stepped inside. At once she saw a patch of moonlight on the floor and feared it might be bright enough to illuminate Zmyrna's face. But even the night sky seemed determined to assist the plot; either that, or from shame, as Cinna wrote, "the silver moon vanished from the sky, and the stars hid behind black clouds."

The old woman led Zmyrna into the dark room. "Take her, Your Majesty," she said in a hoarse whisper. "The girl is yours." The nurse withdrew.

In darkness, Cinyras rose from his bed. His groping hands touched the girl's shoulders. He lifted the sleeping gown over her head, then touched her naked body. He pulled her to the bed.

The girl spoke only in whimpers and sighs. Cinyras gave her cooing words of encouragement. "My sweet little girl," he called her, as he had many times called Zmyrna, and he felt the girl shiver beneath him. She broke her silence and cried out, "Papa!" But her voice in that instant was so strained that he failed to recognize it, and the word itself did not alarm him; it incited him to greater lust. What else should the girl call him— "Your Majesty" or "King Cinyras"? Let her call him "Papa" if she wished. Again he called her "My sweet little girl," and held her more tightly.

When the act was done, Zmyrna left the bed, found her sleeping gown on the floor, and fled back to her room.

In the morning, Cinyras saw a spot of blood on the bedsheet and knew in truth the girl had been a virgin.

The deed was done. But that was not the end. As happens when lust is fresh between two lovers, the appetite of both was only heightened by their first encounter. They were eager to meet again. With the nurse as their go-between, Zmyrna came to her father the next night, and then again the next.

It was at this third meeting, after the act of love, that the king, keenly wishing to see his new beloved, retrieved from an adjoining room a lamp with many flames and brought it to the bedside. The flickering light revealed his naked daughter. She lay with her limbs outstretched and a slack expression on her face, the very picture of passion spent.

Cinyras realized that he had been tricked—by the nurse, by Zmyrna, by his own reckless lust. Horrified, he reached for his sword, which hung on a nearby wall, and unsheathed it. Before Zmyrna's startled eyes and to the sound of her screams, Cinyras cut himself open and fell on the glittering blade.

The nursemaid came running. She saw the corpse on the floor. She swooned. Mad with grief, undone by guilt and shame, Zmyrna fled naked from the room.

Zmyrna ran. Darkness surrounded her. The walls of the palace seemed to melt away. Only an infinite and starless night lay all around her. Across the black sky she ran, and across the sea; across mountains and vast stretches of sand. As she ran, she cried aloud to heaven, begging the gods to give her . . .

Not life—she could not face the living, especially her mother;
Not death—she could not face the dead, especially . . . the other.
What then? Death without death? Life without life?
What place for her, who had lain with her father as wife?

At last, utterly exhausted, Zmyrna began to falter and stumble. How long had she run? For months, it seemed. How far had she fled? Many hundreds of miles. Canyons of red stone surrounded her, as did parched riverbeds choked with sand. In this barren place, she dropped to her knees. Stern Venus, looking down, at last took pity on her. Zmyrna shuddered, and then . . .

"And then what?" I said, lowering the book to my lap, for the scroll had come to an end, with the poem in midsentence. There was no more papyrus to unroll, no more words to read. "What in Hades happens next?"

XXII

"Let me see." Meto took the scroll from me. "You're right. The end of the poem is missing."

"Curse that bookseller! He sold me a defective copy."

"Yes, he did. Well, we shall have to go back in the morning and ask for—"

"But don't you remember? He said he would have no more copies of the *Zmyrna* for at least a month."

"Ah, yes, so he did."

"Well, this is very frustrating." I looked about the room, fully aware of my surroundings for the first time since our reading began. The jarring exit from the world of the *Zmyrna* was disorienting. I longed to still be immersed in the web of language spun by Cinna. And I felt greatly cheated that I had not been allowed to reach the climax.

"I suppose I could tell you how it ends," said Meto, frowning. "I'm not sure how many lines I can recite with complete accuracy—"

"Settle for a paraphrase? I think not. Having read thus far, I intend to read, or have recited to me, the rest of the poem, exactly as it was written. I want to know the whole work, word for word. How otherwise will I know what to make of it?"

Meto smiled. "Would that every literary critic was as scrupulous as you, Papa. Many readers seem to think they're entitled to have an opinion about a book before they've finished it—sometimes before they've started it. Indeed, the less they know, the stronger their opinion." He shook his head. "But you can't wait a month to read the rest. Surely we know someone who owns a copy." He turned the scroll in his hands, looking thoughtful. "Caesar has a copy, of course, but I'm not sure in which house he keeps it. And he shall be very busy tomorrow, as shall I . . ."

"Caesar? We needn't bother him. I shall go straight to the poet himself."

"Of course. Why didn't I think of that? Cinna's sure to have an extra copy that he can loan you—"

"An extra copy? For me to read? No. I shall ask him to recite the ending for me himself."

"Are you sure you want that?"

"Why not? He'll be delighted to do so. He's always after me to read the *Zmyrna*—"

"I'm sure he'd gladly recite the whole thing to you if you asked. Poets live to recite their work. But consider: He's likely to be looking at your face the whole time. He'll see exactly what you're thinking. Do you want that?" Meto looked at me curiously. "Just what *do* you think of the poem, Papa?"

"Unfair, Meto. Didn't I just tell you that I must know the whole of a work before judging it?"

"Yes. But you must have some reaction you can share with me."

"No."

"I think you're evading my question on a technicality."

"Perhaps. But not a word shall I utter about the *Zmyrna* until I've reached the end."

In fact, the poem had stirred very strong and very mixed feelings in me, as I suspect Meto knew already, having observed my face and heard my voice during those passages when I read aloud. But I was honest when I told Meto I wasn't ready to talk about the poem. The truth was, I didn't know what to think.

The language was undeniably extraordinary, and the textual allusions were exquisitely erudite, at least insofar as I could judge them, since I had surely missed a great many of them. At times the verses and the multiple layers of meaning they contained were truly sublime. This was a work that would reward many readings.

But what was one to make of the *story*? To be sure, Cinna had not invented it. It was a very ancient story, and if it were true, then if anyone was to be blamed for the sequence of events, it was Venus, for inflicting such a terrible curse on a hapless mortal like Zmyrna. Many of the greatest poems, including the *Iliad* and the *Odyssey,* were full of the caprices and cruelties of the gods, and the foolishness and suffering of mortals. But why choose this particular story, and lavish so much artistry on it? And so much time; the *Zmyrna* had famously taken Cinna almost ten years to write. To return to such a project time and again, month after month, reworking one part or another, bejeweling the whole with all the artifice the poet could devise—what was it about this story that had so attracted my drinking companion?

And what about this poem in particular had earned it such a towering reputation? To be sure, Cinna had his detractors, such as Cicero. But poor Cicero counted for less and less these days, not just as a politician but also as a thinker. Most of the respected intellects I knew, including Caesar, and Meto for that matter, had the highest praise for the *Zmyrna.* It was the fashion these days for poets to dwell on themes that were convoluted or even grotesque, but was the tale of a tortured young girl's conniving incest with her unsuspecting father really the stuff of great poetry?

I had known not one but two men who laid claim to being the greatest poet of his generation—and their poetry could not be more different. Antipater of Sidon had never written anything remotely like this! The *Zmyrna* was a world away from the standards of excellence I had been taught as a boy, like the staid poetry of Ennius. Even Catullus at his most scabrous had never written anything with such a twisted theme.

Meto and I rose, stretched in unison, and made ready to go to bed.

He would spend the night under my roof but planned to leave at the first cock's crow, long before I was up and about.

"There is one thing I'd like to ask you," I said. "What do you make of the nurse's claim?"

"What's that?"

"In the poem, the nurse speaks of incest as being perfectly normal among animals—and even among humans, 'somewhere far away.' Can that be right?"

"Well, I'm not a farmer, Papa, so I can't speak to the erotic dalliances of livestock. Nor am I a hunter, so I don't know about wild animals, either. But among mortals, doesn't Cleopatra come from a long line of intermarrying siblings?"

"Siblings, yes. But not parent and child. At least, I don't think so. . . ."

"Caesar dreamed of copulating with his mother, the night before we crossed the Rubicon," said Meto, sounding wistful. "Perhaps Cinna indulged in a bit of license with the nurse's speech. The *Zmyrna* is a work of poetry, Papa, not animal husbandry."

I nodded, and the two of us headed to our bedrooms. As we left the library, a slave slipped silently into the room to extinguish the lamps.

Lying beside Bethesda, who snored ever so gently, her face turned away from me, I closed my eyes and pulled the coverlet to my chin. Phrases from the poem echoed in my ears, and images conjured by the poet flitted and floated across my eyes as slowly, slowly I drifted from wakefulness to sleep.

DAY FOUR: MARCH 13

XXIII

The next morning I longed to sleep late, but Bethesda kept slipping into the room to pester me, reminding me that I must be off to find that bothersome toga.

"Yes, yes, my love," I whispered, pulling the coverlet over my head and dozing, until at last it was yanked away by my demanding wife.

I dressed and made my way to the garden. Diana brought me a steaming bowl of crushed millet with goat's milk and scattered bits of dried fruit. I ate what I could and gave the rest to Davus, who had already consumed his serving.

Rather than setting out at once, I dawdled for as long as I could. Something told me that Cinna was not an early riser. Bast sat on my lap and submitted to my caresses.

At last I set out with Davus beside me, only to realize that I didn't know the exact location of Cinna's house, having never been there. I seemed to recall that it was somewhere on the Aventine Hill, and so we headed in that direction.

After only a short walk, our path crossed that of a rotund figure in a senatorial toga, accompanied by a considerable retinue of scribes, bodyguards, and hangers-on. He looked vaguely familiar. As he passed by, I thought of his name.

"Senator Casca," I called. "May a citizen have a word with you?"

He stopped and turned toward me. Since the end of real elections, politicians were not as responsive as they once had been to any questioner or complainer in the street. The fact that so many Romans had recently sent their fellow citizens to Hades also gave men pause when accosted. One of Casca's bodyguards moved to shield his master from any sudden move that Davus or I might make. After studying my face for a moment, the portly senator waved the bodyguard aside.

"Gordianus, isn't it? The one they call the Finder?"

"Why, yes. Though I don't think we've ever—"

"No, but someone—Cicero, I think—once pointed you out to me. He said you were not a bad sort."

"Did he? How kind of Cicero."

He grunted. "You wanted a word?"

"Only a quick question. Do you happen to know where Cinna lives?"

"Of course. I dropped in on him only the other day. Over on the Aventine Hill . . ." He proceeded to give me directions.

"Thank you, Senator."

Casca nodded. "I'm happy to help you, citizen. Give Cinna my regards." He turned and walked on.

The directions he gave were clear, and I knew the various streets he had mentioned. In a short time, Davus and I arrived at the house. It was not what I had expected. The tile steps were chipped and weeds grew from the cracks. The yellow-washed plaster on the walls was spotted with bits of mud and mold from the winter rains. The door was very weathered and without ornament. It seemed odd that Cinna should live in such a drab house. Could it be that all his elegance had been invested in his poetry and his personal appearance, with none left over for the place where he lived?

A slave answered the door. He, too, was not what I expected. The man had a stooped back and a furtive manner. He wore the expression of being accustomed to long abuse.

"Is your master up yet?" I asked, smiling to show that I meant no harm.

"Of course. The master rises before the rooster."

This, too, did not fit my picture of Cinna. "Then tell him that his friend from the tavern has finally read the poem—well, almost all of it—and wants to pay his respects."

The man gave me a very strange look but scurried off, muttering the message aloud to memorize it.

I expected the slave to return and conduct me to his master, but instead another figure appeared. He was a jowly, scowling middle-aged man with a self-important look, wearing an expensive-looking orange tunic—surely a citizen, not a slave. Had I not known better, I would have thought he was the master of the house—which in fact he was.

"You're looking for the other one," he said brusquely.

"I beg your pardon?"

"Oh, you're not the first to arrive at this door, making the same mistake. When the slave mentioned 'tavern' and 'poem' in the same sentence, I knew. It's the other one you want, not me."

"I see. But I was told that this was the house of Cinna."

"So it is. Lucius Cornelius Cinna, *not* Gaius Helvius Cinna. Cinna the praetor, *not* Cinna the tribune. The cognomen is the same, but we are quite different, I assure you. *Quite* different."

"How so?"

He snorted. "I'm not a poet, for one thing. Nor am I a drunkard. And you'll never see me playing lapdog to the Dictator." His scowl deepened.

"I don't suppose you could tell me where the *other* Cinna lives?"

He grunted. "If it will get you off my doorstep, yes." He gave me directions.

"Thank you, praetor."

"On your way, citizen." He slammed the door.

The house was not far. Even at a glance, it appeared more suitable for the Cinna I knew. The steps were swept, the walls freshly coated with a pale green wash, and the door of highly polished oak was adorned with a large bronze medallion that depicted Orpheus playing pipes for an audience of animals.

The slave who answered looked more appropriate, too—a well-groomed, cheerful young man who laughed when I asked if his master was receiving visitors. "At this time of the morning? Well, I suppose if you're very, very important . . ." He saw the look on my face and laughed again. "I'm only joking. Whom shall I say is calling?"

"Tell him that his friend from the Salacious Tavern has some questions for him."

The young slave bowed—mockingly, I wondered?—and hurried off. After a short wait, he returned and led us through the house. The furnishings, as I would have expected, were elegant, and the various paintings and sculptures quite refined. From our conversations I had gathered that Cinna's father was fabulously wealthy, having been one of the Roman officers who reconquered Asia from King Mithridates. Among the booty was the famous poet Parthenius of Nicaea, who had tutored Cinna and greatly influenced both the style and substance of Cinna's poetry.

We arrived at a room that opened onto a peristyle with a garden. The green space was decorated with a fountain populated by marble fauns and dryads. The room was painted to resemble a wooded glade with wildflowers all around. The only furnishings were a dozen or so chairs, all different but each exquisitely crafted, made of exotic woods with inlays of abalone, silver, lapis, onyx, and other precious substances. Two of the chairs were occupied. Cinna and his guest rose to their feet as the slave led Davus and me across the garden.

"Gordianus!" said Cinna, smiling. "I thought it must be you. I hoped it was. And it is."

"You already have company," I said.

"A citizen who's come to ask a favor of a tribune. But our business is done." He said a few words of parting and the visitor left, led out by the slave who had led me in. Cinna sat and gestured that Davus and I should do likewise.

"Not only up, but already conducting business," I said. "I thought you might still be in bed."

"By Hercules, no! It's hard work being a tribune. Public service is no job for laggards. Let no one tell you otherwise. The fellow who just left wants me to petition the Dictator for the return of a pigsty that was seized by soldiers during the war and then auctioned as public property. Oh, the endless litigation and mitigation required to effect such a miracle!" He laughed.

"You almost put me off becoming a senator," I said. "What if Caesar gets it into his head to make me a tribune, or whatever?"

"All appointments have already been filled for the foreseeable future, or until Caesar returns from Parthia—whichever happens first. So you needn't worry on that count. Unless, of course—ah, but that would never happen."

I raised an eyebrow.

"Oh, no, the Finder with his penetrating gaze compels me to speak!" He laughed. "Well, I suppose I'll tell you. It's not absolutely certain yet, but . . ."

"From your repeated hesitation, I assume it must be something quite important."

"So it is. But will I attract the Evil Eye if I boast prematurely? Ah well, your son will probably tell you if I don't. While Caesar himself has not yet confirmed it, I've been told that he wants me to come with him to Parthia."

"As an officer?"

Cinna shook his head. "My father was the military man, not me. No, Caesar will take me along as an observer."

"Observing what?"

"The Dictator's brilliant campaign, of course. It's because he admires my poetry, don't you see? While he fully intends to write up his own account of the war, as he's done so successfully for his previous conquests, he wishes that this campaign be commemorated with something more in the vein of a heroic epic. Something Homeric, if you will."

"I'm not sure I would call the *Zmyrna* a heroic epic. . . ."

"Because it isn't. But Caesar trusts that I can write in any form I turn my hand to. But anyway, the only reason I mentioned that I may be leaving is that someone will have to be appointed to finish my term as tribune. Caesar will announce his choice on the Ides, I presume, and alas, it won't be you, because he would hardly make you a senator and a tribune in one day, would he? Cicero and his crowd might drop dead of heart attacks on the spot. Well, I've digressed enough. I don't suppose you've had any new thoughts about that warning?"

"Warning?"

"You know, I told you about it—the word 'beware' in Greek scratched in the sand before my doorstep."

I sighed. "Apologies, Cinna, but I've hardly given it a thought. I've been rather busy the last few days, with . . . one thing and another."

"As have I. Packing for Parthia is no small task! But never mind. I'd almost forgotten that word in the sand myself. Seeing you reminded me. But wait a moment. By what right do you state any opinion whatsoever regarding the *Zmyrna*? You haven't even read it. Or . . . have you?"

Once again he had exercised the power men attributed to me, perceiving the purpose of my visit before I could state it. He had only to glance at my face to see that he was right. Davus gave me a sidelong look, amused to see the table turned on his father-in-law.

"You *have* read it, haven't you? Ah, well, then, my existence here in Rome is complete and I can happily go traipsing off to Parthia, for at long last Gordianus the Finder has read the *Zmyrna*."

"Almost," I said.

"How can one *almost* read a poem?"

"I mean that I've read almost all of it, but not quite. Meto bought me a copy yesterday, as a gift in anticipation of my birthday. We read it aloud to each other last night. But the copy was defective. The end is missing."

"Oh, Gordianus! How terrible for you. To be left in such suspense. However did you manage to sleep?" He spoke sincerely, without a shred of irony.

"To be honest, my sleep was uneasy. The poem put some . . . strange images . . . and strange ideas . . . in my head."

"My verses *have* been known to cast a spell. Naevius said it well: 'Women may have witchcraft, but we men have poetry.' Where did the poem break off?"

"After King Cinyras kills himself, and Zmyrna flees. She finally drops from exhaustion, and Venus at last takes pity on her—"

"And the poor girl feels a change come over her, yes." Cinna narrowed his eyes. "Shall I recite the final verses to you?"

"I came here hoping you would."

Cinna summoned a slave and whispered in the man's ear. The slave vanished—off to fetch us some wine I thought, mistakenly.

Cinna opened his mouth and began to speak.

XXIV

I had never heard anything like it.

I wouldn't have recognized Cinna's voice. Reciting his verses, it became a musical instrument of extraordinary range upon which the suffering of Zmyrna was conveyed to the very depths of my being. To hear Meto read the poem aloud, and to read passages aloud myself, had been a heady undertaking. But to hear the poet himself recite its climax was an experience of an altogether different magnitude, far more wrenching and powerful than I had expected.

Having fled to the ends of the earth, and having reached the end of her mortal existence, Zmyrna does not die. By the mercy of Venus she is spared from both the unbearable misery of life and the equally unbearable shame of a confrontation with the shade of her father in the underworld. Some parts of her body stiffen. Other parts stretch. She expands in one place and contracts in another. In her transformed state, she begins to give birth to the child conceived with her father.

The baby breaks from her womb—no longer a womb of flesh and blood but a cavity of wood that splits and splinters as the baby emerges. With her eyes, the last vestige of her humanity, Zmyrna beholds the child Adonis, perfect in every part, destined to become even more beautiful than his father, the only mortal who could ever break the heart of Venus herself—and thus avenge his parents on the cruel goddess.

Zmyrna weeps. But even as she weeps, her eyes are transformed, and the tears she sheds are not of water and salt, the tears of a woman, but the tears of a tree, a kind of sap—but a sap like no other. When burned, it exudes a fragrance unique in the world, which bewitches all who smell it—the smell of myrrh, the tears of Zmyrna.

As she loses the last shred of her humanity, Zmyrna's thoughts are of her father.

"Father, I'd have kissed your mouth a thousand times before I fled—
But never will you know our child or see the tears I shed."

As Cinna recited the last words of the poem, I actually smelled burning myrrh. The hallucination was startling, a genuine act of magic achieved with words alone—or so I thought. Davus, who sat as spellbound as I, must also have smelled it, for he let out a small gasp as the sweet, musky odor permeated the room.

The slave dispatched by Cinna had been instructed not to fetch wine but to bring a censer charged with myrrh, then to stand just out of sight and set the substance aflame as his master spoke the word "myrrh" aloud.

The experience—the final verses of the poem, the revelation of Zmyrna's fate, the actual smell of myrrh in the room—was exquisite beyond words. Davus bowed his head and began to weep. Cinna gazed at the hulking, shivering figure in the chair beside me, and smiled. We sat in silence for a long moment, as the slave gently fanned the censer and sent thin streamers of fragrant smoke wafting among us.

"But . . . what did the poor girl do . . . to deserve such a fate?" Davus said haltingly, covering his face to hide his tears.

"He doesn't know the rest of the poem?" Cinna arched an eyebrow.

"Davus was elsewhere, fast asleep, while Meto and I read to each other."

"Yet see what an effect even the last few verses have on him," said Cinna quietly. "And you doubt that I can write an epic fit for Caesar?"

"If I doubted before, I doubt no longer," I said.

"Do forgive that bit of stagecraft at the end. I always finish any public reading of the *Zmyrna* with a pinch of burning myrrh. The audience is invariably enchanted. Well, then . . ." He leaned back and crossed his arms. "You've known the two of us—you're perhaps the only man alive who can make such a claim. Which of us is the greater poet?"

"Do you mean . . . ?"

"I do. Antipater of Sidon or Gaius Helvius Cinna?" He gave me a piercing look.

"Your power to compel my honesty will do you no good in this case, Cinna. How could I possibly choose between two poets so unalike? You're not just of different generations. Your poems are in different languages. How could I compare your Latin and his Greek? It's not just pointless, but impossible."

"Ha! I thought I could force an answer from you. But you deflect the question, and for reasons entirely valid. I say, Gordianus, does the big fellow often weep like this?"

After a brief respite of dabbing his eyes and wiping his nose, Davus had begun to weep again. "I can't help it," he muttered. "So sad . . . so beautiful . . ."

"By all means, weep!" Cinna leaned forward and touched Davus's arm. "You pay me the highest compliment, to be moved to an emotion beyond your control. Your tears are more precious to me than pearls. If I could string them on a necklace, it would be valuable beyond reckoning."

We sat for a while without speaking, while the poet basked in the tears of my son-in-law.

"And you, Gordianus? What did you think of the poem?" asked Cinna.

I spoke slowly, carefully choosing my words. "You make a great deal of the extraordinary beauty of Cinyras, and the power it exercises over his daughter—"

"Only because she's been smitten by Cupid, at Venus's behest."

"So Cinyras is blameless. All fault lies with the women—first with Queen Cenchreis, who blasphemes against Venus by claiming her daughter is more beautiful; then with Venus, who takes offense and craves vengeance; then with Zmyrna, who burns with a secret passion for her father; then with the nurse, who conceives a sordid plot to bring them together; and finally with Zmyrna again, who acts on her mad passion, carries out the scheme . . . and drives her father to suicide."

Davus, finally done with weeping, wiped his nose with the back of his hand and cocked his head. "What sort of story is this?"

"A story of long ago and far away," said Cinna, "which is invariably the setting for any tale in which mortal men and women attain the utmost lineaments of gratified desire. You make an interesting point, Gordianus. But you omit the fault of King Cinyras."

"But he was duped. He's blameless."

"Is he? The man betrays his wife, and for what? The chance to sleep with some nameless girl the same age as his daughter. Is there not some part of the man that desires to copulate not with a facsimile but with the daughter herself? And in the groping darkness, does he not imagine it's Zmyrna in his arms?" He saw the frown on my face and nodded slowly. "You see, Gordianus, I have given some thought to the deeper meanings of my poem. I did spend nine years writing it!"

"But then . . . Zmyrna acts knowingly. She wants it, invites it, enjoys it. Cinyras acts unknowingly—"

"But invites it, enjoys it."

"And both are punished quite horribly."

"Yet something beautiful comes of their union—the child Adonis. And from Zmyrna's agony come the tears of sweet-smelling myrrh."

"A strange tale," I said.

"But a haunting one."

"Upon which you chose to lavish your talent. Of all the tales you might have recounted, this is the one you chose to make immortal."

"You flatter me, Gordianus. Only time will tell if the *Zmyrna* is immortal."

"How could it not be?" I said, and meant it. "Someday I hope you'll recite the whole poem to me, from start to finish."

"Someday I will, Gordianus. I promise." Cinna appeared to savor the moment. At last, I had not only read his poem, I had succumbed to it. In unison, the three of us each took a long, deep breath and shivered slightly, as if waking from a dream.

"So, Gordianus, what business has kept you so occupied the last few days?"

I shook my head. "Matters so trivial I hate to mention them. Most aggravating of all is my quest for a senatorial toga. Everyone says I must go to Mamercus, but when I do, he has nothing to offer me. Now it's only a matter of hours until the Ides. I suppose I shall spend the rest of the day—"

"But why didn't you come to me?" asked Cinna with a laugh. "I'll be glad to loan you a toga. I think we're not too different in size. The garment will probably need no alterations at all."

"But Cinna, I could hardly impose—"

"Mind you, it's my summer toga you'll be getting. My winter toga, which is thicker and rather warmer, I shall be wearing myself, in case of inclement weather, always a possibility in Martius. And that big assembly chamber at Pompey's Theater can be awfully drafty. But let me think: Where is my summer toga? Sappho will know. Since the death of my wife, she's the woman of the house. Polyxo!"

He called to a slave who happened to be passing in the garden, a stooped woman with jet-black skin and snow-white hair. The woman crossed the garden, walking a bit stiffly, and stepped into the room.

"Master?" she said.

"Go and find Sappho. Ask her to locate my summer toga. I intend to loan it to this brand-new senator."

"Yes, Master." The woman turned and began to leave the room.

"Getting a bit slow, this one," said Cinna, suddenly speaking Greek. "Been with us a very long time, since Sappho was a baby. Remind me to tell you the story behind her name. Oh, don't worry, she doesn't know I'm talking about her. She doesn't know a word of Greek."

"She's as black as ebony," said Davus, enunciating the obvious in Latin, now that Polyxo had disappeared from sight.

"From Nubia, where everyone is black skinned," said Cinna, also returning to Latin. "Nubia lies closer to the sun's course year-round, so it's always summer there. Just as you and I grow darker in the summer, the Nubians have grown permanently dark, as dark as Polyxo. As I said, she doesn't know a word of Greek. Can't read or write, either, unusual for a slave in this household. My late wife used to converse in Greek with no fear of being overheard, even if Polyxo was right there in the room."

"Good luck, keeping secrets from a slave," I said.

"How true! Yet slaves always manage to keep secrets from their masters. A subject for a small poem, perhaps. Do you know what? Along with the toga, I shall give you something else today—a copy of the *Zmyrna,* with every line intact."

"You're too generous, Cinna."

"Nonsense. I always keep a few extra copies. Wait here. I'll fetch it myself."

Davus and I were left alone in the room full of empty chairs. Though the smell of myrrh lingered, the slave with the censer had vanished as discreetly as he had earlier appeared. I gazed out at the garden, watching the play of sunlight and shadows on the greenery as clouds crossed the sky. Davus sniffled, weeping yet another tear for Zmyrna.

A young woman appeared, bearing a folded toga over her arms. She was followed by the Nubian and another slave, a man of middle age.

I rose to my feet and gestured for Davus to do likewise, for despite her plain yellow gown and her long, undressed hair, as black as the slave behind her, I realized she must be the mistress of the house, Cinna's daughter. She was young but not a child, still in her teens—old enough (and certainly pretty enough) to be married by now, though clearly she was not.

"You must be Sappho," I said.

"And you must be the fellow who needs a toga," she answered.

"I am." I introduced myself and Davus.

"Would you like to try it on? You can use that room across the garden. Myron will help to dress you." She gestured to the male slave.

"Perhaps we should wait until your father returns."

She gave me a sidelong look. "Because you don't want to leave me alone with your son-in-law?"

"Decorum would prescribe—"

"That there be a suitable chaperone in the room with an unmarried Roman girl and a young man, especially one as virile-looking as this. There will be: Polyxo. Don't worry. My father has trusted her with every part of my upbringing. There could be no better chaperone."

"Very well." I followed the slave Myron to the other room, where he proved to be quite expert at winding and draping the toga on my person. The garment fit perfectly and hung at just the right length, as if it had been tailored for me. Even so, I felt uncomfortable wearing it. How could I dare to appear in public dressed as a senator? The idea suddenly seemed more preposterous than ever. Nevertheless, I walked across the garden wearing it, so that Cinna could see for himself how well it fit.

Cinna had not yet returned, but his daughter looked me up and down.

Sappho smiled. "You look very handsome, Senator. Very handsome, indeed." Was she flirting? That possibility seemed almost as preposterous as the fact that I was wearing a senator's toga. But her words gave me a dose of confidence.

Sappho turned to the old nurse. "What do you think, Polyxo?"

For the first time I actually looked at the slave's face. It was lined with wrinkles, and quite striking thanks to the white nimbus of her hair and her white eyebrows, and also the color of her eyes, a very bright shade of green, like the emeralds mined on the banks of the Nile.

"I think," Polyxo said, speaking very slowly and with a distinctly Nubian accent, "I think he looks perhaps as your father might look, if your father should live to be so old."

I looked at her blankly, but Davus laughed aloud. "I'm not sure if that's a compliment or not," he said, voicing my own thought.

Sappho said something to Polyxo, and the nursemaid replied. The language they spoke was neither Latin nor Greek, perhaps Nubian, and something funny was said, for they both laughed.

"Sappho! Polyxo!" Cinna had finally returned. He spoke sharply. "You know I don't like it when the two of you speak that gibberish to each other, especially in front of visitors." In his hand he clutched a leather pouch containing a scroll. Before he could say another word, a slave appeared and spoke in his ear.

The scowl on Cinna's face vanished. He raised both eyebrows. "You'll have to excuse me, Gordianus. There's a messenger at the door and I must see what he wants. I'll come back as quickly as I can." He pressed the scroll into my hand. Then he was gone.

XXV

Sappho sat. She gestured to Davus and me to do likewise. Polyxo and Myron remained standing and discreetly stepped to the far corners of the room, as slaves are trained to do.

"A copy of the *Zmyrna*?" said Sappho, nodding to the scroll in my lap.

"Yes. Thanks to your father's generosity."

She smiled. "Thanks to his pride. He loves to share that poem."

A silence ensued. Sappho seemed content to simply sit and look at me, which after a few moments I found unnerving. Had she been staring at Davus, I would have understood. At my age, a man grows used to not being looked at, especially by pretty girls.

"Your nursemaid," I said, in Greek, at last thinking of something to talk about. "Your father said there was an interesting story about her name." I glanced at the slave, who gave no sign of understanding.

"Yes. Do you know the story of the women of Lemnos?" said Sappho, also in Greek, and with an accent far more refined than mine. Cinna must have given her a good education, for only children with excellent tutors can speak Greek as elegantly and effortlessly as Sappho did.

"The women of Lemnos?" I said. "Let me think . . ." Every Greek island has numerous stories attached to it, and there are a great many Greek islands. Even Homer couldn't have known all their stories.

"It's part of the tale of Jason and the Argonauts. They stop at Lemnos on their journey."

"Ah, yes, it comes back to me. There were no men on the island, only women. But I can't recall why."

"Because the women had killed all the men." Sappho finally turned her gaze to Davus and smiled, for my son-in-law looked quite appalled at such an idea. "Well, not quite all of them. And thereby hangs the tale."

"Which you are about to tell us, I hope." It is always good manners to encourage one's host or hostess when they seem ready to tell you a story.

"The trouble began when the Lemnian men sailed off to make war," she said. "When they returned, having slaughtered a great many Thracians, they brought back as booty all the possessions of those they had killed, including their daughters and widows. But instead of treating the Thracian women as slaves, the Lemnian men took the most beautiful of them as second wives. They lavished all their attention on their new brides, and treated the Lemnian women like servants. Any who dared to protest were thrown into the streets, along with their daughters, reduced to beggars. The Lemnian women were furious. They held a secret meeting at a clearing in the forest. Among them was the unmarried daughter of the king, the princess Hypsipyle, attended by her nursemaid—Polyxo."

I saw the slave look up at the utterance of her name, then look elsewhere as Sappho continued in her elegant Greek. "So furious were the women of Lemnos, they decided to kill every man on the island. Even the old men. Even the little boys."

"But that's terrible," said Davus, whose Greek was surprisingly good. "Tell me that the princess stopped them."

"No, she did not. Their wrath was too great to be stopped. They disbanded and went their separate ways, each going home to slaughter the males of her household. Wives killed husbands. Sisters killed brothers. Mothers killed sons. Daughters killed fathers. And of course the new Thracian wives were killed as well.

"All the Lemnian women took part in the massacre—all except Princess Hypsipyle. She, too, was caught up in the madness—until she saw a friend, a girl no older than herself, walking through the streets carrying the severed head of her own father. Hypsipyle loved her father, King Thoas. With the aid of her nursemaid, the loyal Polyxo, she contrived to smuggle him off the island.

"While the other women raged through the streets like frenzied Maenads, covered with blood and gore and crying out to Bacchus to bless the slaughter, Hypsipyle dressed her father in the ivy wreaths and sacred robes of Bacchus, covered his face with a mask of the god, and led him onto a wagon. While King Thoas stood upright, impersonating a statue of the god, donkeys pulled the wagon through the streets thronged by the Bacchic worshippers.

"The wagon reached the deserted outskirts of the city. Hypsipyle led her father into the woods and down to the seashore. They waited for days, attended only by Polyxo, who smuggled food and drink to them until at last a ship sailed close enough for Hypsipyle to summon help. The sailors agreed to allow her father aboard and to take him to safety.

"By the time Hypsipyle returned to the city, the frenzy had died down. The corpses of the dead had been burned. Not a single male was left alive. She was declared queen and ruled over an island of women. Nor did any men dare to stop at the island, because the sailors who rescued King Thoas spread the news of what had happened. For years the women lived without men, unmarried and childless, until at last Jason, ignorant of the story, decided to cast anchor off Lemnos."

"And then what happened?" asked Davus, who stared at her spellbound.

"What happened next . . . is another story," said Sappho.

"You tell the tale very well," I said. "I think you must have inherited your father's gift for storytelling."

"Do you? My father always hoped it would be so, I think. Why else did he decide to call me Sappho when I was still just a child? I do attempt to write poetry, from time to time. Mere trifles. Nothing worth reciting. Certainly nothing to compare to the work of my namesake, or the work of my father."

"Few poets can be compared to Sappho of Lesbos, or to Cinna of Rome," I said. "Still, there must be room in the world for other poets and other poems. I would be honored to hear some of your verses."

I thought my words would please her. Instead, her proud bearing vanished and she turned bright red. She averted her eyes and stuttered.

"No, no, no, that would be im-im-impossible . . ." She folded her hands in her lap and took a deep breath. "The point of the story was to explain my father's inspiration to name my nursemaid Polyxo. Her Nubian name was something im-im-impossible to pronounce and not pleasing to the ear—gibberish, as my father would say. So he gave her the name of the loyal nursemaid of Lemnos, who helped a devoted daughter to save the life of her father. A lovely gesture, don't you see? My father would make everything around him—his life, his house, his household—a work of art, as perfect and pleasing as his poems. What more appropriate name for his daughter than Sappho? What better name for my nursemaid than Polyxo?"

She had regained her composure and again stared at me. "Is my father in danger, do you think?"

"I beg your pardon?"

"The word that was written in the sand in front of our doorstep—'beware,' in Greek. What do you make of it?"

"Did you also see it?"

"I did, before father scratched it out."

"What did *you* make of it, Sappho?"

She sighed, then shrugged. "They call you Finder, don't they? Is that why father asked for your advice, about the warning?"

"I suppose it is." An awkward silence ensued, for I hesitated to share with her my private dealings with her father.

"What are you thinking, right now?" she asked.

I smiled. "I was thinking that you women often know more than we men give you credit for. And you do things about which your menfolk know nothing. My own wife and daughter have surprised me sometimes . . . and not always in a good way. You have your own ways of knowing."

"Our own ways?"

"Witchcraft, I mean. There, I've said it. Magic. Sorcery. Spells. Every woman resorts to the supernatural from time to time."

"Yes, well, Papa writes a bit about that in the *Zmyrna*, doesn't he? When the nursemaid helps Zmyrna to summon the courage to go to her father the first time, she says to her:

'*Spit three times into your hand, virgin. Like this; watch me.
Jupiter Magus, king of sorcery, delights in the number three.*'"

"Yes, I remember that part," I said.

"As do I," said Cinna, stepping into the room.

"But I don't think I've ever before heard the epithet 'Magus' attached to Jupiter," I said. "Do women in their secret rites really call on 'Jupiter the Magician'?"

"I have it on good authority that they do," said Cinna. "A great deal of research went into that poem, one of the reasons it took so long to write. But don't tell me the three of you have been talking about nothing but the *Zmyrna* since I left you."

I shrugged. "We talked of many things. Such as—"

He clapped his hands, too excited to hear me out. "But I have news. Splendid news! Not only am I traveling to Parthia—a message from Caesar himself confirms it—but I am to join you and your son for dinner with Caesar tomorrow night."

"Splendid news, indeed," I said.

Cinna paced about the room, too excited to sit. I had never seen him so animated. I was struck by how handsome he looked, with his eyes ablaze and a broad grin on his face. "But look at you, Gordianus, dressed in my summer toga. Stand up so that I can see. Yes, turn around for me. The garment fits as if it were tailored for you. With that toga, and a trim to neaten your beard, you shall look quite presentable on your first day as a senator. Now if only you can assume the pompous bearing of a senator, people will think you've been one all your life. That may take some practice."

"Should I wear the toga tomorrow, at the dinner?"

"I think not. The occasion will be elegant, but not formal. Let Caesar see you in that toga for the first time on the Ides. I think he'll be quite happy to see the last of his new senators turned out so smartly— an omen that the rest of the day's business will go smoothly."

"Is there any reason to think it won't?"

"You never know. This will be the last chance for the envious and the grudge holders to express their discontent before Caesar leaves Rome. Who knows what mischief they might get up to?"

DAY FIVE: MARCH 14

XXVI

The next morning, Bethesda and Diana descended on me as the harpies descended on the feast of Phineas. No visible part of me was left ungroomed. My hair was washed and combed, then given what Diana assured me was a fashionable cut for a man of my age and station. My beard was also neatly trimmed, as were my eyebrows, and various hairs were plucked from various places where hairs tend to grow as a man gets older, such as his ears. My nails were also trimmed.

With the help of a slave, I donned the toga Cinna had given me. Diana clapped her hands with joy. Bethesda looked ready to swoon. But as I paced back and forth across the garden, trying to assume the "pompous bearing" Cinna had talked about, Diana stifled a laugh. Bethesda raised an eyebrow and clucked her tongue.

"Do I look that absurd?" I asked.

"Of course not, Papa" said Diana. "Pay us no attention. We're only teasing you."

Nevertheless, I banished them from the garden, drained of my confidence and feeling more nervous than ever at the prospect of wearing the toga in public. I set about pacing again, trying to find a gait that felt natural to me.

A slave came to tell me that I had a visitor in the vestibule. It was Tiro. I told the slave to show him in.

Tiro's jaw dropped when he saw me. He grinned and laughed, and then with some effort assumed a more serious expression. "Gordianus, of course I've heard the news, but to actually see you—I mean to say, you look quite—yes, *very*—but why shouldn't you?—I mean to say—congratulations!"

"Thank you, Tiro. Does Cicero send his congratulations, as well?"

Tiro skirted the question. "No other man in Rome is more deserving of the honor than you. I mean that sincerely. Yes, there may be some who complain or express doubt. It may take some getting used to. Even Cicero, perhaps—"

"Just how bad a tantrum did he throw when he heard the news?"

"Tantrum? I would hardly call it that. He did throw a rather heavy bronze stylus at one of the slaves, and almost blinded the fellow, but he felt terribly sorry afterward. But never mind. Every senator in Rome, all of them, including Cicero, shall be won over by your dignity and gravitas, I have no doubt. Just look at you! Born to wear that toga, I would say."

" 'Clothes make the man,' as Plautus says."

"Exactly." Tiro flashed a crooked smile. "To be honest, I was afraid you might turn up wearing something—well, something not quite—that is to say, not all togas are equal, and to obtain a really fine one, especially at short notice. . . . Where *did* you get that toga?"

"That, Tiro, is a state secret. To reveal the source of my toga would compromise not only myself but also a high-ranking magistrate of the Roman people. I shall say no more."

"You know I could find out if I really wanted to."

"I'm sure you could. You and Cicero must have a network of informers second only to Fulvia."

"That woman does set the standard for spycraft. But that brings me to the purpose of my visit." He lowered his voice. "Have you anything to report to me, Gordianus? I know you've been out and about the last few days, paying calls on various people—Fulvia, included."

"Yes. I made it seem that I was testing the waters, seeing how those 'various people' would react to my impending appointment."

"And while doing that, did you also happen to learn anything that might be of interest to Cicero, regarding the matters the two of you discussed?"

I grunted. "Caesar will outlive us all, I suspect."

"You detect no current of anger or resentment against him? No thread of envy or spite? No tide of discontent?"

"No such current or thread or tide, by themselves, ever killed any man, as far as I know. Of course there are those who might wish Caesar gone, if they could do so by snapping their fingers. The world would suddenly be quite a different place, wouldn't it? A better place, in Cicero's judgment. Don't deny it."

"Cicero accepts the dictatorship and conducts himself accordingly."

"I'm sure he does, holing himself up and writing dissertations—on divination, of all things! How he must long for the days of great speeches in the courts and fiery debates in the Senate. How he must wish that the dead Republic could be brought back to life. But I've never seen a dead body get back on its feet."

Tiro sighed. "Then Caesar is safe. No one will be brave enough, or mad enough, to change the course laid out for us by the Fates."

"The Fates always have surprises in store, Tiro—as this garment demonstrates." I felt the weight of the toga wrapped around me and sensed the elegant rise and fall of the folds as I shrugged. "Wait a moment—that's why Cicero decided to devote all his energies to a study of divination, isn't it? Not to debunk it, but to see if in fact there might be some supernatural means of seeing the future, of discovering where and how and by what means the thread of Caesar's life will reach its end. Instead, Cicero found nothing in divination to help him—so he turned to me. That would bring us full circle, wouldn't it, taking us back to the very beginning of his career, when you and he and I all got the better of that other dictator, Sulla. Oh, Tiro, what your master . . . forgive me—Cicero, I mean to say . . . what Cicero needs is a magical spell to rid him of useless nostalgia. Sulla was long ago. Caesar is now. Cicero must learn to live in the world as it is."

"And what world is that?"

"A world where Caesar is dictator for life. Where men forget all those speeches by Cicero that you transcribed so carefully, because the ideas in those speeches no longer make sense. A world where Rome is ruled by a dictator, and that dictator rules an empire bigger than that of Alexander, stretching all the way to Parthia, maybe even to India. A world where Gordianus the Finder is a senator, no less than Cicero—unthinkable as that may be."

Tiro shook his head. "It seems that neither you nor I have learned anything in the last few days to contradict the future you describe. By every indication—every bit of gossip, every scrap of information I've managed to collect—the future will be as you say. Nothing will happen in the next few days to change it. No person or persons will *do* anything to change it. There is no conspiracy against the Dictator. If there were, then surely Cicero and I would know about it."

"There, your duty is done, Tiro. You have my final report. Cicero won't like it, but there it is. I know of no imminent threat to the Dictator."

We were both silent for a long moment.

Tiro finally spoke. "Well, then. That's that. But we haven't seen the last of each other. Far from it. I still attend meetings of the Senate, as secretary to Cicero. No one can take down spoken words as quickly or as accurately as I can, using my shorthand. Others have learned the method, but I'm still the best. I shall be there on the Ides to take down your remarks after Caesar announces your appointment."

My pulse quickened. "By Hercules, I hadn't thought of that. I'll have to *say* something, won't I?"

Tiro smiled. "No one will expect an immortal speech. Most new senators say just a few words—honor the ancestors, praise the institution of the Senate, acknowledge friends and allies. Men used to thank the citizens of Rome who elected them to their first magistracy and thus set them on the Course of Honor. These days, they give thanks to Caesar, since voters no longer matter. Then you'll take the oath that's now re-quired of every senator, to protect the life of the Dictator with your own."

"A speech *and* the oath. With everyone looking at me?"

"I'm afraid so. Pretend they're not there, that it's just you and Cae-sar. He's the only man in the chamber who matters, anyway. Or picture your fellow senators with animal heads, like those absurd Egyptian dei-ties. I sometimes do that to amuse myself when the speeches are espe-cially long-winded."

"I can see I'll be coming to you for advice on a regular basis, Tiro."

"I shall be honored to give the new senator any assistance I can."

On an impulse, I stepped forward and embraced him, as I would a son. He returned the embrace, then stepped back.

"You really do look quite splendid in that toga," he said.

"Thank you. But I'm a bit uncertain about how to carry myself. Especially when I'm in the Senate House."

"I can help with that, if you wish."

There was no one whose judgment I trusted more. "I would be very grateful."

"Walk to the peristyle and back. Yes, like that, but a bit slower, and with your shoulders back. . . ."

By the time Tiro left—after midday, having been treated to the most lavish luncheon I could put before him—my confidence had returned. Even so, it was with some relief that I took off the toga and put on a simple tunic, suitable for taking a nap in the garden under the mild Martius sun with Bast the cat snuggled beside me.

Aside from napping, I spent the rest of the day doing very little. It seemed to me that my work was done. I had not only obtained the toga I needed but I also had received expert advice on how to wear it. The investiga-tion assigned to me by Cicero—a task I had never accepted in the first place—had ended with my report, such as it was, to Tiro. The more spe-cific task given to me by Caesar, to look into the affairs of certain men on a list, had reached its end as well. I could give that report to the Dic-tator in person that night at dinner, if he wished.

Caesar was notorious for mixing business with pleasure at his meals. Meto had told me of a dinner party in Egypt where the Dictator interrupted an anecdote being told by Cleopatra not once but three times to whisper memoranda in Meto's ear, so that Meto could jot down the ideas while they were still fresh in Caesar's mind. "But he made sure to laugh quite heartily when the queen finally finished her story," said Meto. "He's not ill-mannered. He just has a great deal on his mind. The queen showed not the least displeasure. She's one of the few people on earth who can even begin to understand how great a burden Caesar bears, every moment of every day and night."

The day passed without incident and with no more visitors, until, as the sun began to sink behind the rooftops of Rome, Meto arrived, wearing a splendid green tunic with gold embroidery. I had chosen to wear a more understated tunic of very dark blue, with a Greek key pattern in white at the hems. The women of the house made a great fuss over us both, and then Meto led me through the vestibule and out the door.

"Are we going far?" I asked, stepping into the quiet twilit street and seeing a very large, very fine litter. The cushions and curtains were of a sumptuous fabric with a pattern of checkered black and gold. The slaves assigned to carry it were all very large and fine to look at. Half were black-skinned Nubians with tightly curled black hair, and half were Scythians with white complexions and golden hair. They were interspersed so that the bearers themselves formed a sort of black-and-gold-checkered pattern around the litter's perimeter.

Meto laughed. "We're not going far at all. We dine at the house of Lepidus, who provided the litter. Somehow Caesar has got it into his head that you're an old man and shouldn't be made to walk."

"I'm only ten years older than Caesar," I said. Did Caesar think that in ten years he would be a doddering old man? No wonder he was in such a hurry to conquer Parthia. "Surely no task for an old man," I muttered.

"What did you say, Papa?"

"I said, walking to the house of Lepidus is no task for an old man. Help me into the litter and let's be off."

XXVII

I had never met Marcus Aemilius Lepidus, our host. About him I knew
only what most Romans would know. He was of patrician birth, about
my age, and had been allied with Caesar for a long time. When the civil
war began, it was to Lepidus that Caesar entrusted the keeping of Rome
while Caesar chased Pompey to Greece. It was Lepidus who put forward
the motion that granted Caesar his first, temporary, dictatorship. Later,
Caesar dispatched Lepidus to Spain to quell a rebellion there, and was
so impressed that Lepidus was granted a triumph when he returned to
Rome. While Lepidus's procession paled compared to the staggering
grandeur of Caesar's own four triumphs the following year, a triumph is
never a small affair, and that of Lepidus had been sufficient to impress
his name on the minds of even the least attentive citizens. Currently, he
was serving as Master of the Horse, essentially a deputy of the Dictator.
On Caesar's departure to Parthia, Lepidus was to leave Rome and become governor of Spain.

Among his family connections was his marriage to a half sister of
Marcus Brutus, which united two of the oldest and most distinguished
patrician clans in Rome. But Lepidus and Brutus had never been political allies. Lepidus had always been loyal to Caesar.

Lepidus's house followed the rule of inverse opulence that I had often observed when admitted to the homes of the powerful in Rome: The more austere the exterior—in this case, a very simple white plaster wall fronting the street, and a wooden door without a single ornament, not even a bronze knocker—the more sprawling and opulent the interior. The vestibule, crowded with wax images of ancestors, was the size of my garden; the garden, populated by some notable Greek bronzes, was the size of my house. The dining room, open on one side to the garden but warmed by two massive braziers, was small but exquisitely furnished with three very fine dining couches. On the walls, painted roses bloomed and peacocks displayed shimmering plumage.

The three long couches were arranged at right angles to one another with the open side toward the garden. By custom, no more than two guests would share a couch, each reclining on one elbow, head to head. With only three couches for six guests, the dinner was not to be a grand affair, where a simple guest like myself could recede into the background, but something more like an old-fashioned Greek symposium. There would be a host, a guest of honor to his right on the center couch, and two pairs of guests on the couches to either side, with food and entertainment arriving from the open side facing the garden.

Our host stood at the center of the dining room. Meto, who had been acquainted with him for years, introduced us. Lepidus was clean shaven. His full head of silver hair was stylishly cut to look a bit tousled and unkempt, but I had no doubt that each lock had been carefully laid in place by the slave who groomed him. He stepped forward to greet me and clasped my right hand in a firm grip.

"Gordianus, father of our esteemed Meto—it's so good to finally meet you. You're something of a legend, you know."

"Am I?"

"Oh, yes. At this dinner, only legends! Well, for guests, I should say. I won't presume to use such a word for myself."

"Nor would I for myself," I said.

"Humble." Lepidus nodded thoughtfully. "Yes, Meto says as much, but that's a son speaking about his father. One doesn't expect it to be true. I so often find myself surrounded by men who are the opposite of humble that I forget the virtue actually exists."

"If it *is* a virtue," said Meto. "My father has no reason to be humble, not after the life he's led."

"The same could be said of you, Meto." Lepidus smiled. "I think you must be the only man still alive who actually fought alongside Catilina in his revolt. Now *that* is the stuff of legend. You rose from slave to citizen, and now you are to be the son of a senator. And then there are your literary achievements, for which you receive no credit whatsoever, though I know for a fact how scrupulously you attend to Caesar's grammar and syntax, not to mention his occasional factual errors. Oh, yes, Gordianus—even Caesar, like Homer, sometimes nods, and your son is there to ever so gently open his eyes to any small oversight in the text. Thus are Caesar's memoirs made perfect before they're copied for an eager readership."

"I assure you, Master of the Horse, there is no such thing as a perfect text." Meto shrugged off the compliment, but I saw that he was pleased by Lepidus's words.

"Ah, but I think the man himself is about to join us." Lepidus looked past us, at a slave who was gesturing to him from across the garden. "Yes, not only Caesar, but my other guests as well. They must all three have come in a group." He clapped his hands. Two slaves seemed to appear from nowhere, each bearing a tray of three silver cups filled with a dark red wine. "That means we can at last quench our thirst. It would have been rude to begin without the guest of honor. And here he is!"

Lepidus strode forward, across the garden. He embraced Caesar, who was dressed in a shimmering tunic with long sleeves. The fabric was silk, woven in a very complex design; one could see all kinds of colors amid the interwoven patterns. Caesar would later tell us that the fabric came all the way from Serica, beyond India. Once Parthia was conquered, and its trade routes claimed by Caesar, we might expect such exotic fabrics to become common in Rome.

To Caesar's left stood Decimus Brutus, dressed in a dark green tunic. The woolen garment was gathered at the shoulder with a golden brooch and cinched at the waist with a golden belt. Even at a distance I could see that the dragon-headed clasps were of Gaulish design. The Gauls have no peers when it comes to such metalwork.

To Caesar's right stood Cinna, wearing a white linen tunic without ornament. The belt was of black linen, cinched with a simple silver clasp. When Cinna saw me, he gave me an impish wink, as if to say, *Here we are, among the stars. Can you believe it?*

Lepidus turned about and led the other three toward us. To either side of me, braziers burned. Torches flickered from various sconces in the surrounding portico. The last faint light of day lit the ashen sky, in which the first stars had begun to shine. The four men moved amid green shrubs and tall statues. The ever-changing light, the men in their finery, the looming figures of marble and bronze—all combined in a moment of surpassing strangeness. I looked at Meto, wondering if he, too, felt it. On his face I saw a look of deep contentment that increased with each step that brought Caesar nearer.

The two of them embraced. I acknowledged Decimus and Cinna. Meto, stepping back from Caesar, gave each a friendly nod. We were offered wine. I noticed that my cup was exquisitely decorated with an image of Silenus quaffing wine from a Greek krater, surrounded by wildly cavorting nymphs, dryads, and satyrs. The flickering light on the embossed silver seemed to make the figures tremble ever so slightly, as if alive and merely holding a pose.

Of the wine, I remember nothing. Nor can I recall any of the food I was served that night. Those details, so vivid at the time, are lost to memory. Yet I remember Silenus and those satyrs on the silver cup, and I remember what each of us was wearing, as clearly as if Cinna, Caesar, Meto, Decimus, and Lepidus stood before me, all of us still alive, as we were on that torchlit, starlit night.

Before we reclined on the couches, Caesar drew me aside. "The list?" he said.

I shook my head. "I have nothing to report, beyond the comments I made to Meto. That was the day before yesterday."

"Yes, he passed along to me the thoughts you expressed."

"I fear I've been of no use to you."

"Of no use? Never. Of little use? Perhaps. But even an empty report may signify something. Or rather, nothing. Which is what I hoped for. Calpurnia will be greatly relieved that the Finder found nothing to fear. For some reason, she has a very high estimation of your talents."

"My talents, such as they are, have usually been employed in finding the truth of some event that's already taken place. I've never claimed to have any talent for prevention or precognition. I can't foretell the future."

"No man can. Not even Spurinna, though I know he means well. As I say, your lack of alarm will comfort Calpurnia."

"And you as well, Caesar?"

"Any worries I may have had are now in the past. I have no fear of anyone on that list I gave you, or of anyone else in Rome, for that matter."

He flashed a smile that did not seem quite appropriate, and in his eyes I saw a feverish glint that was the first indication of the singular mood he was to display throughout the evening—a strange excitability, an animation out of proportion to the moment, an occasional, vaguely manic laughter that set my teeth on edge. No one else seemed to notice these things, not even Meto. I told myself that Caesar was simply excited at the prospect ahead of him, so close now—the conquest of Parthia and the unprecedented, almost inconceivable power it would give him, the power to marry multiple queens, to sire many princes, to become more godlike than any mortal before him, to be remembered for all time.

We took our places on the dining couches. I reclined next to my son, Cinna beside Decimus, and Caesar beside our host.

At first we talked of practical matters. We spoke of my elevation to the Senate and Cinna's solution to my toga dilemma. A great deal was said about the preparations of everyone except myself to depart Rome—Decimus to govern Gaul, Lepidus to govern Spain (a full legion was encamped on the Tiber Island just outside the city to escort him), Cinna and Meto to travel with Caesar.

Cinna had been with Caesar for most of the day, the two of them holed up at Cinna's house ("the only place where I can escape from all

other concerns," Caesar explained) to work on the speech that Caesar
would deliver to the Senate the next day. This was to be no ordinary oration, but a combined farewell speech and valedictory address, in which
Caesar would put forth for posterity his version of the civil war (briefly,
so as not to dwell on the past) and his vision for the future of Rome as
the capital city of the world—not Alexandria or Troy, as some rumors had
reported. The speech, Caesar declared, was a masterpiece—thanks in no
small part to the contributions of Cinna.

"This is to take nothing away from you, Meto," Caesar said. "You
helped with the initial draft, which shaped the basic arguments, but the
final version required a poet's touch. And not just any poet, but our own
dear Cinna, the greatest poet alive. Cinna, you blush! Or is that the braziers' flames reflected on your cheeks?" Here Caesar delivered one of
those laughs that set my teeth on edge. "I say it without hesitation, you
know—that you are our greatest poet. A month ago, I might not have
done so. But a month ago, I had not yet read your *Orpheus and Pentheus.*"

"The great work is at long last finished, then?" asked Lepidus.

"It is," said Caesar. "And I was honored to be the first reader."

"And so far, Caesar, you are the *only* reader," said Cinna, whose cheeks
were still flushed.

"And what is the judgment of Caesar?" asked Lepidus.

"My opinion I will gladly share with you, but you can judge for
yourselves—because Cinna has agreed to recite the poem in its entirety
this evening."

"Hear, hear!" said Lepidus, clapping his hands. Decimus did likewise,
though it was hard to imagine him a connoisseur of poetry, and so did
Meto, though less enthusiastically. I think Meto was a little jealous of
Cinna. Over the years I have observed that every writer seems to be jealous of all other writers.

"The very conception of the poem is brilliant," said Caesar. "One
wonders why no poet thought to do it before—to recount in a single poem
the deaths of both Orpheus and Pentheus, so similar in some respects,
so different in others. I think you may have created a genre, Cinna, for

surely others will follow your example, historians as well as poets. Imagine a series of life stories told in parallel, to compare and contrast the careers and fortunes of great men."

"I foresee a poem combining Alexander and Caesar," said Lepidus, flashing a knowing look at Cinna.

"Perhaps," said Cinna. "If I am so fortunate as to follow in Alexander's footsteps, side by side with Caesar, I pray the Muse will grant me the inspiration and longevity to express the wonder and the glory of both expeditions, then and now—perhaps in parallel, as you suggest, Lepidus."

"I like that bit about longevity," quipped Meto. "The *Zmyrna* did take you almost ten years to write. And so, I gather, did the *Orpheus and Pentheus.*"

"But surely it won't take ten years for Caesar to conquer the East," said Lepidus. "You must learn to write faster, Cinna. Faster!"

"No, no," said Caesar. "One cannot hurry perfection. Let Cinna take whatever time he needs to create his masterpieces. The world will be forever grateful."

"You flatter me, Caesar," said Cinna.

"No, I do not!" Caesar sounded almost angry. His eyes glittered with manic fire. "Caesar flatters no one. Caesar has no need to. I surround myself with men of supreme ability. If they disappoint, I discard them. If they match or exceed my expectations, I give reward and encouragement—but never flattery. So when I speak highly of your poetry, Cinna, I mean every word I say. If anything, I understate my high regard. As an orator I've trained myself to avoid the appearance of hyperbole. So let me be clear and speak without equivocation." He drained his wine cup, handed it to a slave, and gestured to another, who produced a scroll. The ornate dowels were carved from ivory with inlays of carnelian and caps of gold. "When you gave me this copy of the *Orpheus and Pentheus,* you told me it is the only copy in existence. I felt a grave responsibility to have in my keeping a thing so precious and rare. I began to read it as soon as I had a spare moment, thinking to read only a little and then get back to work. The moment grew to hours. I couldn't put it down. Nor could Meto pry it from my hands."

"It's true," said Meto. "I had to turn away one visitor after another."

"From the very first words, I felt a curious premonition, a stirring of something like . . . fear."

"You, Caesar? Fearful?" said Cinna.

"Yes. So dreadful a thing it is to explore the inmost secrets of such stories—think of the *Zmyrna* and the secrets it reveals. Nor did this feeling diminish as I proceeded. It deepened into a sort of . . . terror . . . almost a horror . . . of what might come next. Fierce, fiery, incandescent—a firestorm of words ablaze with dazzling images, words that conjure utter ecstasy and utmost despair. I trembled, as one must in the presence of such a singular masterpiece. There is nothing in the whole length and breadth of Latin literature with which to compare it, not even the *Zmyrna*. Whatever great works you've given us before, Cinna, the *Orpheus and Pentheus* outshines them with a furious brilliance."

There followed a long silence. Caesar's listeners sat stunned and speechless. I looked from face to face. Most stupefied of all was Cinna. He had blushed before but now looked ashen. His hand trembled so violently that he had to put down his silver cup. I thought he might be ill. Then he put his face in his hands and began to weep, as men do when overwhelmed with joy.

XXVIII

By custom or instinct, one does not closely observe other men when they bathe, or eat, or weep—especially when they weep. Taking my eyes from Cinna, I gazed at the nearby statues in the garden. Situated atop a marble pedestal not far from the dining room, there happened to be a rather magnificent statue of Orpheus.

The handsome youth was depicted, as usual, wearing a Phrygian cap and holding a lyre, surrounded by numerous animals. The son of the Muse Calliope and a mortal king, Orpheus had been revered for centuries as the greatest musician who ever lived, able with his songs not only to charm birds, beasts, and fish, but also to inspire trees and rocks to dance, and rivers to change their course. When his beloved Eurydice died from the bite of a viper, Orpheus descended to the realm of Pluto, using his music to charm the watchdog Cerberus and the ferryman Charon. Even the god of the dead was susceptible. After hearing Orpheus sing, Pluto agreed to relinquish Eurydice. But there was a condition: Orpheus, ascending from the Underworld, must not look at his beloved until both of them emerged in the world of the living. Orpheus ascended, step by step, playing his lyre so that Eurydice could follow, but she uttered no response to his song. He listened for her footsteps but could not hear them. In an agony of doubt, he dared to look back. Their eyes made contact, they reached for each other—and then Eurydice tumbled back, back, back to the Underworld, never to be seen by Orpheus again.

That was the most famous story about Orpheus, but there were many more. His songs, handed down through countless generations, were now known to only a handful of initiates. These special acolytes, keepers of the Orphic Mysteries, were said to possess magical powers.

As I was soon to learn, Cinna's poem dealt only in passing with the life of Orpheus. The singer's gory death was its chief concern.

Of Pentheus, the other subject of Cinna's poem, there was no image in Lepidus's garden—indeed, I had very seldom seen Pentheus depicted by statues or paintings, only by actors on the stage. (How actors love to play a doomed man driven mad!) But there was, not far from the Orpheus—facing it, in fact—a statue of Bacchus, the god whom Pentheus so gravely offended that he was punished with a fate almost too horrible to imagine—a death in many ways similar to that of Orpheus.

The statue depicted Bacchus as a voluptuous youth with a handsome face that betrayed no emotion whatsoever. His brow was wreathed with ivy and his shoulders clothed with a mantle of grapevines heavy with fruit. Wine—or more precisely the wild intoxication that comes from wine—was a gift to mankind of Bacchus, who inspires not only drunkenness but all manner of madness and frenzy. For centuries, women have been known to worship Bacchus in secret. No man knows the exact nature of these rites, which are said to turn sane women into Maenads, mad creatures clothed in animal skins who run headlong through the woods playing shrill music, singing ululating songs in praise of Bacchus, attacking and annihilating any living creature they encounter. Maenads are the stuff of nightmares—for men, at least. The word is Greek for "raving ones." In Latin we call then Bacchantes, after Bacchus, and so they were often referred to in Cinna's poem.

I knew the tale of Pentheus mostly from the famous play by Euripides. Young Pentheus, king of Thebes, was so disgusted by the behavior of the local Bacchantes, including his own mother, that he banned the worship of Bacchus altogether. But no mortal dishonors a god without consequence. Bacchus decided to wreak a particularly terrible vengeance on Pentheus. Looking at the statue of Bacchus in the garden of Lepidus—youthful, serene, the giver of wine and joyful abandon—it was hard to imagine such a benevolent divinity inflicting such cruelty. . . .

Regaining his composure, Cinna spoke, drawing my attention away from the nearby statues in the garden.

"After words that do me such honor, Caesar, I hesitate to utter a single verse of my poem aloud, for fear that I must surely disappoint my listeners."

"Nonsense, Cinna," said Caesar. "These men will fall under the poem's spell as surely as I did. Recite to us now. Do you require the written words?" He gestured to the scroll with its ornate ivory dowels.

Cinna shook his head. "I've labored so long over every word, the verses are engraved in my memory."

He rose from his couch and stepped to the outer edge of the dining room, standing almost in the garden, so that he was framed by the moonlit statue of Orpheus on one side and Bacchus on the other, with his own face brightly lit by the flaming braziers. The placement of poet and statues was so ideal, so theatrical, it seemed almost contrived, not mere coincidence—but by whom? Not by any of the men present, I thought; by the Fates, perhaps.

As when Cinna had recited for me the ending of the *Zmyrna,* I was again spellbound by his voice: the timbre, the cadence, the flood of words—words beautiful and terrifying, uplifting and appalling, majestic and overwhelming, sometimes seeming to come from a great distance, like heavenly pronouncements, and at other times as intimate as a whispered kiss upon the ear. Caesar was right to praise him, I thought, but what Cinna had wrought was beyond praise. It was like a thunderstorm or avalanche or raging flood, a phenomenon overwhelming to mortal senses, demanding complete attention but beyond human judgment.

Caesar was also right in saying that the new poem was greater than the *Zmyrna*. Not merely greater, but ten times greater, dwarfing anything any Roman poet had done before.

The story of Orpheus was briefly recounted: his gift for music, his journey to the Underworld, his loss of Eurydice.

Then Cinna came to the death of Orpheus.

Beside the banks of the Hebrus River, attempting to console himself for the loss of Eurydice, Orpheus devised the most beautiful of all his songs, a song of lamentation but also of deep and endless love, love that transcended time and death. So compelling was his song that all creatures stopped to listen. Lions and lambs alike gazed at Orpheus, their eyes brimming with tears. The trees bent toward him, striving to embrace him with their leafy branches. Rocks, enraptured, rose into the air, arranged themselves in fantastic shapes, and swayed to the rhythm of his verses in a kind of dance.

Only Maenads were immune to his music. A group of Bacchantes, rampaging though the woods, came upon Orpheus as he sang. They covered their ears and shrieked, for the sweet music threatened to draw them out of their frenzy, to tame them as it had all other creatures and even the elements themselves.

"See, see the man who scorns us!" cried one of the Bacchantes. She hurled a spear at Orpheus, but being made of wood, the spear fell prostrate before the singer, then rose before him and twirled about, dancing in time to his song.

Another Bacchante reached for a stone and hurled it at Orpheus, but the other stones formed a wall to block its passage, so that it recoiled and fell to the ground—then rose up and joined its fellow stones in the dance.

The furious Bacchantes began to howl, and those with instruments—flutes, tambourines, braying horns, drums made from animal hides—created such a din that even the song of Orpheus was drowned by the discord. Now the stones could no longer hear his song, and neither could the wooden spears. The animals that surrounded Orpheus scattered and fled. The rocks fell to the ground. The trees drew back.

The howling Bacchantes surrounded Orpheus. They pelted him with stones, beat him with sticks, stabbed him with spears. Still he sang, though now only the Bacchantes could hear. His song became a cry for mercy, a song that would make even Medusa weep, but the Bacchantes were unmoved.

They laid hold of him and began to gouge his flesh. They tore off the hands that played the lyre so lovingly. They tore off his arms and legs. Some of them bit into the quivering flesh still warm with blood, while their sisters chanted a hymn to Bacchus Carnivorus, Eater of Raw Flesh—an ancient name of the god no one alive dared whisper except the Bacchantes.

Still Orpheus sang. They gouged his neck with sharp fingernails and ripped his head from the body. Into the Hebrus they threw his lyre and his head. His lips still murmured, his tongue still moved, but no sound issued from his breathless mouth to charm the river that carried him swiftly to the sea.

A wave chanced to toss his head onto the lyre, which cradled it as gently as a pillow. As the head, lifeless now, rolled over the strings, the motion produced the strangest and most mournful music ever made, with no mortal to hear it.

At last the lyre and the head were tossed upon the sandy shore of Lesbos. The head rolled away from the lyre and suffered the fate of all flesh: Insects consumed the eyes, all else besides the bones rotted and withered, and even the sun-bleached skull finally crumbled and turned to sand.

But the lyre of Orpheus remained intact and undamaged. It was undiscovered for many years, until the day a young woman walking on the beach, anxiously searching the horizon for the sail of a longed-for ship, came upon the lyre and picked it up. Her name was Sappho. . . .

Beside me on the couch, Meto drew a sharp breath. On his face I saw an expression of wonderment. Lesbos was famed in legend as the destination of Orpheus's severed head—no doubt a shrine or temple on some

Lesbian beach commemorated the event—but I had never heard of a link between Orpheus and Sappho. This was Cinna's own invention, the kind of liberty that modern poets allowed themselves.

"Brilliant!" Meto whispered, and I knew he was praising Cinna's bold innovation.

If Cinna heard, he gave no sign. He appeared to be almost in a trance, his eyes nearly shut, his arms at his sides, and his shoulders held stiffly back. He took a deep breath and resumed . . .

Watching all this from the heavens was the god Bacchus, whose only reaction to the mad destruction of his Maenads was a sly smile.

Then the smile of Bacchus faded.

He turned his attention to Thebes, which he saw at a great distance, like a city in miniature that rested on the palm of his hand. It was the city of his origin, for Bacchus had been born of the union of a Theban princess with Jupiter. The royal house of Thebes had refused to accept the divinity of Bacchus, who left the city to wander through the world, spreading the cultivation of the grape and inspiring the frenzy of his Bacchantes.

It was the singular wailing of a Bacchante that drew his attention to Thebes. She was Agave, Bacchus's mortal aunt, and one of his most fervent acolytes. Agave was mother of young King Pentheus, the first cousin of Bacchus but as unlike Bacchus as any mortal could be: stern, humorless, rigidly disciplined, completely and devoutly sober.

Agave wailed because her son had outlawed the worship of Bacchus in every form. Even the drinking of wine was forbidden. What insanity was this? Surely the banning of madness was itself a mad act.

Bacchus descended to earth and set foot on the woody slopes of Mount Cithaeron, above Thebes. As he walked toward the city gate, he covered himself with a mist to hide his divinity, especially his horns, from mortal eyes. Despite the royal ban, the streets were thronged by Bacchantes, whose drunken carousing seemed more joyous than threatening. The women had enticed young men to join their celebration, and the men, too, carried ivy-twined wands, wore ivy wreaths and fawn skins, played tambourines and finger cymbals, whirled about and shook their hips. Delighted, Bacchus joined the dance. He appeared to be just another drunken mortal amid the throng.

Pentheus appeared, furious at the debauchery. He called on the men to throw aside their wands and take up swords again, to cast off ivy wreaths and put on helmets. Suddenly ashamed of their uncontrolled behavior and their womanly appearance, most of the men obeyed. Those who came to their senses arrested those who did not—including Bacchus, who allowed himself to be led away in chains. The Bacchantes fled in panic to the woods of Mount Cithaeron.

In his prison cell, Bacchus brooded. What fate would be appropriate for Pentheus? Bacchus recalled the death of Orpheus. . . .

The chains fell from his wrists. The iron door of the cell sprang open.

The guards, bewildered, took Bacchus to the king. Pentheus demanded to know how he had escaped. Bacchus declared himself a magician and a master of disguise whom no prison could hold. He offered to advise the king in his program to eradicate the frenzied debauchery on Mount Cithaeron. Pentheus decided to trust the smiling stranger.

It was essential, Bacchus said, that the king should first spy on the Bacchantes, to discover their plans and weaknesses. To penetrate the ranks of the Bacchantes, the king would need to pass as one of them. Bacchus replaced the king's diadem with an ivy wreath, and his scepter with an ivy-wound wand. He took off the king's royal robes and clothed him in animal hides. He convinced Pentheus to leap in the air, twirl about, and gyrate his hips as the Bacchantes did, and drilled him in these movements until the beardless king could pass as a woman among women.

Bacchus hid his laughter behind his hand. Pentheus meanwhile began to feel strangely elated. From time to time, for only an instant, he thought he caught a glimpse of horns amid the stranger's curling locks.

Bacchus led Pentheus out of the palace, through the city gate, and up the woody slopes of Mount Cithaeron. They wandered past ancient trees hung with moss, standing stones that seemed to have faces, and drifts of dry leaves that crumbled with a crepitating protest under their feet. Soon they came upon the Bacchantes. Pentheus was aghast at the strange things he beheld. A bull was being sacrificed, but there was no altar and no ceremonial knife. Instead, the Bacchantes killed the creature with their bare hands and tore off its flesh, laughing as they did so. Their mad cachinnations rang through the forest.

Bacchus convinced the king to join in the frenzy. Pentheus at first merely whirled about, mimicking the dance, but then, with mixed loathing and elation, he found himself reaching for the bull, rending its flesh with his bare hands, and devouring pieces of the steaming, bloody flesh. Then Pentheus caught sight of his mother among the screeching Bacchantes and felt ashamed that she should see him in such a state. He turned and ran back toward the city.

The god cast a spell on the Bacchantes, including Agave, so that Pentheus appeared to them as a lion. They ran after the beast, howling as they did so, turning the secret names of their god into a shrill, ululating chant: "Euhan! Euhius! Eleleleus! Euhan! Euhius! Eleleleus."

As he ran, Pentheus came back to his senses. With mounting terror, he realized where he was, how he came to be there, who had tricked him—and who pursued him.

Agave was first to overtake the lion. She leaped on the beast and brought it down, then tore at it with her teeth and sharp nails, ignoring its bleating cries, which sounded almost human. She gorged on its flesh and drank its blood. The other Bacchantes arrived and tore the limbs from the living body. Using only her teeth and fingers, Agave tore off the head.

Gripping the mane, Agave proudly held the lion's head aloft. She displayed it to the raving Bacchantes, then ordered them to follow her into the city. They arrived at the gate and ran through the streets, spreading panic. Agave reached the palace, mounted the steps, and turned to face the crowded square. Aghast, the people of Thebes beheld the head of their young king held aloft by his mother, who was covered with gore. Blood streamed from her babbling mouth.

The lips of Pentheus still writhed, as if trying to scream. His wide-open eyes looked this way and that. His face was a mask of utmost terror. The Thebans could not bear to look at him. The Bacchantes clapped their finger cymbals and howled their ululating chant.

Bacchus arrived. He mounted the steps. He took the head of Pentheus from Agave and peered into the wide-open eyes that stared back at him. Smiling, Bacchus stilled the wriggling lips with a kiss, and with his fingers shut the eyes, allowing Pentheus, who had dared to deny him, the gift of death.

XXIX

Cinna bowed his head. He had come to the end of the poem.

My eyes moved to the statue of Bacchus in the garden. By some trick of illumination—subfuscous moonlight and starlight, flickering torches and braziers—the beautiful face of Bacchus, expressionless before, now seemed very faintly to smile.

With a shiver, I tore my gaze from the statue. Cinna meanwhile had resumed his place on the couch he shared with Decimus, who averted his eyes and drew back slightly as Cinna settled himself. Cinna held up his cup, which was filled by a slave who then disappeared into the shadows. Cinna drained the cup at a single draft, then held it out to be filled again.

There followed a long silence, which became more awkward the longer it lasted. I had no intention of speaking first. I looked at Meto, who would not look back at me. No one in the room seemed to be looking at anyone else, except me—the ever-inquisitive Finder, never afraid to look or listen, only to speak.

Caesar finally cleared his throat, and then spoke. "However did you . . . I was going to say, 'find the words,' but what I truly wonder is, however did you summon the *strength* to write such a poem?"

"And the stamina," added Meto.

"It was the labor of many years," said Cinna. "And the product of much wine. I never fail to honor Bacchus each and every day. I never stint the god, or myself."

Caesar shook his head. "You deprecate yourself, Cinna. Here there is no need for modesty, false or otherwise. It's not just the subject matter, and the power of the scenes—it's the language. Featherlight yet sturdy as a pyramid. So complex and so obscure at times as to be mind-wounding, yet even then delivering an intense, peculiar sort of pleasure. As beautiful and serene as the face of Bacchus in the garden there, but also . . . macabre . . . grotesque, like a . . ."

"Like a statue of Aesop, perhaps?" suggested Meto. "Withered, hunch-backed, horribly misshapen?"

"If you like," said Caesar. "As *wise* as Aesop, too, and yet . . . there seems to be something almost frivolous hidden inside in the words, something debauched, and rather wicked—yet irresistible . . . taunting . . ."

"Like the comminatory smile of Bacchus," suggested Meto, gazing at the statue.

Caesar nodded.

"Romulus, too, was torn to pieces," said Lepidus.

"What's that?" said Caesar, who had become lost in thought.

"I say that King Romulus also was torn to pieces. Or cut up, with sharp knives, I suppose. And presumably beheaded as well. The first king of Rome, all those hundreds of years ago, assassinated by the first senators. So historians tell us. There was a ceremony of some sort, a sacrifice over which Romulus presided, and then a storm broke, so that darkness and rain hid the deed from sight. The assassins killed him, then chopped him up and carried off the pieces under their togas. Nothing was ever found of him."

"Curio, too, was beheaded," Caesar said quietly. "His beautiful head, taken as a trophy by King Juba. How Fulvia wept. And so did I! Well, Juba is dead now, and Curio is well and truly avenged." He gazed into the shadows of the garden. "I wonder, Cinna, have you ever actually *seen* a man beheaded?"

Cinna looked thoughtful. "No, I think not, Caesar."

"I ask because your descriptions of the severed heads of Orpheus and Pentheus are so vivid, and seem so keenly *observed*. If not from your own observation, then I wonder if perhaps you extracted some details from Gordianus during your research."

"Me, Caesar?" I said.

"You and Cinna are drinking companions, are you not? I thought perhaps the subject had come up between you. Because you did witness the beheading of Pompey, did you not, when those accursed eunuchs slew him on that beach in Egypt?"

I nodded. "Yes, I saw it happen. But only from a great distance. I was on a ship, and the murder took place on shore." In memory I beheld the desolate beach, the sparkling surf, the confusion in Pompey's small boat as it came ashore, the flashing daggers, then the head of the Great One held aloft. "But I don't think I've ever spoken of it to Cinna. His imagination far outstrips my faulty memory, I'm sure. Though, as I recall, there was only *one* eunuch involved in the murder of Pompey. 'Accursed eunuchs,' you said, using the plural."

Caesar snorted. I saw the manic sparkle in his eyes. "I use the word in this instance as a derogatory term for all Egyptians."

"That seems hardly fair," Lepidus said mildly.

"Come, come, even Cleopatra says it! I think I picked up the habit from her. The young queen of Egypt says the most appalling things, even about her own people—and can do so in almost any language you can think of."

Everyone laughed at this. We drank more wine.

"Yes, the beheadings are very vivid," Caesar said thoughtfully. "The way you describe the death of each man is so wrenching, almost unbearable— I swear, reading those passages silently to myself was bad enough, but to hear them recited aloud, it was all I could do not to cover my ears. And no man has ever called me squeamish."

"Your response to the verses has less to do with squeamishness, I think," said Cinna, "and more to do with *horror*—something very different, and from which no man is immune. We can all be made to feel horror."

"But how do you achieve this horror, as a poet?" said Lepidus.

Cinna answered slowly, carefully choosing each word. "I tried to imagine the worst possible death, and then write about it. Surely no death could be more horrible than being torn to pieces while still alive. I had to imagine exactly what that might feel like—not just the physical pain, but also the anguish of seeing your body ripped apart. To see your hands torn off, your arms and your legs, and to know there can be no turning back, no possible recovery—no hope. Utter horror, utter hopelessness. To *see* oneself destroyed, to *know* what is happening, even while suffering unimaginable agony . . ." He took a sip of wine. "But do you know, once I had committed those descriptions to verse, I felt somehow relieved . . . unburdened . . . as if I had faced my worst fear, and by admitting it, describing it, dwelling on it, I had overcome it."

"You stared down the enemy!" said Decimus with a laugh.

"If you like."

Lepidus nodded. "Now, thanks to Cinna and his *Orpheus and Pentheus,* we all know what the worst death would be. But I wonder, what would be the *best* way to die?"

"Not so fast!" said Caesar. "I'm not sure that Cinna has described the very worst way to die. Dismemberment by Maenads would at least be relatively quick, however agonizing. I'm not even sure dismemberment would be that painful. The body seems not to feel pain after a certain point. I've seen more than one man pick up his sword and keep fighting after having a hand or an arm lopped off—the wounded man seems not to feel his wound at all. Nor would death by daggers necessarily be so terrible, as happened with Romulus . . . and with Pompey."

"After which, each was beheaded," noted Decimus, staring into his wine cup.

"Yes, well, the desecration of one's corpse is a whole other question," said Caesar. "The beheaded are said to stay that way even in Hades. But as for the worst way to die, I think it would be a long, lingering illness. To see yourself wither, to become increasingly helpless and derelict, to lose appetite, to lose control of one's bladder and bowels, to know for a long time that the end is drawing closer and closer."

"King Cyrus of Persia died like that," said Cinna. "So Xenophon tells us in the *Cyropaedia*. He saw his end approaching. He even planned the details of his own funeral."

"Well, then, let me *not* die like Cyrus!" said Caesar. "Yes, by slow degrees would be for me the worst death. Far better to die quickly . . . unexpectedly . . ."

"Even if by violence?" asked Decimus, gazing into his wine cup. "Like Romulus? Like Pompey?"

Caesar smiled. "I was thinking of the way my father died, actually. He sat on a bench one morning, bent down to put on a shoe—and fell over, dead. A terrible shock for my mother, and for me—I was only sixteen—but I imagine he felt little or no pain, and had no anticipation of death. Or if so, only for an instant."

"Do you fear death, Caesar?" I asked.

"Fear it? I think not. But nor do I desire it. To desire death is against nature. One hopes always to achieve more fame, more glory. To do so, one must keep living."

"But can't a man live long enough to satisfy nature?" I said. "Can he not achieve *enough* glory?"

"Perhaps," Caesar said thoughtfully. "Yes, I think so. I have lived long enough, for nature or for glory."

Decimus raised his eyes to meet those of Caesar. "Sudden death is best, then?"

"Undoubtedly," said Caesar.

There was a break in the conversation, the natural silence that falls when people have had their fill of food and wine and talk. The quiet was broken only by the crackling of the fires in the braziers, a comforting sound. I heard the distant soughing of wind in treetops, and then gusts of wind in the garden, shaking the foliage, stirring dry leaves, and whistling past the statues.

"Do you smell it?" said Caesar. "The smell of approaching rain. How I love that!"

Meto laughed. "How I hate it! It makes me think of muddy campsites and wet boots. Oh, there is nothing so miserable as a leaky tent some-where in the middle of Gaul!"

"I wish I were in Gaul this very minute," Decimus said wistfully.

"Soon enough, you will be," said Caesar. "But if we've descended to talking about the weather, I think that must be the signal for the end of this most pleasurable and memorable occasion. Thank you all for com-ing. Thank you especially for your hospitality, Lepidus. And thank you, Cinna, for the recitation. No one here will ever forget the night he heard the *Orpheus and Pentheus*."

Cinna stood and bowed. "To recite for such august company was my deepest pleasure."

"If we're leaving, we should probably do so quickly, or else we're likely to be drenched," said Meto, who sprang up from the couch and stepped into the garden to peruse the night sky. "The moon and stars have disappeared behind clouds. I see lightning to the west."

A few seconds later, a peal of thunder rumbled through the garden.

"You'll come with me to the Regia, Cinna, as we planned," said Cae-sar. He didn't spring to his feet, like Meto, but stood slowly, grunting as his limbs straightened. "I may yet want to do a bit of revising on that speech before I sleep tonight, or first thing in the morning, when my mind is fresh."

"It will be my honor, Caesar."

"And you, Gordianus . . ."

"Yes, Caesar?"

"Come to the Regia the second hour after sunrise, and wear your sen-atorial toga. I want you and your son to be in my entourage when I walk to the Senate meeting."

"Are you sure, Caesar?"

"When I am unsure of a thing, Finder, I do not say it." He stared at me for a long moment, then finally released me from his stern gaze with the faintest hint of a smile.

As we stepped into the garden, a bolt of lightning split the sky and struck the earth somewhere very near. The thundercrack was so loud it made my heart jump in my chest. I happened to be glancing at Caesar when the lightning flashed. By its searing illumination he seemed transformed into a statue of white marble.

The illusion ended in the blink of an eye, but Caesar remained unmoving, statue-like, for so long that Meto touched his arm. Caesar blinked and gave a slight jerk, as if coming to his senses. He touched his forehead and winced, then brushed aside Meto's hand, as if to assure him that nothing was amiss.

"All of you, to bed," said Caesar, addressing us as if we were soldiers on the eve of a battle. "Sleep well. Tomorrow promises to be a very memorable day."

DAY SIX: MARCH 15

The Ides

XXX

There was thunder and lightning all night long. Sheets of rain pelted the roof above my head.

By daybreak the storm had passed. The world seemed sparkling and newly made. The streets were washed clean and the air was so clear that from my doorstep I could count every stone of the distant Temple of Jupiter atop the Capitoline.

Dressed in my borrowed toga, breathing in the fresh, moist air, I made my way with Meto down the steep road that descended from the Palatine Hill to the Forum, and then toward the Dictator's house.

When staying in the city, Caesar, as Pontifex Maximus, resided in the Regia, which since the earliest days of Rome had been the official residence of the head of the state religion. The mansion had been subject to numerous renovations over the centuries. The latest addition was a magnificent marble pediment to decorate the facade. Caesar had petitioned the Senate for permission to add this pediment. The effect was to make the mansion look more like a temple—suitable housing for a descendant of Venus.

Outside the Regia, a large number of lictors were milling in the street. Roman magistrates are traditionally accompanied by these ceremonial bodyguards, armed with fasces, axes bundled in wooden rods—the ancient weapons for protecting the person and dignity of Rome's rulers on official occasions. As dictator, Caesar was entitled to twenty-four lictors, apparently. They were no substitute for the Spanish bodyguards that Caesar had dismissed—hulking, war-hardened brutes— but at least they would provide a dignified escort for Caesar and his entourage as we made our way to the Senate meeting. While the rest of us walked, it appeared that Caesar would be conveyed in a gilded litter with purple cushions. Among the four slaves who would bear this small but splendid vehicle I recognized Hipparchus, who had waited for me outside the Salacious Tavern.

The doors of the Regia were wide open. Meto and I ascended the short flight of steps and joined the toga-clad crowd gathered in the vestibule. On the occasion of his final address to the Senate before leaving Rome, the Dictator had invited a great many magistrates and senators to join his retinue. I felt honored to be among them and at the same time not so special after all, seeing how many of us there were. Standing out in the crowd was the imposing figure of Marc Antony in his consul's toga, talking to Cinna. When the two of them saw Meto and me, they both nodded. Antony turned to talk to someone else. Cinna made his way through the crowd to join us.

He looked rather haggard, as if he hadn't slept well, but his face lit up as he looked me up and down.

"Gordianus, how splendid you look! Clearly, this was the toga the gods meant for you to wear on this day. What do you think, Meto? Doesn't your father look splendid?"

"He does, indeed. But where's Caesar?"

"Already out and about. There was some ceremony he had to attend at daybreak at Calvinus's house, not far from here, something to do with Calvinus being named Master of the Horse for the coming year. But Caesar should be back at any moment, and then we'll all head for the Senate meeting."

"How did the speechwriting go?" I asked

Cinna shuddered. "What a ghastly night! Caesar was up and down, up and down, waking me at all hours to do a bit of tinkering to this passage or that. Really, if Caesar is to be this demanding during the campaign, I think I shall expire from exhaustion."

"He does ask a great deal from his collaborators," said Meto with a thin smile.

"But the speech is good?" I asked.

"Yes, yes. 'Quite the finest speech I will ever have given,' Caesar told me, when at last he let me flee to my bed and catch an hour of sleep." Cinna flashed a crooked smile. "But his voice was so oddly strained when he said that, it rather spoiled my enjoyment of the compliment. What a peculiar mood he was in last night. Didn't you think so?"

This question was addressed to Meto, who slowly nodded and lowered his voice so that only Cinna and I could hear. "I've seen Caesar like this before. Sometimes, when the demands on him are very great, he falls prey to the falling sickness."

"You mean he falls unconscious, or suffers a seizure?" said Cinna. "So I've heard, though I've never witnessed it. Nor did I witness such a thing last night."

"Ah, but the sickness takes many forms," said Meto. "Sometimes he merely suffers a headache, or dizziness, or moods that change without reason. He laughs too much, or loses his temper, or doesn't remember something I told him just a moment before."

"I see. Yes, he did seem to be in a bit of a fog when he left for Calvinus's house this morning. But I put that down to his lack of sleep, and Calpurnia's pestering."

"Calpurnia?" I said.

"While we were going over the speech one last time, she burst into the room, raving about some nightmare she'd had. Something about the pediment of this place crashing down and trapping Caesar underneath. Well, that dream was caused by all that crashing thunder, don't you think?"

At that moment I happened to spy Calpurnia herself. She had just stepped into the room in a surprising state of undress, wearing house slippers and a thin cloak pulled over her nightgown. She cast an anxious gaze over the crowd—seeking Caesar, I thought—and then her eyes fell on me. She made an emphatic gesture that I should come to her, then stepped back, out of the room.

Meto and Cinna, having seen, both gave me an understanding nod when I excused myself. I slipped across the room and then down a short hallway. A hand seized my arm and pulled me into a small, windowless chamber lit by a single lamp. Its flame illuminated the face of Calpurnia.

Never a great beauty, but handsome in an austere way, she looked considerably aged since I had last seen her. Rather than giving her face a warm glow, the flickering light made her look sallow and deepened the wrinkles around her eyes and mouth. She looked very pale and drawn, almost ill.

"Finder, you must help me." Though it seemed impossible that any-one could overhear, she spoke in a hushed voice.

"Of course."

"Caesar must not attend the Senate meeting today."

"I'm not sure I could—"

"You must convince him."

"How?"

"I know he gave you a list of men he's worried about. Caesar told me."

I nodded. "Did he also tell you that I had nothing to report?"

"Make up something."

"Invent a threat? Accuse someone falsely? I don't think so."

"Then think of something else!" Her voice broke. She clutched my arm so fiercely that I felt the sharpness of her fingernails through the thin wool of Cinna's summer toga.

"What is it you fear, Calpurnia?"

"Something terrible is going to happen. I know it! Last night, when the two of us were in bed, the doors of the room flew open—yet no one touched them."

"The wind, Calpurnia—"

"No, not the wind! This was something else. There was . . . a pres-ence . . . something . . . *someone* . . . in the room with us. . . ."

"Who?"

Her face became even paler. She wrinkled her brow. "Pompey?"

I shook my head. "A nightmare, and the storm, and the wind—"

"No! Caesar and I were both wide awake when the doors opened. He felt it, too. The expression on his face—I've never seen him look like that. He looked . . . afraid."

This was hard for me to imagine. Once I had stood beside Caesar on a pier in Alexandria while catapult bombardments fell all around us, and he had shown not the least trace of fear. My task at that moment, it seemed to me, was not to prevent Caesar from going about his business but to somehow calm Caesar's wife. Before I could say anything, she spoke again.

"Then I had a dream. The pediment of this house broke in two and fell on us—on Caesar and me—right there on our bed—and he was trapped beneath it. I saw blood—a pool of blood, spreading across the floor. I tried to lift the pediment, but the marble was too heavy and the corners were too sharp. They cut my hands. . . ." She stared down at her open palms and then held them before me, as if to show me wounds, but the flesh was intact.

"Calpurnia, you've had a terrible night. A sleepless night, full of bad dreams. You're worried for Caesar. Of course you are. He's about to set off for the ends of the earth. And I think perhaps Caesar is a bit unwell. That must worry you, too—"

"Yes, that's it! You must convince him that he's not well enough to go to the Senate meeting. There's too much at stake. His speech is too important. He's not well enough to properly deliver it—"

"I'm not a physician, Calpurnia."

She clutched herself and rolled her eyes. "Perhaps the sacrifice at Calvinus's house will indicate a warning. Perhaps the divination performed before the Senate meets will be so unfavorable—"

"I'm not a haruspex, either. You should be talking to Spurinna."

"He's with Caesar, at Calvinus's house. Spurinna warned him already, a month ago—"

"But the month has come and gone."

"Not quite! The Ides haven't yet passed. This is the final day before the period of greatest danger passes. Caesar must somehow survive the Ides. . . ."

"Calpurnia, he'll be surrounded by friends and supporters all day. Where is he safer than at a meeting of the Senate, where every member has taken a sacred vow to protect him?"

"The Senate! A nest of vipers. Vipers, one and all!" She stared at me with a wild look, then seemed to notice that I was wearing a senatorial toga. "Not you, Finder. I trust you! Do you know how rare it is, that I can say such a thing? That's why I plucked you out of that room, you of all men."

"You can also trust my son. Meto would die for Caesar," I said. *And probably he* will *die, or lose an eye, or a limb,* I thought, *somewhere off in Parthia, far from home, far from me, serving your husband and his never-ending quest for glory. . . .*

"Yes, Meto I also trust. The two of you, then—the two of you must help me! Say or do something, whatever you must, to persuade Caesar to—"

We heard shouts from the vestibule. Men called out Caesar's name. The Dictator had just returned.

"Go to him, Finder."

"And you?"

"I'll stay here. A woman has no place in that gathering. Go, now! Convince him to stay home. Say or do whatever you must. I beg you!"

I left her and headed back to the vestibule.

XXXI

Everyone in the vestibule had gathered around Caesar, pressing as closely as they could. Like bees in the hive clustered around the king bee, the drones all alike in white togas, Caesar resplendent in the toga of a triumphing general, solid purple with gold embroidery, with a laurel wreath on his brow—the clothes which by order of the Senate he alone was allowed to wear on formal occasions. How was I to get close to him, let alone do as Calpurnia asked?

I was struck by how vulnerable he seemed at that moment. Any one of the men in that room, armed with a dagger, could conceivably land a fatal blow before anyone else could react. Why had Caesar given up his Spanish bodyguards and made himself so accessible, not just to friends like these but also to anyone he passed in the street? But Caesar's safety was a matter for Caesar to judge, not me, and not Calpurnia. I wasn't there to do her bidding, never mind that her lavish compensation had altered my fortunes and set me on my present course. I was here for my own sake and that of my family, not just my children and grandchildren but all the generations to come. On this day I was to become a senator.

Meto approached and spoke in my ear. "He's not going. He's staying home!"

"What?"

"Caesar isn't attending the meeting today. He's just sent Antony to inform the Senate."

I looked across the room and saw the back of Antony's head as he moved toward the front doorway. "So the Senate won't meet today?"

"Perhaps they will, with Antony presiding as consul. But they won't attend to business of any great importance without Caesar there. The question of Dolabella's consulship, and Cinna's proposal about foreign wives—"

"And my installation?"

Meto sighed and shook his head. "Caesar himself must nominate you. It won't be done in his absence. This delay may even postpone our departure for Parthia. It's not every day the Senate can legally meet. . . ." He squinted, as if visualizing a calendar in his head.

I felt profoundly disappointed, yet oddly relieved. A part of me still found the notion that I was to become a Roman senator too far-fetched to ever come true, and perhaps it was. Beyond Meto's shoulder, I saw Caesar wave his hands to disperse the tangle of togas around him. As he left the vestibule, heading toward the private quarters he shared with Calpurnia, he passed just behind Meto, so close I could have touched him. How different he appeared from the glittering dinner companion the previous night. Like Calpurnia, he looked pale and drawn. Neither had gotten much sleep during the long, stormy night.

As soon as Caesar departed, the vestibule was abuzz with hushed conversations.

"Why will Caesar not attend?" I asked Meto.

"I'm not sure, Papa. Cinna told me that Calpurnia is set against it—"

"As she's just told me."

"But I can't imagine that alone would convince him to stay home. The warnings of an anxious wife—"

"It was *my* warning that convinced him," said Spurinna, suddenly joining our conversation. He was dressed in the traditional yellow robes and conical hat of a haruspex.

"Your warning? How so?" I asked.

"We've both just come from Calvinus's house. I was there when Caesar arrived. I could see that he was worried, as well he might be. Fretful. Distracted. Not at all his usual self. He tried to make light of it. 'Ah, Spurinna,' he said to me, 'the Ides have come, yet here I stand before you, alive and well.' And I answered, 'The Ides have come, Caesar, but are not yet gone. *Not yet gone!*' That gave him a start. Every drop of blood drained from his face! He performed the ceremony, but his mind was elsewhere. When he was ready to leave, he insisted I come with him. 'I'll let you explain to everyone,' he said, though I wasn't sure what he meant until we got here and he dispatched Antony to give the Senate his regrets. Well, better to take heed of my warning at the last moment than not at all! I can't tell you what a relief this is. The past month has hung heavy over me. The dread I've felt, fearing at every moment that something terrible might befall the Dictator. But as long as he spends the rest of the day here in the Regia, I'm sure that Calpurnia will keep him safe and sound."

Meto snorted. "Caesar is having you on, Spurinna."

"What do you mean?"

"I think it must amuse him to see you so puffed up and self-important. Do you think it's your warning that's made Caesar cancel his plans? No, you put your finger on it when you said he's not himself today. He wasn't entirely well last night, and he looks more unwell today. Now *that's* something to worry about. Caesar unwell is Caesar *not* on his way to Parthia. After all our months of preparation—"

"What an uncouth little freedman you are!" said Spurinna. "How selfish, to put your own hopes for glory above the safety of the Dictator."

"You sniveling Etruscan!" Meto raised a fist. Had I not restrained him, he would have struck Spurinna squarely in the face.

"Not in the house of the Pontifex Maximus!" I hissed. Meto stepped back. "Though I have half a mind to punch you in the nose myself, Spurinna!"

As I had restrained Meto, I in turn was restrained by Cinna, who suddenly appeared and grabbed my upraised fist. "All of you, be calm!" he said. "I'm not sure what this altercation is about, but no one is more upset than I that Caesar will not be addressing the Senate today. After all the hours we spent on that speech! Ah, well, it shall sound just as sweet another day, if Caesar is unable to do it justice today."

"Caesar's health is not the issue," said Spurinna. "He has decided to stay home because of my warning."

"Come now," said Cinna, "we all know how little regard Caesar gives to omens and portents. If he took your warning seriously, Spurinna, he'd have hidden himself away for a whole month! Just now, before he left the room, he confided to me that he's feeling quite dizzy. He can hardly address the Senate if the room is spinning. But what a disappointment for you, Gordianus, looking as splendid as you do in that toga. Don't you agree, Senator Spurinna? But why are *you* not wearing *your* toga? Were you not planning to attend the meeting today?"

"Of course I was!" snapped Spurinna. "But I was appointed to take the haruspices first, outside the Senate chamber, to determine if the day is propitious. Only after that was I going to change into my toga." He frowned. "Perhaps I'm still expected to take the haruspices, if Antony convenes the meeting without him. Oh dear, I suppose I should hurry after the consul." He turned and began shoving his way through the crowd.

"I'm not sorry to see the back of him," said Meto.

"Nor am I," I said.

"Spurinna? But he's such a charming fellow," said Cinna with a straight face, then smiled to show he was joking. "But what a disappointment this is, for all of us. Ah, well. Caesar shall deliver that speech, and Gordianus shall become a senator, and I shall propose my brilliant bit of legislation permitting the Dictator his foreign marriages—all on some other day. I think Caesar is simply overtired, from having stayed up all night, working with me on the speech, and doing his best to calm Calpurnia. . . ."

He fell silent and turned his head, distracted by a booming voice from the far side of the room. Decimus had just arrived. If the departure of the imposing Antony had left a gap in the room, Decimus filled it. I couldn't make out what he was saying as he queried one man after another, including Spurinna, who hurried past him, but I could see that he looked quite perturbed.

Seeing his dinner companions from the previous night, he strode toward us.

"What is this nonsense?" he said, looking at each of us in turn. "On my way here I crossed paths with Antony, who claims that Caesar isn't coming. Just now I heard Spurinna spouting his usual nonsense about bad omens. I can't believe Caesar is staying home, on this of all days. What is this about, Meto?"

"Caesar has said nothing to me. But you saw for yourself how he was last night."

"He was in high spirits."

"He was a little *too* high-spirited. I've seen this before. After such a night, the next day he suffers one of his spells."

Decimus frowned. "A seizure, you mean? I thought he hadn't suffered those for a long time."

"But he's dizzy. So he told me," said Cinna.

"A bit of light-headedness should hardly prevent him from attending a meeting of this importance."

"Perhaps . . ." I began, but bit my tongue. It occurred to me that Caesar, judging his own symptoms, was perhaps afraid of suffering a seizure in front of the Senate. What would men think if they saw the Dictator in such a helpless state, tumbling out of his golden chair to writhe on the floor?

"No, this won't do!" Decimus scowled and shook his head. While the rest of us were disappointed or puzzled or concerned for Caesar, Decimus seemed almost angry. Some powerful emotion flashed from his eyes, but I couldn't make it out. He had been among Gauls too long, I thought. His expressions had become inscrutable to a fellow Roman.

"I'll talk to Caesar myself!" Decimus declared. He strode toward the private quarters and disappeared from sight.

Despite Caesar's change of plans, no one in the vestibule seemed ready to leave. Men milled about, rearranging the folds of their togas and talking quietly. It was as if we all awaited a further announcement.

Time passed slowly.

It was perhaps half an hour later that Decimus reappeared, followed by Caesar, who cast a stern gaze around the suddenly silent room, as if to forestall any questions. Decimus, whom I might have expected to look pleased with himself, having evidently convinced Caesar to reverse his decision, instead wore an expression as grim as Caesar's.

Caesar's harsh gaze abruptly softened. He smiled very faintly, as if to admit that he felt every so slightly chagrined. Meto laughed with relief, and others around the room did likewise.

"Hail, Caesar!" shouted Cinna, clapping his hands.

"Hail, Caesar!" Meto shouted. Others joined in the salutation.

I, too, at that moment, in that place, raised my voice in acclamation of Rome's dictator. "Hail, Caesar!" I shouted, feeling slightly foolish, but also genuinely excited and sincerely grateful to the man who in a single stroke was about to elevate my fortunes and the fortunes of my family forever.

Caesar looked in my direction. His eyes met mine. I said it again: "Hail, Caesar!"

"Enough of this!" he said. "Decimus, send a swift-footed messenger to countermand the order I gave to Antony. I shall attend the Senate, after all. Citizens, colleagues, friends—let us be off!"

With Caesar leading the way, we filed out of the vestibule and into the street. As Decimus passed by me, I heard him mutter, "After today, may I never have to deal with that woman again!" Even with Calpurnia begging Caesar to stay, and Caesar in a muddle, Decimus had persuaded him to go.

I hung back, deferring to the more senior members of Caesar's entourage, so that I was the very last man to step through the doorway. As I did so, I turned back and saw Calpurnia across the room, standing in the hallway. Her body was mostly hidden by shadows, but her face caught the late morning light. It was stark white, cold and remote, the color of a full moon.

Though she spoke barely above a whisper, I heard her clearly across the empty room. "Stay close to him, Finder. Are you armed?"

"Of course not. No senator is allowed to carry arms into the Senate House. Even I know that."

She hung her head and stepped back, vanishing amid shadows.

XXXII

The Roman Senate meets in various venues. All are technically temples; the Senate can render official decisions only in a space consecrated to the gods. On this day they were convening a considerable distance from the Regia, in the area of the city still called the Field of Mars, despite the fact that little in the way of open space is to be found amid the jumble of tenements and temples that have sprung up in my lifetime.

Preceded, followed, and flanked by his twenty-four lictors, and carried aloft in his golden litter by four slaves, Caesar led his large entourage down the Sacred Way, through the heart of the Roman Forum and past the city's most ancient temples and shrines. We then skirted the slope of the Capitoline Hill, passing by Caesar's new Temple of Venus, and entered the Field of Mars. By this time, a great many ordinary citizens had joined the retinue, tagging along at the end or, where the way was wide enough, walking alongside.

Meto had a habit of walking faster than most people. Keeping up with him, I soon found myself near the front of the entourage, where I had a clear view of Caesar in his litter. At one point we were so close that I overheard Caesar remark to Decimus, who was walking alongside him,

"What need have I for those Spanish bodyguards? Everywhere I go in the city, I am surrounded by friends."

Decimus nodded, then looked about, a bit nervously, I thought.

The Senate had been scheduled to meet not long after dawn, but Caesar had dawdled so long that the noon hour was approaching. This was the day of the festival of Anna Perenna, and I saw many courting couples and their chaperones with food baskets heading for the sacred grove of the goddess outside the city, as well as older couples who no longer needed a chaperone but who still enjoyed an amorous holiday and the chance to drink, eat, and carouse outdoors. Many of the young people stopped to stare at the Dictator and his entourage, then went about their business, more interested in each other than in the pomp and ceremony of affairs of state.

"They shall have wet ground to lie on," noted Meto.

"Who?"

"All those young lovers hoping to escape from their chaperones into the bushes."

"And all the older couples still young enough to enjoy such a frolic," I said.

"Diana and Davus are going to the festival."

"They are?"

"Yes, while Bethesda looks after the children. Diana helped to plan the Anna Perenna celebration this year, just as Bethesda is helping to plan the Liberalia a few days from now."

"Really?"

"Papa, do you pay no attention to what's going on under your own roof?"

"I *am* aware that Bethesda and Diana have been going to meetings at Fulvia's house," I said, with a vague wave of my hand. "Thanks to Caesar . . . and Cicero . . . and you, I've had more important things on my mind."

As we passed the crowds along the route, men and women gawked at Caesar in his golden litter, and many called out his name, as we in his retinue had done before we set out. "Hail, Caesar!" they would cry, waving to the Dictator and then shouting his name again if he saw them and waved back. Some ran toward Caesar, reaching past stern-faced lictors to hand him bits of folded parchment. Caesar made a show of reaching out to accept each of these written requests for favors. He collected them all in his left hand, keeping his right hand free to wave to the crowd or reach out to accept more bits of parchment.

As we were going down a particularly narrow street of ramshackle tenements, "Hail, Caesar!" cried a figure leaning from an upper-story window. The man who looked down at us had long, unkempt hair, a scarred face, and a patch over one eye. "Go show the Parthians!" he cried, shaking his fist. "Show them what Romans are made of, the way we showed those Aedui up in Gaul."

Caesar leaned out of his litter to peer up at the man, then signaled to the bearers to stop. "You were with me when we laid siege to Bibracte?" he asked.

"That I was, Imperator. The day we breached the walls I killed fifty men—and raped a dozen boys while I was at it!" He laughed harshly. "But I did pay a price." He pointed to his eye patch and then inserted his thumb into his mouth and made a popping noise, as if to replicate the sound of an eye plucked from its socket.

Caesar stared up at him. "Yes, I remember you," he said. "Marcus Artorius, centurion of the Seventh Legion."

The man's disfigured face lit up. "That I am, Imperator. Or was. And you remember me, after all this time? Imagine that!"

"I don't forget a citizen who served bravely in a distant land, fighting for Rome."

"Fighting for *you,* Caesar!"

"How are you faring now?"

The man's smile faded. "Not so well as I might, Imperator. Fallen on hard times. No one's fault but my own. Spent all my booty on boys and wine. Just to kill the pain, you see." He grimaced and raised his left arm, to gesture at his scarred face, I thought, until I saw there was no hand at the end of the arm.

"That won't do," said Caesar. He summoned a nearby scribe and spoke in the slave's ear. The scribe nodded and then stepped into the building. "I'm sending a fellow up to see you," Caesar continued. "He'll take down your name and some other details, and I shall see that you are properly cared for from now on. A man who's made the sacrifices you've made for Rome should never go hungry."

"Or thirsty!" said the man, and laughed.

Caesar smiled up at him, then gave him a wave and signaled the litter to move on.

I turned to Meto. "Caesar actually remembered the man's name, out of all the thousands of soldiers he commanded. No wonder everyone calls him such a great leader."

Meto flashed a crooked smile. "It's a bit of a trick."

"What do you mean?"

"Of course you're impressed that Caesar remembers such an insignificant fellow. And it *is* remarkable that Caesar can hold so many names and faces in his head. But if he *hadn't* recognized the fellow—which is much more often the case—he'd have simply waved and nodded to the man and moved on, and you'd have thought no more of it. But since he *did* recognize the man, *and* remembered his name, Caesar put on a bit of a show, knowing how much that sort of thing impresses those who witness it. He did this virtually every day when we were fighting in Gaul—recognizing soldiers and calling them by name. He had me make a note: 'When you see a man whose name you remember, demonstrate it—and all the many whose names you've forgotten will assume that you remember them as well. Good advice whether in the field fighting Gauls, or fishing for votes in the Forum.'"

"I don't remember reading that in his war journals."

"It was edited out!" said Meto with a laugh. Then he wrinkled his brow. "'Good advice whether in the field fighting Gauls, or fishing for votes in the Forum,' he repeated. "But of course votes—and voters—don't really matter anymore, do they?"

"Not once a man is dictator for life," I said.

"But old habits die hard. Caesar took advantage of that chance meeting as if by reflex. I would never have remembered the man. And I'll have forgotten him in an hour. But we'll both remember that Caesar greeted him by name, honored his service, and rewarded his sacrifice."

"Even a dictator must give the people reasons to love him."

"And you have more reason than most, Papa."

I suddenly felt ill at ease in my borrowed toga. No voters had ever elected me a magistrate, and thus set me on the Course of Honor, with a place in the Senate. The honor of wearing a senator's toga had been bestowed on me by one man. I owed the voters of Rome nothing. What did I owe to Caesar? What did all the other appointed senators owe him? How and when might he call in the debt?

We entered a wider street and continued past the newer tenements and marketplaces of the Field of Mars, until at last the Theater of Pompey loomed before us.

The wing of the structure in which we would meet was still called the Senate House of Pompey, despite the Great One's defeat in the civil war and his ignominious death. When Pompey, at the peak of his career, decided to erect a gigantic theater on the Field of Mars—the first permanent, purpose-built theater ever to be constructed in Rome—to satisfy old-timers with religious objections he added a temple to Venus at the top, above the last row of seats, and to bring in some rental income he also added a sprawling portico with shops and warehouses, and, since there was still marble in the quarry, he also constructed a chamber built specifically for meetings of the Roman Senate—all of which he named for himself: the Theater of Pompey, the Portico of Pompey, the Senate House of Pompey. As the Capitoline Hill dominated the city of Rome, so the vast, towering complex erected by Pompey dominated the Field of Mars.

As we drew closer to the theater, I heard a roar from within. At first I thought the cheering must be for Caesar. Then I remembered that a gladiator show was being presented that day, with the combats and killing to take place on the stage. Apparently the program was already under way.

"A gladiator show, on the festival of Anna Perenna," I remarked. "And from the sound of it, the theater is packed. Who would want to watch gladiators hack each other to death on such a fine spring morning?" I sighed. "I suppose those of us too old, or too married, or too chaste, or too sober to celebrate Anna Perenna can enjoy a bit of bloodshed instead."

"That's Rome. Something for everyone!" said Meto with a grin. How happy he was that day, walking beside his father in Caesar's entourage.

We rounded a corner and passed by one of the main entrances to the theater. I saw a great many gladiators milling about. None of them appeared to be handling swords or tridents, but some were wearing armor, and all looked restless and surly.

"Why are those gladiators outside the theater, instead of inside?"

Even as I asked, I saw Decimus leave Caesar's side and walk to the man evidently in charge of the gladiator troupe. Decimus, looking quite serious, appeared to be giving the man instructions.

"I think those gladiators are owned by Decimus," said Meto. "There's some dispute between him and the presenter of today's show about a valuable gladiator who was stolen or lured away. I suspect Decimus's men are here to take back his property—by force, if necessary."

"What if a brawl breaks out?" I said.

"Then the audience will get more bloodshed than they bargained for."

Decimus finished talking to the man in charge of his gladiators, then hurried to catch up with Caesar's litter. Caesar, glancing at the gladiators, appeared to ask a question, and Decimus appeared to answer.

"Caesar probably wishes he were attending the gladiator show today, instead of addressing the Senate," said Meto.

What an appetite our dictator has for bloodshed and suffering, I thought. *What a connoisseur he is, of all manner of mayhem and death. And now he is about to head for Parthia, to unleash untold havoc in a whole other part of the world, carnage and destruction on an unimaginable scale. . . .*

But all I said to Meto was, "I, for one, have no wish to see blood shed today."

Looking back at Decimus's gladiators, I felt suddenly apprehensive. I was merely nervous, I thought, as any man would be on the day he was to stand before the Senate and give a speech, however simple and brief, with the likes of Cicero and Caesar watching and listening to every word.

XXXIII

We arrived at the large courtyard outside the Senate House of Pompey. Crowds of senators milled about, some standing on the broad steps leading up to the building's entrance. Many hailed Caesar; others kept their mouths shut. Some looked restless and bored after waiting hours for Caesar to arrive. Cicero, standing on the steps and attended by Tiro, looked particularly petulant. Side by side, Brutus and Cassius were pacing back and forth at the top of the steps. They looked especially uneasy, but also relieved, I thought, like men who had pressing business to attend to, and now, with Caesar's arrival, could at last get on with it.

Antony, with a smile on his face, came striding down the steps to meet Caesar as he stepped from his litter. "So you decided to come, after all," I heard him say. "Very good! As soon as we've taken the auspices, we can all get to work."

On a raised platform at the foot of the steps, Spurinna stood before a large stone altar. There were also a number of priests holding ceremonial knives for slaughtering and cutting open sacrificial animals. As presiding haruspex, Spurinna would examine the entrails and determine whether the auspices were good or bad for the Senate to meet on this day. If necessary, more than one animal might be sacrificed. Amid the throng of togas in the courtyard I caught a glimpse of the pens in which they were kept and heard the bleating of goats.

Caesar strode through the crowd of senators and mounted the raised platform, facing Spurinna across the altar. Meto and I stood in the crowd behind Caesar, so that I could clearly see the face of Spurinna on the opposite side. As Pontifex Maximus, it was up to Caesar to signal that the taking of auspices could begin. He raised his hand and nodded.

A goat was brought forth on a leash held by a priest. The animal willingly stepped onto the dais—a good sign. The priests proceeded to bind the animal's legs and lift it onto the altar. The goat bleated loudly, but kicked and struggled only a little—another good sign. The more willingly the animal meets its death, the more likely the auspices will be good. Caesar nodded approvingly.

One of the priests raised a knife high in the air, recited a prayer, then deftly cut the goat's throat. The animal convulsed. Priests twisted the goat's head to one side so that channels carved into the altar would carry off the spurting blood. The animal's legs were quickly unbound. Each taking hold of a trembling foreleg and a hindleg, two priests exposed the goat's underside, allowing Spurinna, at the exact moment of death, to slice the goat open from the base of its throat to its navel.

Spurinna put aside his knife and peered at the exposed entrails. He frowned. He shook his head. He grunted.

"By Jupiter, man, what is it?" demanded Caesar.

"Dictator, part of the liver is missing. And the color of the viscera around the heart is . . . abnormal. There's a greenish tinge—"

"What of it?"

"Dictator, the omen is not good. Not good at all. Any deformity of the liver speaks of danger. Green viscera, too, signals a threat—"

"Spurinna, I'm not having this," said Caesar, leaning forward and speaking so quietly that I heard him only because every senator around us was completely silent, as we all held our breath.

"Dictator, I can only report what I observe—"

"Bring forth another sacrifice!" said Caesar, raising his voice.

The operation was repeated. This time Spurinna observed a knot in the bowels that indicated aborted plans and disappointments. Caesar was again displeased.

Another goat was brought forth. Perhaps alerted by the smell of blood and the bleating of the previous sacrifices, this one struggled at every stage, refusing to step onto the dais so vigorously that it almost escaped, then kicking and thrashing as its legs were bound, then twisting so violently that the priest charged with killing it had to make not one but two cuts with his knife.

As the animal died, Spurinna stepped back and lowered his knife. "Dictator, the resistance of the sacrifice speaks for itself. There's no need to cut it open. I can already tell you—"

"You will say not another word, haruspex," said Caesar, in a tone I had never heard from him before. Spurinna shut his mouth and trembled, as if a chill wind blew over him.

Caesar instructed the priests to untie the goat and take it away. He looked at the silent, grim-faced senators gathered in the courtyard and on the steps. He smiled. "Something very similar happened in Spain, when I was about to engage with Pompey's forces there. Three goats were said by the haruspex to be unfit, all three ill-omened. Do you know what happened? I went into battle anyway, and on to victory. Had I listened to the haruspex that day, it would be Pompey standing here instead of me. The auspices can be very difficult to interpret. Even the most experienced haruspex . . ." Here he looked at Spurinna. "Even the most experienced haruspex can be mistaken. As Pontifex Maximus, I declare the taking of these auspices to be inconclusive. The will of the gods cannot be clearly discerned. In light of the importance of this meeting, we shall proceed."

The senators began moving across the courtyard and up the steps.

Caesar lowered his voice. "Now lend me your arm," he said to Decimus, who was standing nearest, "while I step down from the platform. The last thing we need now is a misstep!" He smiled to make light of the moment, but Decimus looked very serious as he helped Caesar descend. With Antony on his right and Decimus on his left, Caesar headed for the steps. He looked over his shoulder.

"Stay close by me, Gordianus. I shall tend to your induction early on, so that you can join in the voting right away."

There was a fluttering in my chest. My heart lurched into my throat. In a matter of minutes, I would be standing before the Senate, having to speak. My mouth was dry and I felt light-headed. I was also hot, so hot I thought I might faint, despite the thinness of Cinna's summer toga.

"Papa, are you all right?" said Meto.

"What? Me? Of course I am."

"Papa! I don't know if I've ever seen you like this. You mustn't worry. Everything will go smoothly, I'm sure. Caesar knows what he's doing."

"Yes, I'm sure he does."

"If only I could be there with you. But only senators are allowed in the chamber during meetings. Well, senators and a handful of secretaries and official scribes, like Cicero's man Tiro."

I was to be on my own, then, in a room full of the most powerful men on earth, some of whose darkest secrets were known to me from past investigations. Some of those men liked me, perhaps. Some loathed me, I was certain. Would a single one of them welcome me as an equal, even at Caesar's behest?

"Where will you go, Meto?"

He shrugged. I knew he was trying to behave as nonchalantly as possible, for my sake. "Perhaps I'll sneak into the gladiator show. Yes, I just might. Even if you have no taste for it, Papa, I enjoy seeing a bit of bloodshed now and then. Why not today?"

Midway up the steps, Caesar stopped and turned back. "Meto! Here, take these." He thrust out his left hand, in which he clutched all the petitions that had been given to him on the way to the Senate House. "Read through them for me, will you? See if there's anything so important that I should attend to it before we leave."

Meto took the petitions, nodded, and was off.

Caesar continued up the steps, with Antony on his right, Decimus on his left, and me a step behind.

Suddenly, Cinna was beside me. "I just passed your son, who made me promise to stay close and look after you today. And so I shall. Take heart, Gordianus! Really, old fellow, you look like a ghost. Or like a man who's seen a ghost."

I tried to smile. Coming rapidly up the steps behind us I saw a figure in a dark green tunic, conspicuous amid so many white togas. By his red beard, I recognized Artemidorus, whom I had seen at the house of Brutus and Porcia, the tutor of their young son. Artemidorus's father had taught Caesar, I recalled, which perhaps explained the man's boldness in approaching Caesar at that moment, only a few steps from the entrance of the Senate House.

"Caesar!" he called. "Caesar, please, I have something for you."

Decimus turned around and stiffened, as if he feared some threat, but all that Artemidorus held in his hand was a small piece of parchment, rolled tightly like a scroll.

Caesar also stopped and turned to face Artemidorus, who now stood a step below me and Cinna, panting as if out of breath.

"Please, Caesar, take this!"

Caesar saw the parchment. "Go find Meto, Artemidorus. There he is, just past the altar. He'll take that from you and put it with the other petitions."

"But this is for your eyes only, Caesar!"

"Then tell Meto not to read it. Tell him to leave it rolled up until he can give it to me."

"No, no, Caesar, you must read it now!"

Decimus scowled. Looking past him, I saw Brutus and Cassius huddled beside a column at the top of the steps, gazing down at the scene. Cassius's face was a blank, but Brutus looked acutely uncomfortable. Was he embarrassed to see his son's tutor make a spectacle of himself?

Decimus reached past me, toward Artemidorus, as if to repel him, but Caesar raised his hand to intervene. "No, Decimus, leave him alone. I shall take the thing, if he insists. Gordianus, you take it from him and hand it up to me."

Artemidorus reluctantly pressed the scrap of parchment into my hand.

"Let Gordianus keep it for you," said Decimus, sounding strangely insistent.

Antony looked faintly amused. Caesar glowered. "Stop this fussing, Decimus! Hand it to me, Gordianus."

I looked down at the parchment. I felt a sudden impulse to unroll and read it. I hesitated, and almost did so—but Caesar, sensing my presumption, snatched the scrap from my hand.

"Now be off, Artemidorus!" he snapped.

"Caesar! Please! Read it at once!"

Caesar paused. He studied Artemidorus for a moment. He started to unroll the parchment. Then we were all distracted by the sudden arrival of a man who grabbed Antony's shoulder and shouted, "Antony! Antony! I've been looking everywhere for you."

"Trebonius," said Antony, a bit tentatively, as if neither sharing nor comprehending the man's enthusiasm.

"Antony, I haven't seen you in a Titan's age! Listen, there's something we must talk about before the Senate convenes."

"Yes?"

"Stay behind, just for a moment. No need to make the Dictator more tardy than he is already!" Trebonius smiled at Caesar. Caesar smiled faintly in return, then nodded to Antony, granting permission for him to leave his company.

Cinna, observing my wrinkled brow, whispered in my ear, "Trebonius and Antony are old comrades in arms. They go back to the Battle of Alesia."

"Seems fonder of Antony than Antony is of him," I said, as Trebonius led Antony down the steps.

"Probably wants a favor—like this pest!" whispered Cinna, who then grunted as Artemidorus attempted to step past him.

"Artemidorus, enough of this!" said Caesar sharply. He made a gesture with one hand that brooked no argument. In the other hand he clutched the rolled parchment, now somewhat crumpled. "I shall read your message the moment I'm settled in my chair."

"Yes, Greek, desist!" Decimus said sharply, placing a hand on Caesar's shoulder and leading him onward, up the steps. Cinna followed close behind, but I hung back, seized by sudden, acute curiosity. As Artemidorus turned to go, I grabbed his arm.

"What's in the message?" I said.

His face was impossible to read, but he was clearly experiencing some desperate emotion. Anger? Sorrow? Fear?

"Not your business!" he whispered. "Just tell Caesar to read it *now*—before he sits on that throne. He must!"

"His golden chair is not a throne," I said, trying to make light of his insistence. "Only kings have thrones—"

Ignoring me, Artemidorus turned and practically ran down the steps, taking two at a time, never looking back. His dark green tunic vanished amid the toga-clad crowd ascending the steps.

"How very strange," I said to myself. I turned around and looked upward to see the reactions of Cassius and Brutus, but they had both disappeared, as Caesar was about to do, having taken the final step. Decimus still touched his shoulder, escorting him. Cinna was a step behind them. I hurried to catch up.

Why was Artemidorus so insistent? Why had he disappeared so quickly, with such a look on his face? Was the Greek tutor trying to beg Caesar for a favor—or trying to warn him? And of what? Of whom?

My heart lurched in my chest—because I was an old man walking too quickly up a flight of steps, I told myself. My vague apprehension was nothing more than a distraction I was foisting on myself, to quell the anxiety I felt as the moment of my induction drew ever closer. My dread of that moment was the source of my uneasiness—not Artemidorus and his message, or the mortified look on Brutus's face, or Antony's sudden absence, or Decimus's single-minded determination to shepherd Caesar into the Senate House.

I hurried up the steps, my heart pounding in my chest.

Ahead of me, I heard Caesar laugh as he entered the Senate House.

XXXIV

Even as Caesar was passing through the wide doorway, I stepped past Cinna and attempted to draw next to Caesar, but Decimus quickly stepped between us, as if intentionally to keep me from him. Perhaps it was customary for one of Caesar's intimates to assume the task of delivering him to the Senate House, escorting the Dictator every step of the way to his golden chair; otherwise Caesar would never get there, dogged by petitioners and well-wishers at every turn. Antony, as consul, was probably supposed to be doing Decimus's job, but Antony had been distracted and taken aside.

I felt Cinna's hand on my arm.

"Gordianus, calm yourself! Take a deep breath. I fear those steps have winded you."

"I'm all right."

"Are you? Your face is quite red. I've never seen you in such a state. Have you let Artemidorus distress you? The Greeks, bless them, do have a way of injecting drama into every situation. The man's a mere tutor, you know. Not even a poet. Making a fuss over nothing, I'm sure."

Side by side we entered the vestibule of the Senate House of Pompey. The walls and the floor were covered with a sort of marble I had never seen before, yellow veined with black. The space was dominated by a very large painting, so famous that even I had heard of it, though I had never actually seen it. It was called *The Warrior with a Shield Ascending*, by Polygnotus of Thasos, brought to Rome by Pompey after one of his successful campaigns. The painting was more than three hundred years old but looked as if the dazzling paint was still fresh on the wood. Against a black void, the warrior, naked except for a Greek helmet, appeared to be suspended in midair. His arms and legs were outstretched and his head tilted up, as if he gazed heavenward. In one hand he held a sword. On his other arm, thrust toward the viewer so that it dominated all else, was a shield covered with intricate designs and fabulous images of gods and monsters, as finely detailed as the famous shield of Achilles in the *Iliad*. For a moment I was distracted from all other concerns, my attention riveted on a famous work of art few men in the world were privileged to see, due to its location. Caesar, too, paused to look at it, though he must have seen it many times before.

He looked back at me. "What do you think, Gordianus? Is the warrior ascending, like Hercules, to join the gods on Olympus? Or is he plummeting from some great height, heading straight for Hades as he gazes toward the heavens?"

I stared at the painting. "It hadn't occurred to me that the warrior must be dead."

Caesar laughed. "Still, he's either going up . . . or down. How Pompey loved this painting. How generous he was to share it with his fellow senators."

He moved on, with Decimus beside him. Cinna and I followed them through another doorway and into the main chamber. I sucked in a breath, struck by the loftiness of the ceiling. From windows high in the walls a diffuse golden light illuminated a milling sea of white and red. The number required for a quorum, if I remembered correctly, was two hundred, and I judged there must be at least that many senators already in the room, with more arriving every moment. The tall chamber resounded with the echoes of many voices. The hubbub grew louder as the Dictator's arrival was noticed.

Caesar steadily made his way through the crowd. Decimus fended off any interruptions from the right, while Caesar himself declined any demand for his attention from the left, holding up the parchment from Artemidorus as if to show that he had already received enough petitions for the day.

Among the senators, I saw Cicero. He stepped back and bowed his head slightly as Caesar passed, and in return received a slight nod from the Dictator. As I walked past him, Cicero gave me a baleful stare.

"I saw that!" said Caesar, looking over his shoulder. Cicero looked chagrined. Turning back for a moment, Caesar said to me in a low voice, "It was worth making you a senator, I think, just to see that look on Cicero's face! Why, Gordianus, I've put a smile on your face. A good omen, at last! If I can put you at ease, Finder, then surely I can charm even the most recalcitrant senators today."

Caesar headed toward a raised platform at the far end of the chamber. On this dais, set atop a high pedestal, stood a statue of Pompey, the great commander's arm raised as if to greet his fellow senators. The figure was extremely lifelike, one of those statues that seem almost to breathe and to look back at you. Its face bore an extraordinary likeness to its model. The sculptor had captured exactly the plump roundness of Pompey's face and the bland smile he bestowed on friends and enemies alike—the smile of a man who might be about to kiss you . . . or kill you. The way the statue loomed above us on its pedestal, and its uncanny resemblance to a man I had seen beheaded, made it seem strangely monstrous. I shivered, at once fascinated and repelled by the image of Pompey.

Many had thought that Caesar would remove this image of his vanquished rival and rename the chamber for himself. Instead, he had allowed both the name and the statue to remain. Meto called this a sign of Caesar's magnanimity in victory. It might also be that Caesar felt some lingering obligation to Pompey, and even affection for him, especially now that he was dead. As we traversed the long room and drew nearer to the looming statue, I saw Caesar gaze up and heard him mutter under his breath, "We meet again, old friend. But while you stand, I shall sit."

Then Caesar abruptly stopped and turned his head, looking from one side of the dais to the other. "My chair," he said in a quiet voice, and then louder, "My chair! Where is my chair? Why is my chair not ready for me?"

"I think," said Decimus, "that someone must have ordered it to be removed and put away, thinking you had decided not to come. It's far too valuable to be left out unattended, as you must agree. I'm sure it's being fetched even as we speak—yes, look there, two slaves are bringing it in."

The gilded chair was carried onto the dais, where the diffused sunlight from the high windows caused it to glimmer like a throne made of golden fire.

Caesar stepped onto the dais. Decimus followed him. I hung back, not sure if it was proper for me to stand on the raised platform. Cinna stayed beside me, but a number of senators felt no compunction about stepping onto the dais. Among them I saw Brutus and Cassius, and also portly Casca, the man who had mistakenly given me directions to the house of Cinna the praetor. That other Cinna, too, I had seen among the senators in the chamber when we entered, scowling as on the day I had met him and wearing his praetorian toga with a red border, but he was no longer in sight.

A train of slaves entered the room carrying leather barrels for storing scrolls. This seemed to be the usual procedure; no one took notice of them. These barrels were set along the far edges of the dais, and some of the senators moved toward them, as if eager to lay hands on some piece of proposed legislation.

"Cinna," I said, "there's something odd about those containers, don't you think?"

"Is there?"

"They look . . . too heavy. The way the slaves carried them . . . they seem to contain something other than scrolls."

"Slaves can make any burden appear heavy, even a pillow stuffed with feathers," said Cinna with a smile.

I shook my head, not quite satisfied with this explanation. Then I saw two slaves set a small tripod table beside the golden chair. Perhaps it was Caesar's habit to take notes during the proceedings, for on the table I saw a wax tablet and a rather heavy-looking metal stylus with a sharp point for scraping letters in the wax. The stylus had the unmistakable gleam of silver—a worthy instrument for a dictator's hand. Before he sat, Caesar picked up the stylus. Perhaps he had thought of something he wanted to write down, for he seemed about to put down the piece of parchment in his left hand, which would have allowed him to pick up the tablet. Then something distracted him, and he kept his grip on Artemidorus's message as well as the stylus as he turned about and gazed over the noisy, crowded room. One of the slaves who had delivered the chair moved it so that Caesar could sit without bothering to look behind him. The slave stepped back, out of the way. Someone in a toga took the slave's place and stood directly behind Caesar, as if stationed there.

"Are there always so many senators on the dais with Caesar?" I asked.

Cinna cocked his head. "No, but with Caesar about to depart, this is their last chance to pester him for favors. See how they keep their heads down and hands inside their togas, looking meek and respectful. Look, there's Tillius Cimber, the old reprobate. No doubt he's here to beg Caesar to recall his brother from exile."

Cimber was a tall man whose most noticeable feature was a very red nose, the sign of a hard drinker. He and a score of others swarmed about Caesar, like flies around honey.

"Soon enough he'll shoo them all away and the meeting can begin," said Cinna. "As consul, Antony is the one who should call us to order. Where is Antony? He's not still outside, is he?"

Like Cinna, I turned and looked around the room, and so it was that I missed something that happened on the dais, for when I looked again at Caesar, seated in his chair, someone had grabbed hold of his toga. It was Cimber, whose back was to me. Beyond him I could see Caesar's face. He looked at first puzzled, and then angry. He seemed to be trying to rise from his chair, but Cimber clutched his toga so tightly that Caesar couldn't get up.

"What in Hades does that fool think he's doing?" said Cinna.

The strange battle of wills continued for a heartbeat, and then Cimber pulled at the toga so forcefully that it slipped from Caesar's shoulder, baring his neck.

"This is violence!" snapped Caesar, as if rebuking an outrage to his dignity.

Then I saw a figure behind Caesar. It was Casca. He seemed to exchange a look with Cimber, then raised his arm.

In Casca's hand I saw a dagger.

XXXV

In such moments, time becomes attenuated. The normally stiff and unyielding stuff of reality is suddenly in flux. Many thoughts take place in the blink of an eye.

One of these thoughts, briefly foremost in my mind, was this: *Where did the dagger come from?* And the answer appeared in my mind at once: It had come from one of those heavy-looking leather drums—heavy because they were filled not with scrolls but with daggers.

While I stared at the dagger in Casca's upraised hand, at the peripheries of my vision points of light flashed amid the crowd of togas on the dais, and I knew that these flashes must be the glimmer of reflected sunlight on metal. There was not one dagger in Caesar's presence, but many daggers.

Casca stabbed downward. If the blow was aimed at the vein in Caesar's neck, he missed, for Caesar jerked backward, toward Casca. The knife struck Caesar's breast, cutting through layers of wool and striking flesh. Blood erupted at the site of the blow, a dark stain on the purple wool that began as a small point and then blossomed to the size of a man's fist.

Caesar whirled around in his chair and stabbed blindly with the stylus in his hand. The pointed instrument struck Casca somewhere, but whether it drew blood or not I couldn't tell. Casca yowled like a dog and sprang back, dropping his dagger. "Gaius!" he cried—the name of his brother.

Caesar tried to spring up from the chair, but Casca's brother lunged forward and stabbed him in the ribs. Knocked from Caesar's hand, the stylus fell to the floor with a loud clang. Another blossom of dark red erupted on Caesar's toga.

On his face I saw many emotions. Fear was not among them. Shock was there, and loathing, and anger. "Curse these Cascas!" he shouted. The brothers had always been Caesar's friends and allies. Perhaps he thought it was only the two of them who were attacking him and was calling on the others to hold the brothers back.

Instead, more men with daggers stepped forward. Caesar raised his hands to defend himself, but a frenzy of stabbing ensued. The repetitive motion made me think of augury chickens pecking at sacred grain, their heads bobbing up and down. So moved the flashing knives, as if powered by some mindless force of nature, up and down.

Some of the senators struck no more than glancing blows, but others ripped wool and penetrated flesh with a sickening, slicing sound. Some failed to strike Caesar altogether, and some—to judge by the screams and shouts—accidentally struck each other.

Somehow Caesar managed to stagger to his feet, or else he was driven forward by blows against his back. Before my eyes, his purple toga became many shades darker, almost black, as blossoms of blood spread and merged into one another.

On Caesar's face I now saw a look of utter confusion. He seemed to be thinking what I was thinking: *Can it happen so quickly?* Could a man like Caesar—known to everyone, everywhere—a man who had conquered nations, enslaved tribes, slaughtered entire cities—a man without fear or trepidation or doubt, seemingly incapable of error—a man as close to godhood as any mortal who had ever lived—could such a man be alive one moment . . . and dead the next?

It seemed somehow against nature that what I was witnessing could actually be taking place. For one instant, with a terrible jolt, I was certain that I truly *was* imagining what I saw. I felt utterly detached from my own senses, unmoored from the world around me. It was as if a trapdoor opened beneath my feet. But the next instant, with an even more terrible jolt, I knew that what I witnessed was entirely, horribly, irreparably real.

Will no one defend him? I thought. *Where is Antony? Where is Decimus?* Then I saw that at least two senators on the crowded dais were shouting and waving their arms, begging the others to stop. But they were unarmed and vastly outnumbered. The assassins forced them off the dais at knifepoint.

I turned my head and looked at the crowded chamber behind me. The men nearest to me saw what was happening, but farther back, toward the entrance, the crowd was still conversing and milling about, oblivious of the carnage. No one outside the Senate House of Pompey could yet know what was happening. Soon enough, everyone in Rome would know. Eventually, everyone in the world would know. But not yet . . .

I thought of Meto. Had he managed to get into the gladiator show in the theater? I imagined I could hear a distant eruption of cheering above the hubbub inside the Senate House. Then the noise inside the room began to change, as screams and cries of alarm broke out. Like a bloodstain, knowledge of the events on the dais spread rapidly.

"They've killed Caesar!" someone shouted. "They're going to kill us all!"

Who were the "they" killing Caesar? Who were the "us" they would kill next? Many other confused shouts and cries of panic echoed throughout the chamber.

Amid the crowd I spotted Cicero. Tiro stood next to him, holding a wax tablet and stylus. While others turned and scuttled past them, heading for the exit, they both stood still, as if transfixed. On Tiro's face I saw a look of shock. On Cicero's face I saw something else. He was surprised, yes—but also delighted. There was no other word for it. He looked like a man whose wife has just given birth, or a politician who's just won an election. He opened his mouth and emitted a series of sharp, nervous laughs. He trembled and swayed. He was giddy with joy.

I looked back to the dais. Cassius stepped forward and slashed awkwardly at Caesar, cutting his cheek. Blood spurted from the wound. Caesar grimaced and staggered back.

Then I saw Decimus. He had clung to Caesar at every step on the way to the golden chair. Where was he when the carnage began? No matter, he was present now. Was it too late for him to put a stop to the stabbings? Might Caesar yet survive, and this moment become another testament to his divine good fortune?

If anyone could save Caesar, I thought, surely it would be Decimus.

Then I saw the dagger in Decimus's hand. He lunged forward and stabbed Caesar's ribs, forcing him backward so that Caesar collided with the golden chair, knocking it over.

Cinna was as shocked as I was. He gripped my arm and gasped.

Caesar staggered sideways. He collided with the pedestal of Pompey's statue. He leaned against it, barely able to stay upright. One at a time, senators lunged at him to deliver shallow stabs. They were like men taking turns to prove their commitment to some cause, then stepping aside to let another man do the same. *Yes, I, too, shall stab Caesar! And I! And I! And I!*

The last was Brutus. He stood to one side. One of his hands was bleeding, apparently from an unintentional jab he had received in the confusion. Cassius, next to him, stared at him sidelong and gritted his teeth. "Do it!" he whispered.

Brutus clenched his dagger and stepped toward Caesar.

Caesar tilted his head and squinted his eyes. He shook his head. "Not you!" he wailed. "Not you, too, my boy . . ."

Without pausing, eye to eye with Caesar, Brutus stabbed low and hard, thrusting his dagger into Caesar's groin.

When Brutus removed his dagger, Caesar slid downward, his back against the pedestal and his feet spreading before him. His toga was unwound and in shreds. The loincloth beneath was so loosened that it barely concealed his genitals. His mouth bubbled with blood that ran over his chin. Caesar gazed down at himself. Awkwardly, he gripped a fold of his toga with his right hand and tried to cover himself. Perhaps he was trying to stanch the wound made at his groin by Brutus, which gushed with blood.

Caesar's eyes rolled up. His arms fell to his sides. His body slumped. His left hand, still clutching the note given to him by Artemidorus, opened, so that the little scroll rolled onto the floor.

"Jupiter help us," whimpered Cinna. "He's dead!"

The assassins surrounding Caesar all took a step back. They stared at their handiwork. Some looked appalled, others jubilant.

"We've done it," said Cassius. "We've actually done it."

Brutus raised both fists in the air, one bleeding and the other clutching his bloody dagger. "The tyrant is dead!" he shouted. "Long live the Republic!"

Others joined in the cry. "Long live the Republic!"

They were shouting to an empty chamber. Even before Caesar was dead, the retreat of their fellow senators had become a stampede. No room had ever been emptied of so many occupants in so short a time. So much for the steadfastness of the Roman Senate! Men loyal to Caesar feared they would be next to die. Men sympathetic to the assassins also fled, being unarmed and having no idea what might happen now. Even Cicero had vanished.

Brutus looked disappointed, like a man ready to make a speech who suddenly has no audience. "Where in Hades have they all gone?" he muttered.

"Cowards and sycophants, every last one of them," said Decimus. "They have the courage of slaves."

"Never mind, we shall make our arguments directly to the people under the open sky," said Cassius. "The citizens of Rome will rejoice, now that the Dictator's dead. They will welcome the gift of liberation with open arms. Mark my words, Lepidus and the rest of Caesar's

lapdogs will be as meek as lambs once they see the mood of the city.
Watch out, or they'll try to take credit for the tyrant's death themselves!"

I saw Gaius Casca stare at Cinna and then at me. "What about these
two?" he said.

"Perhaps we should kill them as well," said his brother.

"And Antony. Don't forget Antony!" said Cimber.

"We discussed this already," snapped Cassius. "We are *not* going to
kill Antony, or anyone else, unless they give us just cause." He looked
askance at Cinna. "We are certainly not going to kill Rome's foremost
poet, never mind his slavish devotion to the Dictator."

"What about the other one?" said Cimber. "The upstart in the toga?"

Brutus stepped toward me. "It's certainly tempting. Do you want
to know a secret, Finder? I hesitated for a long time before deciding
to throw my lot with these brave men. I was torn. I suffered an agony of indecision. Do you want to know what made up my mind?
It was the idea that Caesar was going to put the likes of *you* in the
Senate. Gauls and Etruscan soothsayers were bad enough, but Gordianus the Finder, senator of Rome—*that* was the last straw! Well, you
can take off that toga and leave it right here. You shall never be a
senator now."

I took a deep breath. I straightened my back and felt the weight of
the toga on my shoulders. Instead of retreating, I stepped onto the dais.
I met Brutus's gaze as I passed him and strode toward the pedestal where
Caesar's body lay slumped.

I looked up at Pompey's statue. How dignified the Great One
looked—the stately pose, the lofty brow, the enigmatic smile. Then
I looked down at Caesar. How common and tawdry he looked, like any
other corpse. Even the brightest flame leaves behind only cinders.

Flies had already found a patch of blood next to the scroll that had
slipped from Caesar's fingers. I knelt down, flicked the flies away, and
picked up the little scroll. It was smeared with blood. No one saw me
take it, or if they did, no one cared.

I returned to Cinna and took his arm. We began the long walk across
the chamber, toward the entrance.

"Write a poem about *this*!" shouted Cimber. Beside me, Cinna flinched and then began to weep.

When at last we stepped outside, onto the porch of the Senate House, I could wait no longer. I unrolled the blood-smeared piece of parchment.

The first word was Greek:

προσοχή

"Beware"—the very word that had been written in the sand in front of Cinna's house. I felt a chill.

The next word was also in Greek, and meant "today."

This was followed by a list of names. I whispered as I read them.

"Marcus Junius Brutus. Decimus Junius Brutus. Gaius Cassius Longinus. Gaius Servilius Casca. Publius Servilius Casca. Lucius Tillius Cimber. Gaius Trebonius . . ."

There were many more names, all written in very small letters by a very fine hand.

Artemidorus, working in the house of Brutus, trusted by him, had become aware of the conspiracy. Somehow, he had even discovered the names of the conspirators and had written them down. And he had decided, at the last moment, to warn Caesar. But too late . . .

Artemidorus had discovered what I had failed to discover, what Caesar himself had vaguely suspected, what Cicero had suspected as well. Cicero's name was *not* on the list—a relief to me, if only because it meant that Cicero had not made a complete fool of me by feigning ignorance and playing a part to distract me. . . .

"Out of the way!" shouted a voice behind me.

Leaving the chamber, led by Decimus, the assassins pushed past Cinna and me. They proudly held their daggers in the air. Caesar's confused and frightened lictors, stationed in the square below, scattered before them. When Decimus reached the foot of the steps, he put fingers to his mouth and made a shrill whistle. A moment later his troupe of gladiators came pouring out of the nearest theater exit. Now it was clear why Decimus had devised a pretext for having his gladiators close to the

Senate House—to fight for the survival of the assassins if things had gone badly, or to provide an armed escort if things went well.

Suddenly, I spotted Antony in the courtyard below. He was alone. Staying far to one side, keeping his distance from the assassins, he rushed up the steps toward Cinna and me. His face was ashen.

"Is it true?" he asked.

"You see the bloody daggers, don't you?" I said.

Antony moaned. "Trebonius lured me away. I should have known. I should have suspected something." He shook his head. "His body . . . ?"

"Inside," I said. "See for yourself."

Antony swallowed hard and stepped past us into the Senate House. A few moments later he emerged from the chamber. Instead of his consular toga, he wore a plain brown tunic.

Cinna peered at him. "But—where did you get those clothes?"

"From a scribe I found cowering behind Pompey's statue. He'll take good care of my toga and deliver it to me later, or else I'll find him and beat him senseless."

Antony's consular toga would make him recognizable at a distance, a possible target. "They have no plans to kill anyone else," I told him. "So Cassius said."

"And you believed him?" Antony snorted and hurried down the steps.

"Where are you going?" I said.

"Home to Fulvia!" he shouted, not looking back.

Word of what had happened spread quickly. People began exiting the theater, only a few at first but then a great many at once. Someone fell. There was panic. People screamed and tripped over one another. Those at the front of the crowd saw the assassins with their bloody daggers, flanked by Decimus's gladiators now openly brandishing their weapons, and turned back in terror, causing even more confusion, more collisions, more screaming.

Then I saw Meto. He must have been in the theater, for he emerged from the churning crowd, stared at the assassins, then ran past them and up the steps.

I said nothing. He read my expression and knew the truth. The look on his face broke my heart. I tried to touch him, to embrace him, but he rushed past me. A moment later, from the open doorway, I heard his anguished cry as it echoed throughout the empty chamber.

XXXVI

Feeling utterly drained, I sat on the steps of the Senate House. In silence, Cinna sat beside me.

For a while, as the Theater of Pompey was emptying, the assassins attempted to address the surging crowd. Brutus and Cassius seemed to have speeches ready to deliver. But the crowd was too loud and disorderly. Shouted rumors of riot and looting drowned out the would-be speakers. Rather than listen, the crowd hurriedly dispersed.

At last the assassins moved on. From the words they shouted to one another, I gathered they intended to station themselves atop the Capitoline Hill, a precinct that could easily be fortified. Centuries ago, when Gauls breached the walls of Rome and ransacked the city, a handful of stalwart citizens made their last stand atop the Capitoline, which was never taken.

With the courtyard below us empty, I saw that Caesar's golden litter was still there, set on blocks. The four litter-bearers cowered behind it. It was almost comical to see such big, strong men so confused and frightened.

At last Meto stepped out of the Senate House. His face was red from weeping, but his voice was steady. He seemed hardly to notice me as he shouted to the litter-bearers.

"You men, there. Come. Now!"

Reluctantly, with Hipparchus leading, three of the bearers ascended the steps. The fourth ran away.

The bearers followed Meto inside. A few moments later they emerged carrying the body of Caesar in his blood-soaked purple toga. Meto led them down the steps.

"Where are you taking him?" I said, following after him.

"To his house, of course." Meto's voice was calm and quiet, almost matter-of-fact. The task at hand—delivering Caesar's body to Caesar's widow—had steadied his nerves.

Rather clumsily—the handling of a dead body is never easy—Meto and the bearers managed to load Caesar into his litter. They rearranged the purple cushions so that he lay on his back with his arms crossed over his chest, then they drew the curtains shut. The costly cushions and drapes would all be ruined with bloodstains, I thought. Thus do mundane misgivings intrude on the most extraordinary moments.

With Meto taking the place of the missing bearer, and Hipparchus across from him at the front, the four men lifted the litter and headed back by the route we had taken that morning. Cinna and I walked alongside. Of the grand retinue that had attended Caesar that morning, only we six remained.

Meto stared straight ahead. Occasionally he shuddered as if he wept, but he never made a sound.

People who had thrilled to draw close and get a glimpse of the Dictator that morning now fled before us when they saw the litter approach and realized what was in it. Perhaps they feared that assassins with daggers would follow, or perhaps the idea of confronting Caesar's corpse filled them with superstitious dread.

At some point, one of Caesar's arms was jostled and fell past the curtains so that it hung outside the box, limp and lifeless and smeared with blood. I watched it sway this way and that, horrified and strangely fascinated. I didn't presume to touch it, and neither did Cinna, so there it dangled, all the way across the Field of Mars and through the Forum. Young women, rushing home from their aborted celebration of Anna Perenna, saw the bloody limb and screamed. Men saw it and broke into tears, confronted with the reality of what until that moment had been only a rumor. From windows and rooftops I heard groans and cries of lamentation.

But some who saw the lifeless arm of Caesar smiled and shouted with joy.

"It's true!" one man cried. "It's true! The tyrant's dead! It's a new day in Rome! Come, everyone, follow me! Come hear the heroes who did this thing—they'll be speaking soon, at the other end of the Forum. Come hear what the saviors of the Republic have to say!"

Meto ignored the man. He looked straight ahead and said nothing. The litter-bearers pressed on, until at last we came to the Regia.

Calpurnia somehow knew of our approach. She came running out of the house, followed by female attendants. As the litter was set on blocks, she pushed Meto aside. She saw the dangling arm and let out a stifled scream. She pulled open the curtains of the litter, saw the body of her husband, and wailed with grief.

I stepped closer, thinking to comfort her. She turned to face me, then beat her fists against my chest.

"You were supposed to stop this!" she screamed. "He counted on you. *I* counted on you! Why didn't you keep him from going this morning? How could you let this happen?"

"Calpurnia, you're being unfair," Cinna said quietly. He put his hand on her shoulder.

"Don't touch me, you filthy beast! I know all about you!" She spun around and slapped his face.

Cinna staggered back. His face turned bright red. He touched his cheek. At every moment during the long walk back to the Regia, he had been close to tears. Now they welled in his eyes and came spilling out.

"You, there!" shouted Calpurnia, glaring at the three litter-bearers.

"Don't stand there sniveling. Take your master inside, at once! I won't have strangers gawking at him, here in the street."

She paid us no more attention as she oversaw the conveyance of her husband's body into the Regia.

"I should go to my house, at once," Cinna whispered.

"So should I," I said. "Meto, are you staying here . . . with Caesar?"

He shook his head, not looking at me. "He's work for the women now."

"Then come with me. Bethesda and Diana will need us—"

"No," he said sharply, and began walking resolutely back the way we had come.

"But where are you going, my son?"

He stopped and turned his head, finally looking me in the eye. "You heard what that fool said. The killers are giving some sort of public address. I want to hear what they say."

"But Meto—the danger. There's no telling what may happen."

"Good! If the mob tears them limb from limb, I want to be there."

"And what if they incite the mob to join them and start killing Caesar's supporters?"

"Then I shall put up a good fight."

"Meto, you're not even armed. And there's blood on your hands . . . and on your tunic . . . from carrying the body—"

"*His* blood," Meto said, his stern voice breaking. "I wear it proudly." Then he turned and strode swiftly away.

Hours later, after darkness fell, Meto came home.

He looked worn with care and utterly exhausted, too weary even to speak. He was still wearing his bloodstained clothes. Without protest he allowed Bethesda and Diana to pull the tunic over his head, to bathe him with wet sponges, and then to dress him in an old tunic suitable for sleeping. He collapsed onto a chair beside a flaming brazier in the garden, too tired to stand a moment longer.

After eating a bit of food and drinking some wine, he finally spoke.

"They came down from the Capitoline . . ."

"Who, Meto?"

"The killers. Most of them. Or some of them. And among them were some who weren't in on the plot but now are quite happy to join the men who killed Caesar and sing their praises. A huge crowd gathered in the Forum—people who'd heard the rumor and couldn't believe it. Some wept. Some danced with joy. . . ."

"Was there violence?" asked Bethesda.

"Not at the beginning. Decimus's gladiators were there to protect the speakers. I saw some fistfights. Most people were there to find out what really happened . . . and what might happen next. That's the Roman way, isn't it, when there's a crisis? Citizens gather and listen to speeches. That's what sets us apart from the barbarians. Anyone can sack a city, Caesar used to say, but only a Roman can make a proper speech to justify doing so. . . ."

"They spoke, then? The assassins?" I said.

Meto shuddered and shrugged. "Cassius, Decimus, the Casca brothers, several others. They all took turns boasting and congratulating each other."

"Boasting?" said Diana.

"They've saved the Republic, don't you know? Killed a tyrant even more wicked than the old kings of Rome, a monster who ruled by fear and violence. Now everything can go back to the way it was before, back when—yes, *when,* I wonder? When was that Golden Age they hearken back to? Certainly no time since I was born, or in your lifetime either, Papa. It's always been violence and disorder and the likes of Brutus and Cassius fighting among themselves and ruling over the rest of us. That's what Caesar put an end to. Or tried to . . ."

"What else did they say? How did the crowd react?" I asked.

"Oh, the crowd seemed to love it. For a while, at least. Cassius made a great point of promising to restore free and open elections—no more of having one man decide who gets which magistracy and for how long. It was quite clear what he meant—free meals and gladiator shows put on for the voters by candidates from a handful of the 'best' families, who can get back to splitting the real power and wealth among themselves. Shameless pandering to the plebs, distracting them from the fact that Cassius and the rest are murderers, oath breakers who betrayed the man they were sworn to defend, who spilled blood in a consecrated space . . ."

"No one spoke against them?" asked Diana.

"Not one man. They convened the meeting as if it were a legitimate public debate, but only one side was allowed to speak. Only Caesar's enemies were on the platform, men who hated him enough to kill him. Dolabella was among them, can you believe it? The man Caesar insisted on naming as consul, despite Antony's objections. And daring to wear his consul's toga!"

"Surely Dolabella didn't speak," I said.

"Yes, he did. Not for long, and not to much effect, but he wanted everyone to know that he was on the side of the assassins, now the deed is done. Too cowardly to raise a dagger himself but smiling at every filthy word that came out of their mouths. What a viper!"

Meto paused for a moment to collect his thoughts. "Brutus gave the speech of his life, I'll grant him that. How Caesar would have loved that speech! Brutus must have been practicing it for months. Every rhetorical flourish and orator's trick in the book. Praising his ancestor for driving out the kings, saying he had no choice but to do the same thing himself. Appealing to everyone in the crowd who's lost a son or a brother or a father in the civil wars, saying their sacrifice was not in vain, for now the Republic will be reborn. He even took advantage of his injured hand, wincing and making sure we all saw the bloody bandage—never mind that it must have been another of those vultures on the stage who cut him by accident. Cicero couldn't have done better."

"Cicero? Did he speak? Was he on the stage?"

Meto shook his head. "I didn't see him. I'd have spotted that gray head. Come to think of it, I saw hardly any older men among them. They were mostly my age, the men on that platform. . . ."

"What did the crowd make of Brutus?"

"They loved him! They applauded. They cheered. They practically blew kisses. Oh, it was vile to watch, how he made them hang on every word and bent them to his will. Caesar . . . Caesar also knew . . . how to do that. . . ."

Meto seemed about to weep. I gestured to a slave to offer him more wine, which he eagerly accepted.

"But there *was* violence?" I said. "Earlier, you said something to that effect. 'Not at the beginning,' you said."

"Yes, that's right. It happened so suddenly. Like *that*," he said, and from the way he turned his gaze to the dark sky above, I knew he meant the abrupt change in the atmosphere felt by everyone in the garden, the precursor to a storm. The wind rose. The smell of rain was on the air. The sky flashed, and from somewhere far away I heard a peal of thunder. There had been a storm the night before—it seemed very long ago—and now there would be another.

"After Brutus spoke, the crowd was clearly on his side. I looked around me in disgust, wanting to shake every smiling, mindlessly clapping man I saw by the shoulders. And then Cinna spoke."

"*Cinna?*" I said.

"Oh, not *your* Cinna, Papa. The other one, the praetor. Believe me, two men could hardly be more different."

"Yes, I've met that other Cinna. By accident, thinking I was at the poet's house. And I saw him today, in the Senate House. But not . . . on the dais."

"That's right, he wasn't among the killers. But he felt inspired to speak up for them nonetheless. People were shocked to see him on the platform. His late sister was Caesar's first wife, you know. He was Julia's favorite uncle, before she died. He and Caesar are *family*. Caesar made him praetor this year. But what an ingrate! He didn't have a speech ready. He made it up as he went along. He started with some crude jokes about Caesar—so stupid I can't remember them. People booed. And then he began to gush about the killers, saying we must all vote them public honors, even erect statues to them! Make the Ides of March a holiday, he said, the birthday of the reborn Republic. Celebrate it every year—an act of murder in a consecrated space! Then someone in the crowd challenged him, saying he was ungrateful for the robe Caesar had put on him. 'This rag?' he said, and then he pulled off his praetorian toga, tossed it to the ground, and stamped on it. People were outraged. The fickle mob! The same men who cheered Brutus rushed the platform and tried to grab hold of Cinna. There was a riot. I've never seen anything like it. In the blink of an eye. Complete chaos."

"And Cinna?"

"He picked up his praetorian toga and rushed off in a panic, followed by Brutus and the rest of that rotten bunch. Decimus's gladiators closed ranks behind them while they retreated up to the Capitoline. Down in the Forum, I saw blood spilled, but I can't say how much or whose blood it was—I just wanted to get away, as quickly as I could. It wasn't easy. Everywhere I went, lawlessness. Looters. Men with knives and cudgels out to settle scores. Women screaming—gangs of rapists on the prowl. I had to circle back and make one detour after another. The darker it grew, the wilder the streets. Then things quieted down, quite suddenly. There's a rumor that Lepidus has brought his legion stationed on the Tiber Island into the city—"

"Which is against the law," I said.

"As is murder," said Meto. "I'd have gone to join Lepidus, but I wanted to come here first . . . to make sure all of you were safe . . ." He closed his eyes for a long moment. His shoulders slumped. I thought he might be asleep, until he spoke. "Papa, what did I see on the small table in the vestibule? The garment draped across it?"

"What do you think? It's the senator's toga that Cinna—*my* Cinna— lent me to wear today."

"But why is it in the vestibule?"

"So that I'll remember to return it to him, as soon as I safely can."

"Return it? But what will you wear when the Senate meets, as they surely will, maybe as soon as tomorrow?"

I sighed. "Meto, despite Caesar's intention, I was never formally inducted as a senator—"

"That makes no difference. Caesar made you a senator, he entered your name on the list, and a senator you are, as much as any of those others."

"I don't think—"

"If Dolabella is consul and entitled to wear his toga, then so are you! You were appointed by Caesar no less than he was." The first scattered drops of rain fell. Meto turned his face up, as if eager to receive them. I heard another peal of thunder. "This will be a huge question," he said. "Are all the acts and appointments of Caesar still in force? They must be. Even the assassins will agree, since they were appointed to their magistracies by Caesar. Watch how they cling to their offices—the ungrateful bastards!"

"Brutus, for one, will dispute that I'm a senator," I said, remembering his harsh words to me.

"Then ally yourself with those who'll agree to confirm your status. Antony, perhaps. And Lepidus—the man with whom you shared Caesar's last supper."

"I shared it with Decimus, as well."

"The most treacherous viper of all!"

"I'd rather not ally myself with anyone."

"But you must, Papa. You'll have to. Now, more than ever. Everyone must take sides."

Not again, I thought, remembering all the suffering and horror I had seen over the long course of the civil war. Had a new war begun?

Like a vast spiderweb, jagged lightning bolts crisscrossed the sky.

"Not again," I said, but my words were overwhelmed by a thunderclap so near and so powerful that it shook the ground beneath my feet.

DAY SEVEN: MARCH 16

XXXVII

The next morning, as soon as I'd washed my face and had a bite to eat, I called for a slave to help me put on the toga Cinna had lent me. Meto was already gone; no one could say where. I roused my sleepy son-in-law from my daughter's bed and told him to comb his tangled hair and put on his best tunic. Whether as bodyguard or entourage of one, I wanted him to look his best when I paid a call on Cicero.

Why I felt compelled to visit Cicero I couldn't say. Perhaps, like the dutiful but often diffident Finder I had been for so many years, I felt obliged to give him a final report, never mind that I hadn't accepted his commission or that he already knew how the matter in question had turned out.

We walked down the rain-washed street to Cicero's house. No sooner had I given my name to the door slave than Tiro appeared in the vestibule.

"I knew that had to be your voice," he said. "I was thinking you'd come today."

"Then we shared the same thought," I said, "and perhaps you can tell me why I've come, since I can't say myself."

"Today is a new beginning." I could tell that Tiro was deliberately suppressing any emotion in his voice. He was too well mannered to gloat over any man's death. "When there's a new beginning, it's only fitting that friends should pay calls on one another."

"Am I Cicero's friend?"

He raised an eyebrow. "You're mine, I hope."

"And mine as well!" said Cicero, stepping into the vestibule. "Gordianus, old friend, it's good to see you!" It had been years since I'd seen Cicero in such high spirits, not since the first days of his short-lived marriage to his teenage ward. "But don't stand here in the vestibule. Come along to the garden, and bring that strapping son-in-law with you. That's where we've all gathered."

As I followed him through the house, I heard voices, growing louder and more distinct as we drew nearer.

"And the look on Antony's face," I heard Cassius saying, "when he finally got away from Trebonius and came around the corner and saw us, with our daggers held high. He knew what had happened in an instant. He was like a wineskin that's gone flat, all the juice sucked out of him! A pity you weren't there to see it, Cicero," he added, raising his voice as his host came in sight.

In the garden, I saw not only Cassius but also Brutus, Decimus, and scowling Cinna the praetor, all dressed in plain tunics rather than togas. They stopped their conversation and turned to stare at me. There was a long silence.

"I thought the four of you were all barricaded on the Capitoline Hill," I finally said.

Cassius put a finger to his lips. "Don't tell anyone we're here! This little party is strictly sub rosa."

"We're not prisoners," said Cinna. "We are free men. Free at last, thanks to these brave fellows!"

"Yet you are not wearing your praetorian toga, Cinna," I said. "You're all in plain tunics. You've skulked down from the Capitoline at the break of day, incognito, to pay a visit to the man you left out of your conspiracy. Before you skulk back, are you finally ready to let Cicero in on your plans? Or are you here for his blessing?"

"Cicero is essential to our plans," said Brutus, putting a hand on his host's shoulder. Cicero beamed. "No other man in Rome has his prestige and his reputation for honor and decency. No other man has his skill as an orator. We look to you, Cicero, to put into words the justification for what we did, to persuade our fellow citizens who may not understand the righteousness of our cause."

"Like the citizens who chased you out of the Forum and back up to the Capitoline yesterday?" I said.

"Were you among them, Finder, stirring up trouble?" Brutus glared at me.

"I was not. But I heard about it from someone who *was* there."

"Let me guess—that adopted son of yours, Caesar's little Ganymede," said Cassius. He smirked. "And what are *you* doing, wearing a senator's toga? Did you not hear Brutus yesterday tell you to take it off and never put it on again?"

"Friends, desist from bickering," said Cicero.

"But Cicero, don't you see?" said Brutus. "This fellow still imagines he's one of us! Daring to go about in that toga. Why not dress your son Meto in a senator's toga as well? I'm sure Caesar would have done it sooner or later. Yes, elevated even a freedman to the Senate, as a sort of thank-you gift to his . . . what did you call him, Cassius? Caesar's little Ganymede? Exactly! Shall we be seeing wives and whores in the Senate as well? Why not Cleopatra?"

"Yes, why *not* Cleopatra?" said Cinna, his scowl becoming a leer as he rudely mimed the act of penetrating someone from behind, clutching invisible haunches and thrusting his hips.

"Now, now, Cinna," said Cicero mildly, "we must be diplomatic in our dealings with foreigners, even with Egyptians. But I wonder, what *is* the queen up to today? What must she be thinking, holed up at Caesar's villa outside the city, all her plans in shambles?"

"I imagine she'll scuttle back to Egypt as quickly as she can," said Cassius. "In my mind I picture her as a beetle, rolling a ball of dung—onward, onward, always busy. Don't they worship dung beetles as gods in Egypt? Roll your little Caesarion all the way back to Egypt, queen beetle—and drown him in the Nile when you get there!"

Cicero and Cinna laughed, but Brutus kept scowling at me.

"I wear this toga because Caesar bestowed it on me," I said, very quietly, so as to get their attention. "Just as Caesar named you to be governor of Syria, Cassius, and you, Decimus, to be governor of Gaul, and you, Brutus, to become consul in due course. Will you give up those offices now that he's dead? Will you nullify the appointments of others and not your own? Will you have Dolabella for consul but not Antony? That could become very tricky, especially with Lepidus's legion camped in the Forum."

From the sobered look on their faces, I knew the rumor Meto had heard the previous night must be true. To bring soldiers within the city was strictly illegal, but which laws applied now and which did not?

I looked at Decimus. "You he suspected least of all. Caesar trusted you implicitly. You dined with him one day and put a knife in him the next. Caesar spoke of the best way to die at that dinner—and your face betrayed no sign that you planned to murder him in a matter of hours."

"A trick he learned from the Gauls," said Cinna. "They're masters at showing no emotion."

"And at feigning friendliness?" I asked. "When you called on me ahead of the dinner to introduce yourself, Decimus, what was your intention?"

Decimus cocked his head. "It certainly wasn't to make friends with you."

" 'Scouting the terrain,' my son called it."

Decimus nodded. "You might say that. You were a blank to me. I knew you only by hearsay. I was curious to see if you might pose any threat to our plans—especially given your reputation for perceiving what others do not. Were you a man to watch out for? Perhaps even an agent for Caesar? But when I met you, any worries I had were put to rest. A nonentity, Brutus called you, and so you are, no matter that you dare to put on that toga and traipse about in public."

I looked at our host. There was something almost comical about the way Cicero was wincing and wringing his hands. "Friends, there's no need for harsh words, especially on such a happy day—"

"Come, Davus, it's time for us to go. We'll show ourselves out."

Cicero didn't call me back. Nor did Tiro run after me to say farewell. I straightened my toga as I stepped into the street, feeling more awkward than ever inside it.

XXXVIII

I arrived home to see a very ornate litter outside my house. Neither the well-dressed bearers nor the expensive litter looked familiar to me, until I saw a golden lion's head embroidered on the red curtains. That was one of Antony's favorite images, a link to Hercules, who wore the skin of the Nemean lion as a cowl and cape. It seemed unlikely that Antony himself would use such a vehicle. He preferred to walk. ("Those legs were made to be used," my admiring wife had observed, after seeing Antony run naked through the streets of Rome during the Lupercalia.)

When I stepped into the vestibule, the excited door slave opened his mouth to speak, but I silenced him with my hand. "Fulvia is here," I said.

The slave nodded.

"But why, I wonder?"

The slave gave me a blank look and shrugged, as if to say that the motives of a woman such as Fulvia were beyond his comprehension.

"Beyond my comprehension, as well," I muttered to myself. "What in Hades is she doing here, on such a day?" It did not occur to me that she had come to see not me but my wife and daughter.

I heard women talking. As I stepped into the garden, Diana rushed to my side.

"Daughter, what are all these women doing here?" I asked, for along with Fulvia I saw a great many other well-dressed matrons, among them Bethesda, who smiled at me serenely, looking very pleased with herself.

"Oh, Papa, you don't mind, do you? It's a rehearsal for the Liberalia, and we were supposed to do it at Fulvia's house, but that's simply not possible, or so she says, because Antony and a great many other men are coming and going and trying to organize some sort of meeting—well, you can imagine why."

"Yes, I can. What do you mean, a rehearsal?"

"Oh, Papa, the rituals are very complex and must be carried out perfectly. And the Liberalia is tomorrow! We all need much more practice if we're to do it properly. We don't want to disappoint Father Liber, do we?" She smiled as if making light of the matter, but in her eyes I saw steely determination.

"Disappointing your mother—I mean to say Father Liber, of course—is the last thing I wish to do," I said

"Then you don't mind vacating the house?"

"What?"

"Along with all the other males in the household. Only for a couple of hours."

I grunted. It was too early in the day to visit the Salacious Tavern, even for me, even on such a day. Or was it? "Is that strictly necessary?"

"Absolutely!" said Fulvia, who had overheard our conversation and now stepped up to me.

"Welcome to my house," I said, seeing her with fresh eyes. With Caesar gone, it struck me that the single most devious and ambitious mortal in Rome might well be the woman standing before me.

"Thank you, Finder, but your wife already welcomed us." She laughed at the look on my face. "I'm teasing you, of course. But you *will* have to leave the house for a while."

"You seem to be in very high spirits," I said.

"Why not? The Liberalia is tomorrow."

Why not? Caesar is dead, and no one knows what terrible things will happen next, I thought. "Will the Liberalia even take place? I should think . . . in light of what's just happened . . . and the uncertainty . . ."

"In uncertain times, the only certain thing we have are the gods," she said, "especially Father Liber. Of course the Liberalia will take place. We may have to cancel the public procession, and we may not accomplish all we would like to. . . ." She looked past me, into the middle distance as her voice trailed away.

"And every male must leave the house? Even me?"

"Especially you. Any man who witnesses the secret rites invites divine retribution. I would never wish the wrath of the Bacchantes to be visited on *you,* Finder."

I briefly thought of Cinna's poem, and of Orpheus and Pentheus, both decapitated and torn limb from limb by the mad female worshippers of Bacchus, also known as Father Liber. "That sort of thing happens only in the old myths, not nowadays."

"Is that correct? Let's not test the will of the god, Finder. You really must leave us while we practice. No man can ever witness the secret rituals of the Liberalia. Not even the Pontifex Maximus—" She stopped, realizing she was speaking of Caesar. Who would be Pontifex Maximus now?

I looked past Fulvia, at my wife. Standing in a crowd of wealthy-looking Palatine-dwelling Roman matrons and their daughters—now her peers, I thought with amazement—she had never looked happier. I sighed. "Of course I'll do as you ask. I suppose I can think of errands to keep the male slaves busy for a few hours. What parts of the city will be safe, I wonder? And Davus and I will think of somewhere to go. . . ."

Fulvia touched my shoulder affectionately and actually leaned forward to give me a kiss on the cheek. "How smart you look in that toga," she said. If Bethesda was her peer, was I now the peer of Antony? The idea seemed absurd—Brutus would say so—but the thought sent a shock through me. I was still realizing, in stages, the profound changes that Caesar had set in motion when he granted me the right to wear a senator's toga, culminating now in a kiss—from Fulvia!

. . .

As promised, I thought of places to send the male slaves. As they dispersed down the street in front of my house, and the door closed behind me, I drew Davus aside.

"As for you, son-in-law, go to the Salacious Tavern—if the streets are safe enough—and see if my friend Cinna is there. Ask him for any news he may have, and tell him I hope to see him soon."

"But aren't you coming with me?"

"No. I have something else to do."

"By yourself? Shouldn't I be with you, for safety?"

"No, Davus. I'll be in no danger. Or rather, any danger I may face would be doubled if you were there—and neither of us could protect the other."

"Your words are mysterious, father-in-law." He looked at me earnestly. "I have no idea what you're talking about."

"Good. Now be on your way."

So it was, stealing into my own house (every house should have a secret entrance known only to its owner) and using certain secret passages (built during the civil war, when it became sensible to have hiding places in the home), I was able to ascend to the tiled roof, and there to lie in a spot above the garden where the sun-dappled, leafing branches of a tall tree concealed me from the women below, though I was able to see them by peering through the leaves.

I did what I did on impulse, and not without a shiver. From earliest childhood it is deeply ingrained in every Roman male that he must never under any circumstances witness those religious rites that are to be performed, seen, and heard only by women. The rites of the Bona Dea are one example. Fulvia's first husband, Clodius, had once dressed as a girl and taken part in those ceremonies, and had suffered no immediate retribution, though some speculated that his fate on the Appian Way had been the goddess's deadly, if long-delayed, punishment. To violate the secrecy of any rites having to do with Bacchus and his female worshippers was particularly dangerous, considering the way a malefactor like Pentheus had died, ripped apart by rampaging Maenads including his mother.

How did I justify such an impious act? For one thing, I was an old man. How much more life was in me for any god to snatch away? For another, I was simply curious—and would I ever have such an opportunity again?

Still, I watched with mounting trepidation as the women in the garden below, led by Fulvia, began their practice. My heart beat so loudly in my ears I could hardly hear their chanting.

What I witnessed over the ensuing two or three hours filled me with nothing so much as . . . disappointment.

Was this assortment of skipping dances (such as one might see any group of little girls on any street corner in Rome performing), repetitious chants (accompanied by the ear-splitting music of shrill flutes, banging tambourines, and clattering finger cymbals), and banal incantations (irrythmic hymns that could have used a good polish from Cinna)— was this all there was to the secret rites of the Liberalia?

I had expected something at least slightly shocking, or even very shocking, some titillation so unheard of it would make my hair stand on end, or some divine revelation so awesome it might cause me to spontaneously combust. (What a blow that would have been to my wife's social standing, for her newly minted senator of a husband to burst into flames while perched on his rooftop, violating the secrecy of the female followers of Bacchus!)

Presumably the ritual being rehearsed would take place in Fulvia's garden, with no men allowed. Set up in the middle of my own garden was the focal point of this ritual, a painted wooden idol of the youthful, unbearded Bacchus, complete with horns sprouting from his thick locks. In one hand the god held an upright spear twined with ivy, and in the other a cluster of wooden grapes. Instead of legs, the figure ended in a pole about the thickness of my forearm. This pole was set into a curious mechanism with various metal gears. When a rope was pulled by some of the women, the idol turned slowly around, so as to face each of the surrounding worshippers in turn. I must admit this device was slightly unnerving, especially as it rotated. The motion was by turns smooth and jerky, graceful and halting. The face of the idol was so lifelike that whenever it came into view I felt a slight shiver.

The women put on costumes made of fawnskins strung with golden beads, and headbands ornamented with jewels. Censers of myrrh were lit, filling the garden with fragrance. (*Myrrh,* I thought—*the residue of Zmyrna's tears!*) Bowls of water were produced, and there was a great deal of ceremony having to do with the washing of the wooden wand each woman carried and the wrapping of the wand with ivy. The idol itself was carefully washed, to the singing of prayers. Fulvia explained that first this dance and then that dance would need to be performed before the statue, and then this dance again, and then that dance again.

The songs were all about Bacchus, especially about his death as an infant and subsequent rebirth. Many versions of the story exist. In the one sung by the women in my garden, baby Bacchus was the child of Jupiter and Proserpine, the consort of Pluto. In a typical fit of jealousy, Jupiter's wife, Juno, dispatched a group of Titans to destroy the bastard infant, whom they lured with toys, then viciously tore to pieces and devoured. Jupiter blasted the Titans with thunderbolts, turning them to dust; all that remained uneaten of Bacchus was his tiny heart. But that was enough for Jupiter to reanimate the infant demigod. Jupiter placed the heart in the womb of Semele, who gave birth to Bacchus a second time. Thus the twice-born god is also called Bimater, child of two mothers.

I had forgotten the part about the Titans tearing little Bacchus to pieces. I thought of Cinna's new poem and realized that, long after the death of Bacchus, the maddened female followers of Bacchus were to inflict the same fate on Orpheus and then again on the impious Pentheus, tearing them limb from limb, though neither of those victims would be given rebirth. Surely there was some connection between the way baby Bacchus was killed and the way his followers later killed Pentheus, some thread of reason that connected these bizarre, bloody deaths.

I suddenly understood how certain rumors had come about, concerning the secret female worship of Bacchus, namely, that in their rituals these modern-day Maenads not only sacrificed an animal—some said a baby—by tearing it apart with their hands but also devoured the sacrifice, eating the raw flesh in an orgy of bloodshed and gore. Perhaps the Bacchantes of ancient days had practiced such rites, but nothing remotely like that took place in my garden.

Instead, I saw a great deal of skipping and bowing and pirouetting. And, this being a rehearsal, the various components of the ceremony were performed again, and again, and again—and there was I, trapped on my rooftop, afraid to make my escape lest the rattling of a loose tile might give me away. Would the Bacchantes below tear me to shreds? I doubted it, but Bethesda would be mortified, perhaps even expelled from the group. I didn't dare move, and so all the starting and stopping and endless repetition of the rehearsal below me became a punishment in itself.

Despite my dwindling interest, I was happy to observe that the conduct of my wife and daughter was above reproach. They carried themselves with dignity and grace, and the other women seemed to accept them as equals. Fulvia, whom I had long known to be a born leader, proved herself to be so on this occasion. Whenever any question arose, it was to Fulvia that the other women deferred. They obeyed her without hesitation.

From time to time I spotted Bast the cat perched on the edge of the roof across from me, peering down. As a female, she had not been banished from the house, but she kept her distance from the worshippers below.

Banal, I have called the ritual, and thus disappointing to a forbidden watcher who expected something dangerous. And yet . . . two or three times in the course of those hours, and for only an instant, like figures seen by lightning flashes in the dark, the women in their fawnskins below seemed no longer women but something else, not quite human, unspeakably ancient, primordial, malevolent. In the same instant, the wooden idol of Bacchus seemed not to rotate because of a mechanism but to move of its own volition.

But as I say, this weird warping of my perception took place only a few times, and very briefly; it came and went in the blink of an eye. I attributed these hallucinatory flashes to the extreme stress of the previous day, lack of sleep, and the inbred religious shame I felt for what I was doing. They had nothing to do with Dionysus—or so I told myself.

XXXIX

On that first day after Caesar's death, Rome was like a man with a fever, twisting and turning and muttering in delirium. In countless houses all over the city, countless men (and many women, no doubt) asked themselves and each other what had happened, and how, and who had done it, and why, and what was to be done now. And countless answers were given and pondered and rejected or provisionally accepted until some new idea or question or fear intruded, and the feverish delirium spiraled ever deeper. How many false rumors were spread, how many crimes great and small committed, how many plots and counterplots hatched that day?

While I was watching Fulvia and the rehearsal of the Liberalia in my garden, Lepidus was holding a public meeting in the Forum, using his troops to keep order. This gathering was very different from the one the previous day. Speakers condemned the assassins. Some demanded vengeance for Caesar and said that Lepidus should order his soldiers to storm the killers' stronghold. Lepidus, acutely aware that the presence of his legion within the city was illegal, declined to compound the crime with a wholesale massacre in the sacred precincts atop the Capitoline. That hill offered excellent vantage points from which to look down on the gathering in the Forum. What did Brutus and Cassius and the rest think, watching as one speaker after another extolled the virtues of Caesar and railed against his killers?

Eventually, Lepidus dispersed the gathering. He posted his troops at various key spots around the city, then went to Antony's house, probably arriving at about the same time that Fulvia returned home from the rehearsal in my garden. After much discussion, Antony and Lepidus and the others convening there decided to take no action against Caesar's killers, at least for the moment. A legal resolution would be pursued first.

Antony sent a message to the Capitoline proposing an emergency meeting of the Senate the next day. Though Brutus and the other assassins refused to come down from the Capitoline, they agreed to send representatives.

Messengers from both sides combed the city, alerting their friends in the Senate of the meeting the next day, each side hoping to muster as many supporters as possible.

At some point that evening, Antony and Fulvia went to the Regia. They offered condolences to Calpurnia, then moved on to more practical matters. I imagine Fulvia guided the conversation, which must have required extraordinary tact. As consul, Antony wanted Calpurnia to give him control of Caesar's state papers. She consented. Then, somehow, Calpurnia was convinced to give Antony control of Caesar's huge private fortune, which amounted to a quarter of a million pounds of silver.

As fevers sometimes temporarily abate, so that night an uneasy peace descended on Rome, allowing its people to sink for a while into the oblivion of sleep.

DAYS EIGHT, NINE & TEN:

MARCH 17, 18 & 19

XL

The meeting of the Senate on the second day after Caesar's death was held at the Temple of Tellus, not far from Antony's house.

Meto urged me to attend. "You won't have to speak, Papa. But you *must* show your face. You must assert your prerogative as a full-fledged senator. Show that you're entitled to be there as much as any of the others." After a pause, he added, "It's what Caesar would have wanted."

Diana also weighed in. "And imagine, Papa, instead of observing from the outside, as you've done your whole life, you can actually see what it's like to be *inside* the Senate. Oh, how I envy you! You'll be doing something I can never hope to do."

Bethesda didn't need to speak. She made her will known by the expression on her face, which countenanced no disagreement.

For their sake, I put on my toga and made my way to the Temple of Tellus.

When I think back to those days between Caesar's death and Caesar's funeral, my mind is a muddle of speeches. Speeches before the Senate, speeches in the Forum, speeches on street corners. Words, words,

words—endless words, as repetitious and numbing as those dances and chants of the Liberalia rehearsal.

At that first meeting of the Senate after Caesar's death, I slipped inside as discreetly as I could. I stood in the most inconspicuous place I could find, feeling much as I had on my rooftop the day before, more spy than participant. I hid myself even from Cinna, whom I saw only from a distance. I said nothing. I only observed.

Those speaking on behalf of Caesar's killers spoke first. They proposed that the Senate should declare Caesar a tyrant and proclaim public thanksgiving to the men who had freed the city from his illegal dictatorship. Further, to forestall any future reprisals, the killers of Caesar should be granted unconditional and irrevocable immunity from prosecution. What of the sacred vows the killers had made to protect Caesar? That vow was made under duress, they said, and was thus invalid.

Speakers rose to vociferously oppose these ideas, arguing instead that the assassins should be tried as murderers. But these men were surprisingly few in number, and their speeches received only scattered support. Already the idea of a world without Caesar was taking hold in men's minds. The new reality obliged every man to think of his own good going forward. Caesar was dead, and no act of the Senate could change that. Vengeance on the killers would only set in motion endless vendettas from their numerous and powerful relatives. Rome had shed enough blood in the civil war.

Antony argued against declaring Caesar a tyrant. If his dictatorship were declared illegal, then it must follow that all his public acts would be null and void, as would the public acts of every official he had appointed. All the public land Caesar had granted to his veterans would have to be confiscated by the state. Further, all Caesar's magisterial appointments, some as much as five years in the future, would be invalid. Hundreds of men, set to become everything from praetors to provincial governors, would be stripped of their promised offices. The state would be in chaos. Violence would certainly ensue.

Antony proposed a threefold compromise. First, the office of dictator, established long ago for emergencies and meant to last only a year, should be abolished altogether. Tyrant or not, Caesar would be Rome's last dictator. Second, the assassins would be granted immunity from prosecution. Third, all of Caesar's appointments, acts, and decrees would remain in force. The sovereign authority of the Senate would be restored. Peace, not bloodshed, would ensue.

Both sides of the chamber resoundingly approved Antony's compromise. Only the most recalcitrant and vengeful partisans objected. From near panic and complete uncertainty, Antony had shown a way to restore order and at least the semblance of unity. He was the statesman of the hour. Messengers were sent to the Capitoline to inform the assassins and beseech them to come down from their stronghold.

It was a remarkable day for me, standing among my fellow senators, listening to the likes of Cicero and Antony and Piso, Caesar's famously learned father-in-law, debate.

And yet, in retrospect, the scene I recall most vividly took place outside the Temple of Tellus, after the surprisingly favorable auspices were taken and before the meeting convened. As I stood on the steps, hesitating to go inside, wondering if anyone would challenge me, Cinna the praetor—the *other* Cinna, as I would always think of him—arrived. Not being one of the assassins himself, but supporting their cause, he had dared to come down from the Capitoline to speak on their behalf.

As he walked up the steps, he spotted me, and seemed about to speak—to challenge me?—when suddenly I heard a voice shout his name: "Cinna! Look, there he is! It's Cinna!"

I looked down at the public square in front of the temple and saw a small but very angry-looking mob rushing toward us. I started back, unsure of what was happening. Fortunately, Lepidus's soldiers were present to keep order. They hastily formed a cordon at the foot of the steps and held the crowd back.

Men jeered and shook their fists. "Look!" yelled one. "The coward is wearing his praetorian toga, the very one he stripped off yesterday."

"Which is it, Cinna?" yelled another. "Are you Caesar's lackey or not?

Betray a dead man, would you, but hold on to the job he gave you? For shame!"

With soldiers to protect him, Cinna stood his ground on the steps, smirking and making rude gestures at the mob, which incited them to greater anger. Someone threw a shoe, which he deftly dodged.

Cicero happened to be nearby. "By Hercules," he shouted at Cinna, "get yourself inside, you fool, and quickly! Stop stirring the hornets' nest!"

Grudgingly, the scowling praetor complied. Cicero followed him up the steps. If Cicero saw me, he gave no sign.

That was the second time in two days that Cinna the praetor had been forced to retreat from an angry mob after inciting the partisans of Caesar, deliberately making himself the target of their rage.

The meeting of the Senate was adjourned and its members made their way to the Forum, where a public meeting was held. The compromises worked out by the Senate were explained to the people. The assassins were invited to come down from the Capitoline and assured they would not be harmed. But Brutus and Cassius wanted more than promises; they demanded that Lepidus and Antony each give them a son as hostage. This the two men did, even though Antony's son was a mere toddler. (Did the boy's mother, Fulvia, approve of this arrangement? Surely she must have, yielding to political expediency.)

The assassins came down from the Capitoline. To demonstrate the steady, peaceful rule of the state, the two consuls, Antony and Dolabella, publicly shook hands with Brutus and Cassius.

That night, it was not until after I ate and was making ready for bed that I recalled that this had been the day of the Liberalia, to which my wife and daughter had been looking forward with such excitement.

Bethesda sat in our bedroom. Diana stood behind her, combing her mother's hair with a silver brush, a task she had enjoyed since childhood. When I asked how the rituals had gone, my wife shrugged.

"Neither better nor worse than expected. The rehearsal was adequate.

No mistakes were made. Nothing pleasing to the god was omitted." She looked thoughtful. "But I could tell that Fulvia was not entirely pleased. For one thing, not as many worshippers attended as usual."

"But surely that was to be expected. A great many women must have shut themselves inside their houses, afraid to go out."

"Yes. Perhaps that explains it. But it's as if Fulvia expected something to happen that didn't. She seemed . . . disappointed."

Diana nodded, to show her agreement, and continued to brush her mother's hair.

"Yet you say that nothing was omitted."

Bethesda nodded. "Still . . ."

"Perhaps Fulvia was too distracted to give her full attention to the Liberalia, and so the day was spoiled for her. This was a very important day for Antony. Her future and his both hung in the balance. And then there was the matter of handing over her little boy to be held as a hostage."

"A barbaric practice!"

"Spoken like a true Roman matron, my dear wife. But it's actually a very Roman thing to do. All the old, powerful families compete and intermarry and sometimes war with each other. Exchanging heirs to assure safety and proper conduct is exactly the sort of thing that seems normal to them. The handover took place late in the afternoon, but Fulvia may have known about it well in advance and been fretful all day. Perhaps it was that, and all her other worries, that you read as disappointment. I'm sure that you and Diana and all the other women did very well and gave her no cause for shame. What do you say, Diana?"

Diana cocked her head and stopped brushing her mother's hair. "Everything you say makes sense, Papa. But Mother is right. Disappointed—not distracted or full of dread—is exactly how Fulvia seemed today. *Disappointed.* When I think of how much she enjoyed the rehearsal yesterday—well, the difference was like night and day."

I shook my head. "As long as the two of you don't blame yourselves . . ."

"I should think not!" said Bethesda rather haughtily. "No one comported herself with greater enthusiasm than my daughter."

"Or my mother!" insisted Diana. The two smiled at each other and intertwined their fingers as Diana kissed her mother's cheek.

In at least one household in Rome, true harmony reigned.

XLI

It was at a meeting of the Senate the next day that Calpurnia's father, Piso, called for Caesar's will to be read in public. Not only was Piso Caesar's father-in-law, but he also had been named by Caesar as the guardian of his last will and testament. The very existence of such a document stirred such great interest that the Senate granted Piso's request.

Piso also asked that his son-in-law be given a state funeral, which was a very rare honor. I could recall only Sulla receiving such a funeral. He, too, had been a dictator who held his office longer than the prescribed one year, but Sulla had stepped down of his own accord and had died of natural causes. Rightly or wrongly, his supporters, victors of the last civil war, had proclaimed Sulla the restorer and savior of the Republic, worthy of a state funeral. Why should Caesar be given such an honor?

Piso argued that any funeral procession for Caesar, no matter how privately it began, would inevitably draw a huge crowd, and emotions would run high. As a cautionary example, Piso reminded the Senate of the funeral of Fulvia's rabble-rousing husband Clodius only eight years ago, an ostensibly private affair that had drawn huge numbers to the Forum and then erupted in a riot that saw the Senate House burned to the ground. If only for public safety, Piso argued that the funeral of Caesar should be organized and carried out by the state, using the Forum as a venue with Lepidus's troops (illegally present or not) to keep order. The actual cremation would take place on the Field of Mars.

The anti-Caesar party was initially against the idea of a public funeral, especially Cassius, who spoke vehemently against it. But, having won from the Senate immunity from prosecution—which some of the assassins construed as an admission that Caesar's death was a good thing—they worried that opposition to the funeral desired by his family would make them look petty and vindictive. To maintain peace with Caesar's supporters (including the veterans of his legions, who were now flocking to the city), they acquiesced to a state funeral. Antony asked for permission to deliver the public eulogy, and this was granted.

Another proposal asked the Senate to confirm Caesar's status as a god. While not worshipped in Italy, in some of the far-flung provinces more amenable to such worship Caesar was in fact acknowledged as a god. If his divine status was not upheld by the Senate, the legitimacy of the statutes he had imposed on those provinces would be undermined. To maintain the rule of Roman law throughout Roman possessions, the Senate confirmed that Caesar was a god.

I had witnessed the killing of not just a man, but a deity. Equally amazing, the same deliberative body that declared him a god declared that the killers of this god were exempt from trial and punishment. Those hectic days after the death of Caesar were rife with paradox.

Even as these meetings of the Senate and the public meetings in the Forum were taking place, negotiations were held in secret between the leaders of the assassins and Caesar's most powerful loyalists. (Caesar's young grandnephew and protégé Gaius Octavius was away from Rome and played no part, though Piso looked out for his interests.) The most important consideration for all concerned was that everything must be seen to be done legally, in accordance with the will of the Senate and the consent of the people of Rome.

In retrospect it would seem quite remarkable, and a testament to the strength of her public institutions, that Rome did not descend into a bloodbath in those perilous first days after Caesar's death.

On the night before Caesar's funeral, Meto came to my house. He was wearing a dark tunic, dressed in mourning, as if he were a member of Caesar's family. I had hardly seen him since the morning after the assassination. He was busy helping with arrangements for the funeral, shuttling between the Regia, where Caesar's body lay in state receiving mourners, and the house of Antony and Fulvia, where the actual plans for the funeral were being arranged.

"You may not see me at all tomorrow, Papa. I may be assisting Fulvia, seeing that all goes according to plans."

"Fulvia?"

"Yes. It's Fulvia who's attending to the details. Antony has no head for such things. He spends all his time pacing back and forth across their garden, practicing his eulogy. You should see the two of them at work. Fulvia occasionally looks up from whatever she's doing to make a comment about the speech, and Antony hums and nods and then changes the speech to suit her."

"Fulvia is planning the funeral?" I said. "I'm not sure I like the sound of that. The last time she was in charge of a funeral, the Senate House went up in flames."

"Better this time if the senators are inside when it happens," Meto said bitterly. "It's what they all deserve, every one of them, after the clemency they've shown to Caesar's killers."

"Dangerous talk, my son."

"Dangerous to me? Or to those craven senators who compromised with the killers?"

"Dangerous to us all. I won't argue the merits of the various compromises worked out by the Senate. But frankly, I'm amazed—and thankful—that there's been no slaughter. The assassins might have killed Antony as well as Caesar, and Lepidus, too, and many others while they were about it. But they didn't. And Lepidus could easily have dispatched his legion to chase Cinna the praetor up the hill the other day and storm the Capitoline. Brutus and the others wouldn't have stood a chance. Instead—except for that wild, lawless night after Caesar's death—not a drop of blood has been spilled."

"And you think that's the end of it? Now the Senate and the magistrates will all get back to work, and Rome will go about its business, as if nothing's happened? No, Papa. There *will* be a reckoning."

The harshness of his voice sent a shiver through me.

"Let's see how the funeral goes," I said.

"Yes, the funeral . . ." Behind the tears that welled in Meto's eyes I saw a glint of pure malice.

DAY ELEVEN: MARCH 20

XLII

"I'm not going unless you go, too," said Cinna.

He had shown up at my doorstep a little after dawn, wearing a long dark tunic and a dark cloak.

"You're not dressed as a tribune, in your toga?" I said, wiping sleep from my eyes. We sat in my small library, where a brazier warmed the chilly morning air. "It's a state funeral, isn't it?"

"I won't be there as a magistrate of Rome but as a friend of the deceased. I'm properly dressed for mourning. I'd suggest you dress in similar fashion, and not in that . . . that toga I lent you."

I raised an eyebrow "You're afraid of violence, aren't you? A senator's toga might make a man a target of the mob, if passions run high. Is that what you think?"

"There *is* that possibility."

"Lepidus's troops will maintain order."

"I'm almost as frightened of them as I am of the mob." Cinna shivered.

"Yet you arrived here with only a single bodyguard." The man was in my vestibule, dressed as somberly as his master.

"More than one bodyguard on such an occasion only draws attention," said Cinna. "I wasn't planning to go to the funeral at all. I told

Sappho last night, 'If I should oversleep tomorrow morning, don't wake me. Better I should sleep though the whole day.' Ha! I hardly slept a wink. And when finally I did . . . I dreamed I saw Caesar. He invited me to dinner. I didn't want to go, but he insisted. And when I followed him into his dining room, he gestured with his hand and there was . . . nothing. Nothing at all before me. An abyss. An emptiness. A void. It's impossible to convey the feeling . . . the terror of it. I turned around, but on all sides I saw the same *nothingness*." He shivered violently. "I awoke to find the bed soaked with sweat, too sodden to be slept in. I went to Sappho's room and lay on the bed beside her. She saw how distraught I was, and held my hand, and even wept a little, the dear, sweet thing. I managed to doze a bit. . . ."

"Yet here you are," I said.

"Before the sun rose, I was wide awake. If the dream means anything, it's that I *must* pay my respects to Caesar, never mind my cowardice." He flashed a crooked smile. "Do you think me a coward, Gordianus?"

I shook my head. "In such times, every man must decide for himself what to do."

"Then you'll go with me today, to the funeral?"

"I never said *that*." I started to laugh, but he looked so wretched I stopped myself.

"I suppose I *am* curious to see how it goes. And Meto will want me to be there, though it's unlikely he'll even see me. He's at the Regia now, helping with preparations to stage the procession. . . ."

"Good! Then you and I shall go together."

"Yes, I suppose we shall."

"And you'll dress as I've dressed? Something suitably dark, to blend with the crowd."

"I *have* grown a bit weary of wearing that blasted toga." I smiled. "We'll have a bit to eat, first. And I'll wake Davus, to come with us. One bodyguard for you, and one for me. Just in case . . ."

While I was putting on a suitably dark tunic, Bethesda crossed the bedroom and took me by the arm.

"You mustn't leave the house today."

"Oddly enough, wife, I was about to say the same thing to you. And to you, too, Diana," I added, seeing my daughter peeking around the doorframe. She stepped in to join us.

"Either the day will be safe or unsafe," said Diana. "If it's the latter, you have no more business being there than we do."

"On the contrary, I owe my place in the Senate—if indeed I have one—to Caesar. It would be an act of crass ingratitude if I failed to pay my final respects to the man. And then there's Meto. How my poor son is grieving. For his sake I have to be there. And then, also, there's my visitor. Cinna wants me to go with him. To give him courage, he says, though what good I'd be to him in a dangerous spot, I can't imagine."

"Exactly, husband! You'll be no use to anyone if something bad should happen."

"Bethesda, you undermine my confidence, which is shaky enough as it is. Desist!"

"Yes, Mother, he's right about going," said Diana. "He really must, out of respect for Caesar, and for Meto. And he's right that we should stay home. Calpurnia hardly knows us. Even if she sees us among the crowd, we'd be of no comfort to her."

"And Fulvia?" said Bethesda.

"If Fulvia wanted us to be there—if she needed us to play some part among the mourners, or perform some other function—she would have asked us. No, Mother, it's altogether proper that Papa should go, and take Davus with him, and that we should stay at home, so that neither of them has to worry about us. They'll tell us all about the funeral when they come home, safe and sound. Won't you, Papa? And you, too, Davus?" she added, as her husband entered the room, turning a bit sideways to fit though the doorframe.

Davus embraced his wife, and I did the same. Again the thought struck me: *In at least one household in Rome, true harmony reigns.* What a lucky man I was.

The funeral procession would begin at the Regia, whence Caesar's body would be taken to the Forum, where Antony would deliver the eulogy from a platform on which a gilded shrine had been erected to hold the body. This shrine was shaped like the new Temple of Venus, which had been built and dedicated by Caesar for the worship of his ancestress. After the speech, the body would be removed from the shrine and the procession would continue to the Field of Mars, where a pyre had been erected for the cremation in an open area large enough to accommodate tens of thousands of mourners.

As Cinna and I proceeded down the slope of the Palatine toward the Regia, with Cinna's bodyguard before us and Davus behind us, I could see that a vast crowd had already assembled in the Forum, thronging every step of the Sacred Way. They were dressed in various shades of brown and gray, but mostly in black.

"From a distance," said Cinna "they look not unlike a huge flock of ravens, don't you think? Black birds . . . filling the Forum . . ." He hummed and nodded vigorously. "Oh, yes, that's good. Quite good. A vast flock of ravens to attend the funeral . . . of an eagle! Or something like that . . ."

"Cinna, what are you going on about?"

He looked a bit chagrined. "Did I not tell you? No, I haven't seen you at all these last few days, have I? So much going on. But there's a reason, you see, that I really must attend the funeral, must see it with my own eyes. What did Naevius say? 'The poet must be a witness first.'"

"What are you talking about?"

"Do you remember what that beast Cimber yelled at me, as you and I were leaving the Senate House of Pompey?"

"Something like . . . 'Write a poem about *this*!'"

"That's right. He wasn't serious, of course. He was mocking me. But later, I thought: Why not? Indeed, how can I have witnessed such a thing and *not* write about it?"

"You mean . . ."

"Exactly! Now that the *Orpheus and Pentheus* is finished . . . and Caesar's Parthian campaign will never come about . . . what subject might I turn to next? I said to myself: Why write of gods and heroes of long

ago, when I witnessed the death of the greatest man since Alexander—
a living god, struck down before my very eyes?"

"You intend to write an epic poem about Caesar?"

"Perhaps. Imagine a poem that charts the fantastic arc of his career,
from beginning to end? Oh, a veritable river of phrases and metaphors
is already rushing through my head! Or . . . I've always wanted to write
a play. What do you think, the death of Caesar recounted as a tragedy
for the stage? No Roman has ever written a really good tragedy, you
know. This might be the chance to do so. It would have to be a work of
the most elevated language, the most vivid insights, the sharpest irony.
But if I could achieve such a work, what more fitting memorial could
there be to a man who was both my friend and a true lover of poetry, a
lover of *my* poetry?"

The thought again struck me: *Already the idea of a world without Caesar was taking hold in men's minds. The new reality obliged every man to
think of his own good going forward.* An event that had shaken the whole
world might now serve to give Cinna material for a poem or a play.

"If anyone could do justice to such a subject, I'm sure it would be
you," I said.

Cinna nodded. "My thought, exactly!"

We arrived just as the bier carrying Caesar's body was departing from
the Regia. Calpurnia stood at the top of the steps, her face very pale amid
her black garments, surrounded by women all in black, all gazing down
at the bier. Among the men carrying it I saw Antony, wearing his consul's toga for the state occasion. If his fellow consul Dolabella was also
a bearer, he must have been on the other side, where I couldn't see him.
Upon the bier, the body of Caesar lay on an ivory couch, concealed beneath purple and gold coverlets so that only the shape of the body could
be perceived. Flowers and aromatic herbs were strewn around the couch,
to overcome the stench of putrefaction.

Preceding the bier were five actors, each dressed in one of the five triumphal togas worn by Caesar in recent years, with laurel wreaths on

their brows. Each actor wore a painted wax mask that had been molded on Caesar's living face. Turning this way and that so that all could see them, the actors skillfully reproduced Caesar's gait and oratorical gestures.

"Remarkable!" said Cinna. "Also a bit unnerving, as if Caesar is still alive—and there are five of him."

"Perhaps there *were* five Caesars," I mused. "He did seem capable of being in more than one place at a time. Uncanny, those masks. As if Caesar himself is looking at us. His expression—so thoughtful . . ."

"Thoughtful?" Cinna cocked his head. "I think Caesar must have been rather glum the day he sat for that wax mold. From some angles death looks like a fit of the sulks."

Along with the men in masks, a company of musicians played shrill funeral music that rose and fell like the loud chirring of a cicada, fitting accompaniment to the ululations of the wailing women all around. The music set my teeth on edge. It was not meant to be comforting.

The procession continued. I had already seen five Caesars. Now I saw another, so shocking it took my breath away. Upon a wagon pulled by men in black, an effigy of Caesar had been mounted on a pole. Like the masks worn by the actors, the head of the effigy was made of wax and looked eerily like the man himself, but on this mask wounds had been carved and stained red to reproduce the cuts inflicted on his face. The limbless torso of the effigy was clothed in the last garment Caesar had worn in life, his purple-and-gold toga. Stiff with dried blood and rent with many cuts, the hanging folds flapped fitfully in the breeze. The effigy was not motionless on the wagon, but by some mechanism, perhaps driven by the wheels, it turned slowly in a circle, so that all could see the wounded face and the full goriness of the toga. This rotation was smooth at times, almost graceful, and at other times jerky. The impression was of a corpse given life, unable to move as a living man would, but moving nonetheless. Many in the crowd gasped when they saw the effigy. Many wept. A few shrieked with terror, so strange and weirdly powerful was the sight.

The wagon with its effigy reminded me of something. Suddenly I realized what it was: the wooden idol of Bacchus I had seen in my garden during the practice for the Liberalia, which had rotated in just such a fashion. This must be the very same device, with the effigy of Caesar mounted upon it rather than the idol of Bacchus. In this novel and striking detail I perceived the hand of Fulvia.

Following the bier and wagon with the effigy were hundreds of senators in their togas. Taking part in this procession was not only a show of mourning and respect but also a declaration of loyalty. I saw none of Caesar's assassins among the senators. Nor did I see any of their supporters, like Cicero and the other Cinna. Many of those men were probably far from Rome on this day, safe at their country villas. Those in the city would have been wise to barricade themselves inside their houses.

Along with the senators were all the priests of the state religion and the Vestals, absent their leader, the Pontifex Maximus.

Then came the dead man's family and household, which included not only blood relations but also many of his slaves and freedmen, hundreds of stern-faced men and weeping women all garbed in black. After they passed, Cinna and I joined the general citizenry who followed the procession as it made its way past the crowded temple steps and altars and statues of the Forum.

At last the procession poured into the vast open area before the Rostra, the speaker's platform from which politicians harangued the crowd. Here the body would be placed in its temporary shrine while Antony spoke. From somewhere there appeared hundreds of armed soldiers, veterans of Caesar's campaigns who had flooded the city since his death. They formed a sort of honor guard around the body, banging their swords against their shields and shouting Caesar's name. Many openly wept.

With Antony as the chief bearer, the ivory couch with Caesar's body was carried up the steps at the back of the Rostra, then placed inside the golden shrine. Here a memorable illusion was created, as if on a stage. Temples are homes for gods, and many contain a gigantic statue of the deity. This miniature Temple of Venus was sized in such a way that the body of Caesar fit quite nicely inside—as if he were a deity no less than Venus, and the temple was his home as well as hers.

If this was a subtle prod to the imagination of the crowd, there followed a more obvious one. The wax effigy of Caesar was detached from the wagon and carried up the steps by two men dressed in black. The effigy was fitted onto a pole in front of the shrine, for all to see. Antony gazed at it in awe, as if seeing it for the first time. He reached out to touch the torn, blood-soaked garment, then drew back his trembling fingers as if appalled, even frightened—a large, theatrical gesture calculated to draw the attention of the multitude gazing at the bloody relic. He was rewarded with a cacophony of wailing and sobbing and a thunderous banging of swords on shields. Caesar himself seemed to be standing on the platform next to Antony, strangely mute and motionless, his waxen face impassive, his garments caked with blood.

Antony might be a fine orator, but he was no master of stage illusions. In the eerie presentation of Caesar's effigy on the platform, which made the dead man seem a spectator at his own funeral, again I saw the hand of Fulvia.

XLIII

Even before Antony began his speech, I felt uneasy.

Somehow, the four of us—Cinna and myself, with Davus and Cinna's bodyguard flanking us—had ended up in the middle of the crowd, surrounded by thousands of people on all sides. I would have preferred to be on the outskirts, with one eye on the speaker's platform and the other on the nearest route to safety.

"So many hoods," I murmured, looking around.

"What did you say?" asked Cinna.

"So many men wearing hoods. You can't properly see their faces."

"Perhaps they don't want to be seen weeping."

"Perhaps. But in my experience, in a crowd such as this, some men wear hoods so they won't be recognized, in case the opportunity arises to do a bit of mischief."

"This crowd seems to me more grief-stricken than angry."

"Yes," I said. "So far. As one senator to another, how would one go about introducing a law to ban the wearing of hoods in any public assembly?"

"Gordianus, surely you don't want to become one of those senators constantly thinking up new ways to curtail the liberties of the people."

"Such a law would free the people."

"From what?"

"From the fear of men in hoods who murder and rape with impunity."

Cinna rolled his eyes. "A hood is just a hood, Gordianus. Hoods don't kill people. Knives do."

"Or hooded men with knives."

"The men who killed Caesar weren't hooded, were they? They were proud to show their faces. They wanted us to see them, wanted everyone to see their bloody knives—remember how they held them up as they marched through the streets? They wanted Caesar himself to see their faces as they stabbed him, again and again." Cinna shuddered at the memory. "Well, Senator Gordianus, I shall look forward to debating the merits of your proposal to ban hoods in the Forum, when and if the Senate resumes normal business. But I think Antony is about to begin."

A hush fell on the crowd. All eyes turned to the speaker's platform.

Antony's speech has since become the stuff of legend. Like most legends, it has been imperfectly remembered and liberally embellished, and multiple versions exist. Often, when some particularly memorable phrase is uttered, someone remarks that it comes from Antony's eulogy. To presume that Antony delivered one sparkling epigram after another does his speech, and especially his performance, an injustice. It began as a very ordinary eulogy, but it turned into something quite different.

He established first and foremost his qualifications to deliver the dead man's eulogy. Antony was not a relative either by blood or by marriage. But he was Caesar's heir—as were we all, he said, every one of us who had gathered there in the Forum.

Antony held up a scroll that he said was Caesar's will—not a copy, but the document itself. He held it delicately and at arm's length, as if it were some sacred text, like a Sibylline Book. Gaius Octavius, he said, was named as Caesar's principal heir, along with Caesar's other two grandnephews, Lucius Pinarius and Quintus Pedius. To act as guardians of these heirs, and to be named as heirs in their stead if the principals could not for any reason inherit, were two of Caesar's most trusted and greatly esteemed friends, men whom he loved as sons or brothers—Antony himself, and one other. . . ."

Antony seemed to be choked with emotion, unable to speak.

"Who else?" people cried. "Who is the other?"

Antony turned his gaze from the crowd to the shrine in which lay Caesar's body. He seemed almost to be speaking to himself, but his trained orator's voice reached my ears clearly. "I find it hard to speak his name—considering what's happened. Certainly Caesar never foresaw . . . such a betrayal. . . ."

"Surely this isn't part of the written eulogy," said Cinna under his breath.

"A stage direction scribbled in the margin by Fulvia?" I suggested.

"His name," said Antony, "is Decimus Brutus. You all know him. You know of his service to Caesar, and Caesar's reward to him—the governorship of Gaul."

"Scandalous!" someone near me shouted. "The ingrate!"

"He should be stripped of his office!" shouted another.

"They should all be stripped of their offices, the men who killed him!" cried another. There were many other outbursts from the crowd.

Antony gestured for silence. "We are here to bury Caesar!" he reminded us. The crowd grew quiet, except for the sounds of weeping, which never ceased.

"Caesar's friend, Caesar's colleague, Caesar's heir—that is why I stand before you today, chosen not just by the Senate but also by Caesar's widow to say a few words of remembrance and admiration. And gratitude! No heir should ever forget to acknowledge gratitude, and as I said, we are all of us Caesar's heirs. In this will . . ." He again held the scroll up for all to see. "In this will, first of all, for the free enjoyment of every Roman and for generations to come, he bequeaths his justly famous gardens outside the city. All have heard of those gardens, but few have seen them. I know them well, and let me tell you, what Caesar created there is a man-made marvel worthy to be ranked with the Seven Wonders of the World, so perfect and tranquil and divinely inspired is that place.

In years to come, when you stroll with your loved ones amid those sweet-smelling flowers and magnificent statues, when you marvel at the views, each more breathtaking than the last, pause and remember the genius of the man who created such a place, and the generosity of the man who gave it to you."

Having seen the gardens, and having seen the Seven Wonders in my youth, it seemed to me that Antony was engaging in a bit of hyperbole.

"I wonder if Cleopatra is aware of this news?" said Cinna in my ear. "She's made herself so at home there, one might think she's taken up permanent residence."

"I suspect the queen will be out of Rome quite soon, if she hasn't departed already," I whispered back. With Caesar dead, what exactly was the status of Cleopatra, who occupied her throne thanks only to the judgment of Caesar? And what was the status of the son she claimed to be Caesar's? If there was any provision for either of them in the will, Antony did not reveal it.

Antony continued. "But as amazing as that gift may be, it pales beside another provision of the will. To every citizen of Rome, without exception—to those of you who loved him, to those who did not, it doesn't matter—Caesar leaves to each and every one of you the sum of three hundred sesterces."

This drew gasps from many in the crowd, including myself. Rumors had suggested that the populace would benefit from Caesar's will, but none had put the figure so high.

"So much?" I muttered.

Cinna raised an eyebrow. "His fortune was immense. As was his generosity."

The weeping grew even louder. "Beloved Caesar!" wailed some, and others, "Father of the Fatherland!"

Antony again motioned for quiet. "How could our inheritance, yours and mine, be so great? Consider his achievements—the lands he conquered, the gold and silver he brought back to Rome, the income from so many provinces and colonies, all accomplished for you and in your name, the Senate and the People of Rome. Father of the Fatherland you called him, and yes, like a father he provided for his family. For you new roads were built, reaching to every corner of the world. For you new temples were constructed, lavish houses for the gods, who in return lavish their blessings on Rome. For you were constructed whole new treasuries to contain all the wealth he brought back to this gods-loving, gods-beloved city. You made Caesar master of the legions. He made Rome master of the world."

Antony looked toward the shrine and the covered body. "And now . . . now he lies dead."

"Show us!" cried someone. "Show us the body!"

Antony stepped toward the shrine. For a moment I thought he intended to pull the couch from the shrine, yank the purple-and-gold cloth from the body, and lift Caesar in his arms, so that all could see the corpse itself. What effect would the sight have on the crowd? Instead he shook his head, then turned and raised his hand, palm toward us, as if to reject the pleading of the crowd. "The widow has asked that the body not be displayed, and we will respect her wishes."

He continued with a summation of Caesar's life. A family history and list of offices are typical of eulogies, but Caesar's biography was anything but typical. As Antony sped though the details, I was struck by just how extraordinary Caesar's life had been. Was he really descended from Venus, as Antony reminded us? Whether born with divine blood or not, Caesar had crisscrossed the world, from Britain to Egypt, from Spain to the Parthian borderland, overcoming every obstacle and conquering all that he encountered.

Antony spoke briefly of the civil war, though his descriptions of events did not quite match my own memories. "None but the Gauls had ever dared to march on Rome and conquer the city, many generations ago. It was Caesar who pacified the Gauls once and for all. Yet even while he was busily occupied in that virtuous endeavor, certain parties here in Rome made evil use of his absence and ventured on many odious schemes, so that we came desperately to long for his return. And so, abandoning fresh victories within his grasp—otherwise all of Britannia would be ours today—Caesar rushed to our assistance and quickly freed all Italy from the dangers that threatened. When he saw that Pompey, who had abandoned his country and was setting up a kingdom of his own, transferring all the wealth of Rome to Greece and Asia, using your own money against you, Caesar at first did his best to persuade Pompey to desist and to change course, sending mediators to him privately and publicly and offering solemn pledges of peace. When Pompey refused all entreaties and cut all ties with Rome, even the bond of friendship that existed between himself and Caesar, and chose to fight against you—then and only then, at last, was Caesar compelled to begin the civil war.

"But what need is there to remind you how daringly he sailed against Pompey in spite of the winter, or how boldly he assailed him, though Pompey held all the strong positions, or how bravely he vanquished him, though Pompey's troops, gathered from all Asia and Greece, were vastly greater in number? I saw! I was there that day in Pharsalia, fighting beside Caesar. With my own eyes I saw how great was Caesar's military genius. The Great One, Pompey called himself, but Pompey was shown to be a mere child, so completely was the great general outgeneraled at every point."

I thought this dig at Pompey might draw some ire from the crowd, but the people surrounding me appeared to be partisans of Caesar through and through. If there were supporters of Pompey or Cato among us, they made not a peep of protest.

He spoke of Caesar's virtues, which went far beyond his military genius: the keen intellect that allowed him to master every situation; the shrewd insight into other men's characters that made him such a natural leader; the piety that made him so eminently suited for the office of Pontifex Maximus; the generosity, of which the citizens of Rome on this day were but the latest recipients; and above all, Caesar's tendency to be merciful and to forgive.

"What other man, having achieved by military might the defeat of all his enemies, ever showed such clemency toward the defeated? Yet Caesar always showed mercy to those who opposed him. Even to Pompey he would have issued a pardon, had not the Egyptians killed him first. Think of the mercy he showed to so many men who joined with Pompey's cause and then, bested by Caesar, had every reason to think that Caesar would put them to death. But did he? No! Quite the opposite. He welcomed those men back to Rome with open arms. He gave them back their houses and their estates. He allowed them to return to the Senate. He even appointed them to high office. In return they took a solemn vow to keep him safe from all harm. If some were ungrateful, if some broke that vow, Caesar was not to blame, though you see before you the price he paid for their ingratitude."

"Miserable wretches!" cried someone, and another, "He should have chopped off their heads while he had the chance!"

Antony waved for silence. "Has any man in all of history ever been so great, not just in power but in spirit? Think of this remarkable fact, that in the case of virtually every man who ever achieved so much power, that power only served to reveal and foster his weaknesses. The more powerful such men became, the more selfish and petty and decadent. Yet in Caesar's case, the exact opposite was true. Every increase in his authority only served to increase his virtues. The more powerful he became, the more virtuous he grew, until, at the end, can anyone deny that he was by far the best among us? Warfare did not brutalize him. Good fortune did not corrupt him. Power did not pollute him. Those things only made him greater of spirit, wiser, more merciful, more just. What an extraordinary man! More than a man! Who can doubt his divinity?

"And yet—this Father of the Fatherland, this Pontifex Maximus, this inviolable being, this hero, this god . . . is dead. Dead! Not taken from us by disease, or wasted by old age, or brought low by witchcraft. Nor was he wounded in warfare, fighting on your behalf in some distant land. No, he died right here within the walls of this city, the place in all the world where he should have been safest. He is dead by violence, because of a plot against him. He was ambushed in the city he loved, murdered in the chambers of the Senate—the man who was building for us a far more splendid new Senate House at his own expense.

"The bravest warrior . . . died unarmed. The most beloved bringer of peace . . . died defenseless. The wisest of all judges . . . died because lesser men decided his fate.

"No enemy of Rome was ever able to bring him down, though his exploits gave them many a chance. Once I asked him what had been the closest of his many close scrapes with death. It was in Alexandria, he said, when in the midst of battle his ship sank in the harbor. Enemy ships converged on him. Spears and arrows and catapulted stones fell all around him. Dead men littered the water. The churning waves were red with blood, as red as his crimson cape, which he refused to abandon, though the weight of it dragged at him with every stroke and threatened to drown him. When at last he reached the shore, by some miracle still alive, any other man would have been shaken and exhausted, weeping with relief. What did Caesar do? Without missing a breath he resumed his command and carried the day for Rome.

"It was not the fate of Caesar to die in battle that day, nor ever to die in battle. As I say, no foreign enemy killed him, though many tried. He was killed by fellow citizens, by Romans, by comrades. Slain not by foes but by friends!"

Antony's words had so stirred the crowd that the sound of men shouting had become continuous, like the weeping that never stopped. It was a testament to his oratorical powers that I was still able to hear every word he said, even above the growing roar of the mob.

"Here he lies now, here in the Forum through which so many times he paraded in glorious triumph. Here lies his mute body on the platform from which so many times he spoke to you. Does it seem impossible that great Caesar is dead? I assure you he is, for I have seen with my own eyes the blank, lifeless eyes of his corpse. I have seen and counted the many cuts that scar his body—so many, so horrible to look at. . . ."

"Show us!" people cried. "Show us the body!"

"I cannot," said Antony. "The wishes of the widow must be respected. She doesn't want your last image of Caesar to be the mangled remains fit now only for the flames. Nor would Caesar want that. Look instead at the masks on those men who represent his triumphs, remember his serene countenance in life, imagine that he still lives and looks kindly upon you—"

The shouting grew louder. "No! Show us the body! Show us what the killers did to him!"

Antony seemed to hesitate, torn by indecision. Again I thought that he might step up to the golden shrine, yank away the cloth, lay hands on Caesar's torn and crumpled body, and hold it up for all to see. I held my breath, imagining the effect on the furious crowd.

Instead, Antony did something even more provocative. He laid aside the will, which he had been clutching all this time, using it to jab the air for emphasis. With both hands he took hold of the pole on which Caesar's effigy was mounted. He raised the effigy high in the air and strode from one end of the Rostra to the other, back and forth, turning the effigy to show all sides of it.

"I cannot show you the body," Antony shouted, "but I can show you the toga he wore on the last day of his life. Every place the fabric is torn and stained with blood marks the cut of a dagger that ripped his flesh. So many daggers! So much blood!"

The effect on the crowd was like a thunderbolt from heaven. The sound of weeping, wailing, moaning, screaming, shouting, and the banging of swords on shields was deafening. Never had I heard such a din. Antony continued to stride back and forth across the platform, holding up the effigy. His mouth moved, but I could no longer hear him. For one uncanny instant, the face of the effigy was turned in such a way that it seemed to look straight at me. The illusion of seeing Caesar again— reduced to nothing more than a head and torso, draped in bloody purple and gold—was so bizarre and so powerful that I felt disconnected from the moment, detached even from myself.

Cinna shouted in my ear. "This is even worse than I imagined. Much worse. We must get out of here at once!"

"Easier said than done," I muttered, coming to my senses and looking all around. The crowd had become a shouting, surging mob.

I saw the flicker of flames from the corner of my eye and looked at the speaker's platform. Men with torches had joined Antony on the Rostra.

"Burn him here!" I heard people shout. "Right here in the Forum! Burn him as Clodius was burned!"

Someone nearby shouted, "Burn down the houses of every assassin! Burn the killers! Set them on fire and watch them burn!"

His eyes wide with alarm, Davus clutched my arm to keep me from being swept away. Cinna clutched my other arm and hissed in my ear, "These fools will burn down the city!"

I looked again at the Rostra. Antony and the effigy on a pole had vanished. More men with torches appeared. Others set about removing the body of Caesar from the golden shrine. Was this what Antony intended? Fulvia had seen Clodius cremated in the midst of the Forum. Was Caesar to be burned there as well?

"There!" cried Davus. "I think I see a way out." He turned to Cinna's bodyguard. "The two of us together can clear a path."

The man nodded. The two of them stepped into a rift that had opened in the mob and elbowed their way forward. Like boys following their elders, Cinna and I clutched at their garments and did our best to keep up.

A tremor of fear swept over me. Death seemed very close.

XLIV

At every turn, voices screamed in my ears. Elbows and knees assaulted me. Faces made hideous by hatred and grief flashed by me, each more contorted and unnerving than the last, like an endless procession of hideous tragedy masks. These were interspersed with shadowy faces I couldn't see—more of those hooded figures that had alarmed me early on.

At some point I was struck by something larger and more unyielding than an elbow. I realized it was a piece of wooden furniture—a chair. Then another piece of furniture went by, a bookcase on its side with a single forlorn-looking scroll still clinging to its pigeonhole. I barely managed to dodge the massive piece. Had I been knocked down I would surely have been trampled.

"What in Hades?" shouted Cinna.

"Fuel for the fire!" I shouted back. "It was the same when they burned Clodius—the mob looted every building nearby for anything that would burn."

The men carrying furniture seemed to be heading in one direction, while we were heading in another. That seemed good. But when I looked around for a familiar landmark, I realized we were no nearer the outskirts of the Forum than we had been when we started. The mob seemed to have carried us in a circle. We were like leaves in a vortex.

"Where is Davus?" I shouted, realizing I had lost hold of his tunic. I couldn't see him ahead of us. "And your man, Cinna? Where are they?"

"I don't know! I can't see either of them!" His shout was close to a wail, verging on panic.

I smelled a wood fire, then heard a great roar that had to be the excited cry of the mob as the first flames leaped up. A makeshift funeral pyre had been built somewhere, perhaps quite nearby. Our goal now must be to head in any direction away from it. But where was it? I could see no flames, only smell the smoke. There were other scents as well—the flowers and aromatic herbs that had been part of Caesar's bier, now set aflame and smoking. How long would it be until we smelled his burning flesh?

More chairs and bookcases went by, as well as tables, cabinets, and curtains. Cinna and I both managed to dodge these moving obstacles, but not everyone was so lucky. More than once I stepped on flesh and heard a scream of pain, but there was no way to stop and help whatever poor mortal had fallen. The surge of the crowd was too strong.

"This way!" I shouted to Cinna, grabbing his arm.

I had spotted the round roof of the Temple of Vesta, as good a place to flee to as any other. We doggedly strove toward it and began to make progress as the crush of the crowd relented slightly. For the first time since the riot had started I felt able to breathe again. The air I desperately sucked in carried less smoke than before, though now I caught a whiff of something else, quite aromatic—the unmistakable scent produced by burning myrrh.

We had almost reached the Temple of Vesta. The crowd grew thinner. Every person we encountered was running in the opposite direction, toward the surging mob and the pyre. It seemed that only we two were attempting to flee.

I stopped to look behind us, hoping that Davus and Cinna's bodyguard had somehow managed to follow us, but I didn't see them. How dearly I longed to see my hulking son-in-law at that moment!

From nearby—from what direction I couldn't tell, for the surrounding walls of marble created strange echoes—a gruff, husky voice cried, "Cinna! It's him! Look, there he is! There is Cinna!"

Cinna also heard and glanced around. On his face I saw the insipid look of pleasure one sees so often on the faces of politicians and actors when they are recognized in public. He smiled as he continued to search for the speaker. "Can it be, even here, amid such frenzy—a poetry lover?" he said, and then more loudly, raising one hand in a friendly wave, "Yes, it is I, Cinna!"

I turned around again and now saw a hooded group approaching from the direction we had come. There were at least twenty of them, perhaps twice that many, perhaps even more—their dark cloaks and hoods made them blend together in a single faceless mass. Cinna, too, saw the group approaching and gave them a broad smile. I reached for his waving arm, thinking to hold him back, but he stepped away from me. Sensing danger, I reached for him again—and the next moment I was somehow on the hard, paved ground, and the world was spinning around me.

My head was struck a second time. The world grew dim.

I didn't lose consciousness entirely—so I later came to think. It seemed to me that I continued to see and hear what was happening around me, but imperfectly, and in flashes, as if the world was suddenly a dark place lit only by lightning, while a continuous peal of thunder muffled all other sounds. I could make no sense of what was happening. Time and space were all askew. I was stunned, frightened, and very confused.

Looking up from the ground, I saw Cinna nearby, then did not see him as he was surrounded by the figures in dark cloaks and hoods. My view of those figures was foreshortened, creating the strange illusion that it was children whom I saw all around us; the hooded figures seemed weirdly small. Could they really all be poetry lovers, mobbing Cinna as one sometimes sees theatergoers mob a famous actor?

Then I heard the same husky voice I had heard before, shouting, "It's him, all right! It's Cinna! The praetor who spoke ill of Caesar the other day and praised his killers! Tear him to pieces!"

Though I could no longer see him, I heard Cinna wailing, as if from some great distance, or as if he had fallen down a well: "No, no, no! You have the wrong man! I'm Cinna the poet, not Cinna the praetor! I make verses!"

Some old crone must have been among the rioters, for I heard a cackling voice cry out, "Tear him for his bad verses, then!"

No! I wanted to cry. *You have the wrong man! This is a horrible mistake! It's the* other *Cinna you're thinking of!* But as the dark world continued to swirl unsteadily about me, I found it impossible to speak. Then, for a moment or two, perhaps I did lose consciousness entirely, for the next thing I saw was something from a nightmare—the severed head of Cinna held aloft by a clawlike hand, dripping blood and gore from the torn neck. On my friend's face was a look of utter shock—his mouth gaped and his eyes were wide open, showing white all around the huge pupils. Then I saw something even more horrible—the lips of his mouth moved, as if trying to speak, and his eyes blinked, not once but several times in quick succession. What did Cinna see? What was he trying to say?

I heard screams—not from Cinna's killers but from other people who had stumbled on the scene and turned to flee in terror. *No, don't leave us!* I tried to cry out. *Come back! Come back! Help us, please!* But my numb, useless mouth made no more noise than the moving lips of Cinna.

Amid the swarm of dark cloaks I saw blood fly through the air—ribbons of blood, jets of blood in all directions. It seemed to me the sky had burst open and was raining blood.

The head of Cinna, still held aloft, was now joined by what appeared to be a severed hand, clutched by a gnarled, hardly human claw covered with blood. Then other parts of Cinna's body appeared, raised high in the air like trophies—another severed hand, something that looked like a forearm, a foot, a stump of flesh that might have been part of his leg, all awash with blood and gore, as were the hands that clutched them. When I saw his severed genitals held aloft, my mind reeled in disbelief. The horror of what I was seeing, the sheer savagery, could not be real. This had to be some hideous fantasy from my darkest nightmare, or some terrible vision conjured up by witchcraft. Or was I dying? Or already dead? Was this the world of the unliving, a place of horrors beyond imagining?

Now the swarming assailants abruptly seemed to grow even smaller—but this was another illusion. It was not they who dwindled but the head of Cinna that suddenly rose higher in the air, mounted above them on a spear. Up and down it bobbed, and from side to side, like some ghastly puppet looming above me. I thought of Caesar's effigy, held aloft for the crowd by Antony—but this was no semblance of the dead, it was the dead man himself. Looking up at his face, I shivered in disbelief. Could what I saw be true—that Cinna's lips still moved and his eyes still blinked?

I heard more screams, but not all were cries of terror. Some people seemed to be screaming in a frenzy of delight. I also heard laughter, and applause, as if the scene I witnessed came from some hilarious comedy.

"Cinna the praetor!" someone shouted. "They came upon Cinna the praetor and look what they've done! Ripped off his head and torn the bastard to pieces!"

"No more than he deserves!" shouted another man.

Out of this cacophony of taunts and shouts, I gradually perceived a chant taken up by the mob:

"I'm glad he's dead," Cinna said.
Now look what's left—Just his head!

Over and over they chanted this doggerel, as the head on a spear spun about and bobbed in time, facing one way and the other, then sped off in the direction we had come, back toward the funeral pyre. From the distant mob I heard rolling peals of laughter and screams as the head made its way toward the center of the Forum. Louder and louder, echoing off marble walls, I heard the chant:

"I'm glad he's dead," Cinna said.
Now look what's left—Just his head!

Thousands were chanting it. I pictured the funeral pyre with Caesar's blazing corpse amid the surging mass of angry mourners, and amid the throng the bobbing head of Cinna and the effigy of Caesar, like two puppets meant to amuse children at some mad festival of death.

How Cinna would have despised that vulgar ditty! How unthinkable that such vile doggerel should celebrate the death of Rome's greatest poet!

I somehow managed to get to my hands and knees. Nearby I saw the crumpled, tattered remains of the dark tunic Cinna had been wearing. It was completely soaked with blood, and blood was everywhere on the paving stones. His head, I knew, was gone—but where was the rest of him? There was nothing of his corpse to be seen. Except for the tunic and the blood, and a few bits of slime and gore, no trace of him remained.

"Father-in-law!"

Even amid so much horror I felt a flood of relief—as did my son-in-law, to judge from the tears that flowed down his cheeks as he ran toward me.

"Father-in-law, thank the gods I've found you! But are you wounded? All this blood—"

"No, not wounded," I said, feeling myself to make sure. "Thank the gods you're here, Davus. Cinna's bodyguard—is he with you?"

"No. Lost in the crowd. But where is Cinna? What's become of him?"

I looked around at the pools of blood. Helped by Davus, I staggered to my feet. "I don't know," I whispered. "I don't know!"

DAY TWELVE: MARCH 21

XLV

"This bump on your head is the size of a lemon!" declared Bethesda, dabbing it none too gently with a wet cloth. I winced. "And this other bump is twice that big."

After a restless night filled with terrible dreams, I sat in the garden and submitted to my wife's doctoring. The morning air was still and the sunlight quite warm. It would have been a beautiful day were it not for the pall hanging over us.

"You exaggerate, wife. They're no larger than a small olive, or an almond, perhaps. I've had worse bumps on my head."

"Struck in the head by gods know what, not once but twice! You are very lucky to be alive," she said.

"And not a gibbering idiot," my daughter added. "That can happen sometimes, from a blow to the head."

"I would say that you two are the lucky ones," I said. "Imagine having to bury me, with the city in such a foul temper. Or having to feed me porridge like a baby and wipe the drool from my chin."

Sitting nearby, Davus laughed. This drew sharp looks from both women.

"It's not funny," Diana said gravely. "You might *both* be dead, or horribly maimed. Where would Mother and I be then? Two defenseless women in a city gone mad?"

Something told me that my resourceful wife and daughter would manage without us, somehow. But Davus's smile faded and he hung his head. "I should never have lost sight of you. I still don't know how it happened. You were there behind me one moment, then something seemed to come at me from the side, and I almost fell, and the mob spun me around, and by the time I righted myself, the three of you were gone and I was alone. I should never have let that happen . . ."

"The amazing thing is that you managed to find me again," I said. "You have the perseverance of a hunting dog." *And are almost as smart,* I refrained from adding. "Diana, your husband pulled me to my feet and then practically carried me all the way home. He deserves only praise. I take all the blame for putting us both in danger. I should have known better. I *did* know better. I went only because . . ." *Because Cinna asked me to.* I shuddered. "I suppose . . ."

"Yes, husband?"

"I suppose I should go to his house today."

"To whose house?"

"The house of Cinna."

"I suppose you'll go nowhere at all!" she protested. "Who's to say the streets are any safer today than yesterday? Mobs wearing hoods and carrying daggers, and all those men with torches, set on arson. No, no, no! You'll stay in."

I shook my head. "As soon as you've finished washing my wounds, and I've had a bite to eat, I shall put on my toga. Cinna's toga, I should say. Senator Gordianus must pay a call on the grieving household of his dead friend."

"You can wait for his funeral."

"I think not. Cinna had no close relations, no siblings or even close cousins. So he told me. But he had a daughter. I met her. A visit from me is the least she deserves. I was with her father in his final moments. I was there when he died. I saw—I saw . . ."

What exactly had I seen? A swarm of hooded pygmies bring down a giant of poetry and carry off his head for a trophy? Had they carried off the rest as well, leaving no vestige of his corpse behind?

So jumbled and confused were my memories, I might have convinced myself that I had imagined it all, except that Davus, when I questioned him on the way home, revealed that he, too, had seen the head paraded on a spear, though he hadn't seen its face. He also heard the ditty chanted by the mob, though the words had seemed mere nonsense to him. What I had witnessed in dim flashes, reeling from the blows to my head, had actually taken place. Cinna had been beheaded and torn limb from limb. It happened so quickly. . . .

Bethesda shook her head. "Do you think it will comfort the poor girl to know that her father was beheaded? Perhaps she doesn't even know that he's dead. Perhaps she thinks he's only gone missing."

"All the more reason I must call on her. If she doesn't know what happened, she'll be sick with worry. And she shouldn't learn the details from some gossiping slave. Though I dread seeing the shock on her face if I'm the first to tell her . . ."

"Papa's right," Diana said quietly. "Cinna was his friend. He should do what he can to comfort Cinna's daughter. Perhaps we should go as well."

"Have you met the girl?" I asked. "At some gathering at Fulvia's, perhaps?"

"No," said Diana. Then she cocked her head. "Actually, we did see her once, didn't we, Mother? She was leaving Fulvia's house just as we were arriving. Fulvia seemed to know her quite well. But when the girl saw us, she became very quiet, and left very quickly, before Fulvia could introduce us. Such a shy thing, I thought. I asked Fulvia if the girl was a relative, and she said no. She told me the girl's name, which I remember only because it was so quaint. Imagine being called Sappho—and having Rome's most famous poet for a father!"

I shook my head. "If you've never met the girl, then I think you should stay at home. First, let me determine the situation at Cinna's house."

There was a black wreath on the door. I felt a flood of relief when I saw it. The wreath meant that his death was known already.

I felt an overwhelming sense of absurdity. First I had seen Caesar die, then Cinna. One death was comprehensible, the other incomprehensible. The murder of Caesar had resulted from a cold-blooded decision made by men for motives all too understandable—jealousy of his success, anger at his rule, fear of his wrath, desire for self-advancement, perhaps even ambition to take his place. The murder of Caesar did nothing to make me think the universe was meaningless. Quite the opposite: The death of Caesar was replete with meaning. But the killing of Cinna, a man of unique and surpassing talent—*by mistake,* for no reason whatsoever—was profoundly dispiriting. The death of Cinna epitomized a capricious, meaningless cosmos. . . .

Davus cleared his throat. "Father-in-law?"

How long had I been standing on the doorstep, staring at the black wreath? I knocked, then announced myself to an eye that peered from the peephole. My temples began to throb, and I reached up to touch the bandages Bethesda had wrapped around my head.

An unseen slave opened the door.

I was not entirely surprised to see Fulvia standing in the vestibule to greet me, suitably dressed in black. She and Antony had been friends of Cinna. With no mother to oversee the grieving of the household, Fulvia had taken responsibility. How busy she was, first with Caesar's funeral, and now with Cinna's.

"Gordianus," Fulvia said, taking my hand. "It's good of you to come."

"I thought, perhaps, I should say something . . . to Sappho. Is that smell—do I smell myrrh?" I suddenly had a powerful sense memory of the myrrh I had smelled the previous day, only moments before Cinna was killed. The smell of it now made me feel nauseated. I broke out in a cold sweat.

"Yes, I thought it proper to scent the house, though there's no actual need for it."

"No need?"

"To cloak any scent . . . from the body. Because there is no body."

"No body . . ." I suddenly realized that if any part of Cinna remained, it would be the head carried on a spear through the Forum. In such cases, when a corpse was intentionally defiled by a mob, it was traditional to throw the remains in the Tiber. Was that what had become of Cinna's head? Or was it still mounted on a spear in the Forum? Surely not. Or . . . was it here in the house, somehow retrieved by his friends or household slaves, the only thing left to display of the man's remains? Was it in the next room, placed on a bier for visitors to see? The thought was too grotesque to speak aloud, but Fulvia read my thoughts.

"No body . . . and no head. There's nothing of Cinna left. No remains to be cremated or buried."

"What became of him?" I asked.

"You were there, were you not? So I was told." As usual, her intelligence was far-reaching and correct.

"Yes."

"And what exactly did you witness?" Fulvia looked at me keenly.

"I was struck on the head. Twice. Thus the bandages."

She nodded. "So I presumed. Yet you're well enough to leave your house?"

"Yes. But what I saw yesterday . . . is a bit of a blur. And so ghastly I had rather forget. But . . . I did see his head, being carried off. Was it not . . . found later?"

"The head has vanished, along with the rest of him," said Fulvia. "Probably thrown into the Tiber."

I nodded. "How much does Sappho know?"

"She knows that her father died by violence, that he was beheaded, that there's nothing left of him to show."

"And the reason it happened? Because the mob mistook him for the *other* Cinna?"

"Yes. As you can imagine, she's quite distraught."

I nodded. "So you've come to help? That's good of you, Fulvia."

"My responsibility is a bit greater than that. I suppose you don't know—why should you?—that Sappho was Cinna's only heir, and that Antony is named as Sappho's guardian in her father's will. When Cinna asked, not long ago, if we would accept the responsibility, Antony and I of course agreed."

"Never realizing . . ."

"Who could have foreseen what happened to Cinna?"

"Only the gods," I said. "If indeed the gods see anything that happens on earth. Or care."

"You mustn't speak impiously, Gordianus. Especially in a grieving household. Here, step through, since you've come to pay your respects." She led Davus and me to the next room, where a funeral bier had been set up, complete with flowers and aromatic herbs. On the bier, where the corpse should have been, was the bloody tunic Cinna had been wearing when he died, flattened and laid out to suggest the form of the missing body. I drew a sharp breath.

"Surely his toga would be better, if there must be a garment to represent him."

"But this is what he was wearing when he died. Caesar's bloody toga was kept and shown to the mourners. Why not the same for Cinna?"

"Yes, I suppose . . ." Again I felt nauseated. I swayed on my feet.

"Are you unwell, Gordianus?"

"It will pass. The sight of so much blood . . ."

"On the day of the f-f-funeral, we shall burn it." This was said by Sappho as she stepped into the room. She wore a black gown with long sleeves and a cowl pulled back to form a plush collar. Her narrow face looked stark white against the black. "Since we have no body, this will have to do. On the f-f-funeral day, we shall burn it, here in the atrium, and the smoke will travel through the opening in the ceiling. If we had nothing to burn . . . how else could the f-f-funeral end?"

Except for her stutter, she sounded quite calm. He face was expressionless, but there were dark circles under her eyes and her cheeks were red and swollen.

"I tried to warn him," she went on. "But he insisted. It was the dream. . . ."

"A dream?"

"His dream of Caesar drove him from the house."

"Yes, he told me about it. Caesar insisted he come to a dinner party. . . ."

"And Caesar showed him the abyss. My father then felt compelled to go to Caesar's f-f-funeral . . . to join Caesar . . . in the abyss. That dream must have been sent to him by a god. Don't you think so, F-F-Fulvia?"

Fulvia stepped toward her and put a hand on the girl's shoulder, but Sappho shrugged it off.

"You were there, weren't you?" Sappho stared at me without blinking. "You saw? You heard? Is it true, what they say—that the crowd took up that awful chant? 'I'm glad he's dead, Cinna said. Now look what's left—just his head!'" She flashed a crazed smile and giggled, as people sometimes do in the most awful situations.

"Who told you that?" I was shocked that anyone had recited such filth to her.

"What more can *you* tell me, F-F-Finder? You must tell me everything."

I shook my head. "I think you know too much already, Sappho."

Suddenly, as if a mask had cracked and fallen away, I saw on her face a twisted expression almost too horrible to look at. She began to twitch and thrash. I stepped toward her, thinking to restrain her, but Fulvia waved me back, then threw her arms around the girl, holding her tightly.

"There, there, you poor grieving child!" cried Fulvia.

The old nursemaid appeared and joined Fulvia in restraining Sappho.

"Where were you, Polyxo?" cried Fulvia, sounding angry. "Why did you let her leave her room?"

"I dozed off—only for a moment," said Polyxo. "I was up all night, tending to her, comforting her. I fell asleep. I couldn't help it."

Fulvia slapped the old slave woman across the face. The noise seemed to shock Sappho, who suddenly became rigid, then shivered and began to weep.

"*Now*, Polyxo!" snapped Fulvia. "Take her to her room."

With one arm around the girl, clutching her tightly, the old nursemaid led Sappho away.

"You must excuse Sappho," said Fulvia, catching her breath. "She has a nervous disposition even at the best of times. She's been that way ever since her mother died, when Sappho was still a child. After all that's happened, she's totally distraught. Her grief has induced a kind of delirium."

"Perhaps reality is too awful to face," I said.

"Yes, that's it," agreed Fulvia. "And when reality is too terrible to bear, who knows what forces may be unleashed?"

XLVI

"I think perhaps those blows to my head did more damage than I realized," I said, gazing into the flickering flames of a brazier that needed stirring. I was standing in the garden, with only Diana nearby. The mild day had become a mild evening, with just enough of a nip in the air to merit a warming fire.

Diana approached and used an iron rod to stir the burning wood. The flames leaped higher. Glowing cinders flew and quickly faded.

"Are you serious, Papa?" She put down the iron and touched my forehead, searching for fever and tilting her head when she detected none.

"Perhaps befuddlement has become my natural state. Your father is an old man, after all."

"What are you talking about, Papa? What's troubling you?"

"I should have foreseen the death of Caesar."

"Oh, Papa! No one saw it coming. Not Meto, not Cicero—not Caesar himself."

"Spurinna did."

"Because he issued a vague warning with a month for it to play out? 'Beware' is hardly a prediction of murder."

"Beware," I whispered, thinking of the Greek word written at

Cinna's doorstep. A prediction of his murder? But how was that possible, since he was murdered by mistake?

"You're a wise and clever man, Papa, but you're not a seer, like Tiresias."

"No. More like Oedipus."

"If you wish. Oedipus was certainly clever, and famous for it, like you. He solved the riddle of the Sphinx."

"Yet he couldn't see the crime in front of his nose. He was blind to his own actions. What a horrid tale, that any man should kill the father he never knew and marry his own mother—and produce a family of fratricides!"

"Poems and plays are mostly horrid tales, Papa. Or hadn't you noticed?"

"Yes, but the incest of Oedipus with his mother . . ."

"Is in a category by itself, I suppose."

"Is it? Caesar wrote a tragedy in verse about Oedipus; did you know that? Cinna's famous poem was all about incest, too. Why do people crave such stories?"

"Perhaps they crave what they cannot have in reality."

"Do they?" I shook my head. "Nothing seems to make sense anymore. My head is filled with such horrors—Caesar stabbed to death in front of me, riots in the Forum, Cinna's horrible end . . . poems and plays about the most forbidden things imaginable . . . yet nothing connects with anything else. It's all loose ends."

"But you know that isn't true, Papa. You've always taught me otherwise. In the end, there are no loose ends. Everything connects."

"What if that's not true? What if there's no sense to anything?"

"Sleep on it, Papa. And pray not to have unpleasant dreams."

The brazier abruptly burned low and then emitted a last puff of smoke. It was time for bed.

I slept. I dreamed.

I was in a dim, formless place. I heard my father speaking to me. "It's best to die with your head on your shoulders, son. So the priests say. Otherwise it goes badly for you in Hades."

My father actually said such a thing to me when I was very small. I would later realize he was only half serious, teasing me, but the words made a lasting impression. For the rest of my life, whenever I saw a severed head—which was far too often, as when the dictator Sulla filled the Forum with the heads of his enemies displayed on pikes—I remembered those words.

In the dream, mists parted, and I found myself on a low spit of land with a muddy shore, beyond which a flat gray sea stretched to a featureless gray horizon. All was lit by a soft light too weak to cast shadows.

"These are the Shores of Ugliness," said a voice in my ear. I turned, but there was no one there.

A foul odor permeated the air. It was the smell of a slaughterhouse or a battlefield the day after. I choked at the stench of clotted blood and flesh beginning to rot.

I mounted a low dune, and from the top saw a vast plain before me with no living thing, not a single tree or blade of grass. But there was movement everywhere, and by the feeble light I perceived to the left a multitude of headless bodies, wandering endlessly and aimlessly, blindly bumping into one another. I looked to the right and saw what I took to be a field of cabbages. Then I realized that the cabbages were in fact heads. They stared upward with wide-open eyes, and their mouths moved constantly, shaping words with no breath to give them sound. I knew they were calling out to their bodies, but the heads had no way to speak, and the bodies no way to see or hear.

I heard a flapping of wings. Hovering above the endless mass of bodies and heads, I saw the three Furies: Alecto, Megaera, Tisiphone. They had snouts like dogs and bulging, bloodshot eyes that glowed like coals. Snakes writhed atop their heads. Their bodies were as black as coal, as were their leathery, batlike wings. Their gnarled hands and feet were like the black talons of some giant bird. Each clutched in her right hand a scourge with brass-studded strips of leather. Occasionally one of the sisters would swoop down and wield her scourge against the headless shoulders of a wandering body, making it grovel and writhe in pain. All three sisters would cackle with delight at the sight of such suffering. Then another would swoop down, snatch one of the heads with her feet, fly high in the air, wheeling like a vulture, then drop the head. All three would flap their wings and cackle as the head opened its mouth in a long, soundless scream and plunged to earth.

"This is the place in Hades where the beheaded dwell for eternity," said the unseen voice.

I shuddered, imagining such endless cruelty. "Is Cinna here?"

"He is."

"But why? What crime could be so horrible that he deserves such punishment?"

"You know."

"I don't."

"You do. You know, and yet you don't know. You see the truth, yet you look away."

"Where is he? Let me speak to him."

Some unseen force pushed me forward into the grotesque cabbage patch of heads. I lurched and stumbled, trying not to step on them. Then I saw the head of Cinna, staring up at me.

"Why are you here?" I asked. "Why did the Furies come for you and bring you to this place?"

His lips moved but made no sound. It was just as when I had seen him last, when his head was held aloft in the Forum. I remembered the fist that had clutched him by the hair—a gnarled, black, clawlike hand, covered with blood—the hand of a Fury? Had they been in the crowd, moving among us, guiding the savagery, delighting in it—even taking part? I reeled at the enormity of it. Had the Furies themselves ripped Cinna to pieces, then carried off his body, flying away with their batlike wings, clutching the various parts of Cinna with black talons? No wonder he had vanished without a trace!

Something changed—not the vague light or the shuffling sound of those aimlessly wandering bodies, but the smell. On the thick, still air I caught a whiff of burning myrrh. But the scent did nothing to relieve the slaughterhouse stench. If anything, it made the heavy air even harder to breathe.

I saw the misery deepen on Cinna's face. Tears streamed from his eyes. He wept without making a sound.

DAY THIRTEEN: MARCH 22

XLVII

"But this can't be right," I said, squinting at the scrap of parchment by the early morning light, as if the words might change if I looked at them hard enough. The messenger had arrived at the crack of dawn. I was already up, having awakened from my nightmare. The message was unsigned, but the slave had been sent by Fulvia.

I shook my head. "Cinna's funeral can't be today. There should be at least a few days of mourning. It's not decent."

"But if there's no body to be shown to visitors, why wait to have the funeral?" said Diana, yawning and stretching her arms. She was still dressed in a sleeping gown of pleated linen. The fabric was rather thin, especially when stretched across her breasts by her upraised arms. The resulting transparency no doubt pleased her husband but made her father a bit uncomfortable.

I stared at the message, which simply said that I should arrive at Cinna's house an hour before midday if I wished to be present at his funeral. "Fulvia was behind Caesar's funeral, and she's behind this one as well," I said.

"What of it, Papa? The two events aren't remotely similar. Tens of thousands of people wanted to attend Caesar's funeral. Veterans rushed to Rome from all over Italy. But for Cinna—well, famous as he may have been among poetry lovers, how many people would risk coming to the city now, with all the rioting, and to attend a funeral with no body and no proper funeral pyre?"

"Is it the corpse people come for, then, and the flames?"

"That means more than speeches to most people, yes: to see the body, and then watch it turn to ashes."

"Is that what a funeral is really about? To witness flesh become ash?"

Diana shrugged. "You can remember the dear departed at any time and in any place, and talk about him whenever and with whomever you wish. But only at a funeral can you see the purification of the mortal remains."

"Perhaps men and women have different ideas about funerals," I said quietly.

"Well, I think it's quite reasonable of Fulvia to have the funeral immediately, if only to put it in the past, for the sake of poor Sappho. If the girl is as fragile as you say, why subject her to day after day of mourning and visits from people she doesn't even know? 'Quickly done is best done.' Didn't some poet say that?"

"Ennius, I think."

"There, then—Fulvia is only taking her cue from a famous poet, and wouldn't Cinna approve?"

The ceremony was held in the room where the bier without a body had been set up. The bier was situated in such a way that a beam of midday sun shone through the skylight onto the blood-soaked tunic. The folds of cloth and clotted blood seemed almost to sparkle, as if the dark garment were strewn with tiny rubies. A small stone altar had been placed in the room as well, on which the tunic could be burned, its smoke escaping through the opening above.

The crowd was sparse, considering Cinna's fame. Perhaps Diana was right, that in the aftermath of Caesar's funeral few people would come to Cinna's funeral no matter how much notice was given or time allowed for travel.

Antony was there, looking grim in his consul's toga. His frown tightened to a wince from time to time. Perhaps he was hungover. It struck me that he was to some degree, at least indirectly, responsible for Cinna's death. His eulogy had provoked the mob's fury—with deadly results.

Fulvia was there, too. Her black gown was an elegant garment with jeweled belts below her breasts and around her midsection. The jewels were quite large and all in shades of red and purple—rubies, amethysts, carnelians. Had she worn the same gown to Caesar's funeral? I tried to remember. Surely she had been among the women who surrounded Calpurnia at the Regia, but I didn't recall seeing her. If she had been there, and had been wearing that dress, I would have noticed and remembered—or perhaps not, given all the distractions and confusion.

Meto stood beside me. This was the first time I had seen him since the day before Caesar's funeral. With Caesar gone, Meto seemed to have placed himself completely at Antony's disposal. He was Antony's man now.

Lepidus was there. With Caesar dead, could it be that he and Meto and I were the only mortals alive who had heard the whole of Cinna's *Orpheus and Pentheus*? But no, that was not correct. I had forgotten the presence of Decimus at that last supper, as if my mind wished to erase him from the scene, to expunge him from memory. How completely normal Decimus had seemed that night. Only hours later he would literally stab Caesar in the back.

My wife and daughter had come. Looking around the room, I saw many more women than men. I didn't recognize most of them. They abstained from hysterical weeping; not family, then. Wives of magistrates? Poetry lovers? From their ages, they looked more likely to be friends of Fulvia than of Sappho. Perhaps they were there simply to fill the room.

The fragrance was more pleasant than at most funerals. There was no decaying flesh to contribute its own odor to the room. I smelled only early spring flowers and hints of cinnamon and frankincense.

After the usual prayers and invocations, Antony stepped forward and cleared his throat. As Sappho's new protector and the guardian in charge of her inheritance, he explained, it fell to him to say a few words of greeting, and also to deliver the eulogy. "But rather than recite one date after another, and list the offices he held—such facts would merely make him sound like any other Roman of his time and class—I think it better to speak those words for which he will be eternally famous, remembered for all time to come." He cleared his throat again. A nearby slave pressed a scroll into his hand, and Antony commenced to read aloud the *Zmyrna* in its entirely.

From time to time he fumbled a word, and a few times he even lost his place—I was certain now he must be hungover—but all in all he gave a very powerful performance. Sappho seemed to think so. At several crucial points in the poem, including the suicide of King Cinyras, she burst into loud sobs. Fulvia and Polyxo each stood to one side of the girl and together strove to comfort her.

Perhaps uncharitably, I wondered if Antony's decision to read the poem was simply lazy, a way to avoid writing yet another eulogy on very short notice. Caesar's funeral must have already sapped his speechmaking faculty. From time to time as he recited, I looked at Fulvia, and from certain of her expressions I suspected it was she who suggested Antony would do better to read Cinna's poem than labor over a new speech.

Whatever the inspiration or reasoning, the few of us in attendance were granted a rare opportunity to hear a gifted orator recite a much-celebrated poem. The ringing tones of Antony's polished voice lent a particular beauty and grace to certain passages that I had not perceived before. By the end, when Zmyrna is transformed into a tree and her tears become myrrh, I, too, was in tears, and so was everyone else in the room.

So powerful was this word-image of the wretched Zmyrna that for a moment I actually smelled the myrrh, conjured up by Cinna's verses—an olfactory hallucination induced by poetry! Then I realized that the fire on the small altar had been lit, and someone had sprinkled myrrh on it at the precise moment of myrrh's appearance in the poem. Cinna had pulled the same trick when he read the final verses aloud to me. I smiled, remembering. But after an instant's pleasure, the scent induced another, quite opposite reaction: I shuddered and felt nauseated. Would I ever smell myrrh again, as I had smelled it just before Cinna's death, and not think of blood and beheading and dismemberment?

Squaring her shoulders and forcing back tears, Sappho strode forward and picked up the bloody tunic, cradling it across her forearm. She stepped to the pyre and spread the tunic on the flames. For a moment I thought the fabric might extinguish the fire and fill the room with smoke, but it caught fire and sent tongues of flames high in the air.

Sappho stared at the flames. Antony stepped beside her. In his hands he held the scroll from which he had been reading. When he laid the copy of the *Zmyrna* on the pyre atop the tunic, I let out a gasp, shocked that the poem we had just heard was to be incinerated before our eyes. Of course, there were many copies of the *Zmyrna* in the world, but even so, was it not a profane act to burn this copy? Then I grasped the symbolism: If Cinna's corpse could not be purified by fire, then let his *corpus* be burned. As the scroll caught fire, belched flames, and shriveled to ashes, the magnitude of our loss was driven home to all present.

Then the nursemaid stepped forward. In her wrinkled, bony hands Polyxo held another scroll. Again I gasped. Most scrolls look much alike, but this one I recognized by its unusually ornate dowels, carved from ivory with inlays of carnelian and caps of gold. I had seen such dowels only once before, at the dinner at the house of Lepidus, the night before Caesar died.

I turned to Meto and whispered, "Is that what I think it is?"

He frowned. "It looks like . . ."

"Cinna's copy of the *Orpheus and Pentheus,* yes?"

He nodded. "The one Cinna lent to Caesar, so that he could be the first to read it."

"Didn't Cinna tell Caesar it was the *only* copy?"

"Yes." Meto furrowed his brow. "Caesar spoke of the grave responsibility thrust upon him, being entrusted with something so precious . . . so rare. . . ."

And yet, with Antony and Sappho standing close by, Polyxo placed the scroll on the pyre, where it quickly caught fire.

In a matter of seconds, while I watched dumbstruck, the world's only copy of the *Orpheus and Pentheus* was reduced to ashes.

XLVIII

"Incinerated before our eyes—the work that Caesar called the greatest poem in the Latin language!"

"That's not exactly what Caesar said, Papa."

"Well, he said something close to that."

After the funeral, Meto had come home with Bethesda and Diana and me. The women had retired to their rooms. My son and I sat in the garden.

"What exactly did Antony tell you, Papa, as we were leaving the funeral?"

"I asked what document had been burned along with the *Zmyrna*, and he said, 'The other poem. The last one. *Orpheus and Pentheus.*'"

"And you asked him if it was the only copy?"

"Of course I did." The circumstances had been quite awkward. After the items on the pyre were consumed, and priests recited the usual prayers, the ashes were gathered and placed in a bronze urn, which was presented to Sappho. She held it as one might hold a serpent, at arm's length. In that urn, symbolically, was all that remained of her father—the tunic stained with his blood, the *Zmyrna*, and the *Orpheus and Pentheus*—never to be read or recited to another mortal.

"But why did Antony allow the Nubian nursemaid to burn it?"

"He said it was Sappho's wish. It was his judgment, as executor of Cinna's will, that Sappho had the right to do as she wished with her inheritance."

"But Antony is also the girl's guardian now," said Meto. "In the absence of a father or brother or husband, he's legally responsible for her. Sappho can't act on her own, not in a matter of such importance. She has to obey his directives. Isn't that the law?"

"You're right—up to a point. Women have no standing and no rights under Roman law. All legal issues concerning a woman are to be decided by the man responsible for her—in this case, now that Cinna is dead, and by Cinna's will, Antony. But the burning of a poem breaks no law that I know of."

"Antony still could have stopped her, and he should have!" said Meto. "If not Antony, then Fulvia. She seems to have a great deal of influence over the girl."

I shook my head. "I can hardly believe it myself. Caesar was the only man ever to read the poem from start to finish. And only a handful of us heard Cinna recite it. How long ago that night seems now. . . ."

"Sappho must know the poem. She must have heard her father reciting it, in bits and pieces, over all the years he worked on it."

"Yes. And even if she never heard or read the entire poem while Cinna lived, she had the opportunity to read that scroll in the hours after he died."

"Surely she did read it," said Meto.

"Unless to do so was too painful, evoking memories of her father. Whether she read it or not, it seems that she deliberately chose to burn it. Not just to burn it, but to erase it from existence."

"The foolish girl! Hysterical, grieving, not thinking straight!" Meto shook his head in disgust. I realized the poem had special significance for him because Caesar had loved it, and the recitation by Cinna had been something Meto shared with Caesar. Now the poem was gone, like so many hopes and dreams that died with Caesar.

"Might it be possible to reconstruct it from memory?" I wondered. "If those of us who heard it combined the bits we could recollect . . ."

"Impossible. Is your memory that exact, Papa? Mine isn't. Perhaps a few phrases linger in my memory, intact. At best, we'd come up with a mediocre patchwork, full of holes and errors—an insult to Cinna, not an homage. Caesar might have been able to recover it, or most of it, having read the poem and then heard it recited aloud. Caesar's memory was quite remarkable. But you and Lepidus and me? I don't count Decimus. I can hardly speak his name."

"Then the poem is gone. Truly gone, irretrievably and forever. Oh, Cinna! It should have been your monument."

No day is more exhausting than a funeral day. Something about it saps all the energy from a man. I went to bed that night thinking I would sleep straight through till dawn. Instead, in the middle of the night I awoke in a cold sweat, with a single word in my mind: *Beware.*

In a dream I had seen the word scratched in Greek in the sand before Cinna's door. Then a puff of wind blew it away. But the word reverberated in my waking mind.

Beware.

The word nagged at me, haunted me, would not be silenced. Who had written it, and why? What did it mean?

Cinna had made light of the incident, but he had been concerned enough to tell me about it. I had given little thought to the matter, even though he'd asked for my help. So much had intervened to distract me.

Was it possible that the word scratched in the sand had been a very real warning, linked somehow to Cinna's death? That would mean that Cinna's murder was *not* an accident—not a horrific, meaningless stroke of bad fortune, but deliberate, targeted, premeditated. There had been a plot, then—just as there had been a plot to murder Caesar, and equally secret. But someone who knew of that plot, perhaps was part of it, had tried, in a roundabout and feeble way, to warn Cinna, by scratching that word in the sand where he would be sure to see it. Feeble or not, the

warning prompted Cinna to ask for my advice—and for my help, for all
the good it did him. I had found his story mildly interesting, then forgot all about it in the hectic days that led up to Caesar's death. I had
done nothing to save him. Now the word wouldn't leave me alone.

Beware.

If in fact Cinna's murder had been the result of a plot, then the circumstances of his death had not been accidental. Someone who wanted
him dead had taken advantage of the violence and chaos surrounding
Caesar's funeral—and the widely known fact that twice already a mob
had wanted to kill the *other* Cinna—to make his death appear not
planned but spontaneous, not deliberate but accidental, a twisted and
tragic case of mistaken identity.

But no, something was wrong with that idea. If Cinna, *my* Cinna,
had been killed on purpose, because of some personal or political grudge,
then how could I account for the frenzy of the killers, who had not only
beheaded him but also torn him limb from limb, leaving nothing behind?
That was not the way hired assassins would have gone about it. Hired
killers would have dispatched him simply by slashing his throat or stabbing his heart, then run off as quickly as possible. They wouldn't have
dismembered him and absconded with the remains.

Nor did it seem likely that members of the mob, enraged at the sight
of a man thought to be the *other* Cinna, would have gone about killing
him in such a thoroughly gruesome fashion. Might it be that the way
Cinna was killed, rather than indicating a spontaneous action, indicated
the opposite, that the killing was completely premeditated? But why the
beheading? Why the dismemberment?

Lying awake at the middle of the night, I tried to remember exactly
what happened, precisely what I had seen—but my memories had become even more hazy and confused. Perhaps that was due to the blows
to my head, or perhaps the late hour. I could recall only fleeting impressions, bloody and horrific, hardly discernible from the sleeping nightmares into which I drifted by imperceptible degrees.

DAY FOURTEEN: MARCH 23

XLIX

The next morning, instead of sleeping late—as would have been my prerogative on my sixty-sixth birthday—I was up at dawn, having been awakened by a visit from Cinna.

In my dozy dream, as I was on the very brink of consciousness, Cinna had appeared before me, his head restored to his shoulders. When he opened his mouth, I heard him very clearly.

"You heard but heard not. You saw but saw not. You know but know not, because you wish not to know."

"What sort of rubbish is that? A poem? A riddle?" I asked—perhaps out loud, for abruptly I was wide awake.

I was not only awake, but trembling, seized by that unique sensation that comes only when one is exquisitely close to some monstrous truth. I tried to pin it down, but the impression slipped away from me; it was like trying to hold down a drop of quicksilver with a fingertip. It tantalized, that sensation of being so close but not quite knowing the truth about Cinna's death, being on the very verge of knowing, apprehending some hint of the truth but not the truth itself, like smelling food before eating it—no, not the smell of food, but another smell . . . the smell of *myrrh*. . . .

When had I last smelled myrrh? At the funeral, of course . . . and in a dream . . . and at the house of Cinna when I called on Sappho. But before that, when had I last smelled it?

It was at the scene of the murder. While all the other details had become muddled in my memory, that smell remained vivid—so vivid that in recalling it I seemed to relive the very moment. Suddenly, I realized where the smell had come from. It was not from Caesar's funeral pyre, which was quite distant, but from somewhere much closer. And it was not the smoke itself I smelled but the scent of myrrh secondhand, as if from garments permeated with the odor—from *clothing*. The smell had grown stronger, not fainter, as bystanders fled and the killers went about their butchery. Had it come from the clothing of the killers, then? Yes, because as they surrounded me and pressed closer together, the smell of myrrh became even stronger, almost overwhelming—and when they departed, the smell faded. . . .

Bothering to put on only a simple tunic—I had no time for a toga—I roused Davus and made him quickly dress, then herded him as a dog herds an ox through the house and out the front door.

"Where are we going?" he murmured, wiping sleep from his eyes.

"To the house of Cinna. Keep up!" I yelled, for I felt compelled to walk very fast.

Even before I knocked on the front door, above my own panting breath I heard the keening wail from within. I kept knocking until a slave opened the door, then pushed the slave aside and ran inside. In the room with the skylight, where the funeral had taken place, Polyxo, racked with sobs, lay prostrate on the floor.

I had come to confront Cinna's daughter, but that would never happen. From a rope with a noose tied to the ceiling hung the lifeless body of Sappho. Directly below her on the floor was the urn that held the ashes of her father's poems. Behind me, Davus gasped at the sight.

You saw but saw not.

What exactly had I seen when he was killed? I had seen a clawlike hand holding Cinna's head by the hair—quite literally a claw, as I later imagined, the claw of a Fury. But it was no Fury holding Cinna's head, nor any other divine or supernatural being. It was the hand of an ordinary mortal woman—gnarled and bony and wrinkled, to be sure, and as black as the talons of a Fury: the hand of Polyxo, the same hand that yesterday I had seen place the scroll of *Orpheus and Pentheus* on the funeral pyre.

The nursemaid looked up and saw me. Her face was twisted with grief, the ebony skin as gnarled and wrinkled as her hands. "I woke and found her . . . like this!" she wailed. "She must have done it . . . in the middle of the night . . . in that still hour . . . when the flame of the spirit burns low. Oh, my Sappho!"

I shivered. Had it happened at the very moment I woke in a cold sweat? Was that the instant of Sappho's death?

"Was this her first attempt?" I asked. Unlike the thoughts raging in my head, the words I spoke were quite muted and calm.

"No. Three times before this she tried to do it. Always I stopped her. I feared, even now, even with him gone, she might try again. But last night I was so weary. . . . Oh, Sappho!"

"You couldn't watch her every hour of the day and night. You're not to blame—not for this death, anyway. Was it your idea to kill Cinna?"

Polyxo stiffened and swallowed her sobs. "No! It wasn't I who thought of such a thing."

"Who, then?"

"Sappho. It was she who first thought of doing it."

"But you approved."

"I told her it would be proper and just. I said to her, 'Instead of killing yourself, dear child, kill the one who made you.'"

"And yet . . . it was Sappho who scratched that word in the sand, the Greek word for 'beware.' It must have been her. You didn't write it. You know no Greek."

"Yes, it was Sappho. In a moment of weakness . . . she wrote that warning. Perhaps she thought he would take heed . . . and stop. But he didn't."

I felt a chill. "You mean, he was still . . ."

"Yes! Right to the end."

"I thought perhaps it was all in the past."

"Oh, no. It never stopped."

I gazed at the girl's lifeless body, swaying slightly despite the stillness of the room. "She wanted her father to die—horribly—but still she warned him. . . ."

"Because the poor child was split in two, don't you see? Body and soul, torn in two—never whole. The master did that to her. A girl raped by her father can never be of one mind again. She would always love him, always want his love in return—and at the same time fear him, hate him. Even, sometimes, I think she desired him—as a wife desires a husband. As if they had truly become husband and wife. But she was his daughter, not his wife! Oh, how she hated him. But she despised herself even more. She wanted to die. She wanted *him* to die—but she wanted to save him. . . ."

"The poor girl," I whispered.

Polyxo gazed up at Sappho's body. She clutched the girl's dangling ankles and sobbed.

"It was your hand I saw, Polyxo, holding up his head."

"Yes!"

"And before that, it was your voice I heard. 'Tear him for his bad verses, then!'"

"Yes."

"I thought those words were a slur against Cinna's poetry—careless, hateful words spoken by some know-nothing. But you meant exactly what you said. You meant that his verses were bad, *truly* bad—"

"Wicked! Impious! Evil! To write about such a thing, to dote on it, to lavish on it so much loving care—and then to *do* it, not once but many, many times. Yes, it was I who said those words about his verses—and it was I who tore off the hand that wrote them!"

Nausea clutched my throat. I swallowed hard. "There was another voice. The one I heard first, that said, 'Look, there he is,' pointing Cinna out to the killers. That wasn't your voice. It was a hoarse, husky voice. Like scratchy wool upon the ear—no, more pleasing than that. Like raw silk. A disguised voice, pitched deliberately low, so as to pass for a man voice. It certainly fooled me."

"But you know now, don't you? You're clever." Polyxo flashed a bitter smile. "She's clever, too, that one. As clever as you. As clever as any man!"

"Maybe too clever. Does she know, yet, about Sappho's death?"

"No. No one knows outside this house."

"Let me go to her, then. Let me be the one to tell her what's happened—what all your secrecy and plotting and bloodshed have finally accomplished."

With Davus beside me, I descended the Aventine and headed for the Esquiline Hill, until at last we came to the House of the Beaks.

In the forecourt outside the front door, a litter was departing. The occupant gave some signal to the bearers, for just as I was passing the litter it came to a halt. It was quite plain, with nothing to distinguish it: closed gray curtains, simple poles, no insignia.

The curtains were parted by a delicate hand adorned with exquisite rings and bracelets, all of gold and set with fiery rubies that glinted by the light of the rising sun.

"Good morning to you, Gordianus-called-Finder."

I stopped and peered though the narrow opening in the curtains. I caught a glimpse of one eye peering back at me. "Is that you, Queen Cleopatra?"

She gave a throaty laugh. "You sound surprised to see me."

"I would have thought the queen of Egypt would be seen in a more conspicuous vehicle, one worthy of your divinity."

"Not in this town. Not at this time."

"You're out and about very early in the day."

"I had some business with your consul Antony . . . some final business . . . before I leave this place for good. It was an amicable parting."

"I'm rather surprised that you're still in Rome."

"It takes time to decamp a royal embassy, even in the wake of . . . such a catastrophe." There was a catch in her voice. "I'll be gone within

...sed litter will be loaded onto a barge on the Tiber. The
...ne to Ostia. From there a ship will take me back to Egypt.
...hat yours should be the last face I look upon in Rome."

...of the queen's strange and twisting destiny. If Caesar had
lived, and...Cinna had successfully proposed the legislation allowing him
foreign wives, Caesar's first act in Egypt might very well have been to
marry Cleopatra and legitimize Caesarion as his heir, at least in Egypt,
where Caesar would have become the legitimate king, not by conquest
but by marriage. All that was impossible now, but Caesarion's legitimacy
might yet be affirmed. "This amicable meeting with Antony—may I take
it that Rome has a royal prince now?"

"Don't taunt me, Gordianus-called-Finder. No, my son is not yet
officially Caesar's heir, at least not here in Rome. But who knows what
the future holds?"

A thought struck me. "The Dictator gave you many gifts. . . ."

"Caesar and I often exchanged gifts, yes."

"Perhaps he gave you books, for that famous library of yours."

"Certainly. He was very generous in that regard. He wished for the
Library of Alexandria to possess all the best that the Latin language has
produced."

"Including poetry?"

"Oh, yes."

"Are you familiar with the poet Cinna?"

"Of course. He was Caesar's friend."

"You know the *Zmyrna*?"

"I do. A charming work. Caesar gave me a copy. I knew he loved it,
so I read it with great interest. I suspect the Library already has a copy
or two, but I shall take the copy he gave me back to Alexandria . . . as a
memento." She stopped speaking for a moment, choked by emotion. "Of
course, no Latin poem can ever match the best of Greek poetry, but Caesar thought it a masterpiece."

"What did you think of the subject matter? The incest, I mean."
Cleopatra's family was notorious for marriages between royal siblings.
She herself had been married to one younger brother, killed in the civil

war between them, and was now married to an even younger brother, on whose longevity I would not care to wager. But as far as I knew, the Ptolemies never sanctioned marriage between parent and child.

"The poem was merely true to the legend," she said.

I nodded. "I don't suppose . . ." My heart beat faster. Was it possible? "I don't suppose that Caesar gave you a copy of *another* poem by Cinna, a new poem, about Orpheus and Pentheus?"

There was a pause that stretched until I found it almost intolerable.

"No," she finally said. "He did mention such a work—something the poet was still working on, or perhaps had just finished? But no, I never saw a copy."

"Ah, well. Safe travels, Queen of Egypt, to you and your son."

"And may your dealings be safe as well, Gordianus-called-Finder, if you choose to remain in this nest of vipers."

The bejeweled hand withdrew. The curtains fell shut. The litter began to move again. That was the last that I, or anyone else, was ever to see of Cleopatra in the city of Rome.

L

Before I could knock, the front door of the House of the Beaks opened for me. I had been observed talking to Cleopatra in the forecourt and recognized. Antony, informed of my visit, had instructed a slave to admit me at once.

I told Davus to wait for me in the vestibule. The slave led me down quiet hallways. I heard the hushed murmurs and soft footfalls of numerous slaves going about their early morning chores.

Antony greeted me in a reception room off the garden. He was casually dressed in a green linen gown, a garment I would have thought more suitable for sleeping or lying about the house than for receiving the queen of Egypt. A bit incongruous was the elaborate silver pectoral he was wearing, a massive thing with jewel inlays depicting a hawk with outspread wings, clearly of Egyptian design.

He saw me staring at it. "Do you like it?" he asked. "A parting gift from Queen Cleopatra. A bit gaudy, perhaps?"

"Quite beautiful, I would say."

"Yes, well, I can't imagine where or on what occasion I could possibly wear such a thing here in Rome. Perhaps in one of the Asian provinces, at some informal gathering not requiring a toga or military dress." Stroking the gleaming silver with a forefinger, he seemed to ponder this idea rather fondly. Did he dream of taking up Caesar's ambition to invade Parthia? "Ah, well, gaudy or not, it's certainly quite valuable."

"A precious gift," I agreed. "The queen must greatly esteem you."

"What Cleopatra esteems is the future friendship of Rome," said Antony with a laugh. "Although . . . well, don't tell my wife I said so, but she's quite a charmer, isn't she?"

"Caesar thought so."

"But you don't? Ah, Finder, always immune to bad influences. But no, I mustn't call you that anymore. Senator Gordianus, I should say."

"If indeed I *am* a senator. . . ."

"Ah, yes, I understand your concern, given . . . how the day of your induction was interrupted." He took a deep breath. "Have no fear, you are as certainly a senator of Rome as I am consul. That's the deal we've struck with . . . the others. All Caesar's appointments must be respected—*all* of them. That includes your appointment to the Senate. I specifically made sure of that, as a favor to Meto."

And to ensure Meto's allegiance to you, I thought. *And my allegiance, as well?* "Thank you, Consul."

"You are most welcome, Senator."

"May I ask you a question, then, as senator to consul?"

"Certainly."

"The funeral oration—was there more than one version?"

Antony gave me the thinnest of smiles. "Astute of you, Senator, to perceive the situation. Yes, ahead of time we considered various scenarios for how the day might play out. Had the crowd been unexpectedly hostile to Caesar, we had a very short and very bland eulogy prepared. If the crowd proved to be . . . volatile . . . we planned for that eventuality as well. And that was how things turned out. Rather more volatile than I expected, in fact. So yes, we prepared more than one version of the speech."

"We?"

"Did I say 'we'?"

"Several times."

"A terrible habit. One should never refer to oneself in the plural."

"I thought perhaps the 'we' included the consul's wife, as his collaborator."

Antony narrowed his eyes. "Nothing slips past you, does it? No wonder Cicero speaks ill of you behind your back, and that you tried even Caesar's patience. I'll only say this: No consul could ask for a better helpmate than my wife. Her contributions to the funeral day were incalculable."

"Yet I didn't see her among the grieving women with Calpurnia. I didn't see her at all."

"No? Well, I hardly saw her that day myself. We were both very busy."

"I was most certainly present at the funeral of Caesar," said Fulvia, who seemed to have appeared from nowhere, as if my words had conjured her. Antony seemed as startled as I was. He frowned for a moment, then gave her a crooked grin.

"Well, Senator Gordianus," he said, "have I assured you of your status? Was that the business you had with me this morning?"

"No. Actually, it was the consul's wife I came to see."

"Oh, yes?" He gave me a quizzical look. "Well, here she is. Are you receiving visitors, wife?"

"No." Like Antony, Fulvia was dressed in a sleeping gown that immodestly left her arms uncovered. "But I'll make an exception for the Finder."

"We must call him 'Senator' now, my love."

She slowly nodded. She studied my face, and frowned. "Is this a delicate matter, Senator?"

I took a deep breath. "Very much so."

"Husband, would you . . . ?"

Antony took his wife's unspoken hint and stepped toward the door. Was he always so obliging to her wishes?

"And Antony, do take off that hideous thing. The fewer people who see it, the better."

Antony lifted the silver pectoral over his head with a sigh as he stepped out of the room, leaving us alone.

Fulvia looked at me steadily, not saying a word, forcing me to speak first.

"When Caesar died . . ." I said quietly. "When I saw him killed before my eyes, it was a horrible thing. A terrible shock. Almost . . . unthinkable. And yet . . . who among us was truly surprised? Only a few days have passed, yet now it seems almost as if his death was preordained. Inevitable. Certainly understandable. And then, I saw Cinna die. . . ."

"Did you actually *see* it happen?" she said sharply.

"Not exactly. I was struck on the head, twice. As I told you the other day."

She nodded.

"However jumbled my senses, what I witnessed that day was even more horrible than what I saw when Caesar died. Cinna was quite literally ripped apart, his head and his limbs torn from his body. Killed as Orpheus was killed, and Pentheus. But why? People say he was mistaken for the other Cinna. Ripped to pieces by mistake! Killed for no reason, his body defiled, his head displayed on a pole. It was incomprehensible. Caesar's death at least made sense. But to be so gruesomely murdered by mistake—except, of course, that it *wasn't* a mistake. Cinna was deliberately killed. There *was* a reason."

Fulvia stared at me, her eyes fixed on mine. At last she spoke. "Father Liber commanded it."

"No, Fulvia. *You* commanded it."

"As a priestess of Father Liber, yes."

For a long moment I was speechless. I hadn't really expected her to admit her guilt. Now that she had, I hesitated to pursue the questions in my head, dreading the answers. "Whom did you command? And why? And what did you do with Cinna's body?"

Fulvia crossed her arms and raised her chin, looking as formidable as any man, so imposing that I took a step backward.

"Which question should I answer first?" she said quietly. "I really shouldn't tell you who was involved. Now that you're a senator, you might actually be able to make trouble for us. But I think you won't, once you know the truth. Very well, then. Do you remember the women who attended the funeral yesterday?"

"I saw them. I didn't recognize them."

"Good. Because those women were the vessels for the divine wrath that destroyed Cinna."

"Women? You're telling me it was *women* who tore Cinna limb from limb? That's not possible."

"No? You think that mere, weak women could never be strong enough? Clearly, Gordianus, you do not comprehend the Bacchic frenzy. Inspired by Dionysus, Father Liber, Bacchus—the god of countless names—and with just a touch of witchcraft, even mere women can exceed your wildest imaginings."

"Witchcraft?" I drew a sharp breath.

"There is a point at which a mortal woman can become a Maenad—not merely *like* a Maenad—a moment of metamorphosis. Certain spells must be cast. Polyxo is a very skillful witch."

"The Nubian nursemaid? Are you telling me Polyxo can transform mortal women into Maenads?"

"With the god's help. Maenads. Bacchantes. Vessels of the righteous anger of Dionysus. Daughters of Father Liber."

"I had thought . . . I dreamed . . . of the Furies—"

"It had nothing to do with the Furies!" Her eyes flashed. "Only Dionysus."

"But you were there to lead them. It *was* your voice I heard, wasn't it? Cinna heard it, too—a voice that called out his name, pointing him out to the others. A gruff, husky voice . . . like raw silk upon the ear . . ."

"Like this, you mean? 'Cinna! Look, there he is! There is Cinna!'" She reproduced the voice exactly as I had heard it that day. Hackles rose on the back of my neck. The voice seemed to come from somewhere outside her body. The effect was uncanny.

I was taken back to that moment: I heard the roar of the crowd, saw Cinna smiling beside me, smelled the first hint of myrrh. "Cinna thought he had been recognized by some lover of his poetry, excited by the sight of him."

"Lover of his poetry? Hardly that!" Her laughter was harsh and cruel.

"Sappho—was she among the women?"

"No. From the beginning, it was decided that she should not be present or take part. There was to be no blood on her hands."

"But she knew, beforehand?"

"Yes, of course. It was done for her sake."

"And yet, she tried to warn her father. . . ."

"Yes, in a moment of doubt, of weakness, Sappho wrote that word in the sand. Poor, sad thing. Was the word a warning or a threat? Did she intend to save her father, or cause him dread? Whatever she was thinking, when I heard about it from Polyxo I told her to stop. I wasn't about to see Cinna wriggle out of his punishment, now that the moment had finally come."

I shook my head. The word "beware" in Greek had been used to warn Cinna. The same word had been used by Artemidorus, in the note I had passed into Caesar's hand. Neither warning had been heeded. And they had nothing to do with each other.

"The moment had come, you say. Why *that* moment? Why *that* day for Cinna's death?"

"We bided our time, thinking to do it after Caesar left for Parthia. With Antony running the city, I'd have a free hand. But then I learned that Caesar intended that Cinna would go with him, so it had to be done quickly, before they departed—"

"Just as Caesar's killers had to act by the Ides of March," I said.

"Yes. First I chose the Liberalia, knowing that the power of Father Liber and the witchcraft of Polyxo would be particularly potent that day."

"Polyxo!" I said, struck by the bitter irony of her name. The Polyxo of legend had helped his daughter to save the king of Lemnos, when the women killed every man on the island. This Polyxo had done the opposite. And to think, it was Cinna himself who gave her the name. . . .

"The Liberalia, you say. But you didn't act then."

"No. After Caesar was murdered, and the other Cinna made himself a target for the anger of the mob—not once but twice, the fool!—it struck me that the funeral day would provide the most opportune moment. Emotions running wild, passions unchecked. Amid the frenzy of the crowd, the frenzy of the Maenads could go unnoticed, especially if we cloaked ourselves and went about our business in silence."

"And the confusion of one Cinna with the other would divert any suspicion about the poet's death."

"Exactly. A horrible accident, people would say. The brainless mob mistook one Cinna for the other."

"You think like a man," I said. It was not a compliment.

"To control men, one must be able to think like one."

"And this was all done because Sappho told you that Cinna . . . she claimed that he . . ."

"*Claimed?* Is that why you're here, Finder, because you think your drinking companion was falsely accused? You imagine his poor, half-mad daughter concocted such a story?"

"What proof did you have that Cinna did such a thing? If it was only Sappho's word—"

"Cinna's own words convicted him."

"Do you mean the *Zmyrna*? It's only a poem, Fulvia. A fantasy, based on ancient legend. Cinna didn't invent the story. Yes, it obviously fascinated him—"

"I don't mean that odious poem. As I said, his guilt was proved by his own words."

"You confronted him?"

"I had no need to." She crossed the room and took a small box from a shelf. From a silver chain around her neck she produced the key required to unlock it. From the box she pulled a small, rolled parchment.

"What is that?" I asked.

"A bit of writing by Cinna that we did *not* burn on his funeral pyre. See for yourself." She thrust it into my hand.

LI

I unrolled the parchment. It was a letter addressed to "My darling Sappho" from "Your loving father."

There were other words, but my eyes seemed of their own volition to land on the most pertinent. The handwriting was unmistakably Cinna's.

Obviously you've enjoyed it, from the very first time. Any child would. I think you invited it. Yet you waste your time (and your art) doting on some imaginary wound I inflicted on you. (Show me no more hand-wringing poems on this topic, I implore you!) Leave behind this invented guilt and face the truth, that the act gives pleasure to us both; that it means everything or nothing, whichever you choose.

I let out a gasp. "But why would he write such a thing?"

"Sappho and her father exchanged a great many letters over the years. Can you imagine? Living in the same house but writing long letters back and forth? It was a queer relationship in every way. I could show you letters with passages even more explicit. But that one gives you a rather good sense of the man, I think—of his absurd self-justification. He actually believed that his daughter invited his attentions, wanted them, craved them. In his mind, it was *she* who seduced *him*—just as in that vile poem!"

"King Cinyras was famously handsome," I said quietly. "Almost divinely so. Irresistible . . . even to his own daughter—"

"As Cinna believed himself to be." She saw me shake my head. "Oh, yes! In some letters he even makes a play on the similarity of their names, Cinyras and Cinna. As if they were one and the same."

"Yet he named his daughter Sappho, not Zmyrna."

"Yes, named her Sappho—and then mocked her poems. That's in the letters, as well. We have some of her letters, but none of her poems, because she burned each one after it earned his scorn. Yet she kept writing new ones. How desperately she wanted to please that revolting man, in any way she could."

"She would never have killed Cinna herself," I said.

"No. Nor would any man ever have seen to his punishment. He broke no law. Within his own home, the supremacy of a father's will is beyond question. Other men might detest his behavior, but no statute forbids it. So it fell to us, to the women, to do what had to be done—with the help of Father Liber."

"The poem was his fantasy," I whispered. "If only the fantasy had been enough for him! He had to make it reality. At such a cost!"

"Like Caesar," said Fulvia.

"What? How, like Caesar?"

"Cinna had a fantasy of rape and power. He made it real, and ruined his daughter's life—and his own, in the end. Caesar, too, had fantasies of rape and power—the rape of whole cities, whole nations; the power to rule over every other man on earth, to the end of his days, and to do so seated on a golden throne! Well, he got his wish, didn't he? Would that such a fantasy had stayed in his imagination! Instead, he made it real, at the cost of hundreds of thousands, perhaps millions, of deaths—not just those in combat, but all the multitudes of women and children who died from starvation and pestilence and the cruelties of enslavement. Caesar was the progenitor of countless crimes."

"And your Antony—how is he any different? Will he not follow Caesar's example, if he can? Does he, too, desire a golden throne?"

She flashed a bitter smile. "Yes, all men are the same. But some are more useful than others. Cinna or Caesar: Which man's fantasy would you have put a stop to, if you could?"

"The question is unfair. Why not imagine a world in which men never have such fantasies?"

"Yes, that might be a better world. Or better still, a world without people in it. Without gods, as well. Or even animals. Only stone and water and sunshine and air. A perfect world without suffering or cruelty or death, unchanging, stretching on for all eternity."

"But we don't live in such a world, Fulvia. We live in a world that teems with life of every sort, with every man and beast in desperate competition with every other, sometimes even with the gods."

"So we must simply put up with men like Caesar, or my Antony—or try to harness them for our own uses. But we need *not* put up with men like Cinna."

For a long moment, I was lost in thought. Fulvia, too, was silent.

I cleared my throat. "I know now who killed Cinna, and why . . . but not how, exactly, or what became of him."

"Are you sure you want to know?"

"Yes."

She stepped away from me and slowly paced the room. "We always planned to behead him, and to tear off certain parts of his anatomy, those parts which had offended all decency—the hand that wrote the words, the vile genitals that committed the outrage. As Maenads, we knew we could rely on the unwavering power of Dionysus to give us the necessary strength. To inspire us further, we burned myrrh to infuse our clothing with the scent—myrrh in honor not of any man or poem but in memory of Zmyrna, defiled by her father, and the tears she shed. Let it be the last thing Cinna smelled, along with the stench of his own blood!"

"His blood," I whispered. "The paving stones were soaked with it—yet afterward, there was no flesh to be seen. . . ."

"The blood was quite important, for the purification ritual."

"Ritual?"

"Thrice we suck a bit of the victim's blood into our mouths, and thrice we spit it out. Thus the act is made pleasing to Father Liber. But there is an even more ancient blood ritual, an act of expiation, almost never performed nowadays. . . ."

"Yes? Go on."

"Because of the crowd all around us, the Maenads had to act almost in silence—no shrieks or shouts to work up our frenzy, for our feminine voices would give us away. Usually her voice is the *only* way a woman is allowed to vent her emotions, either that or some violence against her own body, tearing her hair or rending her cheeks. We silenced our voices, and instead we took action. That enforced silence caused our frenzy to become all the more intense. So frenzied, so intense . . ."

"Yes? Go on!"

"We touched the very face of the god that day," she whispered, staring into the distance. "Thrice we were to lick the blood from his severed parts, and thrice to spit it out—thus those organs could never again harm us, could never take revenge either in this world or the next. Even the Furies would be assuaged. His head, his hands, his genitals—severed and rendered powerless forever. But the Maenads became truly mad, all of us, all at once. We reached back into the deepest, darkest past. We enacted the blood ritual at its most primitive and most powerful. No man can ever hope to reach such a state of divine frenzy—only those of us who follow Father Liber."

"What did you do to Cinna? What did you do to the parts of Cinna after you tore him to pieces?" I knew, but I had to hear it.

"We ate him."

I covered my mouth in horror.

"We devoured his raw flesh. Crushed him with our teeth and swallowed him." She turned toward me. On her face I saw not horror but a kind of ecstasy. "It was the most perfect and most complete rite of Bacchus I have ever experienced, and I doubt that I will ever experience such a thing again—a rite worthy of our most ancient ancestors, of those mortals never to be forgotten who populate the ancient legends and myths. There was no limit to our power in that moment. It was blissful. Exquisite. Indescribably beautiful. It was beyond anything you can ever hope to experience, beyond anything you can imagine."

I shivered. "What about the bones? You can't have eaten those."

"Only the marrow."

The gorge rose in my throat.

"As for the rest of his bones," she said, "by that time there were already bonfires around the Forum, started by men telling the mob to light torches, hoping to burn down the houses of Brutus and the rest. When we were done, we threw the bones and other bits and pieces on the fires. They were burned to ashes and no one took notice."

"And the head?"

"The head was carried off as a trophy by a man I hired to do so, intentionally to distract the funeralgoers and lead them away so that we could carry on our business uninterrupted and unobserved. The man saw to it that the head was eventually tossed into the Tiber. Food for fishes—the traditional end for a beheaded criminal. They say that a man who's lost his head in this world remains without it in Hades as well, body and head severed for all time. A fit punishment for Cinna."

"But how could you have taken such a risk? Cinna had a bodyguard that day, as did I. What if Davus and the bodyguard hadn't been lost in the crowd? What if they had fought back?"

She smiled. "It was Cinna's bodyguard who carried off his head. The man was in my pay, one of my spies in Cinna's household. First he abandoned his master at my signal and saw to it that your son-in-law was separated from you and lost in the crowd. It was he who struck you in the head just before Cinna was taken. I told the man not to kill you, only to daze you. He did well."

"The slave should be crucified for betraying his master!" I said.

"The man is far from Rome by now, with a new name and a bag full of gold."

We looked at each other for a long moment. At last I broke the silence.

"Cinna made the *Zmyrna* come true, using his own daughter. But you made his *Orpheus and Pentheus* come true. You tore a living man apart, you and your Maenads. And then you burned the only copy of that poem on his funeral pyre!"

"Poetic justice, Finder. We couldn't destroy all traces of his vile *Zmyrna*. There are too many copies, in too many hands. But we could see to it that Cinna's final dose of poison was never inflicted on the world."

"Poison? Caesar called it the crowning achievement of Latin literature."

She spat on the floor. "The judgment of men! Men who write poems about rape and incest to titillate other men who declare such pornographic rubbish to be masterpieces. I heard enough of the *Orpheus and Pentheus* to know that it was another foul piece of garbage. Instead of a scheming nurse and a lust-mad daughter, the women were all mad, murdering monsters."

"But you became those monsters yourselves!"

She shook her head. "That which is truly monstrous runs counter to divine will. Everything we did was pleasing to Father Liber. And now that you know the truth, Finder, let me caution you never to speak of it. I should hate for Cinna's terrible fate to befall a man of your qualities. For the sake of your lovely wife and daughter, say nothing."

We were both silent. I searched for the courage to ask a final question.

"Bethesda . . . and Diana . . . ?"

Fulvia's smile was not unkind. "That's the question you really came here to ask, isn't it? You'd figured out the rest already, or most of it, but you don't yet know if Bethesda and Diana took part. They both took part in the Liberalia, after all." She paused, seeming to enjoy the way I fidgeted as I waited for her to answer. She drew a deep breath through her nostrils and narrowed her eyes.

"For better or worse, Senator Gordianus, your wife and daughter played no part in Cinna's punishment. Nor did they have any knowledge of our plans. I excluded them intentionally, for fear they might give something away to you. Also, it's my understanding that once already, some years ago, they secretly brought justice to a man not unlike Cinna. No woman should be called on to do such a thing more than once."

I had been holding my breath, braced to receive a different answer. My gasp was mingled with a sob of relief.

"Now that you have the answer to that question, are we done?" said Fulvia.

I shook my head. "Not quite. There's another reason I came here. There's something I have to tell you."

She raised an eyebrow.

"Sappho is dead."

The sardonic smile vanished. "How do you know this?"

"I came here from the house of Cinna. Polyxo found her this morning, hanging by a rope. I'm very sorry, Fulvia."

At first she looked more shocked than grief-stricken. Then her wide eyes abruptly brimmed with tears. She said not another word but turned and left the room.

A little while later, Antony appeared, dressed now in his consul's toga. From his tone of voice, it was evident he had not seen his wife and her distress. "Are you still here, Finder? Senator, I mean to say."

"I was just leaving."

"I'll walk you out."

The house was noisier than before. As we drew near the vestibule, I heard many voices.

"Another day, another meeting." Antony sighed. "What an awful lot of talk there's been, since Caesar died."

"Better talk than the alternative."

"Perhaps. There'll be plenty of time for bloodshed later. I'll say farewell to you here, before we reach the vestibule. I'm not quite ready to face all that jabbering. By the way, do you know what's become of my wife?"

"She left me rather abruptly. I don't know where she went. Perhaps . . . to the house of Cinna."

"Ah, to comfort Sappho? That poor girl. We're her guardians now, you know. I call her poor, but Cinna left her an enormous fortune, which it is now my duty to administer. Well, I shall leave the financial dealings to Fulvia. She's quite good at that sort of thing."

"She's a most unusual woman, your wife."

Antony smiled. "You don't know the half of it."

LII

"The consul's wife—a cannibal? And all those respectable matrons at the funeral, as well? Perhaps I've not become as Roman as I thought," said my Egyptian wife, tilting an eyebrow.

We sat in the garden at midday, picking at a meal for which none of us except Davus had much appetite. In spite of Fulvia's warning to say nothing—which I took quite seriously, especially since her husband might eventually take Caesar's place—I knew it would be useless to try to keep the truth from my wife and daughter. I told Bethesda and Diana everything.

Their surprise—which seemed entirely genuine—reassured me that Fulvia had been truthful when she told me they had no involvement in the plot. My relief was somewhat lessened by what Diana said next.

"I wonder why Fulvia didn't ask *us* to take part, Mother? I thought Fulvia liked us."

Would you have done so? I started to say, but thought better of it. I might not like the answer. "Fulvia was afraid one of you might give away the plot to me. I might have alerted Cinna, you see. Or done something else to wreck their scheme."

"Ah, that explains it," said Diana. "Though I would never have betrayed Fulvia's trust, not even to—"

"Enough, daughter," said Bethesda, who saw the look on my face. "What's done is done. Fulvia's friendship is genuine. If she excluded us, she was only doing what she deemed wisest."

"Now we shall see if you can keep a secret from Fulvia," I said. "She mustn't know I've told you."

"I suspect that Fulvia will never ask, and we will never tell," said Bethesda.

"Nor shall I," mumbled Davus, with a bit of flatbread stuffing his mouth.

"All the secrets one must live with these days!" I muttered. "The world will think that Cinna's murder was an unfortunate case of mistaken identity and never know the truth of who killed him or why."

"Would you have it otherwise, Papa? If people knew how he came to die, they'd also know what he did to Sappho. Fulvia at least allowed him to keep his reputation as a poet intact."

"Even as she oversaw the burning of his final masterpiece!"

"He insisted on living the *Zmyrna*," said Bethesda. "Fulvia saw to it that he experienced the *Orpheus and Pentheus* as well."

Her matter-of-fact tone made me shiver. "So the world will remember him for the *Zmyrna* only, and for dying a stupid, meaningless death," I said, "and people will think Sappho was a dutiful daughter who killed herself from grief, not guilt."

"I'm sure she felt both," said Diana quietly.

"So you think Fulvia was right, about the incest?" asked Bethesda.

"I doubted it at first—I didn't want to believe it—but Cinna's own written words confirmed it. Fulvia acted righteously, or at least believes she did."

"I'm not completely sure that avenging Sappho was her only motive," said Diana.

"What else?" I asked.

"Cinna was quite wealthy, was he not? With Sappho dead, and no close relatives to make a claim, who's likely to get his hands on the entire fortune now?"

I blinked. "Antony. But surely you don't think Fulvia killed Cinna to get hold of his estate?"

"Fulvia has a great deal of experience at building a fortune through inheritance," noted Diana. "And she'll always need more and more money, if her ambitions for Antony are to be realized. Knowing that Antony would become Sappho's guardian on Cinna's death, and being well versed in the legal means by which a guardian might lay claim to an unmarried girl's estate—well, I won't say that's the only or even the main reason she plotted against Cinna. But things have worked out to Fulvia's advantage, haven't they?"

I shook my head. "She couldn't have foreseen Sappho's suicide."

"Even with Sappho alive, Antony and Fulvia would have controlled her inheritance, and could have scared off any suitors."

"What a schemer you make her out to be! Next you'll be telling me that Fulvia had a hand in Caesar's assassination."

Diana blinked and cocked her head. "That very odd idea came out of your mouth, Papa, not mine. But it would make sense. How else was Antony ever to fulfill the destiny Fulvia has in mind for him and become ruler of Rome? Caesar could only stand in his way."

"Daughter, you're cynical beyond your years. But back to Cinna: Fulvia justified the killing as a pious act. You suggest she was driven by self-interest."

"Perhaps, Papa, like many powerful men in Rome, Fulvia is motivated by both virtues and vices, so mixed together it's impossible to sort them out."

I shivered, despite the warm sunlight.

"But Papa, today is your birthday!" said Diana, clapping her hands. "No more talk of death and deceit and other's people's drama. You must do something special."

"Yes, husband, you must do something to celebrate," said my wife. "Something out of the ordinary."

Davus nodded enthusiastically.

I took a deep breath. "Yes, I've been thinking about that. Today I believe I *will* do something special, something unusual—something I haven't done before, anyway. And so I shall—after a long midday nap, which surely I deserve on my sixty-sixth birthday. Bring me a sleeping couch, and a coverlet, and Bast the cat."

CODA

"Are you well rested, Papa?"

"Yes, Diana. That little nap cleared the cobwebs from my head."

"*Little* nap? You slept for hours. It's almost sundown."

"I blame the purring of Bast the cat. It puts me in a trance. Yes, I'll probably be wide awake well into the night. We have plenty of oil for the lamps here in the library, don't we?" I glanced around the little room that housed my small but precious collection of scrolls. Stacked on a high shelf was the newest addition, my copy of Cinna's *Zmyrna*.

"We can make the room as bright as daylight if you wish."

"You exaggerate. Even with twice as many lamps, this room would be no brighter than twilight. I find it difficult to read, let alone write, by such insufficient light. It's these old eyes of mine."

"If you want to read something, let me do it for you. I love to read aloud."

"Yes, and you have a most pleasant voice. But it's a bit of writing I intend to do."

"Oh?"

"Yes. I shall mark this birthday by embarking on a project that's been in my mind for quite some time. Cinna encouraged the idea. Any time

I shared with him some anecdote from my investigations for Cicero, or my dealings with Caesar, or my travels as a young man, he would say, 'You really must write your memoirs someday.' And I would roll my eyes and tell him that only politicians were vain enough to write down their life stories. And yet . . ."

"Yes, Papa?"

"Perhaps I do have a few stories that might entertain a handful of readers. I may have a worthwhile insight or two about the powerful men and women I've known. I might even dare to reveal a few dangerous secrets, especially now that so many of the people involved are dead and beyond caring."

"That would be splendid, Papa."

"Do you really think so? Of course, some of the most amazing things I've witnessed in my lifetime would be quite hard to capture in words. . . ."

"Such as?"

"I'm thinking of your mother. Stories about lustful girls turning into trees are all very well, but the metamorphosis of a headstrong Egyptian slave girl into a haughty Roman matron—to chart that transformation would surely tax the skills of even the finest poet."

"Such stories are seldom told."

"All the more reason for me to do so."

"You might even tell the story of Cinna's death. The true story."

"I think not! For as long as either Fulvia or Antony is alive—or the witch Polyxo, for that matter—that shall be a tale too dangerous to tell." I shivered. I felt that quicksilver sensation of "already seen" that I had recently discussed with Tiro, the mental phenomenon of re-experiencing an exact moment from the past. I was sure the Etruscans had a word for it, though I couldn't remember it. . . .

"What are you thinking, Papa?"

"I was thinking of Cinna, and Sappho, and I was reminded of my very first investigation for Cicero, involving the murder of Sextus Roscius, and the secrets it revealed—some of those secrets strikingly similar to those surrounding Cinna. Uncannily so! But the case of Sextus Roscius revealed other secrets, too, not just about the crime, but about the whole rotten state of affairs in Rome under the dictator Sulla. The highest perpetrators were too powerful ever to be brought to justice." I sighed. "And so it is with Fulvia. If Caesar were still alive, there might be some appeal to him, especially since Cinna was his friend. But with Caesar gone, Antony and Fulvia are far too powerful to cross. When it comes to meting out justice, not much has changed in my long lifetime. Well, I shall never conduct another such investigation. I am truly retired from all that."

"Never say never, Papa."

I shook my head. "I'll leave that sort of thing to Eco now. And perhaps to you, Diana. Yes, to you and Davus. I know it's what you long to do, to follow in your father's footsteps. I've always opposed the idea. But why not? The fact that you're female shouldn't stop you. You have the brains. He has the brawn. But your dear father shall be retired, here only to give you advice. Perhaps I'll never leave this house."

"Except to attend meetings of the Senate, of course."

"Must I? I suppose I'll have to make an occasional appearance, if only for the sake of my progeny. Hopefully, Senator Gordianus won't get into as much trouble as did Gordianus the Finder! I think I shall spend as many hours as I can here in the library, and in the garden, when the weather permits, dictating my memoirs."

"Dictating them to whom, Papa?"

"You put your finger on the problem: At present I own no slave suitable for such a task. I suppose I'll have to shop around to find a reasonably priced scribe who not only can spell but can also keep his mouth shut. Perhaps Tiro can help me find such a slave. . . ."

"But Papa, why purchase a scribe when you have me?"

"You, Diana?"

"Why not me? I've learned Tiro's shorthand. I can write as fast as you can dictate. You know my spelling is excellent; better than yours, anyway. And I can also correct any grammatical errors you make, even as I'm writing."

"Grammatical errors?"

Diana winced. "Papa, you may have learned your Greek from

Antipater of Sidon, but your Latin . . . well, it's not the most elegant, is it? But never fear, I can fix that."

I raised an eyebrow. "Perhaps I should ask Meto for an editorial polishing. Or Tiro. But I'm sure they'll both be much too busy—"

"Why ask either of those two, when you have me? My Latin is every bit as good as theirs."

I scoffed. "No woman ever wrote a book, Diana."

"What about Sappho of Lesbos?"

"A handful of poems, quite famous, to be sure; the exception that proves the rule. No woman ever wrote a history or a memoir."

"Or at least no woman ever got credit for doing so."

I looked at her steadily. "You make the project sound like a collaboration. My memories, your deathless prose."

"Deathless? You tease me, Papa, but why not? If you can tell an interesting story, and if I can add a bit of luster to the language, then who knows—perhaps your memoirs will be read by your children's children, and by their children as well."

"You forget that even the best books are terribly vulnerable. I saw a considerable portion of the Library at Alexandria burned to ashes when Caesar was besieged in the royal palace."

"And you were there, with Caesar, and with Cleopatra. Yes! That's *just* the sort of story you must include."

"My point is about literary immortality. I know how easily mere parchment and papyrus fall prey to fire and water and mold, war and the whims of thoughtless men. Not to mention hungry insects! The prose may be immortal, but the papyrus is not. Look at what happened to Cinna's final masterpiece, now gone forever." I shook my head. "Who knows what documents will be lost to future generations? Can you imagine a world without Sulla's blood-drenched memoirs, or Caesar's brilliant war diaries? Who knows, perhaps all that survives the ravages of time will be scroll upon scroll of those long-winded speeches of Cicero's, lovingly transcribed by Tiro—and ours will be known as the Age of Cicero, seen through his eyes alone."

"Or perhaps only *your* memoirs will survive, Papa, and this will be the Age of Gordianus."

I laughed.

"Stranger things have happened, Papa."

"I can't think of one! Or perhaps I can. There was that time in Babylon. . . ."

"No, Papa, don't speak. Hold that thought. Let me call for a slave to light the lamps, and I'll collect a stylus and wax tablet, and we can begin."

"Right here? Right now?"

"Yes!"

I shut my eyes and allowed my thoughts to wander. After a little while I perceived the lighting of the lamps though my closed eyelids. Perhaps, I thought, I should compose my memoirs in Greek. There was something to what Diana said, that my Greek was more formal than my street-learned Latin, having been taught to me by none other than Antipater of Sidon. Should I begin my memoirs with him, and with the voyage we took together to see the Seven Wonders? What remarkable things I saw, what unforgettable people I met on that trip!

But no—it would be best to begin not at the very beginning, but somewhere in the middle of the action, as the Greek playwrights do. Perhaps with the day Tiro first came to my house, and I met Cicero—a turning point in both our careers, and perhaps in the history of the Republic.

When I opened my eyes, Diana sat before me, a stylus in her hand, her eager eyes flashing in the lamplight. "I'm ready when you are, Papa."

I took a deep breath, and shivered. Again I felt it, that prickling sensation for which I was sure the Etruscans had a word, never mind that it eluded me. . . .

"The slave who came to fetch me on that unseasonably warm spring morning was a young man," I said, as Diana wrote, "hardly more than twenty. . . ."

DA CAPO

AUTHOR'S NOTE

(This note reveals elements of the plot.)

On a balmy evening in April 2014, in the town of Waco, Texas, I received the seed of an idea from which this novel sprouted and grew.

The Classical Association of the Middle West and South was meeting at Baylor University. I was honored to address a plenary session. At a cocktail party in a hotel suite off campus—no alcohol may be served on the Baptist campus—I shared with one of the scholars the dilemma I currently faced as a novelist. In the ongoing sequence of short stories and novels about Gordianus, sooner or later I would have to confront head-on the assassination of Julius Caesar. A problem: Readers of the Roma Sub Rosa series would expect a murder mystery. But surely there was no mystery about the most famous murder in history.

To be sure, at least one crime novel had been written on the subject— *The Julius Caesar Murder Case* by Wallace Irwin, published in 1935. Irwin, a wisecracking San Francisco newspaperman, had the senators of Rome talk like gangsters in a James Cagney or Edward G. Robinson movie (a decidedly postmodern device that served to show them as the gangsters they literally were). The harebrained plot revolved around the substitution of a ringer for Caesar, allowing the real J.C. to dodge the blades and escape to a quiet retirement—shades of *The Godfather: Part III*. For about two seconds I actually toyed with stealing Irwin's twist.

Jack Lindsay fictionalized the end of Caesar in a clever short story called "Princess of Egypt," included in *Come Home at Last* (Nicholson & Watson, 1936). Lindsay put Cleopatra's kid sister Arsinoë at the helm of a plot to kill Caesar, parallel to the conspiracy of Brutus and company. Lindsay's twist worked well enough for a short story, but wouldn't sustain a novel.

As a rather elaborate stalling device, following *The Triumph of Caesar* in 2008 I embarked on what turned out to be a trio of prequels about the young Gordianus and his far-flung travels (*The Seven Wonders, Raiders of the Nile,* and *Wrath of the Furies*). Taking a break from the straightforward chronology of the series not only allowed me to avoid Caesar's impending assassination; it also allowed my age to catch up (almost) with that of Gordianus, destined to turn sixty-six shortly after the Ides of March, 44 BC.

But I could stall only so long. With a new contract came a promise to my editor to deal at last with the elephant in the room: What was Gordianus up to in the last fateful days of Caesar's dictatorship?

At that cocktail party in Waco, it was James J. O'Hara, George L. Paddison Professor of Latin at the University of North Carolina, Chapel Hill, who solved my dilemma: Make it about Cinna, he said. Shakespeare simultaneously killed Cinna and made him immortal with a single scene in *Julius Caesar*—but surely there was more to the story, some hidden secrets to be revealed about a murder as famous and infamous as that. . . .

In that instant, I was off and running. Thank you, Jim O'Hara.

What can one know about Cinna? More than I expected and less than I might wish. More, because it turns out that Cinna in his own lifetime was a very important poet. Less, because his poems, except for a few threadbare fragments, are lost.

All the scattered bits of Cinna have been gathered and assessed by Edward Courtney in *Fragmentary Latin Poets* (Oxford, 1993) and by A. S. Hollis in *Fragments of Roman Poetry* (Oxford, 2007), who suggests that "after the disappearance of Lucretius, Catullus, and Calvus . . . Cinna could have enjoyed almost a decade as the leading Roman poet." For a penetrating look at Cinna and his place in Latin literature, see T. P. Wiseman, *Cinna the Poet and Other Roman Essays* (Leicester University Press, 1974).

So much for Cinna's tangible corpus. What of his poltergeist? R.O.A.M Lyne (*Ciris: A Poem Attributed to Virgil*, Cambridge, 1978), Richard F. Thomas ("Cinna, Calvus, and the *Ciris*," *The Classical Quarterly* 31:2, 1981), and Peter E. Knox ("Cinna, the *Ciris*, and Ovid," *Classical Philology* 78:4, 1983) all surmise that substantial portions of Cinna's *Zmyrna* may have been cribbed by the author of the *Ciris,* a later poem about a different father and daughter. The *Ciris* survives, while the *Zmyrna* does not, but when we read certain lines of the *Ciris,* we may yet hear a distant, ghostly echo of Cinna himself.

Cinna's mentor (and slave) Parthenius was another major poet of whom little survives, but he did write the book, literally, on modern poetry circa 44 BC, and we still have it: *Erotica Pathemata* (Of the Sorrows of Love), a bare-boned collection of stories intended as "a storehouse from which to draw material." The morbid, sexually convoluted subject matter is eyebrow raising, to say the least.

Born a year after Caesar's death, Ovid tells the fullest and most familiar surviving version of the Zmyrna story, in the *Metamorphoses*. As J. D. Morgan notes in "The Death of Cinna the Poet" (*The Classical Quarterly* 40:2, 1990), "Ovid must have been familiar with the famous poem of his renowned predecessor," but how his version followed or differed from Cinna's we do not know. Variant scraps of the myth are found in Ovid's *Ars Amatoria* (1.285–8); Oppian, *Halieutica* (3.402); Hyginus, *Fabulae* (58, 242, 248, 251, 270, 271, 275); Nonnus, *Dionysiaca* (13); Tacitus, *Histories* (2.2–3); and Antoninus Liberalis, *Metamorphoses* (34).

What drove the killers of the poet to such frenzy? Blame it on the Liberalia, say Francesco Carotta and Arne Eickenberg, authors of "*Liberalia Tu Accusas!* Restituting the Ancient Date of Caesar's *Funus*" (*Revue des Études Anciennes* 113, 2011; online at academia.edu). While untangling the evidence for the date of Caesar's funeral, Carotta and Eickenberg, as Keats might say, "Look'd at each other with a wild surmise"—in particular on page 12, where they make a striking connection between the funeral effigy of Caesar, mechanically rotated for everyone to see, and the ritual image of Dionysus transported on a wagon and mechanically rotated. In another Dionysian leap of logic, they argue that no date but the Liberalia will do for Caesar's funeral, for on what other day could the Roman mob have descended into the "Bacchanalian omophagic ritual" that did away with Cinna? About their conclusion I am skeptical, but their linkage of Cinna's death to the dismemberment of Pentheus (and Dionysus himself) spurred my imagination.

If the reader of these pages has not had enough of beheadings, look to "Maxentius' Head and the Rituals of Civil War" by Troels Myrup Kristensen (*Civil War in Ancient Greece and Rome: Contexts of Disintegration and Reintegration,* Franz Steiner Verlag, 2015; online at academia .edu), where we learn that "a mutilated body could indeed have dire consequences for one's afterlife."

For readers seeking a sound historical account of the assassination, I highly recommend *The Death of Caesar* by Barry Strauss (Simon & Schuster, 2015). My battered copy of this book has dog-ears, highlighting, and scribbled notes on virtually every page.

Antony's funeral speech in this book descends not from Shakespeare (who freely invented) but from Cassius Dio (*Roman History* 44.35–49). One line of Shakespeare does make its way into this novel: "Tear him for his bad verses" (*Julius Caesar,* Act III, Scene III), a line original to Shakespeare that does not appear in any ancient source. Its literal meaning here pays wry homage to the Bard.

Another homage to another poet runs through these pages, in which, like Cinna in the *Ciris,* he makes ghostly appearance. Some of his other (alleged) similarities to Cinna are explored here, between the lines. The first reader to send me this author's name (email throne@stevensaylor .com) will be given a mention in some future edition of this book.

Finally, my thanks to my longtime editor, Keith Kahla, and longtime agent, Alan Nevins, who conspired to make me confront the Ides.

4/23

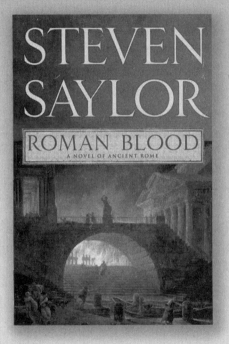